SS, JULY 4, 1776.

hirteen united States of America,

r one people to diffolve the political bands which have connected them with another, and to
Nature's God entitle them, a decent respect to the opinions of mankind requires that they
uths tobe felf-evident, that all men are created equal, that they are endowed by their Creator
— That to fecure these rights, Governments are instituted among Men, deriving their just
of these ends, it is the Right of the People to alter or to abolish it, and to institute new
to them shall seem most likely to effect their Safety and Happiness. Prudence, indeed,
nd accordingly all experience hath shewn, that mankind are more disposed to suffer, while
But when a long train of abuses and usurpations, pursuing invariably the same Object
f such Government, and to provide new Guards for their future security. — Such has
ter their former Systems of Government. The history of the present King of Great
f an absolute Tyranny over these States. To prove this, let Facts be submitted to a candid
the public good. ——— He has forbidden his Governors to pass Laws of immediate
d when so fuspended, he has utterly neglected to attend to them ——— He has refused to
he right of Representation in the Legiſlature, a right ineſtimable to them and formidable
l distant from the depository of their Public Records, for the sole purpose of fatiguing them into
ng with manly firmnefs his invaſions on the rights of the people. —— He has refuſed for
ble of Annihilation, have returned to the People at large for their exercise; the State remain
—— He has endeavoured to prevent the population of these ſtates; for that purpose obstruc-
, and raising the conditions of new Appropriations of Lands. —— He has obſtructed the
He has made Judges dependent on his Will alone, for the tenure of their offices, and the amount
varms of Officers to harraſs our People, and eat out their fubſtance. —— He has kept among
render the Military independent of and superior to the Civil power? —— He has combined
; giving his Aſſent to their Acts of pretended Legiſlation: —— For Quartering large bodies of
ers which they should commit on the Inhabitants of these States: —— For cutting off
depriving us in many cases, of the benefits of Trial by Jury: —— For tranſporting us beyond
bouring Province, eſtabliſhing therein an Arbitrary government, and enlarging its Boundaries
hese Colonies: —— For taking away our Charters, abolishing our most valuable Laws, and

"The dye is now cast, the Colonies must either submit or triumph. I do not wish to come to severer measures, but we must not retreat; by coolness and an unremitted pursuit of the measures that have been adopted I trust they will come to submit...." George III to Lord North September 11, 1774

"The die is cast.... Heaven only knows what is next to take place, but it seems to me the Sword is now our only, yet dreadful alternative, and the fate of Rome will be renued in Brittain."

Abigail Adams to Mercy Otis Warren February 3(?), 1775

GEORGE WASHINGTON. Charles Willson Peale, 1782. Private collection.

"The Dye Is Now Cast"

THE ROAD TO AMERICAN INDEPENDENCE, 1774-1776

TEXT BY LILLIAN B. MILLER
Historian, National Portrait Gallery,

AND THE STAFF OF THE HISTORIAN'S OFFICE:
MICHAEL D. SCHAFFER, *Research Historian*
JEANNETTE M. HUSSEY, *Researcher*
BARBARA H. BARES, *Research Assistant*
CLAUDIA K. JURMAIN, *Research Assistant*

ILLUSTRATIONS SELECTED BY
THE CURATORIAL DEPARTMENT, NATIONAL PORTRAIT GALLERY:
ROBERT G. STEWART, *Curator*
MONROE H. FABIAN, *Associate Curator*

RUSSELL BOURNE, *Editorial Consultant*

EXHIBITION STAFF
BEVERLY JONES COX, *Coordinator of Exhibitions*
JOSEPH MICHAEL CARRIGAN, *Chief of Exhibition Design and Production*

MARVIN SADIK, *Director, National Portrait Gallery*

PUBLISHED FOR THE NATIONAL PORTRAIT GALLERY

BY THE SMITHSONIAN INSTITUTION PRESS

CITY OF WASHINGTON 1975

Library of Congress Cataloging in
   Publication Data

National Portrait Gallery, Washington,
   D. C. Historian's Office.
   "The dye is now cast."

   Bibliography: p.
   Includes index.
   1. United States—History—
Revolution, 1775-1783—Biography.
2. United States—History—Revolution,
1775-1783—Causes. I. Miller, Lillian B.
II. Title.
E302.5.N38 1975   973.3'074'0153
74-24843

SMITHSONIAN INSTITUTION PRESS
publication number 5312

For sale by the Superintendent of Documents, U.S. Government Printing Office
Washington, D.C. 20402 - Price $11.25

Stock Number 047-001-00121-4

Contents

Foreword

The title of this volume and the exhibition which accompanies it—"The Dye is now Cast"—is a phrase which so well characterizes the nature of the events taking place in Britain and America in the 1770s that it was invoked in both camps.

From Kew, on September 11, 1774, King George III wrote his Prime Minister, Lord North:

> ... the dye is now cast, the Colonies must either submit or triumph. I do not wish to come to severer measures, but we must not retreat. ... there is no inclination for the present to lay fresh taxes on them, but I am clear there must always be one tax to keep up the right, and as such I approve of the Tea Duty.

From Braintree, during the first week of February, 1775, Abigail Adams began a letter to her dear friend, Mercy Otis Warren, with the words:

> The die is cast. Yesterday brought us such a Speach from the Throne as will stain with everlasting infamy the reign of George the 3 [delivered at the opening of Parliament on November 30, 1774] determined to carry into Execution "the acts passd by the late parliament, and to Maintain the authority of the Legislature over all his dominions." The reply of the house of commons and the house of Lords shew us the most wicked and hostile measures will be persued against us—even without giving us an opportunity to be heard in our defence. Infatuted Brittain! .... Heaven only knows what is next to take place, but it seems to me the Sword is now our only, yet dreadful alternative, and the fate of Rome will be renued in Brittain. She who has been the envy of nations will now become an object of their Scorn and abhorance, and as it was said of Rome that she governd other people by her will but her own by law, they now behold her governd herself by will, by the Arbitrary Will of the worst of her own citizens, and arrived at that period which has been foretold when the people co-operateing with the Enimies of the constitution by Electing

those to represent them who are hired to betray them, or by submitting tamely when the mask is taken of or falls of, and the attempt to bring beggary and Slavery is avoued or can be no longer concealed.

Clearly, in concluding that the dispute which divided them was irreconcilable, both sides recognized that the real matter at issue was one of principle. Even a nineteen-year-old student at King's College in New York, only lately come to America, named Alexander Hamilton, addressing a mass meeting in City Hall Park on July 6, 1774, knew that the contest was not over "the petty duty of 3 pence per pound on East India tea, [but] whether the inhabitants of Great-Britain have a right to dispose of the lives and properties of the inhabitants of America. . . ."

Mrs. Adams also perceived the causes which lay at the root of the shift from constitutional rights to arbitrary authority. Indeed, in a letter written from London on March 12, 1775, to his fellow Pennsylvanian Joseph Galloway, Benjamin Franklin was even more blunt in referring to "the extreme corruption prevalent among all orders of men in this old rotten state. . . ." Yet there were those in Parliament who fought to reform the government and bring about a reconciliation with the colonies. One of these men, a friend in fact of Franklin's, David Hartley, having failed in his efforts, rose before the House on December 21, 1775, and spoke these words:

The fate of America is cast. You may bruise its heel, but you cannot crush its head. It will revive again. The new world is before them. Liberty is theirs. They have posession of a free government, their birthright and inheritance, derived to them from their parent state, which the hand of violence cannot wrest from them. If you will cast them off, my last wish is to them; may they go and prosper! When the final period of this once happy country shall overtake ourselves either through tumult or tyranny, may another Phoenix rise out of our ashes!

A decade and a half after America had secured her independence from Britain, the Founding Fathers met to form a government for the new nation. On the day this document was adopted, it is said that as Benjamin Franklin was leaving the Constitutional Convention, an old lady stopped him and asked, "What is it to be, Dr. Franklin, a monarchy or a republic?"—to which the Doctor is said to have responded, "A Republic, Madam, if you can keep it."

MARVIN SADIK, DIRECTOR

NATIONAL PORTRAIT GALLERY
SMITHSONIAN INSTITUTION

Lenders to
the Exhibition

CHARLES FRANCIS ADAMS

LADY TERESA AGNEW

AMERICAN ANTIQUARIAN SOCIETY

THE AMERICAN MUSEUM IN BRITAIN, Bath

THE AMERICAN NUMISMATIC SOCIETY

THE AMERICAN PHILOSOPHICAL SOCIETY

VOJTECH BLAU RUGS AND TAPESTRIES

MRS. HENRY A. BOSCH, JR.

THE BOSTON ATHENAEUM

DONALD M. BRAXTON

THE BRITISH MUSEUM

ANNE S. K. BROWN MILITARY COLLECTION, BROWN UNIVERSITY LIBRARY

CARPENTERS' COMPANY OF THE CITY AND COUNTY OF PHILADELPHIA

MRS. ARNOLD B. CHACE

CITY OF CHARLESTON, South Carolina

CHICAGO HISTORICAL SOCIETY

WILLIAM L. CLEMENTS LIBRARY, UNIVERSITY OF MICHIGAN, Ann Arbor

THE CLEVELAND MUSEUM OF ART

THE COLONIAL WILLIAMSBURG FOUNDATION

COLUMBIA UNIVERSITY

THE CONNECTICUT HISTORICAL SOCIETY

THE RIGHT HONORABLE THE EARL OF DARTMOUTH

DARTMOUTH COLLEGE

S. COOPER DAWSON, JR.

DICKINSON COLLEGE LIBRARY, Carlisle, Pennsylvania

HER MAJESTY QUEEN ELIZABETH II

EVANSTON HISTORICAL SOCIETY, Illinois

FORT TICONDEROGA MUSEUM, Ticonderoga, New York

HIS GRACE THE DUKE OF GRAFTON

THE RIGHT HONORABLE THE EARL OF GUILFORD

GUTHMAN COLLECTION

ROBERT H. HICKS

HILLWOOD, SMITHSONIAN INSTITUTION, Washington, D.C.

THE HISTORICAL SOCIETY OF PENNSYLVANIA

THE RIGHT HONORABLE THE SIXTH EARL HOWE

HUGENOT-THOMAS PAINE HISTORICAL ASSOCIATION, New York

INDEPENDENCE NATIONAL HISTORICAL PARK, Philadelphia

INDIANA UNIVERSITY LIBRARY

MR. AND MRS. JAMES DUANE IRELAND

JOHN K. LATIMER

WILMARTH SHELDON LEWIS

THE LIBRARY COMPANY OF
PHILADELPHIA

LIBRARY OF CONGRESS

HERMAN W. LIEBERT

THE LONG ISLAND HISTORICAL SOCIETY

ARTHUR T. LYMAN

TRACY W. McGREGOR LIBRARY,
UNIVERSITY OF VIRGINIA,
Charlottesville

THE RIGHT HONORABLE THE EARL
AND COUNTESS OF MALMESBURY

MARYLAND HALL OF RECORDS, Annapolis

MARYLAND HISTORICAL SOCIETY

MASSACHUSETTS HISTORICAL SOCIETY

MR. AND MRS. PAUL MELLON

THE METROPOLITAN MUSEUM OF ART

MRS. FREDERIC A. MILHOLLEN

VICTOR MONTAGU

MR. EDWARD RUTLEDGE MOORE

A. PERRY MORGAN, JR.

THE MOUNT VERNON LADIES'
ASSOCIATION OF THE UNION,
Mount Vernon, Virginia

MRS. ELIZABETH MURRAY

MUSÉE NATIONAL DU CHÂTEAU
DE VERSAILLES

MUSEUM OF ART, CARNEGIE INSTITUTE,
Pittsburgh

NATIONAL ARCHIVES

NATIONAL ARMY MUSEUM, London

NATIONAL COLLECTION OF FINE ARTS,
Smithsonian Institution

NATIONAL GALLERY OF ART,
Washington, D.C.

NATIONAL GALLERY OF IRELAND, Dublin

THE NATIONAL MUSEUM OF HISTORY
AND TECHNOLOGY, DIVISION OF
MILITARY HISTORY, Smithsonian
Institution

NATIONAL PORTRAIT GALLERY, London

NATIONAL PORTRAIT GALLERY,
Smithsonian Institution

NEW YORK PUBLIC LIBRARY

NEW YORK STATE HISTORICAL
ASSOCIATION

HIS GRACE THE DUKE OF
NORTHUMBERLAND

ANDREW OLIVER

PEQUOT LIBRARY, Southport, Connecticut

PRINCE CONSORT'S ARMY LIBRARY,
Aldershot, Hants, England

THE PUBLIC ARCHIVES OF CANADA,
Ottawa

PUBLIC RECORD OFFICE, London

THE PUTNAM PHALANX, Hartford,
Connecticut

CHRISTOPHER, ANDREW AND HENRY
REED

RHODE ISLAND HISTORICAL SOCIETY

L. G. STOPFORD SACKVILLE

WILLIAM SALT LIBRARY, Stafford,
England

WILLIAM H. SCHEIDE

HERBERT SCHIFFER ANTIQUES

DAVID STOCKWELL, INC.

TRINITY COLLEGE, Hartford

UNITED STATES NAVAL ACADEMY
MUSEUM

VIRGINIA HISTORICAL SOCIETY

VIRGINIA STATE LIBRARY

WADSWORTH ATHENEUM

GENERAL ARTEMAS WARD MUSEUM,
Shrewsbury, Massachusetts

THE WATKINSON LIBRARY, TRINITY
COLLEGE, Hartford

YALE UNIVERSITY ART GALLERY

Acknowledgments

The National Portrait Gallery gratefully acknowledges the many historical societies, libraries, museums, and individuals in the United States and abroad who helped to make "The Dye Is Now Cast" possible.

In Great Britain, for their special assistance, we wish to thank the Duke of Grafton, the Honorable the Earl and Countess Howe, the Earl and Countess of Malmesbury, L. G. Stopford Sackville, Sir John Pope-Hennessey, Director of the British Museum, and Sir Geoffrey Agnew. The National Portrait Gallery in London was especially cooperative in responding to our numerous requests and we are very grateful to John Hayes, Director, John Kerslake, Deputy Keeper, Robin Gibson, Assistant Keeper, and Sarah Wimbush, Museum Assistant. Robin Hutchinson, Keeper of the Scottish National Portrait Gallery, was most helpful in expediting the loan of the portrait of John Murray, Earl of Dunmore.

We were aided in our search for French portraits by Hélène Balstruaitis, Fine Arts Consultant for the United States Embassy in Paris, and Pierre Lemoine, Conservateur en Chef, and Claire Constans, Conservateur, of the Musée National du Château de Versailles were most obliging. James White, Director, and Michael Wynne, Assistant Director of The National Gallery of Ireland, must also be thanked for allowing the portrait of Edmund Burke by James Barry to remain here for our second Bicentennial exhibition.

In this country we are indebted to a long list of people who provided many kinds of valuable assistance: John Melville Jennings, Director, Virginia Historical Society; James E. Mooney, Director, Historical Society of Pennsylvania; Edwin Wolf, Director, and Stefanie Munsing, Curator of Prints, The Library Company of Philadelphia; Clement E. Conger, Curator, The White House; Stephen T. Riley, Director, Massachusetts Historical Society; Albert T. Klyberg, Director, Rhode Island Historical Society; John D. Davis, Curator of Metalwork, Joan Dolmetsch, Curator of Prints and Maps, and Wallace Gusler, Curator of Mechanical Arts, Colonial Williamsburg; Marvin Ross, Curator, Hillwood; Leonard Faber, Exhibits Officer, and Milton Kaplan, Curator of Historical Prints, Library of Congress; Eugenia Holland, Assistant Curator, Maryland Historical Society; Mrs. Thomas V. Lape, Curator,

Acknowledgments

Fort Ticonderoga Museum; Christine Meadows, Curator, Mount Vernon; Richard B. Harrington, Curator, Anne S. K. Brown Military Collection, Brown University Library; Peter O. Marlow, Chief Curator, Wadsworth Atheneum; Carolyn A. Wallace, Manuscripts Curator, University of North Carolina at Chapel Hill; Arlene Kleeb, Assistant Curator of Manuscripts, William L. Clements Library, University of Michigan; and Mildred Steinback and Helen Sanger, Frick Art Reference Library.

The Historian's Office was also assisted in its research by the staffs of the National Collection of Fine Arts-National Portrait Gallery Library and other Smithsonian Libraries, the Library of Congress, and the Martin Luther King Memorial Library.

Prologue

A stranger finding himself in Boston in the spring of 1774 would have been both bewildered and diverted by the unusual curses echoing around him. If a wheel of his carriage ran into a rut, he would hear the imprecation, *"this is Lord North's Road,"* growled to sound like an unholy curse. If the carriage "jolted hard over a Stone, the Rumble was accompanied with a *"Damn Lord North!"* In clergymen's prayers, *Lord North* substituted for the Devil; and if our traveler found himself in a Boston church, the service was apt to start off with something like "O! Thou Lord of the East, & of the West, & of ye South! Defend us against Lord North!" From morning to evening, people of all classes could be heard on the slightest occasion damning Lord North, so that the conservative Peter Oliver, horrified at this degradation of "that great & good Statesman," could only conclude that "Had Lord *North* been vulnerable by the Curses & Prayers of those Carters & Parsons, he would not at this Day have stood at the Helm of Government, but both Pilot & Ship would have foundered long since."[1]

Frederick North, the second Earl of Guilford, was prime minister of Great Britain from 1770 until 1782. As the King's faithful representative and as the head of the ministry that determined colonial policy, he was considered by Bostonians responsible for the series of acts recently passed by Parliament designed to punish their town for allowing the East India tea to be dumped into Boston Harbor. When both Boston and the Province of the Massachusetts Bay refused to pay for the destroyed tea, Parliament had passed several acts, changing Massachusetts's charter, closing the port of Boston, and regulating trials at common law. Trade to the colony was diverted to the port of Salem, and troops were sent to Boston under General Gage to implement and maintain both civil and military government.

General Gage's arrival further heightened the tension in the port city. It was rumored and, indeed, expected that he carried with him orders to apprehend "several Persons, who had been declared by His Majesty's Law Servants to have been guilty of high Treason" and ship them back to England for trial and hanging.[2] Even when no one was arrested or taken into custody, the people of Boston were not placated.

Bostonians were not an easy people to govern, as General Gage soon found out, especially when they believed that their interests were threatened. When Gage ap-

1.
FREDERICK NORTH, second Earl of
Guilford. John Singleton Copley.
Crayon on paper, circa 1779.
The Boston Athenaeum.

2.
PETER OLIVER. William Williams,
1781. Andrew Oliver.

pointed new council members and summoned them to Salem to meet "according to the new Act of Parliament," several of those so honored declined his invitation, "imagining that their persons & Properties would be in imminent Danger, upon their taking it." Boston's mobs had already begun to operate; and, skilled in the art of exerting pressure on uncooperative officials, they knew how to make the lives of those who accepted Gage's summons unpleasant. Some who took the oath of office, as Peter Oliver describes them, "were . . . forced by the Mobs to resign. . . . A great Number did undertake the Office, & hold it; but they were forced to repair to *Boston* for safety, under the Protection of the Troops."[3]

Massachusetts's lower House of Assembly, now in the hands of the radicals, seemed absolutely uncontrollable. Locking themselves into their legislative chamber, the legislators voted "some seditious Resolves; which, when [Gage] understood, he sent the Secretary to dissolve them." Denied admission, the hapless messenger was obliged to order the dissolution of the Assembly from the doorway. When he was forced to withdraw, having been too late to prevent the Assembly from passing their resolves, all "civil Government, both Form & Substance," came to an end in Massachusetts.[4]

Now the town of Boston and the people of Massachusetts took things into their own hands. Organizing themselves into committees and associations, they formed a new extralegal government by means of county meetings, created a militia, passed resolves, and established relationships with the other colonies. All of them, according to Oliver, "interested their Selves in the *Boston* Port Bill; & in a pretended Compassion to the Sufferers of that Town shipped Cargoes of Provision; but it was thought that those who had the Distribution of them fared full as sumptuously upon them as many of those did, for whom they were designed." A "wild Fire" seemed to run through all the colonies, like the eruption of a "Volcano."[5] As Oliver reported, when "the lava

. . . at last settled," it formed an assembly of fifty-two men who called themselves a Continental Congress and met in Philadelphia, September 5, 1774, to devise measures for the aid of distressed Boston and to call to the attention of the governing officials in Great Britain the concern and anger of the American people at the restrictive policies imposed upon them. Thus Americans took the first step toward what was to eventuate in the establishment of a new and united nation.

3.
The Bostonians in Distress satirizes the blockade of Boston after the Boston Tea Party. The caged, starving Bostonians, surrounded by British soldiers, are receiving food and clothing from other colonists. Johann Martin Will. Mezzotint, November 19, 1774. Colonial Williamsburg.

"The Dye Is Now Cast"

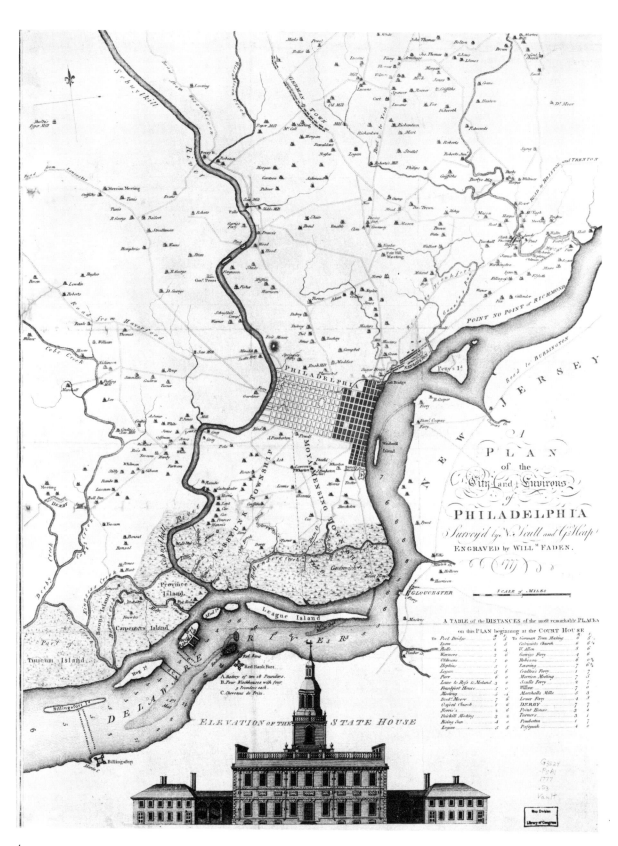

4.
A Plan of the City and Environs of Philadelphia
with a view of the Pennsylvania State House.
William Fadden. Engraving, 1777.
Library of Congress.

I.

The First Continental Congress

The men who trudged the cobblestones from Philadelphia's City Tavern to Carpenters' Hall represented the best in American political leadership. They had been selected by their fellow citizens to come to the City of Brotherly Love to sit as a Continental Congress and settle a family quarrel. They did not come to set in train a movement for independence from Great Britain. Nor did they come merely to register their protests against the Coercive Acts. Rather, the instructions they had received from the various legal and quasi-legal bodies that elected them plainly charged the delegates to find a way to reestablish the harmony that before 1763 had characterized colonial relations with the mother country. The Congress must try again to accomplish what Americans had been trying to accomplish for ten years: to persuade the British government to abandon its efforts to tax the colonies without their consent. In addition, the delegates would have to convince their sovereign, George III, to free his American subjects from the incubus of the Coercive Acts. Battered though it was by a decade of turmoil, hope for reconciliation still lived on the western side of the Atlantic.

The cooperative spirit had never been strong among the colonies. The delegates who came to Philadelphia in 1774 were heirs to a tradition of provincialism, disunity, and collective ineffectiveness. Twenty years before in Albany they had failed dismally to agree to a plan of union. Now, as the Congress opened, this heritage was in evidence. John Adams observed that the Congress included ". . . a diversity of religions, educations, manners, interests, such as it would seem almost impossible to unite in one plan of action. . . ."[1] Many members entertained dark suspicions about the New England—and especially the Masachusetts—delegates. They feared that New Englanders were aiming at establishing independence and substituting their own hegemony for that of England in North America. After the Congress had been sitting for a month, the Connecticut delegates wrote home to Governor Trumbull that work went slowly because each province wanted to make certain that its particular rights and interests were secure. What was of small importance to one colony might be of the greatest moment to another. The decisions of the Congress had to satisfy everybody.[2]

More difficult to cope with as a divisive factor was the disagreement between radicals and conservatives. The radicals, sympathizing with Boston's plight, favored de-

Instructions for the DEPUTIES *appointed to meet in* GENERAL CONGRESS *on the Part of this Colony.*

THE unhappy Disputes between Great Britain and her American Colonies, which began about the third Year of the Reign of his present Majesty, and since, continually increasing, have proceeded to Lengths so dangerous and alarming as to excite just Apprehensions in the Minds of his Majesty's faithful Subjects of this Colony that they are in Danger of being deprived of their natural, ancient, constitutional, and chartered Rights, have compelled them to take the same into their most serious Consideration; and, being deprived of their usual and accustomed Mode of making known their Grievances, have appointed us their Representatives to consider what is proper to be done in this dangerous Crisis of American Affairs. It being our Opinion that the united Wisdom of North America should be collected in a General Congress of all the Colonies, we have appointed the Honourable PEYTON RANDOLPH, Esquire, RICHARD HENRY LEE, GEORGE WASHINGTON, PATRICK HENRY, RICHARD BLAND, BENJAMIN HARRISON, and EDMUND PENDLETON, Esquires, Deputies to represent this Colony in the said Congress, to be held at Philadelphia on the first Monday in September next.

And that they may be the better informed of our Sentiments touching the Conduct we wish them to observe on this important Occasion, we desire that they will express, in the first Place, our Faith and true Allegiance to his Majesty King George the Third, our lawful and rightful

124

[4]

his Majesty's Representative, we would remind him that the Statute 25th Edward III. has expressed and defined all treasonable Offences, and that the Legislature of Great Britain hath declared that no Offence shall be construed to be Treason but such as is pointed out by that Statute, and that this was done to take out of the Hands of tyrannical Kings, and of weak and wicked Ministers, that deadly Weapon which constructive Treason had furnished them with, and which had drawn the Blood of the best and honestest Men in the Kingdom; and that the King of Great Britain hath no Right by his Proclamation to subject his People to Imprisonment, Pains, and Penalties.

That if the said General Gage conceives he is empowered to act in this Manner, as the Commander in Chief of his Majesty's Forces in America, this odious and illegal Proclamation must be considered as a plain and full Declaration that this despotick Viceroy will be bound by no Law, nor regard the constitutional Rights of his Majesty's Subjects, whenever they interfere with the Plan he has formed for oppressing the good People of the Massachusetts Bay; and therefore, that the executing, or attempting to execute, such Proclamation, will justify Resistance and Reprisal.

Defect in the association.
— we are permitted any goods, imported before Nov. 1. 1774.
+ we are not allowed to import the implements of manufacturing nor books
— we may still import wines, coffee &c tho' dutied articles
— we are allowed to continue commerce with the other parts of the British empire, tho' they should refuse to join us.
x the American grievances are not defined
x we are to conform to such resolutions only of the Congress as our deputies assent to. which totally destroys that union of conduct in the several colonies which was the very purpose of calling a Congress.

upon the whole we may truly say,
we have left undone those things which we ought to have done and we have done those things which we ought not to have done.

5.
Thomas Jefferson's copy of Virginia's *Instructions for the Deputies appointed to meet in General Congress on the Part of this Colony*, 1774. Library of Congress.

cisive action against the mother country, specifically in the form of a continental agreement establishing a total embargo on trade with the British Isles and the British West Indies. The conservatives, dismayed by the violence of the Boston Tea Party, thought that such a policy would irritate the British even more and aggravate the Anglo-American quarrel. Besides, they argued, such an agreement could only be executed and supported by illegal means. What they wanted was a plan whereby the colonies would function within the Empire under freer circumstances.

Despite the divisive elements, the Congress did have the advantage of owing its very existence to consensus. Radicals and conservatives alike had agreed in the summer of 1774 that such an assembly was the only solution to the American dilemma—although they expected different things of it and not all were optimistic as to its outcome. The delegates also had more in common personally than was at first apparent. They were all well educated and well-to-do; half were lawyers. Most were in their late thirties or early forties, and they had shared similar colonial experiences in their settlements, their westward expansion, their commerce, and political relations with England. They also shared a sense of a virtuous American identity in distinction to what they perceived to be the corruption of contemporary British society, "The old rotten state," in Benjamin Franklin's words.[3] Thus, even men of such widely divergent viewpoints as Samuel Adams and Joseph Galloway could find common ground on which to meet in discussing the future of America within the British Empire.

CARPENTERS' HALL

The decision of the delegates to meet in Carpenters' Hall was an initial victory for the more radical members of the Congress. Joseph Galloway, Speaker of the Pennsylvania Assembly and longtime political ally of Benjamin Franklin, had offered the Congress the use of the State House (later Independence Hall) in an effort to place the meetings under the influence of the conservative Assembly, or at least to associate them with the Quaker legislature that advocated caution in meeting imperial problems and supported mercantile and property interests.

Boston's fiery Sam Adams, however, held other ideas. Arriving in Philadelphia a week before the Congress officially opened, he had made the most of his time. "He eats little, drinks little, sleeps little, thinks much and is most decisive and indefatigable in the pursuit of his objects," reported Galloway.[4] By opening day Adams had persuaded most of the delegates, with the exception of the New Yorkers and Philadelphians, to vote for Carpenters' Hall, the property of the Carpenters' guild, as a suitable meeting place. The "mechanics and citizens in general," who favored quick, decisive action in defense of American rights, were, of course, delighted with the choice, seeing in it an expression of the Congress's sympathy with their position. The conservatives, however, did not lose hope. Although they had wished that the delegates would do Galloway the courtesy of at least looking at the State House, they read the vote as a reaction to Galloway's domineering personality rather than as a repudiation of their position.[5] Galloway himself believed that he had simply been tricked "by an Interest made out of Doors."[6]

6.
The earliest known view of Carpenters' Hall, published in the rule book of the Carpenters' Company, 1786. The Carpenters' Company of the City and County of Philadelphia.

Joseph Galloway (c. 1731–1803)

Joseph Galloway did not understand the political climate of Pennsylvania in 1774. Although not a member of a Quaker meeting, he had aligned himself with the Quaker antiproprietary interests in the colony and in the city of Philadelphia, which were essentially conservative in local and imperial politics. He had considered Quaker support of his election to the Provincial Assembly in 1756 a sign of popularity; and his eighteen-year stint in the Assembly, half of it spent as Speaker, only confirmed his vanity. Within the Assembly, Galloway had exerted his influence successfully. Together with Benjamin Franklin, he had seen that the colony received adequate military defense; he had compelled the Proprietors—the Penns—to bear a more just share of the burden of taxation; and he had made peace with the Delaware and Shawanese Indians. When Benjamin Franklin was sent to London in 1757 to lobby against the proprietary position and to seek support for transforming Pennsylvania into a royal colony, Galloway took over leadership of the antiproprietary party in the Assembly, a leadership that marked him as a formidable adversary of the Penn family. With his services in constant demand, his strength in the colony's political life increased, until he came to believe, as Robert M. Calhoon has pointed out, that "his dominance was an essential prerequisite to the defense of Pennsylvania's interests."[7]

Legal training, ownership of a large estate, and a prominent family background had also contributed to Galloway's important position in Pennsylvania society and politics up to 1774. As a man of property, he devoted his career as a lawyer to its protection. "Power results from the real property of society," he wrote.[8] He would never accept

5

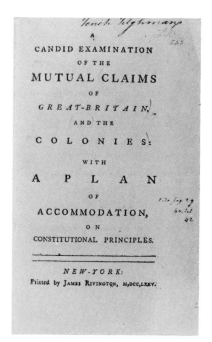

rule by a propertyless mob or approve changes in the *status quo*. When he opposed the Proprietors, he did so because he feared their appeal to the "baser" elements of society. This fear of democracy also entered into his decision in 1764 to refuse representation in the Provincial Assembly to the angry settlers of the western counties of Pennsylvania who had created such a disturbance in the Paxton riots. Since these westerners were also Presbyterian in religion, he equated Presbyterianism with dangerous leveling and rioting. In his mind, only members of the Anglican Church, Quakers, Methodists, Lutherans, and German Calvinists were attached to the mother country.

Galloway recognized the injustice of many of Parliament's colonial taxation policies and desired a redress of grievances; but he believed that the way for the colonials to win their rights was through "decent and respectful" petitions, not through extremist threats and radical action. While he busied himself with the details of the Congress's meetings as a kind of self-appointed committee of arrangements, he kept hoping that he could dominate the Congress sufficiently to prevent lawless behavior, which he feared even more than parliamentary tyranny. He had, after all, been able to influence the Pennsylvania Assembly to exclude from the colonial delegation such despised political opponents as John Dickinson and Charles Thomson. He was certain that with the proper leadership he could similarly influence the entire Congress.

As the delegates began arriving in Philadelphia, Galloway grew more optimistic about his capacity to persuade them to a course of reasonable protest. Their "temper and moderation" impressed him; surely here were the qualities needed to bring about the desired reconciliation with Great Britain. Galloway even began to hope that the Congress would justify the Bostonians' "refusal to pay for the tea until their grievances [were] redressed." [9]

Thus, when the delegates so unceremoniously rejected his hospitable suggestion of convening in the State House and instead chose Carpenters' Hall merely to please Philadelphia's mechanic class, he was disappointed; but he was even more so when against his advice they chose Charles Thomson secretary of the Congress.

Charles Thomson (1729-1824)

Charles Thomson was frequently referred to as "the Sam Adams of Philadelphia." [10] Galloway believed that he was "one of the most violent Sons of Liberty [so called] in America." [11] To have Thomson now brought into the Congress in an administrative capacity, after he had so carefully plotted to have him excluded from the official delegation, was a blow not only to Galloway's prestige among his fellow delegates but to his *amour propre* as well. Stung by this second rebuff, Galloway conceded to William Franklin, royal governor of the neighboring colony of New Jersey, that he was "surprized"—a euphemism for outmaneuvered. [12] The New York conservatives James Duane and John Jay protested that the secretary ought to be an elected member of the Congress. The supporters of Thomson replied that a member would not have the time to do the job properly. Realizing that they were greatly outnumbered, the conservatives prudently dropped their opposition and reserved their fire for more important issues; but they could not fail to realize that the radical delegates were proving to be formidable opponents.

Thomson, who in recent years had replaced Galloway as the principal political ally of Benjamin Franklin, was the leader of the small merchants and mechanics who con-

8.
CHARLES THOMSON. William Rush,
circa 1795. The American
Philosophical Society.

stituted the strength of radical opposition to Britain in Philadelphia. Born in Ireland
and orphaned before landing in America, Thomson was educated in Pennsylvania by
the Presbyterian minister Francis Alison. Young Thomson became a competent clas-
sical scholar who occupied himself in turn as tutor, merchant, politician, and agitator.
Several days before the Congress convened, the Irish orphan had capped his rise to prominence in the Philadelphia community by marrying a wealthy relative of John Dickinson.

The hard times that followed the close of the French and Indian War had
prompted Thomson, then proprietor of a general store, to turn his attention to politics.
The young man made the proper start by becoming acquainted with Benjamin Franklin, and, when Franklin traveled to England as agent for Pennsylvania in 1764,
Thomson became one of his primary correspondents. It was Thomson who convinced
Franklin that "the Prudence and Moderation" counseled by the doctor was not a
proper response to the Stamp Act. Franklin was impressed by Thomson's argument
that American liberties were in grave danger, for "The parliament insist on a power
over all the liberties and privileges claimed by the colonies, and hence require a blind
obedience and acquiescence in whatever they do. . . ."[13] Even more convincing to the
politically sensitive Franklin was Thomson's argument that public opinion would not
tolerate the enforcement of the Stamp Act. Thomson underlined his position by leading the active resistance in Philadelphia against the act and by taking a hand in forcing
the resignation of the stamp agent John Hughes.

7

9.
Peyton Randolph. John Wollaston, date unknown.
Virginia Historical Society.

In 1768 Thomson joined forces with John Dickinson, the "Pennsylvania Farmer," in the difficult task of mobilizing Philadelphia's merchants against the Townshend Acts. By 1770 he had molded the town's shopkeepers and artisans into an effective political force, capable of acting as a counterweight to the conservative element in the Assembly led by Galloway and bringing pressure on the larger merchants to acquiesce to radical policies.

Thomson's success earned the perpetual ill-will of Galloway, for it undercut the Speaker's political control of the province. Galloway warned his friend, Franklin, to beware of Thomson as a man devoid of "Principle or Virtue." Yet, Thomson maintained his standing with Franklin, for it was Thomson who understood better than any other man in Pennsylvania the political temper of Philadelphia's middle classes, with which Franklin identified, and it was Thomson who, alone among the political leaders of his province, remained consistently an opponent of British imperial policies. Now it seemed that the Continental Congress, like Franklin, held Thomson in higher esteem than Joseph Galloway thought proper.

The choice of Peyton Randolph, lately Speaker of Virginia's House of Burgesses, as presiding officer of the meetings satisfied the conservatives more and, indeed, helped to create a harmony of great importance to the eventual success of this first Congress. Nominated by South Carolina's Thomas Lynch, a delegate of radical disposition, as "one who had presided with great dignity over a very respectable society, greatly to the advantage of America," Randolph received the unanimous approval of his fellow delegates and gracefully accepted the title "President of the Continental Congress." [14]

Peyton Randolph (c. 1721-1775)

The portly, affable Randolph was just the man to preside over the Congress (as the delegates officially decided to call their sessions). Discreet, intelligent, and urbane, he was also—and more important—a genuine moderate, a man who could be trusted by both radicals and conservatives. Educated at Virginia's College of William and Mary and the Middle Temple in London, Randolph was of a cautious and deliberate nature, a member in good standing of the colonial gentry, and a staunch defender of colonial interests. As King's attorney for Virginia from 1748 to 1766, he had proved himself adept at balancing the rights of the colony against the demands of the Crown. In 1766 Randolph was elected to replace John Robinson as Speaker of the House of Burgesses. Here he had had to cope unwillingly with Patrick Henry's extremely worded resolutions against the Stamp Act, which had so angered him that he had left the Speaker's chair fuming that he would give a hundred guineas for a single vote to use against Henry.

Randolph was not opposed to protest, however; on behalf of the burgesses he had written to the King his own objection to the Stamp Act. But essentially his was the voice of moderation and caution—which his fellow Virginians appreciated as the quarrel between the colonies and Britain rapidly accelerated. In 1773 they elected him chairman of the colony's committee of correspondence; and in 1774 and 1775 the Virginia Convention, the unofficial surrogate for the dissolved House of Burgesses, chose Randolph to preside over it.

The members of the Congress intended that their president be less an executive officer than a chairman. Still, the president could do much to influence the course of the Congress. The conservatives could have done much worse than the responsible Randolph.

9

From the opening days of the Congress, Galloway had recognized that the delegates were divided into two distinct parties in their attitude toward the mother country: "One intended . . . to form a more solid and constitutional union between the two countries and . . . the other consisted of persons whose design was to throw off all subordination and connexion with Great Britain. . . ."[15] The first order of business confirmed his impression. Once officers had been elected, the delegates had to determine voting procedures. As in the choice of a meeting place and officers, more was at stake than was at first apparent. Not only was each colony apprehensive that it would be forced to sacrifice its local interest in order to make a satisfactory settlement with the mother country, but the larger colonies were also anxious that they might have to yield power to the smaller ones, while the smaller colonies feared the tyranny of the larger. Conservatives, like Galloway and John Jay of New York, saw the danger of establishing democratic precedents if voting was based on population; yet, it was this principle that was sought by radicals like Patrick Henry of Virginia and Thomas Lynch of South Carolina, who wished to break down "the Distinctions between Virginians, Pennsylvanians, New Yorkers and New Englanders" and have all consider themselves "American."[16]

What Henry seemed bent on establishing was a new national constitution; "Government is dissolved," he declared; ". . . We are in a state of Nature." This was too exaggerated a claim for most of the delegates. John Jay spoke the common mind of the Congress when he replied, "I cant yet think that all Government is at an End. The Measure of arbitrary Power is not full, and I think it must run over, before we undertake to frame a new Constitution."[17] Jay's argument prevailed; the Congress adopted a unit rule of voting, allowing one vote for each colony. For the benefit of the radicals, however, the delegates voted a rule of secrecy that later was to permit all disagreement to be expunged from the official record in order to present an appearance of unanimity.

The second day of the Congress an express rider from Boston brought news that emphasized the dangers the delegates would soon be facing: the British, the rider falsely reported, had bombarded Boston. All Philadelphia was in turmoil, Silas Deane wrote his wife, every tongue was crying for revenge. "The bells toll muffled," Deane declared, "and the people run as in a case of extremity, they know not where nor why."[18] The rumor was contradicted in two days, but the strength of the response was ominous. John Adams rejoiced that every member of Congress regarded the attack on Boston as an assault on his own capital. "WAR! WAR! WAR! was the Cry," wrote Adams to his wife, Abigail, ". . . pronounced in a Tone, which would have done Honour to the Oratory of a Briton or a Roman. If it had proved true," he concluded, "you would have heard the thunder of an American Congress."[19] The Congress did not need to thunder, but the delegates were reminded dramatically— if they needed any reminder—that a settlement of the Anglo-American quarrel was becoming every day more urgent.

Nobody in the Congress understood better than the Massachusetts delegation the potential value of religion as an element in political strategy. On the second day of the Congress Thomas Cushing of Massachusetts proposed that the sessions be opened with a prayer. It must have seemed to the conservatives that the radicals had gained sufficient advantage with the selection of the meeting hall and the secretary without being allowed to gain strength by allying with the pulpit. Playing on the distaste of many delegates for the rigid Congregationalist establishment, John Jay complained that the variety of sects in Congress made it impossible to find a form of prayer agreeable to all delegates.

Jacob Duché
(1738/39-1798)

Sam Adams was ready for this; holding his Puritan nose, he countered with the suggestion that an Anglican clergyman lead the prayers. Assuring his colleagues that he was no bigot, Adams maintained that he

> ... *could hear a Prayer from a Gentleman of Piety and Virtue, who was at the same Time, a Friend to his Country. He was a Stranger in Phyladelphia, but he had heard that Mr. Duché (they pronounced it Dushay) deserved that Character, and therefore he moved that Mr. Duché, an episcopal Clergyman, might be desired, to read Prayers before the Congress, tomorrow Morning.*[20]

Adams's strategy worked. Assured that Adams was not trying to propagate the New England way in the Congress, the delegates agreed that the Reverend Duché should lead them in prayer. Adams later admitted that he had made the proposal because "many of our warmest friends are members of the Church of England. . . ."[21] John Adams recorded in his diary that a prominent Pennsylvanian, Joseph Reed, had told him that the Massachusetts delegates "never were guilty of a more Masterly Stroke of Policy, than in moving that Mr. Douché might read Prayers, it had a very good Effect, &c."[22]

Jacob Duché, a graduate of the College of Philadelphia (now the University of Pennsylvania) and assistant rector of St. Peter's and Christ Church, was a man of weak convictions but great eloquence. When requested by his fellow clergymen from New York and Maryland to refrain from lending his influence to the radical cause, he had agreed; but soon thereafter he succumbed to "the more patriotic feelings" of his parishioners.[23] By the time of the First Continental Congress, he was closely identified with the American cause and therefore, from the radical viewpoint, a safe choice for the chaplain's job. Indeed, Duché did not disappoint Sam Adams and his followers on the morning of September 7. The priest had been much moved by the rumor of the firing on Boston that had rocked the entire Assembly the previous day; and when, accompanied by his clerk, he mounted the platform in his lawn sleeves to lead the Congress in prayer, his performance moved all beyond expectation. John Adams found that no one had ever "prayed with such fervor, such ardor, such earnestness and pathos, and in language so elegant and sublime, for America, for the Congress, for the province of Massachusetts Bay, and especially the town of Boston."[24] Silas Deane believed it worth a hundred-mile ride to hear the Reverend Duché preach on behalf of America, while the Congress offered the minister its hearty thanks.[25]

The Reverend Duché's convictions, however, broke down under the strain of independence and war. When General William Howe occupied Philadelphia in 1777, Duché resigned from his post as chaplain to the Continental Congress, and after one

10.
JACOB DUCHÉ. Thomas Spence
Duché, Jr., date unknown. The
Historical Society of Pennsylvania.

night in prison, broke completely with the Patriot cause. The publicizing of his letter to General Washington, in which he urged the commander in chief to surrender his army and reaffirm his allegiance to the Crown was an act of apostasy that no American could forgive. Undoubtedly "dictated [more] by his fears than by his real sentiments," as Washington charitably explained Duché's motive, the timid minister fled to England, not to return until 1792, when, broken down in health and spirit, he awaited a reunion with his former hero, General Washington, and an early death.[26]

THE SUFFOLK RESOLVES, SEPTEMBER 1774

Although the delegates settled down almost immediately to the business that had brought them to Philadelphia, defining committees and determining their membership, little was accomplished during the first two weeks. Galloway called this period a time of stalemate. Within the committees there was desultory sparring between radicals and conservatives, and quibbling on points of political philosophy. None of this, however, could contribute to either the radical or conservative cause. Some dramatic, outside stimulus was necessary to bring the two parties to a confrontation. This came on September 17 when Paul Revere clattered into Philadelphia, carrying in his satchel the Suffolk Resolves.

Boston had been seething during the summer of 1774. Emotions had been running high since the previous spring, when Parliament had sent General Thomas Gage to assume the governorship of the colony. The outraged citizens had not welcomed the dissolution of their Assembly and the arrival of a new military government. Accustomed to autonomy and belligerently independent, Bostonians did everything in their power to obstruct and impede the provision of food and shelter for General Gage's troops.

When the colonial agents in London, Arthur Lee and Benjamin Franklin, sent word to Boston that the King and Parliament had passed a series of punitive acts designed to regulate colonial government in Massachusetts and abrogate the judicial system, the fury of the Bostonians increased. Such coercive measures they saw as "glaring evidence of a fixed plan of the British administration to bring the whole continent into the most humiliating bondage."[27] Even before copies of the acts arrived, all the towns and counties of Massachusetts Bay had united to resist further curtailment of their freedoms. "The whole continent seems inspired by one soul, and that soul a vigorous and determined one," reported the *Boston Gazette*.[28]

In the face of the new threats to colonial liberty, local town meetings assumed extralegal duties of government until Governor Gage, unable to tolerate such blatant flouting of authority, was able with the arrival of the Coercive Acts in early August to squelch these forums of discontent by prohibiting all town meetings and appointing *mandamus* councillors. The radical leaders could not accede to such restrictions. Quickly, they began to organize town and county conventions to provide a legislative substitute. Open resistance to British authority reached such heights that by the fall of 1774 Governor Gage was forced to write to the British secretary of state, Lord Dartmouth:

> ... *Civil Government is near it's End, the Courts of Justice expiring one*

after another . . . so that we shall shortly be without either Law, or legisla-
tive Power. . . . Nothing that is said at present can palliate; Conciliating,
Moderation, Reasoning is over, Nothing can be done but by forceable
Means.[29]

General Gage was not bluffing. When Salem called a town meeting on August 20, 1774, the infuriated governor ordered his troops to advance on the town. Luckily, the town meeting managed to finish its business before any outbreak of violence could occur, but Gage's action further fed seditious fires among the colonists. Realizing the dependence of his authority on military strength, Gage began to fortify Boston.

Meanwhile, throughout Massachusetts Bay, counties quietly continued to hold conventions and meetings to plan their defense and retaliation. On September 9 between sixty and seventy delegates, appointed from towns in Suffolk County, including Boston, met for the third time since August at Milton. The summer's events had readied them for the most extreme measures. Without hesitation, they unanimously approved a set of resolves drawn up by Dr. Joseph Warren that protested the "unrelenting Severity . . . of a licentious Minister" being visited upon the "guiltless Children" of Massachusetts. Bitterly, the resolves insisted that "the hand which would ransack our pockets" be arrested, and "the parricide which points the dagger to our bosoms" be disarmed.[30]

Joseph Warren
(1741-1775)

Dr. Joseph Warren was a man respected and loved in Boston both as a physician and as a Patriot. A friend of both John and Samuel Adams, he had become deeply involved in the politics of his rebellious colony from the first murmurs of discontent with British policies. By writing articles, giving speeches, and organizing meetings, Warren was of crucial assistance to Sam Adams in his attempt to maintain public antipathy to British rule. As Grandmaster of the Masons, through his position and personality, he gave a degree of organization to the political activities of Boston's artisans and craftsmen. And with Sam Adams he initiated the system of committees of correspondence that so effectively established communication among all the North American colonies. Indeed, even British officials in London, who tended to be astoundingly unknowledgeable about the rebel movement and its leaders in America, knew of Dr. Warren as "the greatest incendiary in all America."[31]

A graduate of Harvard and a learned physician, Dr. Warren possessed as much talent with words as with science. "One of our most bawling demagogues and voluminous writers is a crazy doctor," a Tory pamphleteer had written.[32] Although his commitment to politics and consequent neglect of personal affairs involved him in financial difficulties, Warren did not waiver in his activities when faced with what he considered the unbearable insult of the Coercive Acts. These provided exactly the catalyst he believed was needed to unite the colonists against the mother country. "I can assure, you, that I never saw a more glorious prospect than the present," Warren wrote to his compatriot Sam Adams in Philadelphia that fateful summer.[33]

When the Suffolk County Convention met on September 9, 1774, Joseph Warren was ready with nineteen eloquently written resolves, which were unanimously approved by the delegates. Here he sounded the key notes of some of the most important policies to be eventually adopted by the Continental Congress—nonintercourse with

MAJOR GENERAL JOSEPH WARREN
Who gloriously fell in the defence of American Liberty June y: 17ᵗʰ 1775.

11.
JOSEPH WARREN. Attributed to
Samuel Okey after John Singleton
Copley. Mezzotint, circa 1775.
Mrs. Henry A. Bosch, Jr.

15

12.

The Suffolk Resolves, adopted September 9, 1774, by the County of Suffolk, Massachusetts, and endorsed by the Continental Congress, September 17, 1774. Massachusetts Historical Society.

Britain and, if necessary, a defensive war. Acknowledging George III as the sovereign of America, Warren fearlessly went on to indict Parliament's "unparelleled usurpation of unconstitutional power" in the passage and attempted enforcement of the Coercive Acts.[34] He emphatically urged complete resistance to all of the abhorrent acts, the reinstatement of colonial government, and the immediate cessation of all trade with Great Britain, Ireland, and the West Indies. The resolves demanded the resignation of Crown officers in Massachusetts and refused the payment of any taxes to General Gage's government. As a further affront to British authority, the resolves unlawfully fixed a day for the meeting of a new provincial congress and stressed the importance of the formation of a militia. Most importantly, the resolves placed Massachusetts in the position of open rebellion. The unanimous adoption of the resolves by the county convention became in effect an adoption of a posture of defensive war.

Warren's work was not over after the Suffolk County Convention. In 1775 he took a leading role in the creation of a provincial congress and strongly urged preparation for armed resistance if it became necessary. He participated in the fighting at Lexington, encouraging the minutemen with brave words and tending to the wounded. And a few weeks later at Breed's Hill, the newly commissioned major general threw himself voluntarily into the heavy fighting and was killed by a shot from a British musket. The loss of their leader caused great mourning among the populace. Abigail Adams wrote: "Not all the havoc and devastation they have made has wounded me like the death of Warren. We want him in the Senate; we want him in his profession; we want him in the field." [35]

Dr. Warren had won many hearts to his side when he delivered the orations on the anniversary of the Boston Massacre in 1772 and 1775, and he had convinced many minds with his numerous articles and reports criticizing British policies. He inspired many of his fellow Patriots with a vision of a government that would "Most contribute to the good of the whole with the least inconvenience to individuals." [36] But his radical Suffolk Resolves were to have a much larger impact than any of his previous or later work. On September 11, 1774, Warren sent the resolves, in the trustworthy hands of Paul Revere, to Sam Adams and the Continental Congress in Philadelphia.

Samuel Adams (1722-1803)

Sam Adams, hot-headed radical from Boston, was strangely quiet at the opening of the First Continental Congress, and when he spoke, did so judiciously and diplomatically. He still strongly believed that Parliament must be denied authority over the colonies in "all cases whatsoever." As an expert political manipulator, he also knew that many of the other delegates assembled in Philadelphia feared and condemned the intemperance of the Massachusetts radicals. The Continental Congress was far too important to Sam Adams's cause for him to risk alienating any of its members. Normally an ardent critic of the Church of England, which he liked to identify with the "Whore of Babylon," Adams pleased many southerners when he suggested that the Anglican Reverend Jacob Duché offer prayers for the Congress. Although many of the delegates arrived at the Congress fearing the "leveling spirit" of the New Englanders, they were surprised to find, as Caesar Rodney wrote, that "the Bostonians who had been condemned by many for their violence are moderate men when compared to Virginia, South Carolina, and Rhode Island." [37]

Mr SAMUEL ADAMS.

13.
SAMUEL ADAMS. Samuel Okey after
John Mitchell after John Singleton
Copley. Mezzotint, 1775. Massa-
chusetts Historical Society.

Adams's tone may have been moderate and his manner diplomatic, but his intentions were far from conciliatory. The relentless spirit with which he pursued resistance to British policy in Massachusetts continued with full effort in Philadelphia, but in a more subtle fashion. The "Old Roman" sat back in his chair while the young "Turks" from the South, like Richard Henry Lee of Virginia and Christopher Gadsden of South Carolina, indulged in radical oratory. Sam Adams was awaiting the results of the meeting of the Suffolk County Convention, which he had helped plan before leaving Massachusetts. And behind the scenes at Philadelphia he was actively engaged in gathering enough support to force the Congress to support his colony by adopting severe policies against Great Britain, especially a complete boycott of all commercial intercourse. Like his astute cousin John, Sam was impatient with the delegates' indecisiveness. John had written that in their jealousy of each other, the delegates had become "fearful, timid, skittish." Consisting of "one-third Tory, one-third Whig, one-third mongrel," they needed a prod, and through the Suffolk Resolves, Sam Adams planned just that.[38]

As Joseph Galloway, Sam Adams's foremost opponent in the Congress, watched the wily Boston radical, he clearly realized that Adams was attempting to foment rebellion. Although Galloway had little respect for Adams's abilities, he could admire his capacity for political intrigue:

> *It was this man, [wrote Galloway] who . . . managed at once the faction in Congress at Philadelphia and the factions in New England. Whatever these patriots in Congress wished to have done by their colleagues . . . Mr. Adams advised and directed to be done; and when it was done, it was dispatched by express to Congress. By one of these expresses came the inflammatory resolves of the county of Suffolk, which contained a complete declaration of war against Great Britain.*[39]

When Peyton Randolph read the Suffolk Resolves to the Continental Congress on September 17, "the hall exploded" and "men swarmed to the Massachusetts delegation cheering and shouting."[40] Immediately, resolutions were offered and approved expressing sympathy with the plight of Massachusetts and endorsing the stand that the Bay colony had taken "under the operation of the late, unjust, cruel and oppressive acts of the British Parliament."[41] It was "one of the happiest days" of John Adams's life, for now he was sure that the united colonies would "support Massachusetts or perish with her."[42] As for Sam Adams, that "Machiavel of Chaos" as he was branded by his enemies, no victory could please him more than this; in his eyes, the Congress had essentially approved any action that Massachusetts might wish to take to protect its rights against Great Britain.

Conservatives were not so happy, however, and the resolves did not pass unanimously, despite the fact that it was so noted in the official journals. Both Joseph Galloway and James Duane were refused permission to enter in the record their protests against the "treasonableness" of the resolves. The commitment of the Congress to the Suffolk Resolves, said the Tories, "gave such a blast from the trumpet of sedition, as made one half of America shudder."[43] Later, Galloway explained that the radicals had so stirred up feelings in Philadelphia that there was some fear of tarring and feathering if the Massachusetts colonials were not supported. The conservative

Isaac Low of New York, however, refused to suspect Massachusetts of revolutionary designs: "We have too much Reason in this Congress," he remarked, "to suspect that Independency is aimed at." [44]

GALLOWAY'S PLAN OF UNION

The adoption of the Suffolk Resolves brought "tears" into the eyes of "the old, grave, pacific Quakers of Pennsylvania . . . enough to melt a heart of stone," John Adams reported to Abigail in Boston. Adams believed that the tears were signs of "affection, and admiration for the people of Boston"; but it seems more likely that they were tears of despair.[45] The conservatives, however, were not without recourse; and now they looked to Galloway and his Plan of Union to rescue them and the colonies generally from the morass of rebellion into which they believed the Suffolk Resolves had plunged them.

Galloway himself was no longer as confident that his Plan of Union would be adopted, but he hoped it would appeal to the moderates who were still anxious to remain united to the mother country. If these could be convinced that British sovereignty was not a threat to colonial liberty, then they might cease supporting the radicals toward what Galloway clearly saw was revolution. If the moderates had voted for the Suffolk Resolves in the belief that their rejection would signify implicit approval of the British treatment of Massachusetts, so they might be persuaded to approve Galloway's plan because they were not quite yet ready for independence. Moreover, once the Congress was persuaded to open negotiations with Great Britain, Galloway believed, all misunderstandings between the colonies and the mother country would be cleared and harmony once again restored.

Galloway's analysis of the situation was not far from the truth, as the radicals themselves recognized when they mustered their strength against his plan on September 28, the day he presented it to the Congress. Declaring that he was "as much a friend of liberty as exists," Galloway insisted that every government must have a supreme legislature and that America could not exist without the armed protection and regulatory supervision of Great Britain.[46] Therefore, he proposed that an American legislature be formed, consisting of duly elected members from each of the colonies. As "an inferior and distinct branch of the British Legislature," the American assembly would be headed by a president general appointed by the King, with veto power upon its acts; the assembly, or Grand Council, would "exercise all the Legislative rights, powers, and authorities, necessary for regulating and administering all the general police and affairs of the colonies." Legislation could originate in either America or Britain, and "the assent of both [the Council and Parliament] shall be requisite to the validity of all such general Acts and Statutes." Such a plan, Galloway insisted, would draw together "the strength of the whole empire," advance "the interest of both countries," and secure "the rights and liberties of America. . . ." [47]

James Duane *(1733-1797)* Galloway's Plan of Union was seconded by James Duane, a leader of the conservative delegation from New York. Although Duane did not "think it perfect in its present rude form, much less that I am so fond a friend of it as to recommend it to our

14.
JAMES DUANE. Robert Edge Pine,
1785. Mr. and Mrs. James Duane
Ireland.

assembly for adoption," he wanted to see a lasting reconciliation with Great Britain result from the meeting of the Continental Congress.[48] Like Galloway, he believed that the British Parliament was needed to regulate colonial trade, and he feared that a new democratic spirit was beginning to direct the dispute with Great Britain. "A civil war with America would involve a national bankruptcy," he concluded.[49]

A wealthy member of New York's aristocracy, Duane was well known in his province as a conservative citizen and a brilliant lawyer. Since his admission to the bar in 1754, he had earned a reputation as a courageous and independent lawyer who was not averse to defending the cause of the aristocracy against the interests of the Crown when it suited his purposes. Duane was, above all, loyal to his class. Like many wealthy New Yorkers, he indulged in land speculation and had become embroiled in the New Hampshire Land Grants controversy, in which many landholders from New York and New Hampshire had found themselves holding title to the same land. Duane brought his legal acumen to bear on the problem and became a leader in the "Yorkers" fight to maintain ownership. Not completely successful, he suffered financially; and the guerrilla tactics and escapades of Ethan Allen's Green Mountain Boys in protection of the New Hampshire claims also added to Duane's distrust of New Englanders. He certainly did not appreciate Ethan Allen's "joke" of advertising a £15 reward for his capture in response to the reward of £20 offered by the New York courts for Allen's.

The riots that resulted from the Stamp Act in 1765 and the organization of the radical Committee of Fifteen in New York in 1773 made many conservative New Yorkers anxious and frightened. "God forbid that we should ever be so miserable as to sink into a Republick!" Duane had written in the *New York Gazette* in 1770.[50] Shrewdly, the conservatives managed to wrest power from the radicals by forming a Committee of Correspondence, which they called the Committee of Fifty-one, thus submerging the radical members in a superabundance of conservatives. James Duane was one of the fifty-one.

The conservative complexion of the New York delegation in Philadelphia was not unrepresentative, because New York was one of the most loyal of the thirteen colonies. Duane may have been a "cold" speaker, according to John Adams, but he worked diligently to insure that Parliament be accorded the right to regulate external commerce, and he finally won the acknowledgment of the Congress on that point. Forced into signing the nonimportation and nonexportation agreement, Duane thought the Congress had gone too far; but once the decision was made, he supported it.

After the adoption of the Suffolk Resolves, Galloway and Duane exchanged certificates attesting to the fact that both men opposed the action. Later, when Galloway was forced to flee to England, he presented his certificate to Parliament as proof of his loyalty; but James Duane destroyed his:

> *On cool reflection, . . . I resolved to share the fortune of my country; to be buried in her ruins, or at every hazard to shake off the fetters which were forged for her bondage. It appeared to me to be essential for the safety of America, that the resolutions of a majority of Congress should be fully respected.*[51]

Edward Rutledge
(1749-1800)

Many moderate delegates to the Congress agreed with its more conservative members that Galloway's proposal was the most reasonable and proper way to resolve the conflict with Great Britain. Young Edward Rutledge from South Carolina enthusiastically seconded the Plan of Union, stating, "I think the plan may be freed from almost every objection. I think it almost a perfect plan." [52]

Edward Rutledge was only twenty-seven years old, with one year of a promising law practice behind him, when he went to Philadelphia to represent his colony at the Continental Congress. Like many young men in colonial America, and especially those in the southern colonies, Rutledge had studied law at Middle Temple, but had failed to develop a firm attachment to Great Britain while in London. When he returned home in 1773, the plight of the colonies deeply affected him. Although he did not join the radicals or support their violent tactics, his sentiments placed him strongly on the colonial side. Edward was less conservative, or more "warm" than his older brother and fellow delegate, John, "whose sentiments," Joseph Galloway found, "and mine differ in no one particular." [53] However, young Rutledge's intention to "pursue a right line, and meet with the approbation of my countrymen" while at the Continental Congress did not win him a great deal of popularity in either camp.[54] John Adams found the young Carolinian to be "a perfect Bob o' Lincoln—a Swallow—a Sparrow—a Peacock—excessively vain, excessively weak, and excessively variable and unsteady—jejune, inane, and puerile"; while Charleston merchants thought the

15.
EDWARD RUTLEDGE. Attributed to
James Earl, date unknown.
Edward Rutledge Moore.

young delegate contemptible for supporting and helping to frame the nonimportation, nonexportation, and nonconsumption agreement.[55]

Edward Rutledge was, in fact, a competent and conscientious congressman. His loyalty to America and belief in colonial rights were strongly voiced, though leveled at a conservative pitch. Rutledge was not fond of mob rule, nor was he desirous of adopting or approving illegal means to solve the conflict with Great Britain. He feared the "low Cunning" of the New Englanders, "which Men with Character and without Fortune in general possess."[56] Galloway's Plan of Union seemed, at that time, the "perfect" solution to a complicated situation.

Even after the vote on Galloway's plan was tabled, Rutledge continued zealously to participate in the business of the Congress. As violence increased, he attempted to interpret as faithfully as possible the desires of his constituents, while standing firmly for protection of colonial rights. By time the vote on the Declaration of Independence came to the floor, Rutledge was philosophically ready to add his signature to the document. He then returned to the South to work diligently in helping to bring his colony into statehood.

The popular leaders found little of merit in Galloway's proposal, and several took the floor to voice their objections. Richard Henry Lee of Virginia asked rhetorically,

23

"How did we go on for one hundred and sixty years before the year 1763?" Without waiting for a reply, he answered his question: "We flourished and grew." He could not agree to such a profound change in the "Legislature of the colonies . . . without consulting my constituents." Patrick Henry was morally outraged by the proposal. It would "liberate our constituents from a corrupt House of Commons" only to commit them to an American legislature open to bribery by Great Britain.[57] Although Galloway's main purpose in proposing his Plan of Union was "to prevail on Congress to take the ground of accommodation," it was tabled for later consideration after a heated debate.[58] The closeness of the vote revealed that Joseph Galloway, like Sam Adams, had been busily working behind the scenes, or "out of doors" as the delegates called it, to win support for his measures: six of the twelve colonies represented voted to defer the plan, five voted for it, and the Rhode Island delegation split. Even Galloway's longtime and now increasingly estranged friend, Benjamin Franklin, wrote to Galloway from London that

> *when I consider the extreme corruption prevalent among all orders of men in this old rotten state, and the glorious public virtue so predominant in our rising country I cannot but apprehend more mischief than benefit from a closer union.*[59]

The Galloway Plan of Union never again came before the Congress during the remaining weeks of the session. The radicals won most of their platform, and Galloway, though he tried to marshall the conservative forces behind him, failed to stem the tide of insurgency and quickly became the victim of general suspicion. At the closing of the Congress in October, the popular leaders, seemingly embarrassed by the fact that they had once consented to listen to the heretical Plan of Union, had all mention of it expunged from the minutes.

Galloway retired from politics a few years after the First Continental Congress, increasingly disgusted with what he considered to be the lawlessness and extremism of the colonies. During the war, he fled to England, where he continued to seek an acceptable constitutional remedy for the conflict between the colonies and Great Britain. Galloway was not only a casualty of the First Continental Congress, but also of the war. In 1788 he was convicted of high treason by the Pennsylvania General Assembly, and the considerable property he had left behind in America was confiscated.

Boston Revindicated

The satisfaction that many of the radical leaders felt after the adoption of the Suffolk Resolves faded fast during the ensuing debates and business of the Congress. The narrow margin by which the Galloway Plan of Union was defeated and the feverish arguments over nonimportation and nonexportation disillusioned those who hoped that specific plans would be made to alleviate Boston's suffering. Describing, with some irritation, the vacillation of the delegates, John Adams wrote to a friend in Massachusetts: "you ask the Question what is to be done? they answer Stand Still, bear, with Patience, if you come to a Rupture with the Troops all is lost. . . . The Commencement of Hostilities is exceedingly dreaded here."[60] Adams's evaluation was right, for while the vast majority of the delegates desired a redress of grievances, they deplored the idea of a military encounter with Great Britain.

Nevertheless, the Congress did not entirely ignore the continuing complaints from the citizens of Massachusetts. Indeed, they could not for long. On October 6 Paul Revere returned to Philadelphia with a letter from the Boston Committee of Correspondence relating General Gage's attempts to fortify the town.

According to the Boston radicals, Gage's military preparations and the confiscation of the colony's munitions by the King's troops were indications that "the Town and Country are to be treated by the Soldiery as declared enemies" and that the British administration "is resolved to do all in their power to force them to a submission."[61] To this news, the radical Christopher Gadsden of South Carolina responded by suggesting that Gage be attacked before he could build up his forces. Joseph Galloway and George Ross of Pennsylvania, on the other hand, moved that Massachusetts solve its own problems. But the Congress as a whole decided that it could not turn a deaf ear to the pleas from the Bostonians for advice.

As the delegates gave their attention to Boston's new crisis, all discussion of plans of union with Great Britain ceased. The maneuverings of the radicals resulted once more in the adoption of strong language and a strong stance. On October 8 the Congress approved "the opposition of the inhabitants of the Massachusetts Bay, to the execution of the late Acts of Parliament; and if the same shall be attempted to be carried into execution by force, in such case all America ought to support them. . . ."[62] On October 10 the Congress declared that all those who had taken office under the new acts of Parliament, which violated the Massachusetts Charter, "ought to be held in detestation and abhorrence by all good men . . . as the wicked tool of that despotism which is preparing to destroy those rights which God, nature, and compact, have given to America."[63] A committee, consisting of Sam Adams, Thomas Lynch, and Edmund Pendleton, was elected to draft a letter to General Gage.

16.
An Address to New-England: Written by A Daughter of Liberty bemoaning Boston's sufferings, 1774. The Historical Society of Pennsylvania.

Edmund Pendleton (1721-1803)

Quieter and more moderate than his fellow delegates from Virginia, Edmund Pendleton wanted only to "raise the spirits of the timid to a general united opposition" and to oppose "the violent who were for plunging us into rash measures."[64]

Born into a poor, fatherless home in Virginia, Edmund Pendleton had been forced to work hard to gain his education and legal training. First elected to the House of Burgesses in 1752, he was returned to office continuously thereafter. Considering his poor economic background, he was an unlikely choice—although an able one—to lead the "Cavalier" party, which consisted primarily of wealthy landed gentry, in Virginia politics. He quickly made a name for himself as a conservative, dispassionate, and judicious man, and won great respect both as a lawyer and politician. Even the men he opposed, such as the young Thomas Jefferson, admired his statesmanship and valued his friendship. "[T]aken all in all, he was the ablest man in debate I ever met with," Jefferson later wrote.[65]

Unlike many of the men who assembled at Philadelphia, Pendleton had no desire to attain provincial or national prominence. His only goal was to see that war was averted whatever the costs. "[A] redress of grievances and not a Revolution of Government, was my wish," he wrote.[66] His conservatism arose not from his love of Britain, but from his love for Virginia, and the interests of his colony motivated almost every deci-

25

17.
EDMUND PENDLETON. William
Mercer, date unknown. Virginia
Historical Society.

sion he made. Eventually, as the executive head of the colony, Pendleton chose independence as the only course left to Virginia.

The letter to General Gage that was finally accepted by the Congress on October 11 bore the stamp of Pendleton's moderation. Sam Adams, the "one who never failed to animate," had prepared a fiery draft stating that the British fortifications of Boston must cease or such "Animosities between Great Britain and the Colonies" would "produce Consequences of the most serious Nature." This was rejected by the Congress.[67] The draft submitted by the committee and approved instead urged Gage to desist building fortifications while the Congress labored to resolve the quarrel, and it assured him that the intentions of the people of Massachusetts were peaceable. Pendleton expressed the hope that General Gage and the people of Massachusetts would avoid a violent confrontation until harmony could be restored between the colonies and Great Britain.

On October 20 Boston received news of the Congress's resolves of October 8 and 10. Although not intended to be used for such a purpose, radical Bostonians interpreted these as a mandate for arming their province against the encroaching British troops.

THE COMMITTEE ON RIGHTS AND GRIEVANCES

The endorsement of the Suffolk Resolves and the defeat of the Galloway plan did not kill conservatism or make the Congress any less cautious. When, on October 14, after much delay and disagreement, the delegates approved the set of resolutions that constituted their statement of colonial rights and grievances, they revealed their commitment to a course of moderation and compromise.

The Committee on Rights and Grievances had been established almost as soon as the Congress had assembled. On the second day of meetings, the delegates had resolved unanimously

> *That the Committee be appointed to state the Rights of the Colonies in general, the several instances in which these rights are violated or infringed, and the means most proper to be pursued for obtaining a restoration of them.*[68]

After much jealous arguing back and forth about the committee's composition, the delegates had decided to appoint two members from each colony to draw up a declaration. Stephen Hopkins of Rhode Island had been unanimously approved as the chairman, and the committee had set immediately to its assigned task. But as constituted, the committee did not find its work easy. Representing colonies with various degrees of commitment to the Patriot cause, its members reflected the extremes of feeling that permeated the Congress in 1774.

Stephen Hopkins, for instance, was ambivalent in his approach to colonial policy. An adept politician, he had overcome the absence of formal education and had risen through politics from town government to the Rhode Island Assembly, and, finally, to the chief justiceship and the governor's chair. In society, he was charming enough to make even John Adams admire the buoyancy of his personality; but he was also indecisive. Certain that the quarrel with the mother country would be settled by powder and ball, Hopkins yet supported Galloway's Plan of Union, a blueprint for accommodation, and he conceded to Parliament a limited right to regulate colonial trade. In an earlier pamphlet at the time of the Stamp Act, *The Rights of Colonies Examined* (1764), Hopkins had been one of the first to object to Britain's taxing the colonies without according them representation, but his objections had been voiced mildly and in a spirit of conciliation. Hopkins's pamphlet suggested ideas that might have proved useful for resolving the present crisis, especially his vaguely expressed notion that the British Empire was "an imperial state, which consists of many separate governments each of which hath peculiar privileges. . . ."[69] Since this theory formed the basis for the conservatives' plans for a settlement, it became a matter for contention within the committee's deliberations.

Stephen Hopkins (1707-1785)

In contrast to Hopkins's weakly conservative position, committeeman Thomas Lynch of South Carolina was strongly radical. It was Thomas Lynch who was responsible for the maneuvering that had operated so successfully on the first day of the Congress to make Charles Thomson secretary and Peyton Randolph president. Now it was he who would help to promote the radical position within the committee.

Thomas Lynch (1727-1776)

Lynch was a wealthy rice planter, whose education at Cambridge, England, seems to have prepared him to become an early and passionate defender of colonial rights. As a delegate to the Stamp Act Congress, he had opposed sending petitions to Parliament, for he refused to recognize Parliament's authority over the colonies. An ardent proponent of nonimportation, he practiced what he preached. One of the first things about him that struck Silas Deane was that "he wears the manufacture of this country. . . ." [70] Deane added that Lynch was not only a plain dresser, sensible and above ceremony, but that he ". . . carries with him more force in his very appearance than most powdered folk in their conversation." [71]

Lynch was well acquainted with other radical members of the committee. He had met John Adams earlier, in August 1773, and Adams had found him "an hearty friend to America, and her righteous Cause." [72] Lynch had been present at both Sam and John Adams's first "elegant" supper upon arrival in Philadelphia, and John had immediately engaged in conversation with him and his fellow radical delegate from South Carolina, Christopher Gadsden—a conversation that surely must have included discussion of the plight of Boston and Massachusetts. [73]

We do not know what role Lynch played in the committee's deliberations, and especially on the important point of the origin of colonial rights. We can guess, however, given his previous and later utterances, that he agreed with John and Sam Adams and the Virginians, Pendleton and Richard Henry Lee, that American rights derived from nature and not, as Lynch's fellow delegate Edward Rutledge insisted, from the British constitution.

Roger Sherman (1721-1793)

Roger Sherman made his own unique contribution to the debates of the Committee for Stating Rights, Grievances and Means of Redress. Insisting that there was "no other Legislative over the Colonies but their respective Assemblies," he indicated that if the colonies adopted the common law of England it was not because it was English common law but "the highest Reason." [74] Sherman's distinction was important, for it could—and eventually did—serve as justification for placing the rights of the colonies above loyalty to the mother country.

Sherman had educated himself far beyond the cobbler's bench to which he had been apprenticed as a boy in Connecticut. The son of a cordwainer, he had molded himself into what can be called a paragon of Yankee virtue: self-controlled, honest, serious, frugal, pious, industrious. Thus he had moved, in characteristic eighteenth-century American fashion, from one success to another as merchant, lawyer, surveyor, judge, legislator, and—his crowning glory as a self-educated man—treasurer of Yale College. Sherman had even published almanacs that featured his own accurate astronomical calculations.

Cautious and deliberate by nature, Sherman had frowned upon the violence of the Connecticut Sons of Liberty in the Stamp Act period, but he had opposed the act itself and had agreed to serve on his colony's committee of correspondence. As a weapon against the Townshend Acts, he endorsed nonimportation. Fear that the Crown might impose a bishop on the colonies further alienated this staunch Congregationalist from the British, and by 1774 he had, in spite of his inclination to moderation, arrived at the conclusion that only the colonial assemblies had the right to legislate for the colonies.

There was nothing elegant about Roger Sherman. He was, indeed, ungainly in form and clumsy in speech and his clothes never seemed to fit him quite right. Sherman's *nouveau riche* Connecticut colleague, Silas Deane, detested him as a boor. Yet it was Sherman, more than any other man at the First Continental Congress, who epitomized the American character of the day, and it is fitting that Sherman alone, of all his illustrious contemporaries, signed the four basic documents of the American

28

18.
Roger Sherman. Ralph Earl, circa 1777.
Yale University Art Gallery. [Not in exhibition.]

19.
JOHN ADAMS. John Trumbull, circa 1793.
A. Perry Morgan, Jr.

Revolution: the Association, the Declaration of Independence, the Articles of Confederation, and the Constitution.

The experiences of John Adams, the author of the committee's resolutions in their final form, reveal the temper of the Congress. Adams was a member of the Harvard class of 1755. Early in his career he had abandoned ideas of entering the ministry in favor of the law. The Stamp Act crisis brought Adams to prominence in his colony as the author of the Braintree resolutions of protest and an opponent of the closing of the courts, and his reputation as a staunch defender of colonial rights grew during the ensuing decade. Adams possessed a fine mind, a great deal of courage, a high-minded regard for justice, uncompromising honesty, and genuine devotion to republican government; yet he could often be vain, irascible, inflexible, petty, jealous, impatient, humorless, suspicious, and provincial.

John Adams (1735-1826)

In the First Continental Congress, Adams found especially annoying what he considered pretentions to statesmanship held by the other delegates. He was only slightly less impatient with the round of dining and visiting that the delegates seemed to find so necessary, although he was capable of enjoying the many toastings in Madeira and proud of his capacity to hold his liquor.[75]

In the autumn of 1774 Adams was especially careful to keep his irritation with "inferiors" from showing. The desperate need of Massachusetts for support from the other colonies helped the prickly Bostonian discover in himself an unsuspected capacity for accommodation, and he was careful to study his fellow delegates to determine how far the radicals might press their colleagues without scaring them off. "We have been obliged to act with great delicacy and caution," he wrote to his law student, William Tudor, in Boston. "We have been obliged to keep ourselves out of sight and to feel pulses, and to sound the depths; to insinuate our sentiments, designs and desires, by means of other persons, sometimes of one province, and sometimes of another." [76] The result was that Adams, the uncompromising radical and self-righteous Yankee, bent sufficiently to include in his final draft of the Declaration of Rights and Grievances several ideas of a distinctly conservative provenance.

Two major issues in particular almost split the committee. The first was whether rights emanated from the law of nature, as the radicals believed, or whether they rested solely on the British constitution and colonial charters, as the conservatives insisted. The second quarrel was waged on the extent of parliamentary authority over the colonies: Could Parliament tax the colonies in all cases, or simply their trade for revenue purposes? This was the thornier and the more immediately important of the two issues. The discussion over the questions, according to Adams, "spun into great length and nothing was decided." [77] The situation was not helped by the fact that Galloway, as he later admitted, was following a policy of deliberate obstruction.[78] Not until John Rutledge asked Adams to produce a formula was the impasse broken and the problem solved.

Adams's formula may be seen in the draft of a declaration that he prepared for adoption by the Congress. He incorporated propositions made by conservatives like James Duane and radicals like Thomas Lynch. He virtually paraphrased Duane's contentions that the colonists enjoyed the right to a free and exclusive power of legislation within their respective provinces, subject only to the negative of the King; and that they possessed the right to be protected by the common law of England, to benefit from all statutes in force at the time of their colonization, and to enjoy all the immunities and privileges granted by their colonial charters. But Adams also insisted that the colonists were entitled to "all the rights, liberties, and immunities of free and natural born subjects, within the Realm of *England*"; to trial by a jury of "peers of the vicinage"; to peaceable assembly; to petition; to be free of the obligation to support a standing army in times of peace; and to the enjoyment of an independent legislature. British "infringements and violations" of these basic rights, together with those acts of Parliament passed since the cessation of hostilities in 1763, Adams declared, "demonstrate a system formed to enslave *America*."[79]

If the conservatives lost a point in the declaration that colonial rights were derived from "the immutable laws of nature," they gained one in Adams's admission that these rights also derived from the principles of the English Constitution. Where they succeeded in having the declaration end on a "loyal" note, they lost in the recommendation that until colonial rights were restored, the colonies should "enter into a Non-Importation, Non-Consumption, and Non-Exportation Agreement or Association." Thus, the declaration represented something of a compromise between the positions of both conservatives and radicals, and each could take heart from a measure of success. The conservatives were able to prevent the Congress from voting to raise "men or money, or arms or ammunition" to secure colonial rights; but the radicals were able to have the Congress accept the recommendation of an Association—an extralegal, revolutionary body established to enforce the resolutions of an illegal Congress.

John Sullivan   When John Adams later in life summarized the work of the committee appointed to
(1740-1795)   state colonial rights and grievances, he noted that the declarations drawn up by John Sullivan, the delegate from New Hampshire, reappeared two years later in the Declaration of Independence. These two declarations revealed the insistence of the delegates that certain acts of the mother country had to be repealed, or else the colonists would "forever restrain our trade from Great Britain, Ireland, and the West Indies."[80] What Sullivan had in mind was British legislation that interfered with the power of provincial legislatures to regulate their internal affairs, and the Canada Bill, or the Act for Governing Quebec, which, he wrote, was "the most dangerous to American liberties among the whole train"[81] because it established the Catholic Church in that province and continued French civil law.

That Sullivan, a New England son of Irish parents who had come to America as redemptioners, should have insisted upon religious liberty as a cornerstone of American freedoms suggests the strength of the reaction to the Quebec Act among settlers along the northern borders. Although his father had been born a Roman Catholic, he had not maintained his church connections in the New World; and his sons, possibly including John, had joined the local Congregational church. Sullivan's biographer had indicated that "as the years went by . . . [he] became violently antagonistic toward Roman Catholicism."[82]

A rugged and energetic lawyer, John Sullivan had entered upon his career with a ruthless ambition that created some hostility in the small town of Durham, New Hampshire, where he was established as the community's first lawyer. Eventually, his charm, gregariousness, and dignified manners broke down some of the ill-feeling that

20.
JOHN SULLIVAN. Unidentified
engraver (probably English).
Mezzotint, 1776-78. Anne S.K.
Brown Military Collection, Brown
University Library.

surrounded him. When John Adams traveled in York County (New Hampshire) in June 1774, he noted that Sullivan was worth £10,000, owned six mills, was "treated with great respect," and had been appointed major in the New Hampshire militia.[83]

Although during earlier years Sullivan had supported the royalist Governor Wentworth, he became increasingly aware of the Crown's threat to "those Liberties which God of nature had given." [84] In the summer of 1774 he represented Durham at New Hampshire's First Provincial Congress where he was chosen one of the two delegates to the Continental Congress.

When the proud and confident John Sullivan joined the distinguished gathering of provincial leaders in Philadelphia, Joseph Galloway briefly entertained the hope that here he would find an ally. But Galloway's expectations were not to be fulfilled. He had not foreseen Sullivan's zeal in defending colonial rights, nor his strong views concerning the Quebec Act. Galloway could be satisfied, however, that in Sullivan's draft report listing British infringements on American rights he did not mention the problem of trade regulation. Conservatives believed that Parliament had the right to regulate external trade, something which the Committee and John Adams were prepared to accede to in 1774.

When the Congress disbanded in October, Sullivan returned to Durham where he worked to win New Hampshire support for the Association. Appointed by the New Hampshire Provincial Congress to the Second Continental Congress, Major Sullivan was commissioned by that body in 1775 a brigadier general in the Continental Army.

33

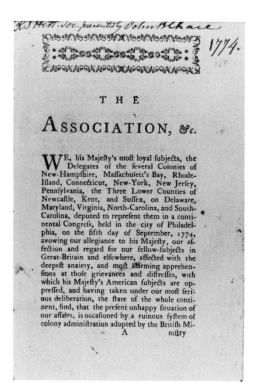

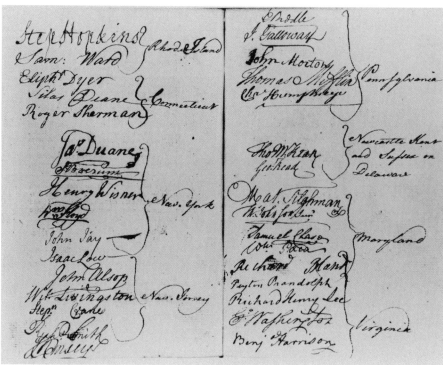

21.

The Association entered into by the American Continental Congress in Behalf of all the Colonies, October 20, 1774. Philadelphia, 1774 (with forty-five signatures of the members of the Congress.) The Rhode Island Historical Society.

THE ASSOCIATION

Although the Congress itself was a symbol of the attempt to achieve colonial unity, collective action on the part of the Americans actually began with the signing of the Continental Association on October 20, 1774. Consisting of fourteen articles and a preamble, the document formally pledged the colonies to unite in a program of commercial coercion against Great Britain in order to "obtain redress of those Grievances, which threaten destruction to the Lives, Liberty, and Property of his Majesty's subjects in *North America*."[85] The final Association agreement signed by "the Delegates of the several Colonies" stated the delegates' belief that "the present unhappy situation" was caused by "a ruinous system of the Colony Administration, adopted by the British Ministry about the year 1763." An embargo on all trade with Great Britain, the delegates asserted, would "prove the most speedy, effectual, and peaceable measure" for effecting redress. Significant in the agreement was the provision that "a Committee be chosen in every County, City, and Town" in the American colonies for the enforcement of the Association, and that offenders' names be publicized so that "all such foes to the rights of British-Americans may be publicly known, and universally contemned, as the enemies of American liberty."[86] Here, then, was the machinery for enforcement of trade suspension with the mother country, as well as the means for unified defense action in the future.

In 1774 the Continental Congress hoped to reestablish the conditions that had existed between the colonies and the mother country before 1763. Guidelines for action had come from the nonimportation agreements of 1768-69 and the Virginia Association of August 1774. Since August the idea of reimplementing a boycott against Eng-

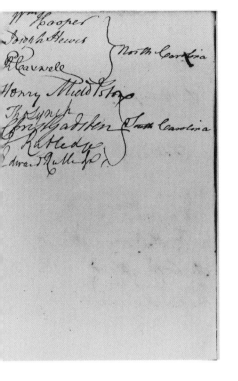

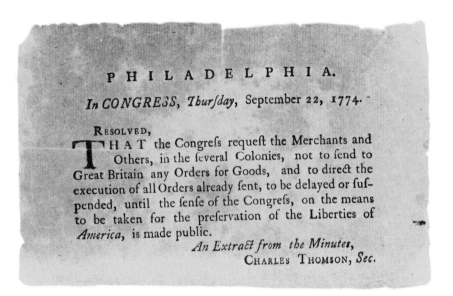

22.
Extract from the minutes of the Continental Congress urging merchants to refrain from trade in British-made goods, September 22, 1774. Library of Congress.

land as a political weapon had been receiving widespread support in colonial newspapers and private conversations. Therefore, when on September 17 members of the Congress began their work on plans for restricting trade with the mother country, they were aware that they had favorable public opinion behind their efforts.

Actually, the Congress had already committed itself to a policy of commercial warfare with Great Britain when it endorsed the Suffolk Resolves. Now, however, faced with the necessity of drawing up plans to implement the trade restrictions, the delegates grew more cautious. To avoid the dangers of too sweeping a commitment, they determined to consider each trade suspension proposal individually before combining them into a general policy.

On September 22, with only brief debate, they resolved to request merchants to stop ordering goods from Great Britain until suitable effective means of opposition could be devised. Five days later, on September 27, they adopted a mild nonimportation resolution setting December 1, 1774, as the deadline for receiving imports from Great Britain and Ireland and for beginning nonconsumption regulation. It was the problem of establishing nonexportation measures, however, that created the most heated dispute, one that truly tested whether or not the colonies could be expected to act harmoniously, or whether, as one unfriendly observer in New York put it, the Congress would end in confusion, since the concerns of its members were so diverse and "Men . . . will . . . stick out anything in prosecuting their Interests."[87]

The debate on nonexportation lasted three days, at the end of which the Congress voted to stop exportation "of all merchandise and every commodity whatsoever" on September 10, 1775, unless the mother country consented to redress colonial grievances. A committee consisting of Thomas Mifflin, Richard Henry Lee, Thomas Johnson, Thomas Cushing, and Isaac Low was appointed to prepare a plan to put into effect all the trade decisions agreed upon.

Thomas Johnson
(1732-1819)

Thomas Johnson shared with Richard Henry Lee the distinction of serving on three of the most important committees of the Continental Congress: the "Great Committee" called "to state the rights" of the colonies, the committee to form a plan to make the nonimportation and nonexportation resolutions effective, and a committee to prepare an address to the King.

A Marylander of distinction and one of the colony's leading spirits in opposing parliamentary efforts to tax the colonies, Johnson had seen a decade of service on numerous committees in the provincial assembly—including the important one established to formulate a "Bill of Rights" for the colony and another to draft a memorial to King George III. Before the clouds of Revolution gathered, he had also played an important role in the Maryland tobacco tax controversy, arguing with the other spokesmen for colonial autonomy—Charles Carroll, Samuel Chase, and William Paca —that the freemen of the province were the ultimate source of authority, superior to the Crown or the Proprietary.

When news of the Boston Port Bill reached Baltimore in 1774, Maryland Patriots assembled in Annapolis to adopt a program of action. Johnson was appointed to a committee of correspondence delegated to make arrangements for a congress of the colonies that would "effect such association" as necessary for securing the rights of freemen.[88]

Impressed by the importance of the task facing the delegates, Johnson was inclined to caution and, like George Washington (whom he later, at the behest of John Adams, placed in nomination for the position of commander in chief of the Continental Army), he "took a legal rather than an economic view of public affairs." He had a "clear and cool Head," wrote John Adams, "and possessed an extensive Knowledge of Trade as well as Law." But, Adams added as qualification, "His Passions and Imagination don't appear enough for an orator. His Reason and Penetration appear, but not his Rhetoric."[89] Later, however, John Adams was to write that Johnson was "the most frequent speaker" from Maryland; and that while the hope for reconciliation had led him "to retard many vigorous measures," "ere long he and all his State came cordially into our system."[90]

Johnson's caution did not inhibit the committee chosen to bring in a plan for a trade agreement from recommending the creation of an American Association, perhaps the most important and radical achievement of the First Continental Congress. Nor did his reputation as "a deliberating man" prevent him from being appointed later by the Maryland provincial committee of correspondence to implement the Association measures.[91] Returning to Annapolis at the close of the Congress, Johnson urged Marylanders to assume the functions of government themselves, and he was one of the members of the Assembly who helped to draft the Association of the Freemen of Maryland—a declaration of rights for a new provincial regime that was signed by delegates to the Assembly in convention on August 14, 1775.

Thomas Mifflin
(1744-1800)

"The animating soul"—as John Adams called him—of not only the revolutionary movement in Pennsylvania but also of the committee appointed to consider ways of effecting the Congress's decision to embark on a policy of economic coercion was

23.
THOMAS JOHNSON and his family.
Charles Willson Peale, 1772.
Private collection.

Thomas Mifflin, wealthy Quaker merchant of Philadelphia.[92] A close friend of Sam Adams and other Boston radicals, with whom he visited and corresponded frequently, he was privy to their hopes and plans for the Continental Congress, which, indeed, he had done much to help to arrange.

Why Mifflin should have become involved with revolutionary politics, given his prominent position in Quaker society, is difficult to determine, except to say that he had been nourished, as a student in a Quaker school and at the College of Philadelphia, in the political philosophy of the English Whig writers Locke and Harrington, and that Britain's oppressive policies began during his days of youthful excitement and idealism. Thus, at the age of fifteen, he was convinced from his readings that "there can be no Right to Power, except what is either founded upon, or speedily obtains the hearty consent of the Body of the People." As a well-trained Whig, Mifflin believed, as did most other members of his well-to-do and propertied class, that "Power wherever lodged will never be stable unless it has large Property for its foundation." However, Mifflin was also taught to believe that people possessed the right to defend

37

24.
THOMAS MIFFLIN. Gilbert Stuart, circa 1800. Private collection.

themselves against abuse of power; even slaves, said Mifflin, may defend themselves against certain kinds of injuries. Therefore, British abuse of imperial power had to be countered by the assertion of the rights of those so abused—the colonists. To this end, Mifflin devoted the greater part of his political life.[93]

In 1772 Mifflin took his seat in the Provincial Assembly as one of Philadelphia's two burgesses. Here, his "very sensible and agreeable" personality soon made him popular among his colleagues, a popularity that extended to the Boston Whigs when he visited that city in the summer of 1773, just before the landing of the East India tea ship.[94] After the Boston Tea Party, Mifflin led his fellow Patriots in Philadelphia in expressing enthusiastic admiration for what some Philadelphia merchants (including Benjamin Franklin) deemed "an Act of violent Injustice."[95]

38

Sam Adams and his Boston Sons of Liberty recognized the importance of Pennsylvania, one of the wealthiest and most populous colonies, to their plan to resist the British. They hoped during the summer of 1774 that Mifflin would be able to arouse Pennsylvanians to cooperate with them by supporting a trade embargo. But Mifflin and his colleague Joseph Reed, who had also visited Boston and formed friendships with leading citizens there, understood the political situation in Philadelphia and had to move more cautiously than Sam Adams would have liked. When a meeting of between two and three hundred people from "all ranks and interests" that the two Philadelphians had arranged fell under the influence of the more moderate John Dickinson and thus rejected resolutions for an economic boycott at that time, Mifflin was "obliged to change our Ground, [as he wrote to Sam Adams] and . . . at last happily engaged their concurrence in a Measure which may in the End secure what you desire and have so much Reason to expect from us"—a continental congress. A congress, he believed, would not offend the people of property and respectability whom he wished to see join the radical cause. "A Non-Importation to be urged immediately," he warned Adams, "without some previous Step taken to obtain Redress, may disunite us & ruin the Cause of America." "Our People are in Earnest," he assured Adams, and proved his point by persuading the Pennsylvania Assembly to recognize the Congress and appoint seven delegates to it, among whom he, of course, figured prominently.[96]

Mifflin's energy and activity made him an important member of the Congress. He was especially active on the committees to plan trade coercion against England, and on the Committee of Five later appointed to make the resolutions of Congress with respect to such trade coercion effective. Under his leadership, the special committee finally recommended the Continental Association, which was adopted on October 18.

The Association document that the committee produced was a refinement and standardization of the delegates' combined experience with trade suspension agreements. For the sake of unity, compromises had to be worked out—for example, the Congress permitted South Carolina to continue to export rice but retained indigo on the nonexportation list. The document further provided for enforcement of the agreement by committees of correspondence; it called for discontinuation of the slave trade and a program of austerity throughout the provinces. Despite the angry protests of some moderates, such as the writer in the Massachusetts *Gazette* who claimed that the terms of the Association "would shock the soul of a savage," the colonial assemblies overrode all objections, and by April 1775 twelve colonies had placed the Association in operation.[97]

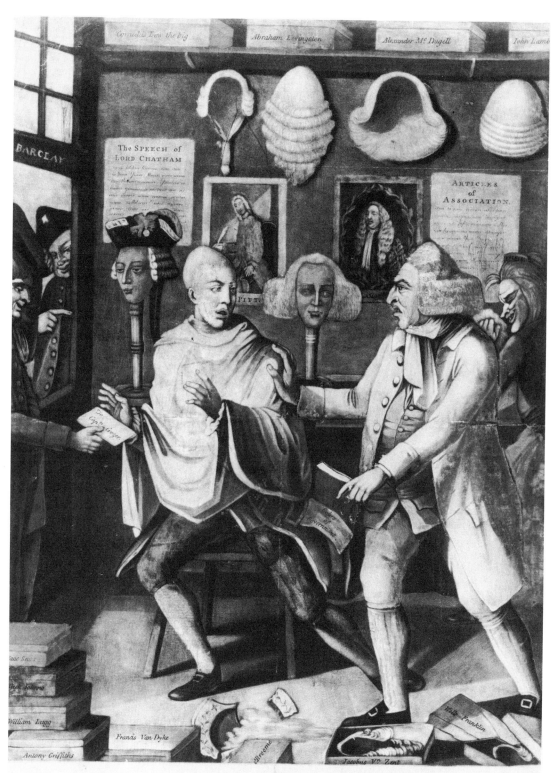

The PATRIOTICK BARBER of NEW YORK.

Plate III.   London Printed for R. Sayer & I. Bennett, Map & Printsellers Nᵒ 53 Fleet Street, as the Act directs 12 Febᵍ 1775.

25.
The Patriotick Barber of New York (or the Captain in the Suds) depicts
the refusal of a New York Patriot to finish shaving his customer
when he learned that he was a British captain. Attributed to
Philip Dawe. Mezzotint, February 12, 1775. Colonial Willamsburg.

The Problem of Persuasion

By the middle of October the delegates to the First Continental Congress were ready to wind up their business and return home. They had been able to agree on what constituted their rights and grievances; they had expressed their sympathy and support for the Bostonians "suffering in the righteous Cause of America"; and, most important, they had agreed upon a general plan and measures for its enforcement that would, they hoped, hit Great Britain where it would hurt most—in her commercial strength.[1] Through economic coercion, they hoped to end further violent confrontations.

Two things more remained to be done before the delegates could pack their bags and prepare for the long and uncomfortable journey to their respective homes. These were to persuade the British colonies in North America to remain united by clearly informing them of the reasons behind their meeting and, secondly, to prove their peaceable intentions by soliciting once again the sympathy of King George III in their fight against parliamentary legislation. On October 11 committees were appointed to draw up four memorials to accomplish these essentially propagandistic purposes: one to the colonists, clearly listing all the acts of Parliament since 1763 that constituted a system "for subjugating these colonies"; the second, to the people of Great Britain, expressing the constitutional and legal reasons behind their protest and their faith in the "magnanimity and justice" of the British people to elect a sympathetic Parliament that would be able to restore "fraternal affection" between the British and Americans; the third, to the inhabitants of Quebec, urging them to join "with your numerous and powerful neighbours . . . in our righteous contest"; and the fourth to the King, listing all offensive parliamentary acts that had been passed since 1763.[2] Whatever was radical in the memorials reflected the extremism of one of the most prominent of the Virginia delegates and a member of most of the committees: Richard Henry Lee, who had already made his force felt in the Committee on the Declaration of Rights.

Richard Henry Lee was committed to a life of statesmanship. A member of one of Virginia's first families, he had studied and traveled in England and on the continent and owned one of the most extensive private libraries in the colonies. A thorough study of law and historical literature gave him a mastery of political ideas and precedents

Richard Henry Lee (1732-1794)

that earned him the reputation (as Silas Deane wrote to his wife) of being the "Cicero of America."[3]

That the aristocratic Lee should have associated himself with liberals and radicals suggests the way in which many southern planters in the mid-eighteenth century became committed to the revolutionary cause, taking over leadership of it within their individual colonies and turning it to their own uses. Through inheritance and education, Lee assumed his right to political leadership as a matter of course; he was also trained to exercise independence in judgment and action. Like most of his fellow burgesses, he resented the restrictions imposed on Virginia's legislature by the governor and the Council, both appointed by the Crown and both possessing unlimited political and legislative powers. The wealthy planters of Virginia ruled with a sense of *noblesse oblige;* but when thwarted by a recalcitrant governor or Council, or by British law, their defense of self-government made them, as John Adams wrote, ". . . intrepid and unchangeable," ready to defend their country "like the Greeks at Thermopylae."[4] Self-interest became identified with the interests of their colony; and limitations on the freedom of the one were considered limitations on personal freedom.

One of Lee's first public appearances in the House of Burgesses came when he spoke for a motion to impose a large duty on slaves imported into Virginia. Lee argued against slavery on economic and social grounds. All fellow creatures were entitled to "liberty and freedom by the great law of nature," Lee declared, and this belief that human rights emanated from natural law underlay his crusade for the preservation of colonial rights.[5] Essentially, as his biographer Oliver Chitwood has pointed out, Lee was a radical conservative, and his spirited opposition to British policy was to a great extent the result of a conservatism in such economic matters as land ownership and such political matters as the maintenance of power in the hands of those born to wield it.[6] The British attempt to tax the colonies in the Sugar, Stamp, and Townshend Acts he believed usurped the colonial legislatures' power to impose taxes on the people they represented; therefore it had to be opposed.

Once committed to a policy of opposition, Lee became unrelenting and ready to adopt extreme measures. With Thomas Jefferson and other young radicals, he "cooked up" the resolution to set a day of fasting in Virginia when the Boston Port Bill went into effect; he served on the committee of correspondence appointed for Westmoreland County; and he suggested a continental congress even before a letter was received from Boston calling for such a meeting in Philadelphia on September 1.

In Philadelphia Lee formed close friendships with both John and Sam Adams. Amidst the drinking of Madeira wine and the consumption of elegant suppers, he found time to contribute to some of the more important documents issued by the Congress during its six-week session. As a member of the committee to compose a memorial to the people of British America he prepared the long, well-written first draft that warned Britain's American subjects that unless the British demonstrated good sense, they would "be reduced to chuse, either a more dangerous contest, or a final ruinous, and infamous submission." The Memorial to British Americans "diligently, deliberately, and calmly" listed the abuses of legislative and executive power by Great Britain, which, commencing after the conclusion of the French and Indian War, represented, in Lee's view, a new imperial policy. Such legislation, Lee insisted, "by rendering Assemblies useless . . . by taking the money of the Colonists without their consent . . .

26.
RICHARD HENRY LEE. Charles
Willson Peale, circa 1795-1805.
National Portrait Gallery, Smith-
sonian Institution.

43

by substituting in . . . place [of Trial by Jury] trials in Admiralty and Vice Admiralty courts, where single Judges preside, holding their commissions during pleasure, and . . . by rendering the Judges thereof totally dependent on the Crown for their salaries," subjugated the colonies "to the uncontrollable and unlimited power of Parliament, in violation of their undoubted rights and liberties. . . ." [7]

Pointing out the "fidelity, duty and usefulness" of the colonies during the last war—particularly the aid rendered by Massachusetts Bay, which raised, outfitted, and supported regiments for the King's service and contributed to the British capture of Nova Scotia in 1710 and Louisbourg in 1745—the Memorial to British Americans defended the "publick spirited Town" of Boston for attacking the "monopolizing combination of English ministers and the East India Company," and it pointed out that the "behaviour of the people in other Colonies" had been equally in opposition. Finally, the Quebec Act came under Lee's fire; it was, said Lee, "an arbitrary arrangement, designed to "extinguish the freedom of those Colonies by subjecting them to a despotick Government." [8] Justifying a "method of opposition that does not preclude a hearty reconciliation with our fellow citizens on the other side of the *Atlantic*" and deploring "the urgent necessity that presses us to an immediate interruption of commerce that may prove injurious to them [the British]," the memorial insisted that the colonists were being driven "by the hands of violence into unexperienced and unexpected publick convulsions and that we are contending for freedom, so often contended for by our ancestors." [9] For the sake of their "salvation and that of your posterity," the colonists should defend their country's honor before the whole world by accepting the temporary inconvenience of a trade embargo. They must be prepared, Lee warned, if "the peaceable mode of opposition recommended by us, be broken and rendered ineffectual, as your cruel and haughty Ministerial enemies, from a contemptuous opinion of your firmness, insolently predict will be the case, . . . to choose, either a more dangerous contest, or a final, ruinous, and infamous submission." [10]

On October 18 Lee presented to the Congress his draft of an address to the people of Great Britain. The document, according to reports, was disappointing. "When it was read in Congress," Edmund Pendleton and Benjamin Harrison reported to Thomas Jefferson,

> *every countenance fell and a deep silence endured for many minutes. At length it was laid on the table for perusal and consideration till the next day.*[11]

Perhaps Lee was too provocative in his document. "We would certainly be Slaves," he told the British people, ". . . we would be unworthy of the British ancestry which is now our boast, if we did not esteem our constitutional liberty far above the possession of Life." As for the Quebec Act, Lee was bitter; the establishment of Catholicism, "this bloody and intolerant religion," was "at such fatal variance with Protestantism, that the inhabitants of that now greatly-extended Country [Quebec] will thereby be well-fitted both from civil & religious Principles to carry Slaughter and destruction into the free protestant Colonies, whenever they shall be encouraged by a wicked Ministry to do so." Americans, Lee assured the British people, had no thought of independence with which "some malignant Spirits in Great Britain" were charging them. But, he added, "this most desirable connection between Great Britain and the Colonies . . . must be interrupted, if the people of America were distressed and ruined by unconstitutional Taxes." [12]

It fell to John Jay to receive the credit for the Address to the People of Great Britain. As a member of New York's conservative Committee of Fifty-one Jay could be expected to be more conciliatory and temperate and thus not frighten the British people with too vehement an expression of protest against the unconstitutional policies of their legislators.

John Jay (1745-1829)

Jay hoped that reconciliation would take place once new elections brought about a change of ministry. He hoped, as the final document indicated, that the British would "furnish a Parliament of such wisdom, independence, and publick spirit, as may save the violated rights of the whole Empire from the devices of wicked Ministers and evil Counsellors, whether in or out of office; and thereby restore that harmony, friendship, and fraternal affection between all the inhabitants of his Majesty's Kingdoms and Territories so ardently wished for by every true and honest *American*." [13]

Jay had joined the New York delegation as the choice of the conservative merchants of New York who feared, as he did, an outright declaration of support for the town of Boston. They were aware that Boston's violence not only might render reconciliation impossible but might also stimulate mob uprisings against property owners as well as against the British. Jay had witnessed "Liberty Poles," the burning of royal governors and stamp collectors in effigy, the rioting of tenant farmers against landowners, and, on April 22, 1774, the "tea party" of New York's Sons of Liberty that had ended with eighteen cases of tea being taken off the ship *London* and dumped into New York Harbor. After news of the Boston Port Bill had reached the city, hotheaded "Mechanics" had organized a committee of twenty-five to supervise the closing of New York's port by means of a trade embargo, and had stimulated a popular resistance movement that threatened to become uncontainable unless taken under control by the city's merchants and upper classes. At least so thought New York's aristocracy, and John Jay belonged by birth, education, and training to this group.

The sixth son of a wealthy New York merchant of Huguenot descent, John Jay, as Samuel Flagg Bemis has written, was "never of a democratic nature or persuasion." His education and family training further heightened qualities of serious contemplation, "strong reasoning powers, comprehensive views, indefatigable application, and uncommon firmness of mind." In his self-assurance, reverence for society, "not disagreeable vanity," and "literary facility [that] sometimes gave way to pretentious oracular utterance," he was not much different from many of his classmates at King's College or from aristocratic friends like Robert Livingston, Jr. and Gouverneur Morris. Like James Otis of Boston, he was seriously concerned lest "when the pot boils, the scum always rises." He was also, however, courageous and charitable, qualities that rendered him popular despite his expressed contempt for the "mobility." [14]

In the Continental Congress, Jay worked (as he had in New York) to mitigate expression of too radical a sentiment and direct the assembled delegates to the path of reconciliation. He approved Galloway's Plan of Union, but he also signed, along with his fellow delegate James Duane, the Association that bound New York to uphold a boycott of British goods until the Coercive Acts were repealed. Although Jay signed the agreement reluctantly, he did so to avoid the appearance of a disunited Congress.

27.
JOHN JAY. Gilbert Stuart and John
Trumbull, probably 1794. National
Portrait Gallery, Smithsonian
Institution.

When he returned to his home, however, he discovered that this act had endeared him to the Committee of Mechanics—New York's Sons of Liberty—who pledged their "readiness in accepting and fidelity in executing the high and important trust" the Association placed in its local committees.[15] Jay and his fellow delegates answered the Mechanics' address with the expected note of conciliation: "Let us . . . endeavor . . . to promote that internal tranquillity which can alone give weight to our laudable efforts for the preservation of our freedom, and crown them with success."[16]

Although Jay's major accomplishments still lay ahead, his most notable achievement in the First Continental Congress was his *Address to the People of Great Britain,* an appeal to the British to understand the American situation in terms of constitutional and political precedents mutually accepted on both sides of the Atlantic. He had been working on a draft appeal since appointment to the committee, although Lee had been formally designated by the committee to write it. When silence followed the reading of Lee's draft, Jay worked far into the night to finish his own. The next morning he gave the draft to Livingston to read to the assembly as being the ideas of a friend. Jay's address as read by Livingston was recommitted to the committee, reported out two days later, and adopted with hardly a changed comma.

"We consider ourselves and do insist that we are and ought to be," Jay wrote, "as free as our fellow-subjects in Britain, and that no power on earth has a right to take our property from us without our consent. . . ." Britain's despotic acts against the colonies could very well become tyranny against the free people of Britain. Ministerial wickedness was responsible for establishing in Quebec "a religion fraught with sanguinary and impious tenets . . . a religion that has deluged your island in blood, and dispersed impiety, bigotry, persecution, murder, and rebellion throughout every part of the world." Assuring the British that Americans were not seditious troublemakers, he appealed to British "justice" and "public Spirit." "We will never submit to be hewers of wood or drawers of water for any ministry or nation in the world," this proud New York aristocrat asserted as he pleaded with the British people to "place us in the same situation that we were at the close of the last war [1763], and our former harmony will be restored."[17]

On the committee to draft an address to the people of Quebec were Richard Henry Lee, John Dickinson, and Thomas Cushing, Boston merchant and Speaker of the Massachusetts legislature. Only three days were required to draft the address, two more for revisions, and on October 26 the Congress approved a final text.

Of the three members of the committee charged with persuading the inhabitants of Quebec to participate in the American cause, Richard Henry Lee was the most radical, but Thomas Cushing was not far behind. Although his was essentially a moderate temperament that ultimately was to find itself uneasy with the extreme measures he had helped create, his temperateness had vanished with the Boston Port Bill, a "cruel and oppressive" example of what Americans might expect from "a parliament who claim a right to make laws binding us in all cases, whatever."[18] In Philadelphia Cushing urged economic coercion as the best way to bring Great Britain around. Britain, he wrote, "has drawn the sword against us, and nothing prevents her sheathing it in our bowels, but want of sufficient force."[19]

Like other New Englanders, Cushing feared the presence of an established Church

Thomas Cushing (1724-1788)

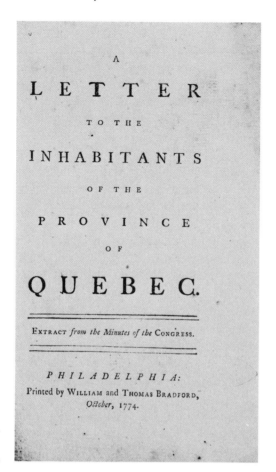

A

LETTER

TO THE

INHABITANTS

OF THE

PROVINCE

OF

QUEBEC.

EXTRACT *from the Minutes of the* CONGRESS.

PHILADELPHIA:
Printed by WILLIAM and THOMAS BRADFORD,
October, 1774.

28.
*A Letter To The Inhabitants Of The
Province of Quebec*, Philadelphia,
October 1774. Library of Congress.

of Rome on the borders of his colony. News of the Quebec Act had evoked horror in his Protestant breast. But when it came to writing the Address to the People of Quebec, Cushing's memory failed, as did Lee's and that of the other members of the Congress who approved the committee's draft. None seemed to remember the uproar against Catholics and Catholicism that had risen just a few months before when news of the Quebec Act had reached them. Now the Congress could only express its joy at this "truly valuable addition" to Britain's free constitutional system. It sympathized with Quebec's plight at being deprived "so audaciously and cruelly" of the "irrevocable rights to which you were justly entitled" and patronizingly assumed the right to "explain" to the people of Quebec, who had been "educated under another form of government," exactly what they had been deprived of in the way of representative government: consent of the governed to taxation, trial by jury, liberty of the person (or habeas corpus), the right to hold lands by the tenure of easy rents, and freedom of the press.[20] Pointing out the limiting aspects of the Quebec Act and appealing to the Canadians' "self-respect" in the words of their "countryman, the immortal Montesquieu," the address urged the inhabitants of Quebec to "join us in our righteous contest, to make common cause with us therein, and take a noble chance for emerging from a humiliating subjection . . . into the firm rank and condition of *English* freemen. . . ." "Nature," Cushing's committee wrote, had joined Canada to the other colonies. "The transcendent nature of freedom" would overcome religious differences. "One social compact" should be formed between the two groups, "based on the generous principles of equal liberty."[21] To this end, the people of Quebec were invited to select delegates to represent their province in the next meeting of the Continental Congress on May 10, 1775.

Perhaps the most delicate task confronting the First Continental Congress was the composition of an address to the King that would be at once conciliatory, dutiful, respectful, and humble while, at the same time, expressing clearly the indignation the colonies felt and the pain they had suffered at the hands of Parliament. Even before a committee was assigned the task of writing the address, the contents of this important statement—especially the list of grievances—were argued and debated by the assembled delegates. Indeed, the composition of the statement became the basis for a tug-of-war between radicals and conservatives, a struggle for power indicative of the tension that existed between the two groups throughout the entire seven weeks of the Congress. If, in the final composition of the statement, the moderates won the day, the radicals were willing to go along, secure in their earlier victory in obtaining the organization of the Association, which they expected would prove to be a more powerful weapon for forcing the issue between Britain and the American colonies.

Patrick Henry
(1736-1799)

The decision to prepare a "loyal address to his Majesty" was reached on October 1. A committee consisting of three radicals and two moderates, headed by Richard Henry Lee and including Patrick Henry, was appointed to bring in a draft statement—a clear victory for the extremists. The draft that was finally presented to the delegates on October 21 was prepared either by Lee or by Patrick Henry in conference with John Adams. "Written in language of asperity very little according with the conciliatory disposition of Congress," in the view of the more moderate John Dickinson, who had joined the Pennsylvania delegation only four days earlier, the statement proved unsatisfactory to the assembly.[22]

Patrick Henry's radicalism had been revealed as early as 1763, when he had censured the King for vetoing salutary laws like Virginia's Two Penny Act, which were desired by the people he had promised to protect. Two years later, during the Stamp Act agitation, Henry again found himself violently denouncing the King: "Tarquin and Caesar had each his Brutus; Charles the First, his Cromwell; and George the Third. . . ." Stopped by cries of treason, Henry had coolly added, "and George the Third may profit from their example. If this be treason, make the most of it."[23]

Henry's "rash heat," as Governor Fauquier of Virginia put it, propelled him to the center of the radical cause, but did not endear him to the British government. His draft of an address to the King could hardly have added to the cause of reconciliation. Although perfectly willing to include such adjectives as "humble" and "dutiful," he was forthright when he talked of "injurys of the most alarming nature" that were "fraught with mischief & destruction to America." "British History," claimed Henry, gave no example of the "Severity of punishment" imposed on the town of Boston and the Province of Massachusetts Bay, nor did "the Annals of Tyranny." Appealing to a King who had sworn to uphold the Protestant faith, he cited Parliament's establishment in Quebec of "the Religion of Rome bloody Idolatrous & strongly inimical to Protestantism" as a "Circumstance . . . dangerous & alarming to the ancient British

49

29.
PATRICK HENRY. Lawrence Sully,
date unknown. Museum of Art,
Carnegie Institute.

Colonys." "Drive us not to Despair," Henry threated. "Urge us not to the last extremity most gracious Sovereign. We can never submit to the Encroachments of the British Parliament. Compell us not therefore to that Situation in which all is Gloom & horror, & from whence no Ray of Peace or Comfort can be discern'd."

In rejecting Henry's draft, the Congress turned to John Dickinson, author of the famous "Letters from a Pennsylvania Farmer," for help, hoping that his temperateness would mitigate Henry's force. Dickinson's final draft of the address was less threatening, more cajoling. Appealing to the King's goodness, wisdom, love of liberty, care for the welfare of his people, and imperial dignity, the address explained in moderate terms the colonists' "apprehension of being degraded into a state of servitude" by "those designing and dangerous men, who daringly interposing themselves between your Royal person and your faithful subjects" abused the King's "authority," misrepresented his American subjects, and created oppressive programs which "at length compelled us, by the force of accumulated injuries, too severe to be any longer tolerable, to disturb your Majesty's repose by our complaints." Much happier would the colonists be to "bleed in your Majesty's service"; but loyalty to the King, his family and government compelled them to send this petition in the hope of obtaining redress of grievances. The address concluded loyally:

We ask but for Peace, Liberty, and Safety. We wish not a diminution of the prerogative, nor do we solicit the grant of any new right in our favour. Your Royal authority over us, and our connection with Great Britain, *we shall always carefully and zealously endeavour to support and maintain.*[24]

With the Address to the King accepted, engrossed, signed, and sent off to the American agents in London with an accompanying letter of explanation, the First Continental Congress had completed its work. Giving thanks to the colony of Pennsylvania for its hospitality, the Congress adjourned, prepared to meet again the coming May to evaluate the results of its effort.

Not all members were sanguine as to their success. In conversation with Henry, John Adams expressed his conviction that "our resolves, declarations of rights, enumeration of wrongs, petitions, remonstrances and addresses, association and non-importation agreements, however they might be expected by the people in America, and however necessary to cement the union of the colonies, would be but waste paper in England." Taking from his pocket a letter from a Massachusetts friend that concluded with the sentence, "After all, we must fight," Adams reported that Henry listened "with great attention, and as soon as I had pronounced the words, "After all, we must fight," he raised his head and with an energy and vehemence that I can never forget, broke out with: 'By God, I am of that man's mind.' "[25]

THE OPPOSITION EMERGES

As the documents issued by the First Continental Congress were published and distributed throughout the colonies, and as towns, cities, and counties began to choose committees to enforce the provisions of the Association, a storm of protest arose from moderates and conservatives who now recognized that during the course of the six weeks in which the Congress had met, it had changed its nature from a mediating body to a revolutionary government.

There was no question that the Congress was an extralegal body that possessed no constitutional power to legislate or dictate procedure for the participating colonies. Delegates to the Congress had been elected by various methods. In some cases, colonial assemblies had selected their representatives, while in others, conventions or committees of correspondence had taken on the responsibility. In no colony did a general election take place, nor was any colony empowered by law to select delegates who would determine the future relations of that colony to the mother country. The idea that had prompted the calling of the Congress had been that here, perhaps, a reconciliation of colonial differences with England might be attempted. The passage of the Association, however, had made such a reconciliation difficult, as most discerning men realized. The Congress now seemed to be intent upon enforcing its will upon the people to prevent them from engaging in trade with England or the West Indies. According to Lord Dunmore, royal governor of Virginia, they were assuming the

> *authority to inspect the books, invoices, and all the secrets of the trade and correspondence of the merchants, to watch the conduct of every inhabitant without distinction, and send for all such as come under their suspicion into their presence, to interrogate them . . . and to stigmatize, as they term it, such as they find transgressing what they are hardy enough to call the laws of Congress.*[26]

Many moderate Americans agreed with Dunmore that the Congress had gone far beyond its mission, and in pamphlets and newspapers they forcefully condemned its proceedings. Such publications were, indeed, the only recourse open to the conservatives who lacked the machinery of organization and the emotional appeal that made the radical cause so effective. One of the most articulate protests came from the pen of Dr. Samuel Seabury, rector of St. Peter's Church in Westchester County, New York.

Samuel Seabury attended Yale College and studied medicine at the University of Edinburgh before following his father into the Anglican ministry. Ordained in London in 1753, Seabury served congregations in New Jersey and on Long Island until 1767 when he was named rector of St. Peter's Church, Westchester County. Physician and schoolteacher as well as pastor, Seabury flourished at St. Peter's and won the esteem of his ministerial colleagues, one of whom described him as "a Man of great good Sense, of a cheerful Disposition, . . . a good Devine and an agreable Preacher." [27]

Samuel Seabury (1729-1796)

For all his cheerful temperament, the rector of St. Peter's was no stranger to controversy. Anglican clergymen were inevitably drawn into constant dispute in a province where sects dissenting from the ecclesiastical establishment of England had struck deep roots long before the first Anglican minister appeared on the scene. Seabury lent his considerable polemical talents to the Anglican efforts to take over King's College (now Columbia University) and to procure the appointment of an Anglican bishop for America. It was not until the time of the Association, however, that he found a topic that moved him to exercise his literary capacity to its most strenuous expression.

Several weeks after the close of the First Continental Congress, the rector, under the pseudonym A. W. Farmer (A Westchester Farmer), fired his opening volley at

30.
SAMUEL SEABURY. Thomas Spence
Duché, Jr., 1783-85. Trinity Col-
lege, Hartford.

radicals and their Association in a pamphlet called *Free Thoughts on the Proceedings of the Continental Congress*. A powerful piece of closely reasoned and persuasive argumentation, the pamphlet was written in a prose style which, like its author, who actually worked his own lands, was plain, blunt, forthright, and muscular.

The Farmer's indignation increased as he came to believe that he and others like him—honest, hard-working, loyal subjects of George III—were being carried down the path to ruin by scatterbrained, antimonarchical political fanatics. It was the farmers, he claimed, who would be hurt most by the Association, not the British, and certainly not the delegates who framed the document. America's rural population was being asked to make sacrifices for a quarrel that city dwellers had started. Nonimportation and nonconsumption would rob the farmers of their best market and deprive them of reasonably priced supplies. The farmers would "have no trade at all, and consequently no vent for the produce" of their farms. Their "wheat, flaxseed, corn, beef, pork, butter, cheese . . . must be left to rot and stink upon our hands." Seabury asked pointedly whether the farmer could live without money. "Will the shopkeeper give you his goods? Will the weaver, shoemaker, blacksmith, carpenter, work for you without pay?" And how would they be able to pay their debts and the interest accumulating on them if they did not sell their produce?

Seabury also warned that the committees established to enforce the Association would erect a tyranny of the mob by arrogating to themselves a privilege that not even the King's magistrates possessed—that of entering a house without a warrant in order to search for forbidden imports. "No *King's* officer" would be permitted to enter his house, he asserted;

> *should any pragmatical committee-gentleman come to my house, and give himself airs, I shall shew him the door, and if he does not soon take himself away, a good hickory cudgel shall teach him better manners.*[28]

To submit to the Association, concluded Seabury, would bring "the most abject slavery on yourselves." His fellow farmers could do as they pleased, but

> *if I must be enslaved, let it be by a KING at least, and not by a parcel of upstart, lawless committeemen. If I must be devoured, let me be devoured by the jaws of a lion, and not gnawed to death by rats and vermin!*[29]

During the next three months Seabury published three more pamphlets under the pseudonym of "Westchester Farmer," progressively expanding the arguments initially laid down in *Free Thoughts*. In a second pamphlet addressed to the merchants of New York, *The Congress Canvassed*, he emphasized the irresponsibility and tyranny of the Congress, a body with no legal authority, which had made "our breach with the parent state a thousand times more irreparable than it was before." The colonies, he insisted, must be reasonable in their demands, or else, in grasping at too much, they would lose everything. "In God's name," he irately exclaimed, "are not the people of Boston able to relieve their own poor?" Did Bostonians "expect a literal completion of the promise that the Saints shall inherit the earth?" Bostonians, Seabury declared, believed that "God had made Boston for himself and all the rest of the world for Boston."[30]

In his third pamphlet, *A View of the Controversy between Great Britain and her*

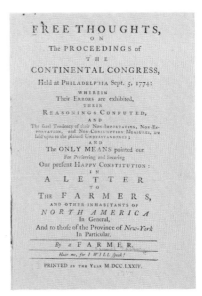

31.
Samuel Seabury's *Free Thoughts, on The Proceedings of The Continental Congress*. New York, 1774. American Antiquarian Society.

Colonies, Seabury undertook an extensive discussion of the constitutional issues involved in the Anglo-American quarrel and proposed a constitution for the colonies that would guarantee them home rule under the ultimate authority of Parliament. And finally, in *An Alarm to the Legislature of the Province of New York*, Seabury warned New York legislators that the Congress, a body with no legal standing, was usurping their right to represent and rule the people of the colony.

The enormous success of Seabury's "Westchester Farmer" pamphlets discomfited the radicals of his colony greatly. Despite the pseudonym, it did not take New Yorkers long to guess that the Farmer was the rector of St. Peter's. When word came in April of Lexington and Concord, public wrath against Seabury spilled over and the pastor was forced into hiding. Late in the year, after he had reappeared, a company of Connecticut militia, outraged by Seabury's articulate Loyalism, seized the minister and carried him to New Haven. Since no substantial charges could be brought against him, he was released after several weeks. The next year he entered the British lines and served as chaplain to a regiment of Loyalists throughout the war. Despite his Loyalism, Seabury was permitted to remain in the United States, and after the war he became Episcopal Bishop of Connecticut and Rhode Island.

Daniel Leonard (1740-1820) The smoke of Seabury's polemical volley against the radicals had not yet cleared when a second attack was mounted in the very stronghold of the radicals, Massachusetts. From December 1774 to April 1775, seventeen articles assailing the radical position appeared in the *Massachusetts Gazette* under the signature "Massachusettensis." Less skillful than those of the Westchester Farmer, these compositions were no less effective in stirring up fears and doubts among those who were not yet convinced of the merits of the radical cause.

"Massachusettensis" (although not identified for another fifty years) was the young lawyer Daniel Leonard, a member of an old Massachusetts family that had grown wealthy in the iron industry. Leonard was educated at Harvard and studied law under the Speaker of the Massachusetts General Assembly. Elected to the General Court in 1770, he took the American side in the quarrel with the mother country at first, but was soon frightened away by the drastic measures advocated by Boston's radicals. Under Governor Hutchinson's persuasion, Leonard became a defender of the Crown. In 1774 he was appointed one of the mandamus councilors created by the widely detested Massachusetts Government Act, and in that capacity was forced to flee with his family to the safety of the redcoat garrison at Boston when the fury of the people against the act threatened reprisals on those designated to implement it.

Leonard's defection from the radical cause was explained by the Patriots as a venal act, undertaken for the sake of Crown money which he needed to satisfy his expensive tastes. Leonard was something of a fop—Mercy Warren satirized his love of finery in her comedy *The Group* (1775) in which Leonard appears as "Beau Trumps." John Adams recalled that Leonard "wore a broad gold lace round the rim of his hat, he made his cloak glitter with laces still broader. . . ."[31] But whether he defected for pecuniary advantage or for ideological reasons—temperamentally Leonard was a thorough conservative—in any case, the young lawyer produced in the "Massachusettensis" letters a profound and devastating critique of radicalism.

Measuring his audience well, Leonard appealed to the law-abiding tendencies and

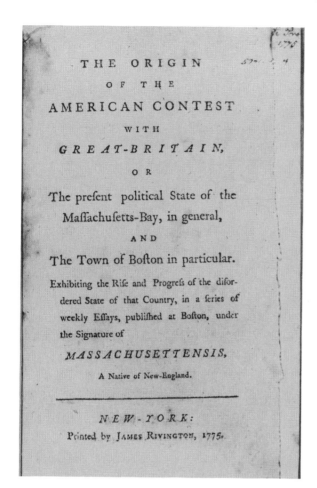

32.
Daniel Leonard's *The Origin Of The American Contest with Great-Britain.* New York, 1775. The Library Company of Philadelphia.

respect for authority that were ingrained in the New England character. He excoriated sedition as a noxious plant; "the vilest reptiles that crawl upon the earth, are concealed at the root; the foulest birds of the air rest upon its branches." [32] It was demagoguery, he argued, that was estranging the good people of Massachusetts from the ancient loyalties. Men were always willing to believe that they were wronged, and political adventurers in Massachusetts had early convinced them that the source of their injury was the Crown.

These men, however, were "cunning animals": "he that would excite a rebellion," declared "Massachusettensis," ". . . is at heart as great a tyrant as ever wielded the iron rod of oppression." [33] Although the Americans had real grievances, which Leonard was prepared to admit, they had no legitimate complaint of sufficient magnitude to justify rebellion.

Using every rhetorical weapon of logic and sentiment, Leonard alleged that the ministry had not overstepped its powers, that the home government had not trampled on colonial rights, and that Parliament did have the right, as old as the colonies themselves, of raising a revenue in America. "Perhaps the whole story of empire," Leonard declared, "does not furnish another instance of a forcible opposition to government, with so much specious and so little real cause." [34] Americans lived under a mild gov-

55

ernment, enjoying "every blessing that is in the power of civil government to bestow." They had no legitimate grievances, and certainly none serious enough to warrant "so unnatured, so causeless, so wanton, so wicked, a rebellion." [35]

The quarrel with the mother country was tearing the province apart, Leonard concluded. Persecution had raised its ugly head, and true liberty had fled from Massachusetts Bay. It was time, he urged, that the colony desist and turn its attention to its own self-interests. America could not win a war with the British, he warned, and the fate of conquered rebel provinces would inevitably be a hard one. "Those that unsheath the sword of rebellion may throw away the scabbard. . . ." [36] Thus the colonists were foolish to provoke the British into armed conflict.

Myles Cooper (1737-1785) — Two other notable pamphlets attacking the decisions of the First Continental Congress made their appearance in the winter of 1774-75: the *American Querist*, published under the pseudonym "A North American," and *A Friendly Address to all Reasonable Americans.*

The *Friendly Address*, like other Tory pamphlets, appealed to the economic interests of the various elements in colonial society. Aiming his fire at the nonimportation aspect of the Continental Association, the author painted a dismal picture of the stagnation of business that would result from such a measure. Ships would rot in the harbor; sailors would drift around the ports without employment and in their aimlessness create riots and disturb the peace; the recently established iron manufactories would close; and both small shopkeepers and large merchants would find their businesses destroyed.

All of this was unnecessary, the anonymous writer claimed. There was hope for Americans within the British Empire, if only Americans would cease talking rebellion and become more reasonable. Whether the British Parliament had been right or wrong, American actions had been "intolerant," encouraged by "rebellious republicans . . . hair-brained fanatics, mad and distracted as the Anabaptists of Munster." Once Americans counted "the cost of rebellion," they would "stop it." Law must be recognized above all else, the unity of the empire above the anarchy of independent existence, monarchy above republicanism.[37] The author was willing to acknowledge that Great Britain had been unjustified in passing the Stamp Act and imposing the tea duty; these were certainly "dangerous to constitutional liberty." [38] But parliamentary abuses must be corrected legally. "A formal allowance of the rightful supremacy in general of Great Britain over the American colonies," coupled with "a declaration of our opposition to a state of independence with corresponding behaviour—a respectful remonstrance on the subject of taxation—an assurance of our willingness to contribute, in some equitable proportion, towards defraying the public expense—and the proposal of a reasonable plan for a general American constitution"—these were the remedies most likely to succeed. "To think of succeeding by force of arms, or by starving the nation into compliance, is proof of shameful ignorance, pride, and stupidity." [39]

It was thought at the time—and the belief endured until the 1930s—that the pamphlets were the work of Myles Cooper, second president of King's College in New York City. It now appears more probable that they were written by Thomas Bradbury Chandler, an Anglican priest from New Jersey. Yet, whether or not Cooper actually

33.
MYLES COOPER. John Singleton
Copley, 1768. Columbia University.

wrote the pamphlets, they reflect his sentiments as the most prominent clerical apologist for the Crown in the colonies.

Myles Cooper was born in England and educated at Oxford. Cultivated, urbane, and articulate, he had joined the faculty at King's College in 1762 and been named president in 1763. The college flourished under Cooper's administration, but his militant Anglicanism, and his efforts to establish an Anglican episcopate in North America, created many enmities among the large number of Dissenters inhabiting the province of New York. Soon, his well-known dislike of radicalism increased the hostility directed at him and led many to credit him with almost every Tory pamphlet or article published in New York.

Cooper had not opposed the calling of the Continental Congress in September. Like other moderate Loyalists, he had hoped that some beneficial result would come from its proceedings, and, indeed, he had rejoiced that it took the quarrel out of the hands of the rabble.[40] But approval of the Association—much to his dismay—spelled the success of the radicals within the Congress and made that body, he believed, an instrument for the promotion of revolution and independence. "Men deprav'd" had taken over the Congress, Cooper later wrote in his long poem, "The Patriots of North America":

> . . . *Half Knaves, half Fools*
> *Whom God denied the Talents great*
> *Requir'd, to make a Knave, complete;*
> *Whom Nature form'd, vile paltry Tools,*
> *Absurder much, than downright Fools,*
> *Who from their own dear Puppet-Show,*
> *The World's great Stage, pretend to know.*[41]

THE PATRIOTS RESPOND

If to conservatives like Cooper the Association represented the victory of "their *High Mightinesses* the MOB," to radicals like the young James Madison, who came to call themselves "Patriots" in response to the Tories' adoption of the nomenclature Loyalists, the Association was the only means by which they could "distinguish friends from foes and . . . oblige the common people to a more strict observance" of the trade boycott.[42] Thus convinced, the Patriots rose immediately to the challenge presented to them by the numerous Loyalist publicists and propagandists, and in newspapers, pamphlets, and broadsides inundated the population with emotionally charged as well as logically reasoned arguments in favor of the course adopted by the Continental Congress. In editorials in the *Pennsylvania Journal and Weekly Advertiser*, William Bradford of Philadelphia—the "patriot-printer of 1776"—pleaded the cause, while in Massachusetts Isaiah Thomas made *The Massachusetts Spy* the very organ of the Patriots' party, blacklisting "traitors" and publishing the names of "infamous Betrayers of their Country" who refused to abide by the promulgations of the Continental Association.[43]

Throughout the colonies, in fact, newspapers with similar political commitment— The *New-Hampshire Gazette*, the *Providence Gazette*, the *Connecticut Courant*, the *Norwich Packet*, the *Virginia Gazette*, among many—dedicated themselves to enforc-

34.
Masthead of *The Massachusetts Spy*, an important Patriot paper, with snake and griffin motif designed by Paul Revere. American Antiquarian Society. [Not in exhibition.]

ing the Association agreement by posting the names of those whom they deemed enemies to their country and forcing them publicly to acknowledge their guilt and pledge reform. "It was by means of News papers," wrote John Holt of the *New-York Journal* to Samuel Adams, "that we received & spread the Notice of the tyrannical Designs formed against America, and kindled a Spirit that has been sufficient to repel them." [44]

Alexander Hamilton (1757–1804)

Not content with limiting their war against the Loyalists to newspapers, the radicals sought to answer the conservatives' attacks with more intellectual and closely reasoned publications. Especially in New York, which was marked by an indigenous conservatism, were the radical Whigs alarmed by the impact of the Loyalist documents, and in particular those written by Samuel Seabury and Myles Cooper. While they were mulling over the selection of a writer capable of dealing with the skillful arguments of the two Tories, they were unexpectedly, and happily, assisted by an anonymous pamphlet that appeared—on December 15, 1774—entitled *A Full Vindication of the Measures of the Congress from the Calumnies of their Enemies.* Soundly and logically argued, full of clever verbiage and brilliant phrases, the pamphlet was addressed specifically to the arguments of the Westchester Farmer.

Speculation as to the real name of the mysterious pamphleteer became the talk of New York that winter. Many people, including Seabury, were convinced that only "an old experienced practitioner" such as John Jay could have written such a learned and eloquent treatise.[45] When it was finally disclosed that the work was that of a young man of seventeen, a student of Myles Cooper at King's College, a native of the West Indies who had been in America for only two years, and a novice in the political arts, there was widespread incredulity.

Alexander Hamilton had made his entrance onto the American political scene six months earlier—on July 6, 1774—when he had addressed a mass meeting in City Hall Park in response to the recently passed Coercive and Quebec Acts. From that time on, he continued to serve the Whig cause with articles in Holt's *New York Journal.* Now he was ready to contribute to the pamphlet war that was raging between Whig and Tory on the question of the legality and appropriateness of the Continental Congress.

Hamilton derived his basic arguments from the principle of "the natural rights of

35.
ALEXANDER HAMILTON. Giuseppe
Ceracchi, 1794. National Portrait
Gallery, Smithsonian Institution.

mankind" to liberty and property. Those who attacked the Congress were enemies to this principle "because they wish to see one part of their species enslaved by another." They failed to see that the contest between America and Great Britain was not over "the petty duty of 3 pence per pound on East India tea," but over the more important question, "whether the inhabitants of Great-Britain have a right to dispose of the lives and properties of the inhabitants of America. . . ." Freedom, Hamilton asserted, rests upon being governed by laws to which one has consented. Since Americans did not empower the British Parliament to legislate for them, Parliament had no "just authority to do it." [46]

What was at stake behind the calling of the Congress and the taking of strong boycott measures, Hamilton insisted, was American "lives and properties." How best to preserve these was what ought to concern Americans, not how whatever measures taken would affect British and Irish manufacturers or the inhabitants of the West Indies. By maintaining neutrality in a fight for civil liberties, these groups had sacrificed their right to be considered by Americans; neutrality, claimed Hamilton, was in effect acquiescence to tyranny: "It is impossible to exculpate a people, that suffers its rulers to abuse and tyrannize over others." [47]

Where Hamilton was strongest was in his economic arguments, which were aimed at refuting the Farmer's claim that the Association would bring ruin to the producers of America. "A temporary stagnation of commerce, and thereby a deprivation of the luxuries and some of the conveniences of life," Hamilton pointed out, were preferable to the loss of liberty, which was "fatal to religion and morality," debasing to the mind, and corruptive of "noblest springs of action." America must develop self-sufficiency, said the future Secretary of the Treasury; necessity would stimulate manufacturing and manufacturing would "pave the way, still more, to the future grandeur and glory of America." [48] If the British Parliament were allowed to have its way, however, it would continue to use every means within its power to restrain American economic growth, out of "fear for the future independence of America." [49]

Hamilton was sure that the Association would be successful in its goal of so distressing the people of Great Britain, Ireland, and the West Indies that they would be obliged to join Americans "in getting the acts of Parliament . . . repealed." Summarizing his closely reasoned economic analysis of the trade and productive capacities of the various groups involved in the contest, Hamilton let his final case rest on an appeal to man's love of liberty, now threatened by British policy. The common people must not be taken in by those whose intentions are to deceive and betray them. "If you join with the rest of America in the same common measure," he promised them, "you will be sure to preserve your liberties inviolate; but if you separate from them, and seek for redress alone and unseconded, you will certainly fall a prey to your enemies, and repent your folly as long as you live." [50]

A Full Vindication was Hamilton's first published pamphlet, and he seems to have been delighted not only with the public and critical acclaim it brought him but also with the sheer fun of indulging in written debate and public controversy. When Seabury answered the *Vindication* with a *View of the Controversy*, Hamilton countered in February 1775, with another longer and no less impressive pamphlet, *The Farmer Refuted*. Here he continued the attack on Seabury personally, accusing him of possessing

JOURNAL

OF THE

PROCEEDINGS

OF THE

CONGRESS,

Held at PHILADELPHIA,

September 5, 1774.

PHILADELPHIA:

Printed by WILLIAM and THOMAS BRADFORD,
at the *London Coffee House.*

M,DCC,LXXIV.

36.
The public eagerly awaited word of what had been accomplished by the First Continental Congress and the *Journal of The Proceedings of The Congress*, printed by William and Thomas Bradford of Philadelphia, became an instant bestseller. The seal on the title page (twelve hands holding a pillar topped by a liberty cap) was a printer's addition and was never adopted by the Congress. The Library Company of Philadelphia.

. . . every accomplishment of a polemical writer, which may serve to dazzle and mislead superficial and vulgar minds; a peremptory dictatorial air, a pert vivacity of expression, an inordinate passion for conceit, and a noble disdain of being fettered by the laws of truth.[51]

But Hamilton's main attack on the "Farmer" was directed toward refuting his assertion that the Congress and the Association were illegal. He continued to maintain, as in his earlier pamphlet, that even if the American attempts to gain redress for grievances were illegal:

When the first principles of civil society are violated, and the rights of a whole people are invaded, the common forms of municipal law are not to be regarded. Men may then betake themselves to the law of nature; and, if they but conform their actions to that standard, all cavils against them betray either ignorance or dishonesty. There are some events in society to which human laws cannot extend, but when applied to them lose all their force and efficacy. In short, when human laws contradict or discountenance the means which are necessary to preserve the essential rights of any society, they defeat the proper end of all laws, and so become null and void.[52]

But in any case the Congress had not acted illegally, Hamilton claimed. There was no law that he knew of that prohibited subjects from stating their grievances and petitioning the King for redress. There could, moreover, be no doubt that when a people were wronged "and their circumstances will not allow them unitedly to petition in their own persons, they may appoint representatives to do it for them." [53]

There is no question that along with such other radical apologists as John Adams of Massachusetts, Landon Carter of Virginia, and Thomas Paine of Pennsylvania, Hamilton in his pamphlets of 1774 and 1775 helped to turn back the tide of loyalist arguments generated by Samuel Seabury, Daniel Leonard, and Myles Cooper and persuade the wavering and ambivalent that the direction adopted by the First Continental Congress was the right one for America.

The Continental Association was successfully implemented, and its success gained prestige for the radicals while forcing moderates to choose between America and England. It provided a source of unity for the people, preparing them emotionally for future events; and through it the Continental Congress achieved its daring attempt to regulate political affairs through the manipulation of public opinion. Of great economic success, it reduced the value of imports from England ninety-seven percent in 1775. Politically, it laid the groundwork for the defense association that would soon change the commercial nature of the Continental Association. For, in the words of one parliamentarian in London,

all the world must acknowledge that when the clearest rights of the Legislative power of a country are invaded and denied, and when in consequence the people so denying are in actual and open rebellion, that then there are points of greater importance to be settled and decided than points of Commerce and Manufacture.[54]

GENERAL the HON^{ble} THO^s GAGE
OB^t 1788

37.
Thomas Gage. John Singleton
Copley, 1768-69. Mr. and Mrs.
Paul Mellon.

64

III.

Lexington and Concord

A s the iron cold of the Massachusetts winter receded before the spring of 1775, the volatile mixture of redcoat garrison and hostile population had not yet exploded into violence in the Bay colony. During the turmoil created the previous September by the rumors of the bombardment of Boston, Americans revealed their willingness to fight if attacked. Yet, there was little heart among the colonists, even in Massachusetts, for an armed conflict with England. Samuel Adams could not arouse the Provincial Congress to support an army for the province; the most the Congress would do was to recommend a policy of defensive readiness for existing bodies of militia. The third week of April, however, saw the explosion finally ignited, and the man holding the match was the one who wanted least to do so: Governor Thomas Gage.

Thomas Gage had the misfortune to be an able administrator in a position where administrative ability no longer counted, and a poor general in a situation where generalship was most required. The second son of an Irish peer, young Gage had decided, like many second sons, to try his fortune as an officer in His Majesty's Army. Promotion through the mid-eighteenth-century British army was by purchase rather than merit, and Gage had sufficient funds to buy himself two handsome commissions. By 1754 he could look forward to a comfortable existence as aide-de-camp to the Earl of Albermarle, but the Seven Years' War intruded on his placid situation as a peacetime soldier.

Thomas Gage (1721-1787)

Posted to America as part of Major General Edward Braddock's command, Lieutenant Colonel Gage was in charge of the forward element of Braddock's army when the force was surprised by the French and Indians near Fort Duquesne. Gage conducted himself bravely enough under fire, but he could not stem the panic that spread with feverish swiftness through his own men and back to the rest of the command, turning the engagement into a hellish rout of the British. In 1758 Gage led an expedition into a similar ambush near Ticonderoga, although with less disastrous results. Even two defeats, however, failed to teach him the vulnerability of a column of infantry marching in formation through the uneven and forested terrain of the American countryside. In 1759 Gage again mishandled a diversionary assignment that was in-

65

tended to take pressure off British forces making crucial moves on Montreal and Quebec. By the war's end, it was clear that Thomas Gage was not an able strategist.

The postwar period tested Gage's capacity for civil administration. Here he was more successful. As military governor of Montreal, he was popular with the King's new Canadian subjects; and when in 1763 he succeeded Amherst as commander in chief of the British army in America, he proved that he was more suited to governorship than generalship, especially if there were no critical decisions to be made quickly.

When Gage was appointed governor of Massachusetts in May 1774, to succeed Thomas Hutchinson, he conducted himself with remarkable restraint and impartiality—too much so, actually, for the taste of Tories like Peter Oliver, who remarked that Gage was "too honest to deal with Men, who from their Cradles, had been educated in all the wily Arts of Chicane. . . ."[1] The general's reputation for fairness impressed even as ardent a Patriot as Dr. Joseph Warren, who conceded in late 1774 that the governor was "a man of honest, upright principles."[2] William Smith, a New York Patriot who had known Gage when the general was stationed in New York as commander in chief, assured John Adams that Gage was "good natured, peacable [sic] and sociable," but not really suited to be a royal governor.[3]

Indeed, Gage was a rather ineffectual man, who found himself in the middle of a controversy in which his efforts to be just could impress nobody—neither the colonists nor his own troops, not even the ministry. Each group, unfortunately for Gage, expected him to take care of its special interests. Paradoxically, too, Gage was hurt rather than helped by the fact that a good name had preceded him to Boston. His popularity in New York, where he had averted bloodshed while serving as commander in chief during the Stamp Act period, and his marriage to an American woman had encouraged the inhabitants of the Bay colony to expect more of him than they should have, given the times. The warmth of their welcome quickly dissipated when Gage, fulfilling his obligations as an officer of the Crown, took steps to implement the Coercive Acts. Disillusionment reached full measure in August, however, when Gage moved to enforce what the people of Massachusetts believed was the most sinister threat to their liberty—the Massachusetts Government Act. They were able to live with the obnoxious Port Act, since they knew that sooner or later it would expire, but the Government Act, which effectively destroyed their charter by reducing the province to military government "from which more numerous and extensive evils will accrue," carried no terminal date and promised, to their horror, to be "perpetual." Finally, Gage's attempt to uphold the Crown's appointment of members of the Governor's Council entirely convinced the people of Massachusetts that they could expect no more from the governor than they could from Lord North.

The implementation of the Massachusetts Government Act undermined Gage's standing at home as well. Having recognized the seriousness of colonial reaction to the act—it would, indeed, have been difficult for him to miss the meaning of the terrorism directed at the Crown-appointed councilors—the governor thought it necessary to warn the ministry that affairs had truly deteriorated in Massachusetts. His warning, however, was regarded by Whitehall less as good judgment than as timidity. In October Gage asked for more troops. In November he sent a warning that the other colonies were prepared to stand with Massachusetts and that only a maximum application of military force could salvage the situation. Now the ministry concluded that his judgment was totally unreliable.

Britain's American policy was obviously confused. The home government wished to preserve peace while maintaining national prestige. How to do this when the ministers had already decided that the Anglo-American quarrel could only be settled "by blows" was a question it found difficult to answer. Unable to provide Gage with the directions he was waiting to receive during the winter of 1774-75, the ministry was still not happy with what the governor did independently. Gage's policy was to display British power but not use it, in order to frighten the colonists into submission. He was willing to take a hard line if necessary, for he understood that "to keep quiet in the town of Boston only, will not terminate affairs; the troops must march into the country." Forced, however, to await "determination from home," he went to great effort to avoid arousing extremists and to maintain peace.[4] Such a policy convinced the King and his ministers, mired in an almost paranoid concern for national honor, that their man had lost his nerve and would end by humiliating the British army.

Gage's troops held an even lower opinion of the Americans than did the ministry. They also taxed the governor with timidity. Wisely seeking to avoid inflammatory encounters with the townspeople of Boston, Gage had been keeping a tight rein on his garrison. In 1775 he wrote with satisfaction to the Earl of Dartmouth, secretary of state for the southern department, that "The Winter has passed over without any great Bickerings between the Inhabitants of this Town and His Majesty's Troops; Some Quarrells now and then happened tho' of no very great Consequence."[5] The soldiers did not, however, appreciate as fully as did Gage the wisdom of not ruffling American sensibilities. Morale sagged, and many of the young officers began to write letters home complaining of Gage's softness with the rebellious provincials. As the complaints circulated in the closed world of the English peerage, Gage's reputation was further undermined. By the end of 1774 the redcoat garrison had nicknamed their commander the "Old Woman."

As the winter wore on, the ministry decided that Gage must be replaced with someone hardy enough to implement the coercive strategy that they sought but could not define. The King and his advisers did, however, want Gage to take some sort of decisive step against the provincials before his replacement, Sir William Howe, arrived. On April 14, 1775, H.M.S. *Nautilus* sailed into Boston Harbor, bringing Gage a letter with secret instructions from his immediate superior, the Earl of Dartmouth. Although Dartmouth was willing to concede the fact that the situation in Boston was volatile and could change from day to day, he emphasized in his message the necessity to repel force by force as well as the hope of the ministry that Gage would "take a more active & determined part" in supporting "the authority of this Kingdom." To do this, Dartmouth finally was able to offer a specific suggestion: the governor should arrest "the principal actors and abettors in the Provincial Congress."[6] Gage believed he had a better idea: he would frustrate any attempt at violence by seizing the stores—muskets, cannon, ammunition, tents, even wooden spoons—that his efficient spy network had informed him were being collected at Concord for the use of the province's militia.

Gage imagined that his expedition to Concord would have the advantage of surprise, but he reckoned without the vigilance of Paul Revere and an efficient corps of observant Bostonians who for several months had been patrolling the town's streets by twos to watch for suspicious movements in the garrison. Gage had attempted forays out of the town before, and the colonials were determined to give him a hot welcome should he do it again.

What Revere and his colleagues saw on April 14 looked very suspicious indeed. Twenty-one companies of light infantry and grenadiers—700 men—were taken off regular duty, allegedly to learn new formations, and the troop transports, previously beached for repairs, were tied under the sterns of the men-of-war anchored in the harbor ready for use. The next day Revere rode to Lexington to warn Sam Adams and John Hancock that Gage might send a force to arrest them. In turn, Hancock sent word on to Concord that the townspeople should begin to disperse and hide the provincial supplies accumulated there.

Francis Smith   More damaging to the British expedition's chance of success than loss of the element of
(1720-1791)   surprise was Gage's choice of Lieutenant Colonel Francis Smith as commander. Fat and physically slow—his only outstanding military trait being an ability to get himself promoted regularly—Smith was hardly the sort of officer to command a lightning strike. But Smith was the senior officer in the Boston garrison, he had been in America twelve years, and he was an old friend of Gage's—sufficient reasons, in Gage's opinion, for him to head the command.

On the evening of Tuesday, April 18, Gage met at eight o'clock with the leaders of the expedition, who were ordered to have their men on the beach at the foot of Boston Common across from the Cambridge shore precisely at ten o'clock. The soldiers were to move to the rendezvous in groups of two and three, as quietly as possible; if challenged, they would give the password "patrole." Colonel Smith was handed sealed orders, which he was not to open until he reached Cambridge, informing him of his destination and mission.

At ten o'clock the troops were on the beach; Smith was not. By the time the slow-moving colonel arrived and the troops were ferried across the Charles River, it was after midnight. The irritation of the wait at the foot of the Common was aggravated by serious discomfort on the Cambridge shore, for, as one junior officer informed Gage's secretary a week later, "the Tide being in we were up to our Middles before we got into the road. . . ."[7] Nor were the annoyances over once the redcoats reached the Lexington road. Lieutenant John Barker of the King's Own Regiment, another of the expedition's junior officers, complained in his diary that

> *. . . wet up to the knees, we were halted in a dirty road and stood there*
> *until two o'clock in the morning, waiting for provisions to be brought from*
> *the boats to be divided, and, which most of the men threw away, having*
> *carried some with 'em.*[8]

When Smith's men finally swung down the road to Lexington, they were already fatigued, impatient, and uncomfortable; worst of all, they were late.

By three o'clock in the morning, as the force moved across Middlesex County, the ringing of bells and the firing of signal muskets made it clear even to Smith that his advance had been detected. The colonel prudently sent a message back to Gage, requesting the governor to dispatch reinforcements. There would be no more waiting,

38.
Page from Thomas Gage's notebook with copy of a memorandum to Lieutenant Colonel Francis Smith advising him to march on Concord "with the utmost expedition and secrecy." William L. Clements Library, University of Michigan.

however; before sending his request, the portly colonel ordered his second-in-command, Major John Pitcairn of the Royal Marines, to press ahead with six light infantry companies, in compliance with Gage's order that "a party of the best Marchers . . . go on with expedition" to secure the two bridges over the Concord and Sudbury rivers. It was this advance party, numbering almost two hundred men, that several hours later confronted seventy local minutemen drawn up in ragged formation across the wet grass of Lexington Common.

John Pitcairn
(1722-1775)

Gage was more fortunate in his choice of a second-in-command. John Pitcairn was a sensible, reliable, and gallant officer, a veteran of nearly twenty years' service in the Royal Marines, and a pious Calvinist, whose popularity with the New Englanders may have been one of the reasons Gage had assigned him to Smith's command. Pitcairn also possessed the good judgment that the mission required. The Reverend Ezra Stiles reflected contemporary American opinion that Pitcairn was "a good Man in a bad Cause . . . a Man of Integrity & Honor."[9]

As Pitcairn led his troops closer to Lexington, he began to suspect that he might meet stiff resistance within the village. His outriders had gathered up country folk on the road who told them that between six hundred and one thousand militia would be waiting for the regulars at the little town. A scouting party, sent out by Gage the previous afternoon and active the entire night, also relayed to Pitcairn the news that Paul Revere, whom they had captured several hours before, claimed that there were at least five hundred minutemen in the town and that Smith's soldiers had been delayed. Believing Revere's fabrication, Pitcairn slowed his advance to allow Smith's army to catch up with him. Revere's story also convinced Pitcairn that his men should be ready to protect themselves. In the pink light of dawn, just before entering Lexington, he ordered his column to stop for priming and loading, a time-consuming operation. The sun had risen and was burning away the mist of early morning when Pitcairn led his men, carrying their loaded pieces, onto the Lexington green.

39.
John Pitcairn's pistols. Lexington
Historical Society. [Not in
exhibition.]

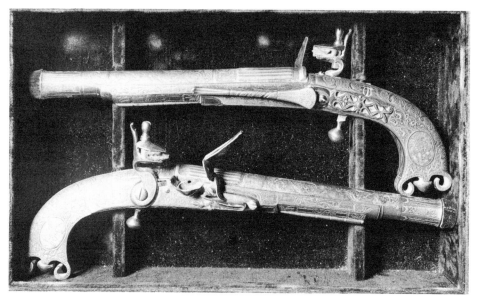

Smith's men had barely disembarked on Cambridge shore when the people of Lexington were alerted to their coming. At ten o'clock in the evening, the hour when the redcoats were supposed to be boarding their boats, Joseph Warren, Boston's Patriot physician and member of the Provincial Committee of Safety, had called his two most trusted messengers, Paul Revere, a silversmith, and William Dawes, Jr., a cordwainer, to his surgery. Arriving before Revere, Dawes was sent by way of Boston Neck around the Back Bay and through Cambridge to Concord in order to alert the Middlesex countryside to the redcoat march, warn Hancock and Adams at Lexington, and rouse the people at Concord.

Revere came to Dr. Warren with plans for the mission already drawn up. Suspecting British intentions, he had agreed the preceding Sunday "with a Colonel Conant and some other gentlemen, that if the British went out by water, we would show two lanthorns in the North Church steeple; and if by land, one as a signal. . . ."[10] Leaving Warren, Revere returned home for his riding boots and surcoat while a friend lit the signal lanterns in the North Church steeple so that the Patriots in Charlestown might know that both Revere and the British were on their way. Two other friends, Thomas Richardson and Joshua Bentley, then rowed Revere "across Charles River a little to the eastward where the Somerset man-of-war lay. It was then young flood, the ship was winding, and the moon was rising."[11] Landing on the Charlestown side, Revere was greeted by Conant, who secured him a horse. By eleven o'clock the bold silversmith was galloping through the night to Lexington.

Dawes was as daring a messenger as Revere. Thirty years old in 1775, he had recently drubbed a redcoat who had behaved improperly toward Mrs. Dawes. He had also won Dr. Warren's admiration by smuggling two cannon out of Boston under the very noses of the guard. He had ridden on many errands for the Committee of Safety, having to masquerade as a miller, an inebriated farmer, or a huckster to get by the various British guards at the check point on Boston Neck. During these escapades, he had made friends among the sentries, an effort that stood him well tonight. While a small group of redcoats passed out, Dawes, pretending to be a spectator, was allowed by one of the friendly guards to slip out with them. Warren's intrepid courier galloped into the night, uninterrupted further in his mission to Lexington.

Revere set out later than Dawes, but his way was shorter and he arrived at Lexington half an hour before the cordwainer. Since no fresh mounts were available in Lexington, the messengers and their animals were forced to rest half an hour before setting out again for Concord. Joined by Dawes and accompanied by "a high Son of Liberty," Dr. Samuel Prescott of Concord, Revere was halfway to Concord when he and his companions were waylaid by one of the British scouting parties sent out the previous afternoon. Captured, Revere attempted to mislead the British by exaggerating the number of militia assembled at Lexington; he was released several hours later—on foot because a British sergeant needed his horse. Prescott escaped and rode on to warn Concord.

Dawes also escaped, but just barely. Horse and rider pounded into a farmyard not far from the ambush and pulled up so hard that Dawes lost his pocket watch. Dismounting, Dawes shouted to the inhabitants of the farmhouse for help. His pursuers, fearing that they were outnumbered, did not wait to find out that the house was empty and beat a hasty retreat. The cordwainer decided to hang up his spurs for the

40.
WILLIAM DAWES, JR. Attributed to
John Johnston, date unknown.
Evanston Historical Society.

night, and, abandoning his horse, walked back to Lexington. Several days later he returned to the farm to recover his watch.

The night was over for Dr. Warren's messengers, but they had done their work well. Dozens of other riders now raced in all directions through the pleasant, moonlit night, spreading the warning that they had first heard from William Dawes and Paul Revere.

When Paul Revere arrived at Lexington about midnight, April 18, he immediately rode to the house of the Reverend Jonas Clarke, pastor of Lexington's First Congregational Church. Clarke had been host to Samuel Adams and John Hancock during the past month while the Massachusetts Provincial Congress had been meeting at Concord. The fact that Clarke's house was guarded by eight minutemen surprised Revere. The minister and his prominent guests had already been warned that nine British officers had been seen on the road between Boston and Lexington, and immediately the orderly sergeant of the Lexington minutemen—William Munroe—had placed a guard on the property.

*Jonas Clarke
(1730-1805)*

It is not surprising that Jonas Clarke should have required protection, even if he had not been host to two of the most important members of the Massachusetts Congress. A huge, impressive man, Jonas Clarke's presence filled the town no less than it did his meetinghouse. A 1752 graduate of Harvard College, the parson was a rationalist and activist who concerned himself less with the esoterica of speculative theology than with the practical application of Christian virtue to daily life. Politics, not theology, was the meat of the minister's intellectual fare, and for half a century it was Clarke who formulated, in masterly fashion, Lexington's response to the events that were shaping an independent American nation. The parson's political arguments were closely reasoned and persuasive, if colored by their author's excitable nature, and through years of sermons Clarke had influenced the political minds of his parishioners. There was not a man responding to the alarm of Dawes and Revere that April morning—including John Parker, captain of the town's minutemen—who did not acknowledge Jonas Clarke as Lexington's *de facto* leader and spokesman. The British would have been glad to take him into custody, for it was he who had been most influential in convincing Lexington's farmers that American liberty was worth dying for.

41.
JONAS CLARKE. Unidentified artist, date unknown. Whereabouts unknown; reproduced in *History of the Town of Lexington*, 1913.

John Parker, a veteran of Rogers' Rangers and a captain in Lexington's militia, had been roused from his bed at about midnight in response to the warning from Boston. Calling out 130 of his men, he had stood with them in the chill moonlight awaiting the intruders. After an hour, with no sign of the British, he dismissed the company, ordering the men to reassemble when they heard the beat of the drum. His intention, he later claimed, was peaceful; he and his man had gathered on the Common

*John Parker
(1729-1775)*

> to consult what to do, and concluded not to be discovered, nor meddle or make with said Regular troops (if they should approach) unless they should insult us; and upon their sudden approach, I immediately ordered our militia to disperse and not to fire.[12]

But surely the Lexington men were not so naive as to suppose that the British would march by a large group of armed men whose intentions were unknown but presumably hostile without taking up arms against them? If the Lexington minutemen believed they would, Jonas Clarke and his house guest, Samuel Adams, certainly did not. It is not difficult to believe, as Harold Murdock has suggested, that Adams, hoping for an incident that would arouse New England to armed resistance, influenced Clarke to have Parker align his men in view of the British as they marched up the road to Concord.[13]

Whatever the intentions of Clarke, Parker, Adams, or the men of Lexington, it is certain that when Parker finally heard, just before dawn, that the British were fifteen minutes from the town, he ordered the drum beat. Seventy men responded. The minutemen established their straggling line beyond the meetinghouse and to the right of the redcoats as they marched toward Concord. When the British noticed the provincials, they swung off the road and started across the Common on a collision course with Parker's command. Pitcairn and several of his officers rode around the meetinghouse and took up a position on the flank midway between redcoats and colonials; from that position Pitcairn thought he could control the situation. What the major intended to do, he later claimed in a letter to Gage, was to disarm Parker's men. Pitcairn recalled that when he came within one hundred yards of the colonials

> *. . . they began to File off towards some stone Walls on our Right Flank—*
> *The Light Infantry observing this, ran after them—I instantly called to the*
> *Soldiers not to Fire &c.—some of the Rebels who had jumped over the Wall,*
> *Fired Four or Five Shott at the Soldiers, which wounded a man of the Tenth,*
> *and my Horse was Wounded in two places, from some quarter or other, and*
> *at the same time several Shott were fired from a Meeting House on our*
> *Left—upon this, without any order or Regularity, the Light Infantry began*
> *a scattered Firing and continued in that situation for some little time, contrary*
> *to the repeated orders both of me and the officers that were present. . . ."*[14]

The American version of the conflict varied from Pitcairn's. Captain Parker claimed that the British troops rushed on his militia without provocation and opened fire. Others of the Lexington company alleged that Pitcairn had damned them as rebels and that the regulars had opened fire on them while their backs were turned as they dispersed. Some claimed that the first shot had come from a pistol, which meant that it was fired by a British officer.

Once the firing had begun, in any case, the British officers tried to stop it. But the redcoats, angered at the colonial fire and frustrated by a miserable winter's confinement in the Boston garrison, were almost uncontrollable. Pitcairn was not one of their regular officers, and they paid no attention to his orders. Having scattered Parker's men, they were about to break down the doors of the houses fronting the Common when Colonel Smith (for the only time in the whole expedition) arrived on the scene quickly enough to salvage the situation. At the drummer's beating the call to arms, the regulars, who recognized Smith, finally heeded. Lexington was saved from looting, but eight Yankees lay dead or dying under the rising sun.

When the soldiers had been restored to order and the rest of the expedition had come up to the Common, the officers faced a critical decision—whether to go on to Concord or, now that American blood had been spilled and the countryside alarmed, to retire quickly to Boston. Several of the officers urged Smith to retreat, but the portly colonel was determined to execute the orders given him by his friend Gage. The column re-formed, the officers permitted their men three cheers over their pitifully small victory (which grated on Jonas Clarke's ears even more than the shooting), and the expedition set off for Concord.

Once the British had departed, Parson Clarke (according to his daughter Elizabeth) sent one of his sons

> *. . . down to Grandfather Cook's to see who was killed and what their condition was and, in the afternoon, Father, Mother with me and the Baby went to the Meeting House, there was the eight men that was killed, seven of them my father's parishioners, one from Woburn, all in Boxes made of four large Boards Nailed up and, after Pa had prayed, they were put into two horse carts and took into the graveyard where your Grandfather and some of the Neighbors had made a large trench, as near the Woods as possible and there we followed the bodies of those first slain, Father, Mother, I and the Baby, there I stood and there I saw them let down into the ground, it was a little rainey but we waited to see them Covered up with the Clods and then for fear the British should find them my Father thought some of the men had best Cut some pine or oak bows and spread them on their place of burial so that it looked like a heap of Brush. . . .*[15]

Obviously, Jonas Clarke, his blood boiling over the massacre of his parishioners, was attempting to have his people transfer their deepest animosity, their implacable hatred, from redskins to redcoats, for he had directed the burial of Lexington's dead as if their murderers were Indians, who customarily mutilated the bodies of enemy warriors fallen in battle. The people of the Massachusetts countryside were now being conditioned to attribute to the British regulars the same ferocity they had customarily associated with the only armed enemy they had known before April 19, 1775.

Having escaped the trap that netted Revere, Dr. Prescott rode on to alert Concord to the British march. Between one and two in the morning the local militia turned out. First to respond to the alarm was the town's minister, William Emerson.

William Emerson (1743-1776)

Emerson, a 1761 graduate of Harvard and grandfather of Ralph Waldo Emerson, did not dominate Concord as Jonas Clarke did Lexington. The young minister had an unfortunate talent for generating ecclesiastical controversy, and he had stirred dissension among his own parishioners and among the neighboring churches. On the quarrel with Great Britain, however, the minister and his congregation were in complete accord. Emerson was an ardent champion of American rights, described by one of Gage's spies as "*un très mauvais sujet.*" [16] The minister assured his people that God Himself was on their side and that his priests were sounding the alarm againt tyranny. Preaching earlier in the year against the Massachusetts Government Act, Emerson had urged his parishioners to resist the measure "even with sword, the firelock and the bayonet, plead with your arms the birthright of Englishmen, the dearly purchased legacy left you by your never-to-be-forgotten Ancestors." [17] Only if their sins testified against them, would God fail to help the colonists against the British. On this day, the minister witnessed the violent resistance he had urged, and the standing of the Concord church with the Almighty was sorely tested.

Amos Barrett
(1752-1829)
and
James Barrett
(1710-1779)

When the British did not soon appear on the outskirts of their town, the Concord men also decided to disperse and reassemble on signal. Meanwhile, they dispatched messengers to other towns in the county and continued to hide what still remained in town of the colonial stores.

Shortly before dawn the Concord men regrouped to consider a scout's report of firing on Lexington Common. Fifty years later Amos Barrett set down his recollections of the occasion. Barrett recalled that the minutemen, who numbered 140, decided not to contest the British entry, but merely to march out and meet the regulars at the outskirts of the town. Barrett remembered that

> *We marched down towards Lexington about a mile or mile and a half and we saw them coming. We halted and staid till they got within about 100 rods, then we were ordered to the about face and marched before them with our drums and fifes going, and also the British. We had grand music.*[18]

The confrontation turned into an incongruous parade, with the ragtag militia escorting the glittering redcoat column into the town of Concord.

It is not surprising that the Concord men did not contest the British entry into their town: still badly outnumbered by the regulars, they knew that their commander, Colonel James Barrett, was at his farm beyond the Concord River, supervising last-minute concealment of contraband. Discretion was, for the moment, in order. The Reverend Emerson reported that when he urged his colleagues to make a stand in the town and die there if necessary, "others more prudent thought best to retreat till our strength should be equal to the enemy's by recruits from other towns that were continually coming in to our assistance. Accordingly, we retreated over the [North] bridge."[19] Once North Bridge was crossed, the militia took up positions on a hill where, according to Barrett, they thought they "could see and hear what was going on."[20]

Left in uncontested possession of Concord, Lieutenant Colonel Smith decided to split his forces for the seizure and destruction of the provincial contraband. Keeping the grenadiers with him to search the town, he sent seven companies of the more mobile light infantry, under the command of Captain Lawrence Parsons, to secure the North Bridge and search Colonel Barrett's farm. Captain Parsons in turn split his command, taking four companies with him to the farm and leaving one company at the bridge, supported by the remaining two several hundred yards beyond the bridge.

Little contraband was found in the town. What the grenadiers did find, they burnt. The flames from their fires, however, excited the minutemen who had taken their stations on the hill beyond North Bridge. Not close enough to see clearly what was going on in the town, the New Englanders concluded that the British were putting Concord to the torch. Strengthened by reinforcements which now were streaming in from the neighboring towns, the men of Concord decided to march back into their town to save it from fiery destruction. Amos Barrett recalled that Colonel James Barrett, back from his farm and now in command, gave the order to load

> *and [we] had strict orders not to fire till they fired first, then to fire as fast as we could. We then marched on. Capt. Davis' minute company marched first, then Capt. Allen's minute company, the one that I was in next. We marched 2 deep. It was a long causeway, being round by the river. Capt. Davis*

42.
AMOS BARRETT. Unidentified artist, date unknown. Whereabouts unknown; reproduced in *Journal and Letters of Reverend Henry True . . . also an Account of the Battle of Concord by Captain Amos Barrett*, 1900. [Not in exhibition.]

had got, I believe, within 15 rods of the British, when they fired 3 guns, one after another. As soon as they fired them, they fired on us. The balls whistled well. We were then ordered to fire that could fire and not kill our own men. It is strange there were no more killed, but they fired too high. Capt. Davis was killed and Mr. Osmore and a number wounded. We soon drove them from the bridge, when I got over, there were 2 lay dead and another almost dead.[21]

As the Americans closed in on him, the British commander at the bridge, Captain Walter Laurie, sent to Smith for reinforcements. Smith himself led the relief, but ". . . being a very fat heavy Man he wou'd not have reached the Bridge in half an hour tho' it was not half a mile to it." [22] Arriving too late to prevent the rout, Smith withdrew into the town and made no attempt to retake the bridge, even though Parsons had not yet returned from Barrett's farm.

Watching the fight from the Old Manse, the Reverend Emerson recorded one of the most brutal acts of the day. A British soldier who lay nearly dead on the side of the road was attempting to rise when

a young fellow coming over the bridge in order to join the country people, . . . seeing the soldier wounded and attempting to get up, not being under the feelings of humanity, very barbarously broke his skull and let his brains out with a small axe.[23]

"The poor object," Emerson added, "lived an hour or two before he expired." Parson's troops, returning from Barrett's farm, saw the mutilated body of their comrade and soon the news spread to the rest of the soldiers that the colonists were scalping and gouging wounded redcoats. The disgust and hatred for a savage enemy that had prompted the Americans at Lexington to hide the graves of the newly killed minutemen now filled the redcoats. The rest of the day's fighting would be marked by unadulterated hatred on both sides.

Meanwhile, Smith, trying to decide what to do next, wasted nearly two hours after the encounter at the bridge, ordering his men into marching formation and then dismissing them time after time, all the while hoping that a relief force would soon appear. Emerson recorded that "the enemy by their Marches & counter Marches discover'd gt. Feekleness [sic] and Inconstancy of Mind, sometimes advancing sometimes returning to their former Posts, till at Lenth [sic] they quitted the Town, & retreated by the Way they came." [24] It was noon when the redcoat column finally set out for Boston.

The British retreat went uneventfully at first, with the redcoat flanking parties keeping the minutemen at a safe distance. But when Smith had to pull the flankers in so that the column could cross a narrow bridge at Meriam's Corner, the situation changed. As the redcoats filed across the bridge, the militia struck with fury. Amos Barrett wrote:

We were soon after them. When they got about a mile and a half to a road that comes from Bedford and Bildrea they were waylaid and a great many killed. When I got there, a great many lay dead, and the road was bloody.[25]

The return march now became a nightmarish rout. Lieutenant Barker recorded in his diary:

> *The Country was an amazing strong one, full of Hills, Woods, stone walls, &c., which the Rebels did not fail to take advantage of, for they were all lined with People who kept an incessant fire upon us, as we did too upon them but not with the same advantage, for they were so concealed there was hardly any seeing them: in this way we marched between 9 and 10 miles, their numbers increasing from all parts, while ours was reducing from deaths, wounds, and fatigue, and we were totally surrounded with such an incessant fire as it's impossible to conceive, our ammunition was likewise near expended.*[26]

In retrospect, the fleeing redcoats could take pride only in the success of the flankers who spread out whenever the columns passed through open country. Most of the American casualties were men who, unaccustomed to conventional warfare, did not think to look behind them as they took cover behind trees and brush, and thus were shot in the back by the flanking parties.

Smith's force was in desperate plight when it approached Lexington. Ensign Henry De Bernière of the Tenth British Infantry noted in his diary that

> *... when we arrived within a mile of Lexington, our ammunition began to fail, and the light companies were so fatigued with flanking they were scarce able to act, and a great number of wounded scarce able to get forward, made a great confusion; Col. Smith (our commanding officer) had received a wound through his leg, a number of officers were also wounded, so that we began rather to run than to retreat in order—the whole behaved with amazing bravery, but little order; we attempted to stop the men and form them two deep, but to no purpose, the confusion increased rather than lessened....*[27]

As the redcoats reeled into Lexington, it seemed to Barker that now "We must have laid down our arms or been picked off by the rebels at their pleasure."[28]

Hugh Percy, Second Duke of Northumberland (1742-1817)

Smith's battered column did not have to suffer the humiliation of laying down arms on Lexington Common. At the far border of the town, the desperately awaited relief column had arrived under the command of Gage's brigadier general, Hugh, Earl Percy.

Percy, later to become the second Duke of Northumberland, possessed the keenest military mind in the Boston garrison and the personal courage that had characterized so many members of his ancient family. A veteran of the European wars and a former member of Parliament, Percy did not regard the colonists as belligerently as did the King and his ministers. But his fortunes were bound up closely with the royal favor. The young earl had married the daughter of George III's mentor, the Earl of Bute; he had been George's aide-de-camp, and he figured among the parliamentary faction called "the King's friends." It was hardly surprising, therefore, that he would offer to command troops in America, whatever his personal feelings about the Anglo-American quarrel.

On the night of April 18, Percy was surprised and not a little dismayed to hear

43.
HUGH EARL PERCY, second Duke of Northumberland. Pompeo Battoni, before 1776. The Duke of Northumberland.

Bostonians talking on the Common of what Gage had assured his officers was a secret expedition to Concord. When the earl told Gage what he had heard, the governor ordered Percy's entire First Brigade of 1,400 men—three infantry regiments, a marine batallion, and most important of all, as it turned out, two artillery batteries—to be under arms at four the following morning, ready to march to Smith's aid. Unfortunately for the ponderous colonel and his men, the First did *not* report under arms at four the next morning; the soldiers were still sound asleep. The brigade major, whose duty it was to assemble the command, had not been in his quarters when his orders arrived. His servant had accepted the message, but forgot to deliver it when the major came in, and not until Smith's request for a relief force arrived at 5 a.m. did anyone realize what had happened. The brigade hastily assembled, but still the marines did not appear; their orders had been inadvertently sent to the quarters of Pitcairn, who,

79

of course, was otherwise engaged. By the time the rescue expedition finally set out, stepping off to a mocking rendition of "Yankee Doodle," it was nine o'clock.

Lord Percy led his scarlet and white array across Boston Neck, through Roxbury, Brookline, and Cambridge, and into the ominously silent and empty Middlesex countryside. As the troops neared Lexington, they could hear distant firing. One of Smith's wounded junior officers, traveling back to Boston in a chaise, told Percy of Smith's plight. The earl hurried his force on to the Boston side of Lexington, where he placed six-pound cannon on two hills and established a line between them. Lieutenant Frederick Mackenzie of the Royal Welch Fusiliers, a member of the rescue force, recorded that "As soon as the Grenadier & Light Infantry perceived the 1st Brigade drawn up for their support, they shouted repeatedly, and the firing ceased for a short time."[29] At 2:30 Smith's harried troops staggered through the First Brigade's line to momentary safety; Percy "had the happiness of saving them from inevitable destruction...."[30]

Percy remained at Lexington for an hour, allowing Smith's men to rest while he planned the return to Boston and the cannon awed the colonials into silence. At 3:30, according to Mackenzie,

> *Lord Percy gave orders for the whole to begin their march towards Boston. Col° Smith's detachment marched in front, as they were a good deal fatigued, and had expended most of their ammunition. Flanking parties were sent out, and the Welch Fusiliers ordered to form the rear Guard. As soon as the rear Guard began to move, the Rebels commenced their fire, having previously crept round under cover, and gained the walls and hedges on both flanks. The firing continued without intermission from Lexington, until the troops passed over Charlestown Neck. Those Rebels who came in from the flanks during the march, always posted themselves in the houses and behind the walls by the roadside, and there waited the approach of the Column. Numbers of them were mounted, and when they had fastened their horses at some little distance from the road, they crept down near enough to have a Shot; as soon as the Column had passed, they mounted again, and rode round until they got ahead of the Column, and found some convenient place from whence they might fire again. These fellows were generally good marksmen, and many of them used long guns made for Duck-Shooting.[31]*

Not all the provincials were content to fire from cover. Some, stirred by that fierce hatred of an enemy that the frontier had produced, were willing to give up their lives for a shot at a British officer. Percy wrote to a friend that some Yankees ". . . advanced within 10 yds. to fire at me & other officers, tho' they were morally certain of being put to death themselves in an instant."[32]

Percy's situation, although not desperate, was far from good. On two occasions the Yankees pressed the British especially hard. Both times Percy used his cannon to relieve the threat. The provincials kept up a galling fire that the commander described as surrounding his men like a moving circle all the way to Charlestown. As the soldiers staggered on under a hail of musket balls, their fury at an enemy that would not stand up and fight in the accepted European fashion increased. "So enraged" were they "at suffering from an unseen Enemy, that they forced open many of the houses from

44.
Handcolored engraving of the uniform of the Royal Welch Fusiliers, one of the British units present at Lexington and Concord. From *Uniforms of the Infantry*, 1768. Prince Consort's Library, Aldershot, England.

which the fire proceeded, and put to death all those found in them."³³ Although this was a justifiable defensive reaction on the redcoats' part, it resulted in the deaths of several innocent bystanders. Even more important for the revolutionary cause, it provided the Americans with a rich mine of propaganda material.

William Heath of Roxbury was a farmer by trade, but his true love was soldiering. In his memoirs Heath, speaking of himself in the third person, recalled:

> *From his childhood he was remarkably fond of military exercises, which passion grew up with him, and as he arrived at years of maturity, led him to procure, and attentively to study, every military treatise in the English language, which was obtainable.*³⁴

Heath moved up through the ranks of the militia, and in February 1775 he was commissioned a brigadier general by the Massachusetts Provincial Congress. On April 19, as the only militia general who showed up, Heath enjoyed the honor of being the first general officer ever to lead an American army in battle.

While out on the afternoon of April 18 Heath had noticed "British officers on horseback, with their swords and pistols, riding up the road towards Lexington. The time of day, and distance from Boston, excited suspicion of some design."

The next day began early for "Our General," (as Heath curiously referred to himself in his memoirs). At daybreak, he "was awoke, called from his bed, and informed that a detachment of the British army were out; that they had crossed from Boston to Phipps's farm, in boats, and had gone towards Concord, as was supposed, with intent to destroy the public stores." After spending most of the morning with the Committee of Safety, Heath was joined by the Patriot-physician, Joseph Warren, and both men set out to join the militia at Lexington.³⁵

At about the time Percy relieved Smith, General Heath joined the Massachusetts militia, which had been scattered by the shot from the British fieldpieces. First devoting his efforts to re-forming the troops, he then led them in close pursuit of the retreating redcoats. Heath, however, never really got control of the provincial forces. The various militia companies were not amenable to taking orders from their own captains, let alone an amateur general. Moreover, he was frustrated by the constant turnover in the American force, as minutemen who had been in the fight since it began dropped out once they had exhausted their ammunition, while new arrivals rushed in and joined the undisciplined firing without stopping to report to a higher command. Consequently, the fighting from Lexington to Charlestown proceeded exactly as it had from Concord to Lexington: in ragged, undisciplined fashion.

Heath was able to execute one tactically sound command decision that might have given his homespun army a stunning victory over the regulars. He sent the Watertown militia to Cambridge bridge, under orders "to take up the planks, barricade the south end of the bridge, and then to take post." In the event that the British should choose that route to Boston, they would discover that the Charles River was, at that point, too deep to ford; and with the bridge lost, they would be effectively trapped.³⁶

Percy, however, foresaw that his return to Boston would be obstructed in Cambridge. As he approached the town late in the afternoon, he feinted to the right, as if making for the bridge, then wheeled his column left and marched for the Charlestown Neck.

William Heath (1737-1814)

45.
WILLIAM HEATH. John Rubens Smith after Henry Williams. Engraving from *Polyanthus*, 1813. Library of Congress.

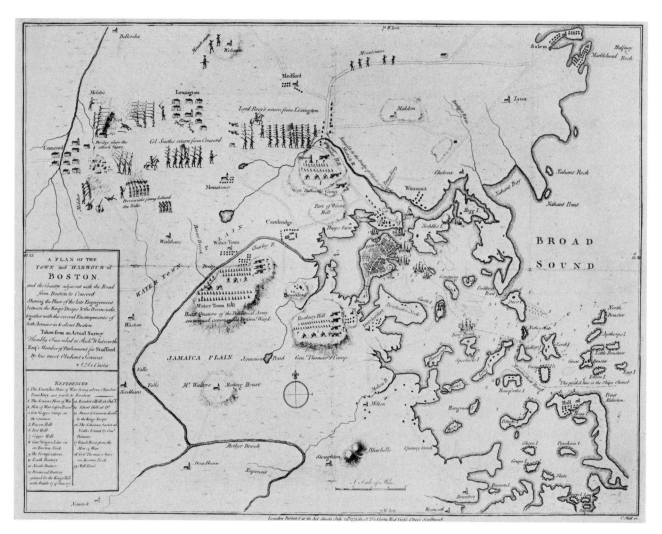

46.
A Plan of the Town and Harbour of Boston . . . Showing the Place of the late Engagement between the King's Troops and the Provincials. C. Hall. Engraving, 1775. The New York Public Library. [Not in exhibition.]

Not surprised at Percy's change of direction, Heath set up a group of militia men to block the path of the redcoats into the Charlestown road—the first American troops to stand in the open against the regulars since the men at Concord bridge early that morning. But Percy merely set up his field pieces and brushed them aside, continuing the march to safety.

Timothy Pickering (1745-1829)

One more possibility existed for Heath's motley army to strike a decisive blow. The chance, however, was slim at best and its success rested on newcomers to the scene: Timothy Pickering and the Salem militia.

Pickering, a 1763 graduate of Harvard College, had been an early and active supporter of colonial rights, turning his hand to pamphleteering and the organization of the Essex County militia. A man of wide administrative ability, which he later demonstrated in various military and public offices, he yet constantly involved himself in controversy. His performance on April 19, 1775, was no exception.

The news of the British march on Concord came late to Pickering, as it did to all

47.
TIMOTHY PICKERING. Gilbert
Stuart, 1808. Arthur T. Lyman.

of Essex County. In 1807 he recalled sitting in his office at the Registry of Deeds in Salem sometime between eight and nine in the morning of April 19, 1775, when Captain Epes of Danvers burst into his office with the news of Lexington. Since the captain commanded a company in Pickering's regiment, he asked for orders; and Pickering "expressed to him my opinion, that his and the other Danvers company should march without waiting for the assembling of the whole regiment."[37]

Pickering himself, however, was not in such a great hurry to get started. In fact, he seems to have misread the situation entirely. Not realizing the distance between Lexington and Boston, he was certain that the redcoats would be safely back in the city before his men could level their muskets at them. He did not reckon with the slowness of Smith, the incompetence of Gage's staff, or the ferocity of the provincial counterattack.

When Pickering finally moved, it was at the importunity of his local Salem companies. Even then, he made no haste, stopping the column at a tavern a few miles from Salem to await the news that the British had arrived safely in Boston. When no such message arrived, the troops grumbled again, and the reluctant commander was forced to lead them forward. As the march continued at a sedate pace, Pickering finally received news, but not what he had expected: the British, not yet back in Boston, were headed for Charlestown. Alarmed at the thought of opportunity about to slip away, the Salem men quickened their pace. As dusk fell they finally came into full view of the last act of the long fight, and Pickering sent a messenger forward to find Heath and obtain news of the enemy's circumstances. When Heath discovered that "about 700 men were close behind, on their way to join the militia," he was chagrined. "Had these arrived sooner," the general believed, "the left flank of the British must have been greatly exposed, and suffered considerably; perhaps their retreat would have been cut off."[38]

Heath was not the only military man in America who lamented Pickering's tardiness. Washington wrote several weeks later that if the Salem men "had happened to be one hour sooner," they would surely have intercepted the British retreat to Charlestown.[39] Actually, the opportunity that Pickering lost was not as great as Washington and Heath imagined. Heath himself replied to Pickering's messenger that an American assault would stand little chance against the British cannon. Thus, "Our General" must take final responsibility for the Salem militia's not getting into action as the long day ended. Intercepting, moreover, is not the same as stopping. The grenadiers who led Percy's column were tough and strong, and they would have liked nothing better than to erase the sense of humiliation they had suffered all day at the hands of the Americans with an effective bayonet charge. It is doubtful that the Salem men, green to battle, could have maintained themselves against such experienced and angry soldiers.

As Pickering rode up to meet with Heath, and muzzle flashes flecked the gathering darkness, the redcoats reached safety on the Charlestown peninsula under the protection of the sixty-four guns of the *Somerset* man-of-war, riding at anchor in the Charles River basin. The next day the British troops were ferried back across Charles River to Boston.

Watertown Wednesday Morning near 10 o'Clock

To all the Friends of American Liberty, be it known that this Morning
before break of Day a Brigade consisting of about 1000 or
1200 Men landed at Phip's Farm at Cambridge & marched
to Lexington where they found a Company of our Colony
Militia in Arms, upon whom they fired without any
Provocation and killed 6 Men and Wounded 4 others. By an
Express from Boston this Moment, we find another Brigade
are now upon their March from Boston supposed to be
about 1000. the Bearer Mr. Israel Bissel is charged
to alarm the County quite to Connecticut and all
Persons are desired to furnish him with fresh Horses
as they may be needed. I have spoken with several Persons
who have seen the Dead & Wounded. Pray let the Delegates
from this Colony to Connecticut see this they know

                    J. Palmer one of the
                    Committee of S—y
(A Foster of Brookfield one of the Delegates. A True Copy
Taken from the Original p Order of Committee of Corres-
pondence for Worcester Attest. Nathan Baldwin T. Clerk
Worcester April the 19th 1775.

Brooklyne Thursday 11 o'Clock. the above is a true
Copy as rec'd Here pr Express forwarded from
Worcester   Test. Daniel Tyler Jr.

Alarm letter advising the Colony
of Connecticut of the attack on
Lexington, April 19, 1775. Guthman Collection.

BALTIMORE: *April 26.*
We have juſt received the following important INTELLIGENCE. viz.

WATERTOWN, (Maſſachuſetts-Bay) April 19.
Wedneſday Morning, 10 o'Clock.

TO ALL FRIENDS OF AMERICAN
LIBERTY.

BE IT KNOWN, that this Morning, before Break
of Day, a Brigade, conſiſting of about 1000 or
1200 men, landed at Phip's Farm, at Cambridge,
and marched to Lexington, where they found a Company of our Colony Militia in Arms, upon whom they
fired, without any Provocation, and killed 6 men, and
wounded 4 others.
By an Expreſs from Boſton, we find, that another
Brigade, are now upon their March from Boſton, ſuppoſed to be about 1000.——The Bearer, TRYAL
RUSSELL, is charged to alarm the Country, quite to
Connecticut: And all Perſons are deſired to furniſh
him with freſh horſes, as maybe needed. I have ſpoken
with ſeveral who have ſeen the deceaſed and wounded.
Pray let the Delegates from this Colony to Connecti-
cut, ſee this: they know Col. Foſter, of Brookfield,
one of the Delegates.
                                        J. PALMER,
                        one of the Committee of S——y.
A true Copy taken from the Original,
By Order of the Committee of Correſpondence,
Atteſt, NATHAN BALDING, Town Clk.
Worceſter. April 19 1775.

THURSDAY, 3 o'Clock.
*Since the above, received the following, by a
ſecond Expreſs.*

SIR,
I AM this Moment informed, by an Expreſs from
Woodſtock, taken from the Mouth of an Expreſs,
that arrived there at Two o'Clock, P. M. That the
Conteſt between the firſt Brigade that marched to Concord, was ſtill continuing this Morning, at the Town
of Lexington, to which ſaid Brigade had retreated.—
That another Brigade, ſaid to be the 2d mentioned in
the Letter of this Morning, that landed with a Quantity
of Artillery, at the Place where the firſt did. The
Provincials were determined to prevent the two Bri-
gades from joining their Strength, if poſſible, and remain in great Need of Succour.
N. B. The Regulars, when in Concord, burnt the
Court-Houſe, took 2 Pieces of Cannon, which were
rendered uſeleſs, and began to take up Concord Bridge,
on which Capt. ——, with many on both Sides were
ſoon killed;—then made an Attack upon the King's
Troops, on which they retreated.
                I am, Your Humble Servant,
                                        E. WILLIAMS.
To Col. Obadiah Johnſton, Canterbury.
P. S. Mr. M'Farland, of Plainfield, Merchant, is
juſt returned from Boſton, by Way of Providence, who
converſed with an Expreſs from Lexington, who further informs, that about 4000 of our Troops had ſur-
rounded the firſt Brigade, abovementioned, who were
on a Hill in Lexington, that the Action continued,
and there were about 50 of our Men killed, and 150 of
the Regulars, as near as they could determine, when
the Expreſs came away. It will be expdient for every
Man to go, who is fit and willing.
*The above is a true Copy, as received by Expreſs
from New-Haven, &c. atteſted by the Committee
of Correſpondence from Town to Town.*

49.
Broadside published in Baltimore,
April 26, 1775, giving news of the
battles of Lexington and Concord.
Library of Congress.

AFTERMATH

When Heath realized that Percy had crossed the Charlestown Neck and gained the unassailable heights of Bunker Hill, he wisely decided that "any further attempt upon the enemy, in that position, would have been futile." Yet, having come so far, the militia were not about to go home and give up the fight. Heath

> *immediately assembled the officers around him, at the foot of Prospect Hill, and ordered a guard to be formed, and posted near that place, sentinels to be planted down to the neck, and patrols to be vigilant in moving during the night; and an immediate report to be made to him, in case the enemy made any movements. The militia were then ordered to march to the town of Cambridge; where, after forming and sending off another guard to the points below the town, the whole were ordered to lie on their arms.*[43]

The next day, as Heath sent out details to bury the dead, the other generals of the Massachusetts militia arrived and began to organize the siege of Boston.

The running battle of April 19, so undistinguished tactically, presented the Americans with a strategic windfall, both militarily and politically. It demonstrated to the British that the Americans would, after all, be formidable opponents in battle. Seventy-three dead redcoats bore mute witness to the prowess of the Massachusetts militia. The twenty percent casualty rate sustained by the Concord expedition led Lord Percy to revise his low opinion of the Yankees. The young earl wrote to a friend that the American insurrection would not turn out as despicable as might be imagined in England:

> *Whoever looks upon them as an irregular mob, will find himself much mistaken; they have men amongst them who know very well what they are about, having been employed as rangers against the Indians and Canadians, and this country being much covered with wood and hilly, is very advantageous for their method of fighting. . . . as the Rebels have now had time to prepare, they are determined to go thro' with it . . . For my part, I never believed, I confess, that they wd have attacked the King's troops, or have had the perseverance I found in them yesterday.*[41]

Of military advantage to the provincials also was the fact that Gage's army was now bottled up in Boston and had become, for all major purposes, ineffective. The coercive power of the royal government was, for the moment at least, nonexistent in New England. More important, the battle of April 19 at last gave Massachusetts a solid foundation for a provincial army. The morning of April 20 revealed 20,000 armed Americans surrounding the town of Boston. From these the Provincial Committee of Safety was able to cull 8,000 who signed hastily formulated enlistment papers that would keep them under service to Massachusetts until the following December. Sam Adams's dream of a provincial army had become reality.

There were political as well as military advantages for the colonials to reap from Lexington and Concord. Sam Adams had taught the Massachusetts radicals that if they could not create events, they could at least improve them, and they improved

86

In Congreſs, *at Watertown, April* 30, 1775.

Gentlemen,

THE barbarous Murders on our innocent Brethren on Wedneſday the 19th Inſtant, has made it absolutely neceſſary that we immediately raiſe an Army to defend our Wives and our Children from the butchering Hands of an inhuman Soldiery, who, incenſed at the Obſtacles they met with in their bloody Progreſs, and enraged at being repulſed from the Field of Slaughter ; will without the leaſt doubt take the firſt Opportunity in their Power to ravage this devoted Country with Fire and Sword : We conjure you, therefore, by all that is dear, by all that is ſacred, that you give all Aſſiſtance poſſible in forming an Army : Our all is at Stake, Death and Devaſtation are the certain Conſequences of Delay, every Moment is infinitely precious, an Hour loſt may deluge your Country in Blood, and entail perpetual Slavery upon the few of your Poſterity, who may ſurvive the Carnage. We beg and entreat, as you will anſwer it to your Country, to your own Conſciences, and above all as you will anſwer to God himſelf, that you will haſten and encourage by all poſſible Means, the Inliſtment of Men to form the Army, and ſend them forward to Head-Quarters, at Cambridge, with that Expedition, which the vaſt Importance and inſtant Urgency of the Affair demands.

JOSEPH WARREN, Preſident, P. T.

50.
Broadside issued by Joseph Warren, president of the Massachusetts Provincial Congress, April 30, 1775, calling for the immediate formation of an army. Massachusetts Historical Society.

WE the Subſcribers do hereby ſolemnly and ſeverally engage and inliſt ourſelves as Soldiers in the Maſſachuſetts Service, for the Preſervation of the Liberties of America, from the Day of our Inliſtment, to the laſt Day of December next, unleſs the Service ſhould admit of a Diſcharge of a Part or the Whole ſooner, which ſhall be at the Diſcretion of the Committee of Safety, and we hereby promiſe to ſubmit ourſelves to all the Orders and Regulations of the Army, and faithfully to obſerve and obey all ſuch Orders as we ſhall receive from Time to Time, from our ſuperior Officers.

51.
Massachusetts enlistment broadside. Guthman Collection.

very well the events of April 19. The Provincial Congress bent every effort to publish its own version of the battle—a version skillfully constructed for optimum propaganda value. For this task the members of the Congress turned to the most imaginative and vitriolic polemicist among them, Doctor Benjamin Church.

Benjamin Church
(1734-1776)

Benjamin Church was a man of facile tongue, nimble pen, and treacherous soul. Educated at Harvard and London, Church was a physician who had early become associated with the radical side of the quarrel with Great Britain. A member of the Provincial Committee of Correspondence and Safety, as well as of the Provincial Congress, Church by 1775 knew as much about the inner workings of Massachusetts radicalism as any man in the colony, including Sam Adams himself. At the same time, however, Church discovered that his elegant taste far outran his moderate means. Seeking to support an expensive house and a no less expensive mistress, sometime in mid-1774 Church ("much drove for money," according to his bookkeeper) became a spy for General Gage. Although the radicals, Paul Revere wrote, realized that "there was a Traytor in the Provincial Congress, & that Gage was possessed of all their Secrets," they did not guess that the traitor was Church.[42]

Yet, Church did not go unsuspected. Dr. Joseph Warren never liked him, and Revere, "a constant and critical observer" of Church, claimed that he never thought him a man of principle. Revere even "doubted much in my own mind, whether He was a real Whig."[43] What saved Church from exposure was his formidable literary talent which the radicals both feared and admired; so that although "it was known," according to Revere, "that some of the Liberty songs, which He composed, were parodized by him in favor of the British, yet none dare charge him with it."[44]

Whatever doubts his colleagues entertained about his trustworthiness, Church did exactly the job they wanted him to do in putting together the provincial account of Lexington and Concord. Church was probably glad to undertake the task in the hope that it would put to rest any suspicions entertained about him. If he thought this a small price to pay for continuing his free operations within radical ranks, he reckoned without the success of his literary handiwork. Church caught at every rumor of British atrocity that the heat and confusion of the day had generated and welded them into an elaborate justification of the militia's actions. The account laid great stress on the claim that the Americans on Lexington Common had been fired upon without provocation. "This small party of inhabitants," Church declared, "was so far from being disposed to commit hostilities against the troops of their sovereign, that unless attacked, they were determined to be peaceable spectators of this extraordinary movement. . . ."[45] The Lexington men had begun to disperse at the approach of the redcoats, "but the detachment, seeming to thirst for blood, wantonly rushed on, and first began the hostile scene by firing on this small party." Church concluded his report by emphasizing the horror visited by the redcoats upon the innocent Yankees:

> *the devastation committed by the British troops on their retreat, the whole of the way from Concord to Charlestown, is almost beyond description; such as plundering and burning of dwelling-houses and other buildings, driving into the street women in child-bed, killing old men in their houses unarmed. Such scenes of desolation would be a reproach to the perpetrators, even if committed by the most barbarous nations, how much more when done by Britons*

88

be away sudden attack made by the troops here for this reason, they are sensible of the impracticability of conducting the affairs of War, without an assumption of the powers of Govern.t for this purpose they must consult the Continental Congress, I am appointed to my vexation to carry the dispatches to Philadelphia, & must set out to morrow w.ch will prevent my writing for some time, unless an opportunity should be found thence by water, The Congress have established a post office and are now appointing riders, Many of our Reg.ts are full, and are recieving their Commissions from our High Mightinesses —
— The Committee of Safety.

we begin to feel very formidable, shall begin to fortify the Camps soon, when they presumes they may be able to frown defiance against all the troops that Britain can send, they will not lay down their Arms unless the acts are all repeald or they are soundly beaten, The Letter becomes difficult every day, Oh for Peace & honor once more —

famed for humanity and tenderness: And all this because these colonies will not submit to the iron yoke of arbitrary power.[46]

Throughout America, Church's account of Lexington and Concord rang with smashing conviction. Militiamen from other colonies shouldered their muskets and stepped off down the muddy spring roads to join their Massachusetts brethren besieging Boston. The name of Lexington, thanks in large part to a traitor, became a new byword in the American mind for British tyranny.

The Massachusetts Patriots thought it no less important to spread their account of April 19 throughout England, in the hope that the British people would rise and make common cause with them in defense of the sacred and ancient rights of Englishmen. The Provincial Congress chartered a fast ship out of Salem to carry the Church report express to the mother country. The Patriot captain crowded on all sail and arrived a full two weeks before the lumbering cargo ship that bore, among its weighty freight, Gage's official report. The propaganda coup of Massachusetts was complete: the ministry, with no word from Gage, could not discredit the story, nor, though they tried, could they keep it from circulating.

Church's efforts in writing the Lexington and Concord story did disperse whatever suspicion remained about his devotion to the Patriot cause. In May the Provincial Congress sent him on a sensitive mission to Philadelphia to ask the Continental Congress to take over direction of the forces surrounding Boston. In June the doctor was deputized to meet Washington, who was coming to Boston to take command of the besieging army. In July the Continental Congress appointed Church director of the army's hospitals. In September, however, a letter that Church had tried to send to the British by way of his mistress was discovered in Rhode Island and turned over to Washington. Church's mistress was arrested, and, though "a subtile, shrewd jade," she broke down under Washington's hard questioning and named Church as the author of the letter. The doctor was arrested on September 29. He was found guilty by a court-martial of criminal correspondence with the enemy (since there was not yet an American nation, the Congress had not defined treason). Church was then dishonorably discharged from the Continental Army and the Provincial Congress and jailed. In 1776 he was allowed to depart for the West Indies, but the ship was lost in a storm with all on board.

52.
A Revolutionary period drum.
Guthman Collection.

The ADDRESS of

LIBERTY,

To the *BUCKSKINS* of *PENNSYLVANIA*, on hearing of the intended PROVINCIAL CONGRESS.

FAIR Liberty, dear Goddess bright—
Wishing to set the *Pennites* right—
Thus from her Throne, in candid Strains,
Addressed her *Pennsylvan* Swains.
Can public Virtue by me stand,
See Faction stalking through the Land?—
Faction that Fiend, begot in Hell—
In *Boston* nurs'd—here brought to dwell
By *Congress*, who, in airy Freak,
Conven'd to plan a *Republick?*
Will Helmsmen let the Ship of State,
Meet with so dire, shipwreck'd a Fate?
Can Judges, fam'd for Probity,
Sit tame Spectators by, and see
The Laws oppugn'd by Committee—
Who laugh at Courts, and Loyalty?
Can peaceful *Quakers,* honest Church,
See Congress leave them in the Lurch,
And o'er their Heads such Vermin perch!
Stop, Independants! Stop, I say!
You mean to fight—*to run away;*
The *British Thunder* you defy,
And Right of Parliament deny;
Revile the kind Peace making *Gage,*
Who with great Prudence would assuage
The Fires lit up by H———k's Rage;
Which unto civil Wars must tend,
Unless the Olive Branch we send
To gen'rous *Britain,* your best Friend.
Stop, Independants, stop, I say!
Attend to my instructive Lay!
Fysham must swing on yonder Tree—
Dear Friends, an *Englishman* you'll see,
Traytor to his King and Country!
With Rope adorn'd on Gallows high,
He'll kick in Air, in Company
With the *Pennsylvan* Farmer *John,*
And *Charley* T———, a Rebel Son,
For Crime by Statute called Treason,
Which they committed without Reason,

Well read in Law *John* seem'd—Oh, Shame!
Not so was it with poor *Fysham!*
For ignorant, alas, was he,
Ignorant as e'er Man could be!
(Ignorance, KNOW YE, in Law's no Plea.)
But Farmer *John* inveigled him,
And *Charles* united in the Scheme;
But Peace the Wight enjoyed—dying—
Both were by his Side a crying,
When Rope about *his* Neck was fix't,—
He clearly saw *they* would be next
Tuck't up aloft on self-fame Tree,
That he, alas, must hanged be!
View, Friends, this sad Catastrophe,—
Three Rebels hanging on one Tree—
Dead as Door Nails—hung for Treason,
Which they committed out of Season,—
Lives lost—Estates confiscated—
Their Fam'lies left discomnited,—
A horrid Scene—dismal Ditty—
Good lack-a-day—what a Pity!
Poor *Fysham* formerly, we're told,
Sold Goods to *France* for Sake of Gold,
'Tis true he did, in Time of War,
Yet he escap'd from Rope or Tar;
But he's o'ertak'n, Hemp has reach'd him—
For *old* Sins his Weight has stretch'd him;—
View, my Readers, this sad Picture!
Hang they will your *Gen'ral Stricture.*
Unnat'ral Deaths some Folk must *dye,*
Sic transit gloria mundi.
Ah, me! Deluded, hoodwink'd Cits,
Rouse from your Sleep, resume your Wits!
Honour the King, obey my Laws!
Don't *forfeit* Life and Lands for Straws!
Had those mad Bandits been discreet,
They ne'er had stretch'd in hempen Sheet.

From the Temple of LIBERTY.
January 7th, 1775.

54.
The Address of Liberty, To the Buckskins of Pennsylvania,
published in Philadelphia, January 7, 1775, warning the citizens
of the dire consequences of rebellion.
The Library Company of Philadelphia.

Preparations for War, Negotiations for Peace

N ews of the battles of Lexington and Concord spread along the Atlantic seaboard like wildfire. The "butchery" perpetrated by the British soldiers hotly stirred enthusiasm among all segments of the American population for fighting the British. The skirmishes between the New England minutemen and the redcoats had propelled the conflict with the parent country into the new dimension of open warfare. All the colonies were ready, as never before, to turn to the Continental Congress for guidance and counsel.

CONGRESS RECONVENES

The Congress was already in the process of reassembling. When it had adjourned at the end of October 1774, after two months of hard work, hopes had been high that the remonstrances, petitions, compromises, and adoption of a firm stand would bring about a reconciliation with Great Britain and a reordering of the status of America within the British Empire. The delegates had counted on the newly formed Association to provide sufficient economic pressure to force England to accede to their wishes. But all hope for reconciliation and a redress of grievances was dashed in the spring of 1775 when George III rejected the Congress's "Petition." Outraged by the Association, he had declared, "The New England governments are now in a state of rebellion; blows must decide whether they are to be subject to this country or independent."[1] When this unfortunate prophecy was realized on April 19 in the villages of Lexington and Concord, many delegates to the Second Continental Congress were already on their way to Philadelphia.

Cheering crowds and fervent welcomes greeted the New England delegates as they traveled southward. In New York City one spectator reported that "the roads were lined with greater numbers of people than were ever known on any occasion before."[2] The delegates interpreted the military escorts and bands of music that ushered them into Philadelphia as "a Strong Testimony of the Spirit and Unanimity of the people through out our long journey."[3]

On May 10 the delegates took their seats, not as before in the uncomfortable Carpenters' Hall, but in the much more elegant—and more private—Pennsylvania State House. Peyton Randolph was reelected the presiding officer and Charles Thomson secretary. The voting procedure and rule of secrecy were readopted, and the Reverend Jacob Duché once more moved hearts and souls with his solemn opening prayers. Immediately thereafter the Congress resolved into a Committee of the Whole to consider "the dangerous and critical situation" of America. In such a consideration, each of the delegations had remarkable latitude, for they carried with them written mandates directing them to adopt all measures necessary for obtaining redress of grievances. In effect, the Congress was empowered to direct the course of the revolution.

A great sense of unity existed among the delegates at this second gathering. The "shot heard round the world" had contributed to that feeling, as it had also created a greater militancy and sternness. Even moderates like John Dickinson of Pennsylvania had come to believe that the only alternative left to them—if they were not to retreat and again submit completely to British domination—was civil war. A small minority still urged submission. The rest of the delegates by now had accepted the challenge of war, but were divided in their estimate of the desired goal. The large group led by Dickinson looked forward to ultimate reconciliation. The radicals, spearheaded again by the Lee-Adams junto, had no such illusions: war meant independence. The confusion of aims irritated John Adams. "I find," he wrote home, "that the general Sense . . . is to prepare for a vigorous defensive War, but at the Same Time to keep open the Door of Reconcilliation,—to hold the Sword in one Hand and the olive Branch in the other—to proceed with Warlike Measures, and conciliatory Measures. . . ."[4]

A NEW PRESIDENT IS CHOSEN

Two weeks after the delegates had assembled, they were faced with the necessity of choosing a new president. Peyton Randolph had been recalled to Virginia to preside over the Virginia House of Burgesses. The opportunity was one that the radicals in the Congress could not overlook. Under the prompting of the two Adamses from Massachusetts, they managed to have John Hancock elected to the presidency of that body on May 24. Hancock was the Massachusetts rebel whose offenses, General Gage had declared, were "of too flagitious a nature to admit of any other consideration than condign punishment."[5]

John Hancock (1737/8-1793) John Hancock had joined the leadership of the revolutionary movement in Massachusetts from the first inchoate mutterings against British laws. Heir to the massive fortune of his uncle, Thomas Hancock, and the directorship of Thomas's many enterprises, Hancock could afford to turn his attention from the problems of making a living to the pursuit of politics. His vanity and pomposity earned him epithets that ranged from "the American king" to "Hancocky" to "Johnny Dupe"; but his liberal sentiments, reputation for smuggling, and flagrant abuse of customs officers made him famous. When Sam Adams recruited him to the colonial cause, Hancock was only too happy to turn over his administrative duties to assistants and devote his time to opposing the King and his officers.

From this time on, he became closely identified with Sam Adams, so that the hostile

55.
JOHN HANCOCK. John Singleton
Copley, 1770-72. Private col-
lection.

chief justice, Andrew Oliver, was impelled to comment that he was "as closely attached to the hindermost Part of Mr. [Sam] Adams as the Rattles are affixed to the Tail of a Rattle Snake." [6] Notwithstanding the ease with which he lent himself to manipulation, Hancock remained popular because of his generous philanthropy. Even when, as treasurer of Harvard College, he became involved in a lengthy scandal in 1773 because of seeming neglect of his duties and the sequestering of college funds, the people maintained their trust in him and elected him to the presidency of the illegal Provincial Congress in 1774.

Hancock continued to bask in the warmth of his reputation as a British outlaw and man of great fortune when he arrived in Philadelphia; and so, despite his mediocre intellectual abilities, he was welcomed to the president's chair. As a result of his experiences as a parliamentarian in Massachusetts, he managed to preserve order, although not harmony, among a body of men of distinctly varied opinions and interests—and the following year, he was reelected to the presidency.

Lord North Extends the Olive Branch and Snaps the Whip

On May 26 the Congress was faced with a decision that went to the heart of the colonial dilemma in 1775. That day Lord North's motion, adopted by the House of Commons on February 27, had to be considered and answered. Ostensibly hoping to conciliate the obstreperous colonies, the Commons had expressed the belief that North's plan would be accepted by all those "who have the least affection for their King and Country, or a just sense of their own interests." It provided for the relief of "every grievance relative to taxation" by the establishment of a compact with Great Britain allowing the colonies to tax themselves for purposes of defense and civil government and Great Britain to impose taxes for purposes of commercial regulation. Parliament would forego its power to tax a colony as soon as the individual colony decided to accept North's plan.[7]

To many delegates this seemed a fair enough arrangement, one which they had been seeking throughout the quarrel with the mother country. But Lord North overplayed his hand: while the delegates were still deliberating about the proposal, a paper written at Lord North's direction by Grey Cooper, joint secretary of the Treasury, was delivered into the hands of Philadelphian Thomas Willing to be laid before the Congress. In the paper Lord North threatened that if the colonies did not accept his conciliatory resolution of February 27, the home government would "pursue the most effectual measures, and . . . use the whole force of the Kingdom, if it be found necessary, to reduce the rebellious and refractory Provinces and Colonies." [8]

Thomas Willing
(1731-1821)

Lord North had chosen a trustworthy emissary. Thomas Willing was a moderate man who represented a large conservative group in Pennsylvania. The son of a wealthy merchant, Willing had spent the impressionable years of his youth at schools in England. A few years after returning home, in 1749, he had entered into a partnership with Robert Morris in the highly successful mercantile firm of Willing, Morris & Company. Although he had taken the side of the colonists in 1765 against the Stamp Act—even to signing a nonimportation agreement—he distrusted the radical elements

56.
THOMAS WILLING. Gilbert Stuart,
circa 1795. Mrs. Arnold B. Chace.

in the Congress that seemed to him intent upon promoting militancy. "Old Square-toes," as he was irreverently called, feared that the Lee-Adams junto would direct its propaganda against the proprietary government, which wealthy Pennsylvanians still found acceptable, in order to win the support of the common citizenry.

Willing exercised strong influence in Philadelphia—as prominent merchant, mayor (1763), member of the Provincial Assembly (1764-1767), and member of the Committee of Correspondence. In 1775 he and his partner were both selected to represent Pennsylvania in the Continental Congress. His presentation to the Congress of Lord North's proposal and threat, then, seemed to many of the radical members an attempt to obstruct the movement toward independence which they hoped to quicken. Willing himself probably believed that Lord North's motion furnished a good opportunity for the colonies to resolve their differences with Great Britain. But with the blindness of his timidity, he was unable to see the compulsory nature of Lord North's "conciliatory" plan, which if enacted would divide the colonies by appealing to their individual self-interest.

The Congress at first tabled the motion for further consideration. Not until July 31 was the issue resolved, when a committee consisting of Richard Henry Lee, Thomas Jefferson, John Adams, and Benjamin Franklin brought in a resolution rejecting the proposal as "unreasonable and insidious." The Congress, dedicated to a course of arms after Bunker Hill, agreed.[9]

97

BOSTON WAITS FOR HELP

On June 2 the Congress received an urgent letter from the Massachusetts Provincial Congress, signed by Joseph Warren, requesting advice on how to exercise properly "the powers of civil Government" of the colony while it lay helplessly at the mercy of Parliament and the King's troops. ". . . [W]e shall readily submit to such a general plan as you may direct . . . as shall not only most promote our advantage, but the union and interests of all America." Furthermore, would the Congress seriously consider taking over "the regulation and general direction" of the New England army in Boston which was "now collecting from different colonies . . . for the general defense of the rights of America?" An army under congressional leadership would be better "able to defend us and all America from the further butcheries and devastations of our implacable enemies." Realizing that its answer to Massachusetts's appeal would, in effect, establish a policy legitimizing the provincial congresses and committees that had been informally established in all the colonies and would make the Congress responsible for ordering armed resistance to Great Britain, the delegates decided that Massachusetts's request was of too great importance to be hastily answered. Therefore, a committee of five was chosen by ballot to formulate a response to Massachusetts Bay.[10]

The members of the committee to answer the Massachusetts Bay queries—John Rutledge, Thomas Johnson, John Jay, Richard Henry Lee, and James Wilson— were preponderantly conservative, with the exception of the fiery Lee. Wilson's approach to the problem and his position with respect to the larger question of colonial relations were quite typical and help explain the compromising nature of the response the committee ultimately formulated, which was adopted by the Congress on June 9.

57.
Permission granted to a Boston citizen to pass over the lines, issued by Thomas Gage, May 1775. Massachusetts Historical Society.

James Wilson (1742-1798)

James Wilson had joined the committee as a moderate and as a freshman delegate from Pennsylvania. His name had come to the attention of the delegates during the first Congress, when his essay, *Considerations on the Nature and Extent of the Legis-*

lative Authority of the British Parliament, was published in 1774. The treatise, which Wilson had originally conceived four to six years earlier, advanced the radical, but able, argument that the American colonies held an independent position within the British Empire. Possessing a facile legal mind and sophisticated intellect, Wilson had reached the conclusion that the dominions of the Empire were separate from each other and Great Britain, connected only by a common sovereign, and completely independent of the authority of Parliament in all instances.

James Wilson had emigrated to Pennsylvania from Scotland in 1765 at the age of twenty-one in search of fortune. Although he had attended both the University of Glasgow and the University of Edinburgh, his professional career in the British Isles was limited by the fact that his father came from the poor farmer class. In Philadelphia Wilson studied in John Dickinson's law office—Dickinson then being considered a radical Whig. After admission to the bar in 1767, he moved to western Pennsylvania where his career as a lawyer enjoyed a meteoric rise. It was in western Pennsylvania, also, that James Wilson was taken with the almost maniacal compulsion to speculate in land and banking enterprises that would color the rest of his career.

Wilson believed that the legal arguments against British rule were irrefutable; but despite his own lowly origins he shied away from popular democracy. While he believed that sovereignty lay with the people, he was skeptical of their ability to govern themselves. Nevertheless, Wilson supported colonial resistance to the Crown and, in 1774, was elected to the Cumberland County Committee of Correspondence, the Provincial Congress, and the Cumberland County militia. In 1775 Wilson tried to have the Boston Port Act declared unconstitutional, which was not possible under British law. His legal reasoning, however, foreshadowed the eventual adoption in America of the doctrine of judicial review. In later years Wilson, sitting on the Supreme Court of the United States, would be one of the first justices to declare an act of Congress unconstitutional.

By the time the Second Continental Congress met, Wilson was more reluctant than many of the New England and southern members to take extreme steps against Great Britain. His early radicalism had changed to strong moderation. Under his committee's direction, then, the Congress answered Massachusetts's questions with halfway measures. Resolving that Massachusetts Bay owed no obedience to "the Act of Parliament for altering the charter of the Colony," it suggested that the offices of governor and lieutenant-governor "be considered . . . vacant." It urged Massachusetts to form a provincial congress through a new election of assemblymen who, when chosen, would elect councillors. The council and assembly would then "exercise the powers of government, until a Governour, of His Majesty's appointment, will consent to govern the Colony according to its Charter." [11]

The provisional government in Massachusetts was disappointed. The colony would not only have to undergo new elections, but the Congress, which had gone so far as to approve the establishment of a revolutionary government, in which General Gage and other royal appointees bore no part, had also successfully avoided recommending a completely independent government which might have become a precedent for other colonies. The next blow was the Congress's deferral of a decision on assuming the maintenance and direction of the army at Boston. James Wilson, among others, was not convinced that the Congress had the authority to assume such a responsibility.

58.
JAMES WILSON. Jean Pierre Henri Elouis, circa 1795. National Collection of Fine Arts, Smithsonian Institution.

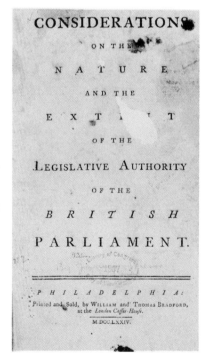

59.
James Wilson's *Considerations On The Nature And The Extent Of The Legislative Authority Of The British Parliament*. Philadelphia, 1774. Library of Congress.

60.
ROBERT TREAT PAINE. Edward
Savage, begun 1802, completed by
John Coles, Jr., 1822. Massa-
chusetts Historical Society.

*Robert Treat Paine
(1731-1814)*

If the Congress was not prepared to take over the direction of the army at Cambridge, it could at least aid in furnishing supplies and munitions. On June 10 a committee was formed to devise ways and means of introducing into the colonies the manufacture and purchase of saltpeter and sulphur—essential in the making of gunpowder.

Robert Treat Paine, delegate from Massachusetts, was appointed chairman of the committee. As a staunch Patriot, anxious to help relieve the suffering of his colony, Paine had worked in the Provincial Congress of Massachusetts to collect supplies for Boston and, therefore, was a suitable choice to head the committee in Philadelphia. He immediately set about establishing government-controlled powder mills and attending assiduously to the task of providing powder where there was none. The distinguished lawyer from southern Massachusetts thus served the colonial cause not through politicking and ideological arguments but through practical means. "[I]t must be a cruel Vexation in the day of decision for Liberty or Slavery," he later wrote a friend,

> *to have the Scale turn against us merely thro' the defect of our own Powder.... I wish the Inhabitants of the United States were more intent upon providing for the means of their defence, than making Governments with [ou]t providing for the means of their Support.*[12]

Although he did not associate with the Boston radicals, Robert Treat Paine had been a supporter of colonial rights from the first incidents of conflict with the mother country. A prominent Taunton lawyer, in 1770 he had served as coprosecutor in the Boston Massacre trials, earning the admission from his formidable opponent, John Adams, that although "Bob Paine is an impudent, ill bred, conceited fellow," he also had "wit, learning, and a great deal of humor." [13] The citizens of Taunton, for their part, liked Bob Paine. In 1773-75 and again in 1777-78 they elected him their delegate to the Provincial Assembly. Paine attended both Continental Congresses, where he made substantial contributions, although they did not attract the same attention as did the more dramatic achievements of some of the other members of his delegation. His most important service to the Continental Congress, and eventually to the war effort, was rendered as a member of the munitions committee and in attending to the manufacture of cannon for the use of the colonial army. Yet, for all of his effort in the preparations for war, Paine vacillated on the question of independence. It was in keeping with his temperament that he signed both the Olive Branch Petition in 1775, appealing to the Crown to restore harmony with the colonies, and the Declaration of Independence in 1776.

61.
View of the old French Fort, Redoubts and Batteries at Ticonderoga on Lake Champlain. Henry Rudyerd. Watercolor, 1777. Fort Ticonderoga Museum.

THE FIRST SPOILS OF WAR: TICONDEROGA, MAY 10, 1775

As members of the Congress assembled in Philadelphia, a group of Connecticut and Massachusetts riflemen were approaching the British Fort Ticonderoga on Lake Champlain in the cold darkness of early morning. The armed band hoped to capture the strategically important fort in a surprise attack before Lord Dartmouth's orders for the renovation and reinforcement of the crumbling post could be carried out. With Ticonderoga in colonial hands, the main entrance into America from Canada would be removed from British control. Of more immediate importance for besieged Boston and the neighboring New England colonies, however, was the capture of the heavy arms and military supplies stashed away at Ticonderoga.

The battles of Lexington and Concord had worried the Connecticut colonists as much as the citizens of Massachusetts. One of the most outraged was a thirty-four-year-old Connecticut captain, Benedict Arnold. "Good God," he wondered, "are the Americans all a Sleep & tamely giving up their glorious Liberties . . . that they don't take immediate vengence on such miscreants?" [14] Quickly assembling a small force of men in New Haven and coercing the town leaders into giving him a supply of gunpowder, the adventurous captain marched to the aid of Boston.

Benedict Arnold
(1741-1801)

Benedict Arnold was always ready for adventure. He had run away at the age of fourteen to fight in the French and Indian War, and when sent home, he ran off again. Finally, he abandoned the battlefront—but only when the drama of a soldier's life wore thin. At the age of twenty-one he had moved to New Haven, where he became a prosperous druggist and bookseller; but the tame life paled as relations between the colonists and England worsened. Joining the Connecticut militia, he had reached the rank of captain when violence broke out in Massachusetts.

Somewhere on the road to Boston, Arnold met up with Colonel Samuel H. Parsons of Hartford, Connecticut, with whom he commiserated on the sorry state of the American forces. Arnold had heard reports of the large number of brass cannon at Fort Ticonderoga protected by only a skeletal force of British soldiers. Capture of the large guns could prove a coup for the Patriots and the salvation of Massachusetts Bay, Arnold confided to Parsons.

Colonel Parsons was excited by the possibilities. Without wasting a moment, he hurried to Hartford where he enlisted the help of two other men who he thought would be sympathetic to the idea of capturing Ticonderoga: Colonel Samuel Wyllys and Silas Deane.

62.
BENEDICT ARNOLD. Benoît Louis Prévost after Pierre Eugène Du Simitière. Engraving, 1779. The Metropolitan Museum of Art.

Silas Deane, a prominent and wealthy businessman and lawyer, had aligned himself with the colonial cause from the beginning of the quarrel with the mother country. Two fortunate marriages by the age of thirty and a natural penchant for self-aggrandizement had relieved him of some of the more tiresome worries of financial security and allowed him to devote his time and energy to the protection of colonial rights. Deane fought against the Townshend Acts, served on the Connecticut Committee of Correspondence, and became one of the most active leaders of the revolutionary movement in Connecticut. The events of the spring of 1775 led Deane to the conclusion that "There is no alternative except to submit or prepare to resist even unto blood." [15] Deane's fellow colonists rewarded his enthusiasm by electing him to represent them at both congresses. He had not yet left for the second session of the Congress when he met with Parsons and Wyllys to plan the first colonial offensive action of the war.

Deane and his two partners realized that the taking of Ticonderoga must be done quickly and quietly. Procurement of the cannon and heavy artillery at the fort was essential to the colonial cause. Furthermore, Deane decided, the threat that a strengthened British fortress on Lake Champlain could pose to the northern colonies must be eliminated. The only force in the area that resembled an organized militia, however, was across the border in the New Hampshire Grants, where the renegade ex-citizen of Connecticut, Ethan Allen, a price on his head since 1771, had established himself as leader of the legendary Green Mountain Boys. What better man to lead an illegal attack against the British fort than a patriotic outlaw? Without authority, Deane and his two conspirators dipped their hands into the coffers of the Connecticut treasury and withdrew £300 to underwrite the expedition. Silas Deane then left to take his seat in the Continental Congress assembling in Philadelphia.

*Silas Deane
(1737-1789)*

63.
SILAS DEANE. Charles Willson Peale, 1776. Connecticut Historical Society.

> *. . . Ethan—Ethan Allen,
> That when with fight he fills a quart
> He up and gulps a gallon.*[16]

Ethan Allen, too, was challenged by the idea of capturing the King's fortress on Lake Champlain after the outbreak of violence at Lexington and Concord. Allen would have found appealing almost any chance to engage in battle. Since 1770 he and his Green Mountain Boys had been "protecting" the New Hampshire Grants from New York settlers and speculators who claimed title to the land. Taking the law into their own hands, the Green Mountain Boys roamed the countryside, raiding, burning, and forcing their will upon trespassing Yorkers. Allen, whose formal education had been neglected due to the early death of his father, had a natural talent for writing that he exercised as forcefully as he did his proclivity for raiding. He produced scores of bombastic and ungrammatical pamphlets and articles supporting the Hampshire claims, writings which nevertheless served to present his case to the public persuasively enough to become offensive to both the New Hampshire and New York authorities.

Allen's eagerness to fight the British arose from a combination of feisty brashness and patriotic zeal. One of the first of a new genre of fearless, bear-wrestling, raw-boned, cussing American frontiersmen, he seemed the perfect choice to lead a group

*Ethan Allen
(1737/8-1789)*

of undisciplined and ill-equipped farmers, who nevertheless were highly devoted to him, in an attack against a heavily armed, if slightly dilapidated, British garrison.

The outlaw possessed a keen intelligence. "There is an original something in him, that commands admiration," was George Washington's assessment.[17] Allen knew that the New Hampshire Grants would be in a precarious position if open war broke out with Great Britain, and he was anxious to mitigate the danger by gaining control of Ticonderoga. Heavily involved in land speculation, Allen also stood to lose a great deal financially if the invading British stripped him and his partners of their land titles. Actually, the holders of the grants had as good a chance of having Great Britain authorize their autonomy as they did of having New York eventually yield their claims. But most of Allen's men, like Allen himself, had moved north from Connecticut, where they had been imbued with hostility toward the mother country.

Whatever the motive, the possibility of having the feather of Ticonderoga in his cap proved irresistible to Allen's vanity. At Deane's request, then, Allen, James Easton, and Seth Warner—second and third in command—assembled 230 men from Connecticut and Massachusetts for the mission. As plans were being laid for the attack, a well-groomed, newly appointed colonel, bearing a commission from the Massachusetts surrogate legislature, the Committee of Safety, appeared at Allen's camp at Castleton.

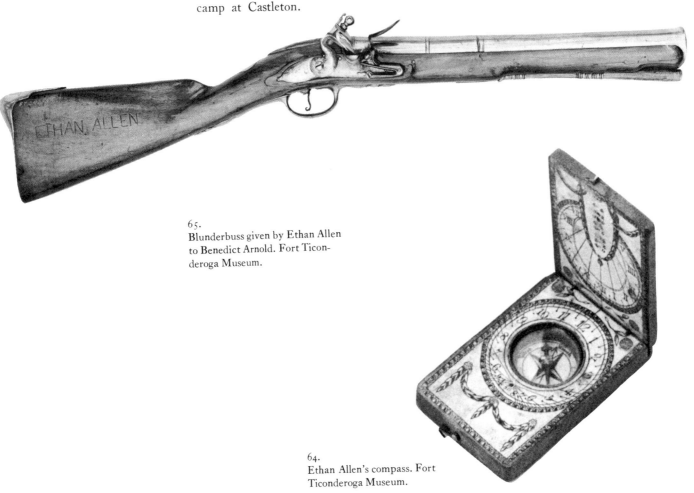

65.
Blunderbuss given by Ethan Allen to Benedict Arnold. Fort Ticonderoga Museum.

64.
Ethan Allen's compass. Fort Ticonderoga Museum.

Convinced that Ticonderoga "could not hold an hour against a vigorous onset," Benedict Arnold was on his way to take possession of the fort in the name of the Massachusetts Committee of Safety. Learning of Allen's intentions, Arnold, according to one of the Massachusetts officers, "presumed to contend for the command of these forces that we had raised . . . which bred such a mutiny amongst the soldiers" that it "almost frustrated our whole design." [18] Slightly worried over the lack of legitimacy surrounding the whole scheme, Allen hesitated before the imperious Arnold. But his men would have none of the officious colonel or his commission. "[T]hey would damn the pay"; their loyalty was only to Allen. Allen was willing to invite Arnold to join his forces, and even offered to let him enter the fort by his side. The pint-sized Arnold had little choice but to concede to the giant woodsman. [19]

The motley company of farmers marched to the east shore of Lake Champlain, anxiously awaiting the arrival of the flatboats that were to take them across to the fort on the other side. By the small hours of the morning, only two boats had arrived. The intrepid Allen, fearing that the approaching dawn would ruin the surprise attack, ferried eighty-three men—as many as the boats would hold—across the lake and recklessly proceeded to march toward the fort, with the small company trailing behind. Luckily, the fort was virtually unguarded; Captain Delaplace, commander of Ticonderoga, had foolishly ignored the orders from Lord Dartmouth and General Gage to fortify the garrison. The one sentry posted at the gate, seeing the approaching men, quickly retreated into the garrison after his musket misfired. Allen then entered the fort and ordered his men to lower their guns at the barracks and give three huzzas to rouse the enemy—forty-seven sleeping soldiers. (The next day, when Allen wrote to the Albany Congress to inform it of the taking of the fort, he generously allowed that "Colonel Arnold entered the fort with me side by side.") [20]

While the stunned British regulars straggled out of bed to see what all the commotion was about, Allen rushed to the captain's quarters demanding an immediate surrender from the first officer he encountered, a Lieutenant Jocelyn Feltham. He was no doubt piqued when he realized that he was dealing with a mere subaltern. The accounts of what Allen actually shouted into the captain's quarters on that occasion have varied from "Come out of there you damned old Rat" to "Come out of there, you sons of British whores. . . ." [21] When the commander, Captain Delaplace, finally did appear and asked by what authority the colonials were seizing the fort, Allen, according to his own "Narrative . . ." written in 1779, thundered, "In the name of the Great Jehovah and the Continental Congress!" [22] (Allen's account of what happened undoubtedly benefitted from his highly developed sense for the dramatic, for none of the other witnesses remembered him uttering the phrase.)

Whether or not Delaplace had ever heard of the Continental Congress is questionable, but it would have been impossible to resist the intruders. The fort was taken without loss of life and only one injury—sustained by a British soldier whom Allen hit with the broad side of his sword as he stormed through the gate. News of the unbelievable victory spread quickly. In Cambridge Dr. Joseph Warren was heard to say, "Thus a War has begun"; while in London, a startled Lord Dartmouth found the whole affair "Very unfortunate, very unfortunate indeed." [23]

Seth Warner
(1743-1784)

When Ethan Allen invaded Ticonderoga with less than half his force, he left the rest of his men on the east shore of Lake Champlain under the command of Seth Warner. Warner had served with his cousin Allen as a leader of the Green Mountain Boys since they first banded together to fight the Yorkers. With only a minimal education and lacking the aptitude for writing which Allen loved to display, Warner was nevertheless as strong a fighter and as well-respected a leader among the Green Mountain Boys as his cousin. The New York Assembly rewarded Warner's enthusiasm, as it had Allen's, by putting a price on his head. Warner's adventurous spirit was slightly crushed and his pride miffed when circumstances kept him from participating in the glorious capture of Ticonderoga.

On the morning of May 10, after the sun rose "with a superior lustre," Warner and the rest of the men rowed across the lake.[24] They arrived just in time to celebrate, for Allen had discovered Captain Delaplace's personal store of ninety gallons of rum, and had distributed the liquor among the victors after politely giving Delaplace a receipt for its cost which, Allen assured him, was redeemable at the Connecticut treasury. The scene that greeted Warner at the fort was one of joyous, drunken revelry carried on under the shocked and disapproving gaze of Colonel Arnold.

Warner was aware, however, that the task of winning control of the base of British operations in the north was not yet complete. A few miles to the north of Ticonderoga lay Crown Point, a small British fort that had not only fallen into disrepair, but had also been severely damaged by fire. Yet, it was a strategically essential garrison—almost as important as Ticonderoga. It was also a storehouse of munitions. Warner asked Allen for permission to take the fort before word could leak out that Ticonderoga had fallen to the Americans.

The following morning, Warner and a band of close to fifty men turned their small boats northward, battling strong headwinds to reach their objective. "[I]n the name of the country"—and without a struggle—the colonial force took Crown Point, which they found guarded by only one sergeant and eight privates.[25] Thus, with a minimum of effort, Ethan Allen and Seth Warner, who, Lieutenant Feltham wrote General Gage, were "as great villains as any on earth," had secured over two hundred heavy guns and "great quantityes of stores." [26] The subsequent effortless capture by Arnold of the third fort on the lake, St. John's, firmly established colonial control of the area. The foundation of British military power in New England was reduced so greatly by the capture of the three forts that the King's troops were never able to regain a strong footing in the north.

John Brown, a Patriot Massachusetts lawyer and soldier at the storming of Ticonderoga, was dispatched to Philadelphia by Ethan Allen to carry word of the victory to the Continental Congress. The news was delivered to an astonished assembly on May 18. The jubilation which followed the victory, however, quickly waned in the face of the responsibility of defending the forts and explaining the action to an outraged British ministry. To the Continental Congress, which was still seeking reconciliation, such an aggressive act began to appear brash and reckless. Ethan Allen's prize brought only confusion to an embarrassed Congress. New York tried to ignore the whole affair; and Massachusetts and Connecticut deferred responsibility to the Continental Congress.

Since the mood of the Congress was still conciliatory, Allen's brazen move had to be discounted as an act of self-defense. Allen and Arnold were ordered to move all of the King's property from Ticonderoga to the south end of Lake George to be held in safekeeping "in order that they may be safely returned when . . . the former harmony with Great Britain and these colonies so ardently wished for" shall be restored.[27] Horrified that abandonment of the area would leave the northern colonies in jeopardy, Allen and Arnold both urged an immediate invasion of Canada. In a decision that it would later reverse, the Congress resolved "That no expedition or incursion ought to be undertaken or made by any Colony, or body of Colonists . . . into Canada." [28] Hoping that Britain would be mollified by this conciliatory stance, the Congress turned back to its self-appointed duties of preparing nevertheless for war.

THE CREATION OF AN ARMY, JUNE 1775

As companies of New England militiamen rallied to the defense of their neighboring colonists in Boston, the delegates in Philadelphia grew less reluctant to assume responsibility for a continental army. If the New England colonies were willing to come to the aid of Boston, the colonies to the south must also share the burden of protecting colonial rights against the redcoats. Since the opening days of the session, the radical members had tried to persuade their more conservative colleagues "out of doors" that the Congress must control the military struggle. In mid-June the whispered persuasions of the radicals came to fruition.

On June 14 the Congress decided that companies of riflemen should be raised in Pennsylvania, Maryland, and Virginia to march to Massachusetts to "join the Army near Boston." [29] War was not declared and hope for reconciliation was not abandoned, but the possibility that the colonies, as a united body, would have to fight for their rights was no longer denied.

The delegates to the Congress saw this fight as a defensive one: blood had been shed on American soil by British troops; security for the future was required before Americans would feel safe again under the protection of the Crown. But there was little security. The King and Parliament had pledged their lives and fortunes to the reduction of America. Considerable British reinforcements under the command of generals Burgoyne, Clinton, and Howe had arrived in Boston providing fresh troops for the besieged Gage. On June 12 Gage had issued a proclamation declaring martial law and calling all who refused to lay down arms rebels and traitors. The delegates had to take cognizance of military realities and, as representatives of the people of their respective colonies, act for their protection. The day after they decided to ask for more troops to go to Boston's aid they resolved that a commander in chief be appointed "to command all of the Continental Forces raised, or to be raised, for the defense of American Liberty." [30]

When John Adams rose from his seat on June 14 to address his fellow delegates on the subject of "the state of the colonies, the army at Cambridge, and the enemy," he had already made up his mind who should be commander in chief of the colonial forces. The virtues of the gentleman he had in mind were well known to his listeners, but Adams did not shorten his address or his praise on that account. Listening to the

*General George Washington
(1732-1799)*

laudatory speech, President John Hancock could only surmise that his fellow Bostonian had him in mind for the great honor. Adams reported that Hancock heard him "with visible pleasure:

> *But when I came to describe Washington for the Commander, I never remarked a more sudden and sinking change of Countenance. Mortification and resentment were expressed as forcibley as his Face could exhibit them. Mr. Samuel Adams Seconded the Motion, and that did not soften the Presidents Physiognomy at all.*[31]

Colonel George Washington, on the other hand, did not receive such public adulation with the same pleasure. "Mr. Washington, who happened to sit near the door," reported John Adams, "as soon as he heard me allude to him—from his usual modesty—darted into the library room." So distressed was Washington by his unanimous election to command the continental forces, that he did not return to the floor of the Congress until the following afternoon, when he met the hearty congratulations of the delegates as they were leaving the State House.[32]

Washington had attended the meetings of the Continental Congress garbed in military uniform—the only member of the group to be so dressed—because he wished to impress upon his colleagues the readiness of Virginia to join the battle that New England now waged alone. Much as he hoped military conflict could be avoided, he was prepared to return to his native colony to lead a Virginia regiment against the British. But upon reaching Philadelphia, he found that many of the delegates wished to place a far larger responsibility on his shoulders.

Washington's reasoned calmness, amiability, quiet manner, and almost excessive modesty impressed the Congress. Eliphalet Dyer thought highly of the "discreet and Virtuous" Colonel Washington, who was "no harum starum ranting Swearing fellow but Sober, steady, and Calm." Tales of his successes and leadership abilities during five years of military service in the French and Indian War were well known. "[T]he more I am acquainted with him, the more I esteem him. . . . ," Silas Deane wrote to his wife, undoubtedly expressing an opinion held by many of the delegates. Even the disappointed Hancock thought him "a fine man" and urged his fellow Bostonians to give him "proper recognition" when he arrived in town. In Washington's diffidence lay another attribute; the Congress felt sure that Washington would not use the newly created and powerful post of commander in chief for self-aggrandizement or the establishment of a military dictatorship.[33]

John Adams had more in mind than Washington's strength and character, however, when he suggested his name to lead the army. Adams wanted the Congress to take control of almost fifteen thousand militiamen maintaining the siege at Cambridge and assume the responsibility of directing the "war" that had already started in New England. He knew also that the choice of a man from a region other than the Northeast made political sense. Offering the name of the "Gentleman from Virginia" would allay any existing fears among the members that radical New Englanders were taking over the conflict with Great Britain and determining its direction. Massachusetts's cause must become the cause of all of the colonies; the appointment of Washington, thought Adams, would "unite the cordial Exertions of all the Colonies better than any other Person in the Union."[34]

66.
GEORGE WASHINGTON. Charles
Willson Peale, 1782. Private
collection.

67.
Trunk used by George Washington during the Revolution. The Mount Vernon Ladies' Association of the Union.

Washington had not commanded, or even drilled, a militia company for fifteen years. After the French and Indian War he had been happy to retire from military life and devote his energies to his beloved Mount Vernon and family. Possessing no appetite for combat, nor pleasure in the life of a soldier, Washington approached military service as a duty. To have refused the appointment of commander in chief, he later wrote to "dear Patsy," his wife, "would have reflected dishonour upon myself. . . ." If his country—which was as yet only an amalgam of individualistic colonies —needed him, he would serve, though reluctantly. Patrick Henry later related that Washington told him with unrealized irony: "Remember, Mr. Henry, what I now tell you. From the day I enter upon the command of the American armies, I date my fall and the ruin of my reputation." [35]

As a very silent member of the First Continental Congress, Washington had conscientiously attended every meeting and consistently voted for measures designed to bring about reconciliation. He honestly believed that none of the colonies "separately or independently" wished "to set up for independency." To Washington, the colonies would have to be pushed to the utmost extremes before they would fight. But if that grim situation should arise, Washington believed that colonial rights must be protected by any means, including force of arms. As a burgess in the Virginia Assembly after 1760 and a justice in the Fairfax County court, Washington had supported the colonial argument that British taxation policies were tyrannical. He sided with his fellow burgesses against the governor and joined the plea for a redress of grievances. "[N]o man should scruple or hesitate a moment to use a(r)ms in defense of so valu-

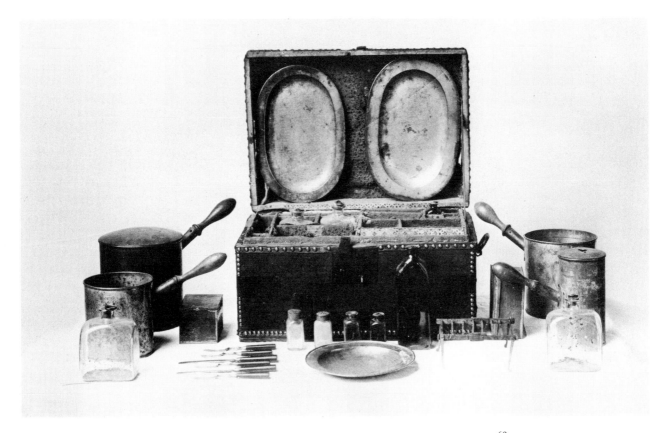

able a blessing," Washington wrote of colonial liberty, ". . . yet a(r)ms, I would beg leave to add, should be the last resource, the dernier resort." [36]

Begging the Congress to remember that "this day I declare, with the utmost sincerity, I do not think myself equal to the command I am honoured with," Washington accepted his appointment on June 16. He did not really know how taxing the job that lay ahead of him would prove to be. In a magnanimous gesture, Washington refused the offered salary of $500 a month and instead agreed to keep "an exact account of my expenses." [37] It was a wise move on General Washington's part; during the eight ensuing years of war his expenses would amount to $160,000.

With the army in a deplorable state and the Congress without funds for its support, "The sword was to be forged on the anvil of necessity," as Washington later wrote in retrospect. The men were poorly clad and undisciplined; there were virtually no arms or ammunition; and officers were elected by their men rather than appointed on the basis of ability. The impossibility of his task depressed Washington considerably. "Could I have foreseen what I have, and am likely to experience, no consideration upon earth should have induced me to accept this command," he complained. The Congress attempted to remedy the dearth of funds by voting, on June 22, to emit two million dollars in bills of credit, optimistically counting on each colony to assume a proportionate share of the burden of payment. The rest of the miracle of creating an army out of chaos was up to Washington. "I am Imbarked on a wide ocean," he wrote his brother, "boundless in its prospect and from whence, perhaps, no safe harbour is to be found." [38]

68.
George Washington's mess kit. Division of Military History, The National Museum of History and Technology, Smithsonian Institution. [Not in exhibition.]

Horatio Gates
(1727-1806)

On June 17, the day that Washington received his official commission, the Congress voted three subordinate generals to assist him in organizing an army. Artemas Ward, commander of the troops in Boston, was appointed first major general; Charles Lee, an expatriate British officer living in Virginia, second major general. "[A]t the earnest desire of General Washington," the Congress appointed Horatio Gates adjutant general with the rank of brigadier. Two days later, upon the recommendation of the New York Assembly, it commissioned Philip Schuyler major general and assigned him to command of the northern army.[39]

George Washington admired Horatio Gates's military ability and experience. Gates had fought in America with the King's troops during the French and Indian War, and probably first met Washington while assigned to General Braddock's army in Virginia. During his service in the French and Indian War, the British soldier was introduced to American Whig principles, as well as to the tactics of frontier guerrilla fighting. When he returned to England he found further advancement in the army blocked by lack of wealth and humble origins (he was the son of a duke's housekeeper). Offended by the British caste system, he retired from the army and returned to America, settling on a Virginia plantation he dubbed "Traveller's Rest."

For several years Gates quietly cultivated his land and watched the contest with Great Britain slowly erupt into armed conflict. On the question of independence, he sympathized with the radicals, and both John and Sam Adams were among his supporters in the Congress. "I am ready," he wrote Charles Lee in 1774, "to risk my life to preserve the liberty of the western world."[40]

With Gates's appointment, Washington gained a very competent officer. In the administration and recruitment of soldiers, and in the organizing of the new American army in Boston, Gates was of enormous help. He could rouse the men to a fighting pitch even while insisting upon discipline. In turn, the common soldier responded to Gates's genuine concern for his welfare and to his democratic spirit. "He . . . has the Art of gaining the Love of his Soldiers," Sam Adams later wrote to Richard Henry Lee, "because he is always present with them in Fatigue and Danger."[41]

Philip Schuyler
(1733-1804)

Not so talented a leader of men as Gates, General Philip Schuyler was particularly skilled in organizing the procurement of supplies. As a member of the landowning aristocracy of New York, he could move easily among the powerful politicians of his native colony. But his assumption of patrician airs offended members of the middle and lower classes, while his unwavering sense of honor and personal integrity frequently expressed itself in a rigidity and self-pity that disastrously affected his capacity to lead men and command their loyalty and affection. The slightest criticism was construed as an insult to his dignity; and, unfortunately, criticism and innuendo plagued him from the beginning of his service in the Continental Army.

A staunch Whig, Schuyler had opposed the royalists who dominated New York politics during the prewar years. Yet, he shied away from radical or mob action and strongly urged redress of grievances and conciliation. His involvement in the political struggle with Great Britain began after he had been elected to the New York Assembly in 1768; seven years later he had achieved sufficient stature within the movement to be selected to join the conservative delegation from New York to the Second Continental Congress. It was, however his admirable record of service in the French

69.
HORATIO GATES. Attributed to
James Peale, date unknown.
Maryland Historical Society.

70.
PHILIP SCHUYLER. John Trumbull,
1792. The New-York Historical
Society. [Not in exhibition.]

and Indian War and his administrative experience in handling the purchase of supplies that encouraged the New York Assembly to vote unanimously for Schuyler when asked for nominations for army officers. But even as he helped the colonies prepare for war, Schuyler continued to hope "that a speedy termination may be put to this afflicting controversy, and Britons and Americans once more regard each other with the fond tenderness of parent and child." [42]

The Hudson River Valley was one of the most strategically important theaters of war. Occupation of the area was imperative for a rebel victory. Philip Schuyler took on a huge job in June 1775, then, when he was sent to organize and command the northern army. The problems he faced were the same as those that troubled General Washington. But where Washington succeeded, Schuyler more often failed. Schuyler had to contend with basic antagonisms between "Yankee" and "Yorker," which grew rather than diminished under his command. His troops included many men from New England and the New Hampshire Grants, who did not trust the general's previous commitment to New York in the New Hampshire boundary disputes. The general's aloofness and superciliousness also alienated the men, while recurrent ill health tended to maintain his isolation and inattentiveness to his troops' needs.

Schuyler's strength lay in his experience in procuring and organizing the distribution of military supplies. But war, as he and other businessmen of his generation were to discover, called for other qualities. Schuyler in particular came to realize this during the campaign into Canada in the winter of 1775-76.

114

General Washington first made Joseph Reed's acquaintance in Philadelphia during the meetings of the First Continental Congress, and his friendship for this "Lawyer of some Eminence" increased during the meetings of the Second Continental Congress.[43] Perhaps Washington responded to Reed's moderation; certainly he appreciated his friend's erudition and political sophistication. Upon being appointed commander in chief, then, Washington turned to Reed for help in the vast task of assembling an army at Cambridge.

Joseph Reed (1741-1785)

After being admitted to the New Jersey bar in 1763, Joseph Reed had spent two years in London, furthering his legal education at the Middle Temple. Vitally interested in the treatment of the colonies by Parliament, he had made a point of making influential friends in England, through whom he would later open a correspondence with the secretary of state, Lord Dartmouth. When his father died, he had been forced to return home to take up the responsibility for supporting his family in New Jersey. In 1770 he arrived in Philadelphia with his new English wife, Esther DeBerdt, and soon became one of the busiest lawyers in the city.

Like many other Philadelphians, Reed approached the growing rift with the mother country with trepidation. He believed that the misunderstandings with the ministry were largely due to misinformation and determined to begin a correspondence with Lord Dartmouth, not to "tell him what he wishes" to hear, but rather "what he ought to know" about colonial discontent. "A gentle tyranny is not more compatible with the rights of an English subject than a violent one . . . ," he wrote the minister. In 1773 he warned Dartmouth that any further attempt to enforce the Tea Act ". . . must end in blood." Although Reed's patriotism was later questioned, his correspondence with Dartmouth, comprising twelve letters in all, never revealed any traitorous purpose. Reed only wanted to alert Great Britain to the seriousness of the colonists' complaints against the hated parliamentary acts. After the battles at Lexington and Concord, Reed abandoned the futile correspondence.[44]

While in Philadelphia attending the First Continental Congress, John Adams recognized Reed as a man of "an amiable disposition, soft, tender, friendly"—a true "friend to his country and to liberty." As a member of the Philadelphia Committee of Correspondence and other radical committees, as well as the Second Continental Congress, Reed continued to maintain a moderate stance. Rather than exult over the battles of Lexington and Concord, he despaired at the idea of war—much like his new friend, George Washington. As the radicalism of Philadelphia increased, however, so did Reed's commitment to the preservation of liberty—regardless of the cost. In 1775 Reed hesitated to accept the job of being Washington's secretary. Not only would it entail great financial sacrifice but he also believed that he lacked sufficient military experience and knowledge. Washington pleaded, and Reed decided to accompany the general as far as New York and make up his mind along the way. At the end of June his friends and family were surprised to learn that Reed had accepted the appointment and would not be returning to Philadelphia. Bound by the "Tye of Duty and Honour" to comply with Washington's request, Reed agreed to stay in Cambridge a few months.

When Washington chose Reed, he chose a confidant as well as a clerk—a man "who can think for me as well as execute orders." Truly gifted as an administrator, Reed helped immeasurably in forming an army out of the chaos at Boston. Many of

71.
JOSEPH REED. Charles Willson
Peale, 1785. Christopher, Andrew,
and Henry Reed.

the eloquent letters and dispatches signed by Washington flowed from Reed's pen. In November 1775, feeling that he had helped Washington "through the See of Difficulties," Reed returned to Philadelphia. Washington suffered the loss of his "good friend" sorely and urged him to return. He could find no other man, he wrote, "with whom I would choose to live in unbounded confidence." Public duties and pressing financial worries, however, kept Reed in Philadelphia until the Congress voted him a raise in salary and a commission of adjutant general that allowed him to rejoin the commander in chief for the summer campaign of 1776.[45]

On June 23 General Washington, accompanied by his generals and aides, set out from Philadelphia with what John Adams described as "the pride and pomp of war." [46] As they traveled northward toward the army at Cambridge, the party encountered indefinite rumors on the road that a bloody battle had been fought on Bunker Hill, or Breed's Hill, in Boston.

BLOODBATH IN BOSTON:
THE BATTLES OF BUNKER AND BREED'S HILLS, JUNE 17, 1775

Alarm over the battles of Lexington and Concord had prompted the neighboring colonies of Rhode Island, New Hampshire, and Connecticut to send forces—under the command of Nathanael Greene, John Stark, and Israel Putnam, respectively—to aid Massachusetts in its fight against the British. As the colonial militia gathered, General Gage also received welcome reinforcements from England. Marines, dragoons, and infantry swelled his troops to well over six thousand men by mid-June. The British ministry, not overly pleased with Gage's performance in Massachusetts, also sent the *Cerberus* with three new major generals on board to help subjugate the tumultuous rebels: William Howe, the senior officer, a firm Whig, brave soldier, and popular officer; the young Henry Clinton, a rather fussy man, but an avid and competent student of military strategy; and "Gentleman" John Burgoyne, a pompous and picturesque character who possessed greater talent with words than with warfare. In England the "triumvirate of reputation," as Burgoyne called the threesome, were not taken very seriously and were even derided in verse by one sarcastic poet:

> Behold the Cerberus the Atlantic plough.
> Her precious cargo, Burgoyne, Clinton, Howe.
> Bow, wow, wow! [47]

On June 12 General Gage, abandoning all hope that he could avoid an encounter with the Patriot troops surrounding the city, issued a proclamation imposing martial law in Boston and declaring all rebels traitors. To show the magnanimity of the Crown, Gage offered to pardon those who would peacefully lay down their arms—except Sam Adams and John Hancock, whose offenses were too extreme to be excused. A few days later, the four British generals met to plan strategy for limiting and containing the provincial troops and gaining control of the town. The generals knew that American occupation of Dorchester Heights and of Bunker and Breed's hills on the Charlestown Peninsula would make the British position in Boston untenable. These points had to be seized before the rebels could mobilize.

By His EXCELLENCY,

The Hon. *THOMAS GAGE*, Esq.

Governor, and Commander in Chief, in and over his Majesty's Province of MASSACHUSETTS-BAY, and Vice-Admiral of the same.

A PROCLAMATION.

WHEREAS the infatuated Multitudes, who have long suffered themselves to be conducted by certain well known Incendiaries and Traitors, in a fatal Progression of Crimes, against the constitutional Authority of the State, have at length proceeded to avowed Rebellion; and the good Effects which were expected to arise from the Patience and Lenity of the King's Government, have been often frustrated, and are now rendered hopeless, by the Influence of the same evil Counsels; it only remains for those who are entrusted with supreme Rule, as well for the Punishment of the guilty, as the Protection of the well affected, to prove they do not bear the Sword in vain.

The Infringements which have been committed upon the most sacred Rights of the Crown and People of Great-Britain, are too many to enumerate on one Side, and are all too atrocious to be palliated on the other. All unprejudiced People who have been Witnesses of the late Transactions, in this and the neighboring Provinces, will find upon a transient Review, Marks of Premeditation and Conspiracy that would justify the fulness of Chastisement: And even those who are least acquainted with Facts, cannot fail to receive a just Impression of their Enormity, in Proportion as they discover the Arts and Assiduity by which they have been falsified or concealed. The Authors of the present unnatural Revolt never daring to trust their Cause or their Actions, to the Judgment of an impartial Public, or even to the dispassionate Reflection of their Followers, have uniformly placed their chief Confidence in the Suppression of Truth: And while indefatigable and shameless Pains have been taken to obstruct every Appeal to the real Interest of the People of America; the grossest Forgeries, Calumnies and Absurdities that ever insulted human Understanding, have been imposed upon their Credulity. The Press, that distinguished Appendage of public Liberty, and when fairly and impartially employed it's best Support, has been invariably prostituted to the most contrary Purposes: The animated Language of ancient and virtuous Times, calculated to vindicate and promote the just Rights, and Interest of Mankind, have been applied to countenance the most abandoned Violation of those sacred Blessings; and not only from the flagicious Prints, but from the popular Harangues of the Times, Men have been taught to depend upon Activity in Treason, for the Security of their Persons, and Properties; till to complete the horrid Profanation of Terms, and of Ideas, the Name of GOD, has been introduced in the Pulpits to excite and justify Devastation and Massacre.

The Minds of Men having been thus gradually prepared for the worst Extremities, a Number of armed Persons, to the amount of many Thousands assembled on the 19th of April last, and from behind Walls, and lurking Holes, attacked a Detachment of the King's Troops, who not expecting so consummate an Act of Phrenzy, unprepared for Vengeance, and willing to decline it, made use of their Arms only in their own Defence. Since that Period the Rebels, deriving Confidence from Impunity, have added Insult to Outrage; have repeatedly fired upon the King's Ships and Subjects, with Cannon and small Arms, have possessed the Roads, and other Communications by which the Town of Boston was supplied with Provisions; and with a preposterous Parade of Military Arrangement, they affect to hold the Army besieged; while Part of their Body make daily and indiscriminate Invasions upon private Property, and with a Wantonness of Cruelty ever incident to lawless Tumult, carry Depredation and Distress wherever they turn their Steps. The Actions of the 19th of April are of such Notoriety, as must baffle all Attempts to contradict them, and the Flames of Buildings and other Property from the Islands, and adjacent Country, for some Weeks past, spread a melancholly Confirmation of the subsequent Assertions.

In this Exigency of complicated Calamities, I avail myself of the last Effort within the Bounds of my Duty, to spare the Effusion of Blood; to offer, and I do hereby in his Majesty's Name, offer and promise, his most gracious Pardon to all Persons who shall forthwith lay down their Arms, and return to the Duties of peaceable Subjects, excepting only from the Benefit of such Pardon, *Samuel Adams* and *John Hancock*, whose Offences are of too flagitious a Nature to admit of any other Consideration than that of condign Punishment.

And to the End that no Person within the Limits of this proffered Mercy, may plead Ignorance of the Consequences of refusing it, I by these Presents, proclaim not only the Persons above-named and excepted, but also all their Adherents, Associates, and Abettors, meaning to comprehend in those Terms, all and every Person, and Persons of what Class, Denomination or Description soever, who have appeared in Arms against the King's Government, and shall not lay down the same as afore-mentioned; and likewise all such as shall so take Arms after the Date hereof, or who shall in any-wise protect or conceal such Offenders, or assist them with Money, Provision, Cattle, Arms, Ammunition, Carriages, or any other Necessary for Subsistence or Offence; or shall hold secret Correspondence with them by Letter, Message, Signal, or otherwise, to be Rebels and Traitors, and as such to be treated.

AND WHEREAS, during the Continuance of the present unnatural Rebellion, Justice cannot be administered by the common Law of the Land, the Course whereof has for a long Time past been violently impeded, and wholly interrupted; from whence results a Necessity for using and exercising the Law Martial; I have therefore thought fit, by the Authority vested in me, by the Royal Charter to this Province, to publish, and I do hereby publish, proclaim and order the Use and Exercise of the Law Martial, within and throughout this Province, for so long Time as the present unhappy Occasion shall necessarily require; whereof all Persons are hereby required to take Notice, and govern themselves, as well to maintain Order and Regularity among the peaceable Inhabitants of the Province, as to resist, encounter and subdue the Rebels and Traitors above described by such as shall be called upon for those Purposes.

To these inevitable, but I trust salutary Measures, it is a far more pleasing Part of my Duty, to add the Assurances of Protection and Support, to all who in so trying a Crisis, shall manifest their Allegiance to the King, and Affection to the Parent State. So that such Persons as may have been intimidated to quit their Habitations in the Course of this Alarm, may return to their respective Callings and Professions; and stand distinct and separate from the Parricides of the Constitution, till GOD in his Mercy shall restore to his Creatures, in this distracted Land, that System of Happiness from which they have been seduced, the Religion of Peace, and Liberty founded upon Law.

GIVEN at Boston, this Twelfth Day of June, in the Fifteenth Year of the Reign of His Majesty GEORGE the Third, by the Grace of GOD, of Great-Britain, France and Ireland, KING, Defender of the Faith, &c. Anneque Domini, 1775.

By His Excellency's Command,   THO'S GAGE.
THO'S FLUCKER, Secr'y.

GOD Save the KING.

72.
Governor Gage's Proclamation of
Martial Law, June 12, 1775.
Massachusetts Historical Society.

Incensed by Gage's proclamation, the Patriots restlessly prepared for a fight. When news of the British plan to storm Dorchester Heights and the Charlestown Peninsula on June 18 leaked out, the Committee of Safety met on June 15, and at the urging of Colonel William Prescott and General Israel Putnam, suggested the immediate occupation of Bunker Hill by American troops "for the Security of this Colony." [48]

From a military standpoint, the American decision to take over Charlestown Peninsula was foolish and impetuous. The colonial troops were undisciplined, untrained, disorganized, and ill-equipped. Brigadier General Artemas Ward, commander in chief of the Massachusetts militia, understood the rebels' weak condition very well. Since receiving his commission from the Provincial Congress on May 19, Ward had been attempting to convert the ragged militiamen into an effective fighting force. He was not convinced that the provincial army was prepared to take Bunker Hill or capable of holding it once taken, but he did believe, with fanatical fervor, in the righteousness of Massachusetts's cause. On June 16 he ordered the immediate occupation of Bunker Hill by a detachment of 1,200 men under the command of Colonel William Prescott.

Artemas Ward (1727-1800)

Ward was a political activist who owed his position as supreme commander of the Massachusetts army not to the military knowledge and experience that he had gained during service in the French and Indian War, but rather to his personal popularity earned by supporting colonial rights against parliamentary infringement. After the passage of the Stamp Act, Ward, already a prominent figure in Worcester County, allied himself with the radical coterie surrounding Sam Adams in the House of Representatives. Basically a "calm, cool, thoughtful man," his ardent patriotism did not generate the same distrust among some segments of the populace that the ranting of Sam Adams often did, and he continued to be effective in organizing resistance to British policy in his colony until he assumed command of the colonial forces in 1775. [49]

Although he suffered continually from poor health, Ward tackled the appalling problems involved in shaping an army out of undisciplined minutemen with enthusiasm. Deeply religious, he came close to losing many of his soldiers when he tried to institute daily prayer in the army regimen. General Charles Lee detested the Massachusetts general and later, when appointed to serve under him by the Continental Congress, called him "a fat old gentleman, who had been a popular churchwarden, but had no acquaintance whatever with military affairs." [50] Regardless of his moral rectitude, however, the "Old Deacon" maintained his popularity and tried his best to mold his men into soldiers. Physically, the troops were far from ready to fight the elite British corps stationed in Boston—a dearth of gunpowder being one of their principal problems. But mentally and emotionally they were primed for battle.

On the night of June 16 Ward dispatched Prescott and his men to fortify Bunker Hill, while he remained at headquarters in Cambridge to observe the British response. He retained with him the greater part of the provincial troops. Had he sent regiments to reinforce Prescott immediately, and had the British decided to attack Boston instead of opposing the Americans in Charlestown, he would not have been able to prevent their capture of the city. Thus, he waited until the British showed their hand. Once he had ascertained that the redcoats were rowing ashore at Charlestown and were advancing on Prescott and his men at Bunker Hill, he deployed all available men to the scene. His action resulted in the containment of the King's troops at Charlestown

Head Quarters 15. June 1775

Resolved in Council of War to take immediate Possession of Bunker's Hill and Dorchester
Neck.   I Ward Secr'y

In Committee of Safety.

Cambridge June 15. 1775

Whereas it appears of Importance to the
Safety of this Colony, that Possession of the Hill called
Bunkers Hill in Charlestown, be securely kept,
and defended; & also some one hill or hills on
Dorchester be likewise secured. Therefore Resolved
Unanimously that it be recommended to the
Council of War, that the above mentioned Bunkers Hill be maintained by sufficient force being
posted there; and as the particular situation of
Dorchester Neck is unknown to this Committee
they advise that the Council of War, take and
pursue such steps respecting the same, as to
them shall appear to be for the security of
this Colony.
                                        Benj.ᵃ White Chairman

Col. Joseph Palmer,   ⎫ Sub Committee from Committee of
Capt: Benj.ᵃ White   ⎬ Safety.
                      ⎭

Gen.ˡ Putnam ⎫
Col.ᵒ Ward — ⎬ Committee from Council War.
Col.ᵒ Gerrish ⎭

the above Committees are appointed to consult with the
Commanding Officers at Roxbury respecting the expediency of carrying the above Resolutions into Execution
                                        I Ward Secr'y

73.
Draft of the decision of the Committee of Safety to take possession
of Bunker's Hill and Dorchester Neck, June 15, 1775. Trustees of
the Boston Public Library. [Original not in exhibition.]

120

74.
ARTEMAS WARD. Raphaelle Peale,
1795. General Artemas Ward
Museum, Shrewsbury, Massachusetts.

(348)

Head Quarters Cambridge June 30th 1775

Sir. –

I have this Day rec.d your Favor of the 22d Ins.t in which you are so kind as to inform me of the general Officers, that the hon.ble continental Congress have appointed. –

I wish, Sir, the Appointments in this Colony may not have a Tendency to create Uneasiness among us; which we ought, at this critical Time, to be extremely careful to avoid. –

I have, Sir, to acknowledge the Rec.t of the Commission of a Major Gen.l; & do heartily wish that the Honor had been conferred upon a Person, better qualified to execute a Trust so important: – It would give me great Satisfaction, if I tho.t myself capacitated to act with Dignity, & to do Honor to that Congress, which has exalted me to be second in Command over the american Army. – I hope they will accept my sincere Desire to serve them; & my most grateful Acknowledgem for the Honor conferred upon me; & pray they may not be wholly disappointed in their Expectations. – I always have been, & am still ready to devote my Life, in attempting to deliver my native Country from insupportable Slavery. –

I am, Sir, with great Respect,
Your most obedient
Humble Servant

P.S Col Gardner is wounded
I hope not mortally. –

Artemas Ward

75.
Artemas Ward's acceptance of
commission as major general,
June 30, 1775. National Archives.

122

and continued colonial possession of Boston, but he was later criticized by James Warren for remaining at headquarters throughout the battle.

Under the cover of darkness on the night of June 16, Colonel William Prescott and a contingent of over one thousand militiamen quietly marched toward Charlestown peninsula armed with spades, tools, and muskets. Halting at the foot of the hills, Prescott hurriedly consulted with General Israel Putnam, commander of the Connecticut detachment that had joined the Massachusetts minutemen, and conveyed Ward's orders to fortify and defend Bunker Hill. "By some mistake" it was decided that Breed's Hill should be "marked out for the intrenchment instead of the other." [51]

William Prescott (1726-1795)

Breed's Hill was closer to Boston and the British fleet and was smaller than Bunker Hill by more than thirty feet. Strong fortifications on Bunker Hill would have commanded the area most effectively; but at midnight Prescott's engineer, Richard Gridley, was quietly setting his men to digging trenches and building a redoubt and six-foot breastwork on the smaller hill. A stone and rail fence was constructed to protect the apron of Bunker Hill, but the remainder of the area was ignored. With dawn only four hours away, Prescott worried that his men would not have time to complete the work before the first light of sunrise would reveal their position to the British.

Unaware that the Patriots had taken control of the peninsula under the very muzzle of their cannon, the British men-of-war—the *Falcon*, the *Lively*, the *Somerset*, the *Glasgow*, and the *Cerberus*—floated quietly at their moorings off the Boston shore. Throughout the night Prescott could hear the sentinels calling "All's well!", reassuring him that his movements were undetected. As dawn began to break over Boston Harbor, men on the *Lively* spotted the hastily constructed redoubt on Breed's Hill and immediately opened fire.

Prescott's men were not conditioned to the noise of battle. Frightened by the roar of the cannonade even more than they were by the actual danger from the guns, from which they were protected by the rude but adequate fortifications, they began to panic. "The Danger we were in made us think there was Treachery & that we were brot there to be all slain," one soldier later wrote. As some of the men began deserting their posts, the tall and confident Prescott, who in the heat of the late spring morning had changed from his heavy uniform into a banyan coat and wide-brimmed hat, leaped upon the parapet—a splendid target to the British—and, pacing backward and forward, encouraged them to stand fast. General Gage, watching the colonel through his field glasses, asked some of the colonials, "Will he fight?" and was warned, "Prescott will fight you to the gates of hell." [52]

A superb commander, brave to the point of recklessness, the nonchalant Prescott was not a soldier by profession. Except for notable service in the provincial forces during King George's War and the French and Indian War, he had lived quietly on his farm in Pepperell, Massachusetts, during the years preceding the Revolution. Only after the argument with England turned to violence did Prescott decide that his place was in the military, and in 1774 he took command of a regiment of militia. Arriving too late to participate in the fighting at Lexington and Concord, Prescott was more than ready to lead a regiment of Patriots to take Bunker Hill.

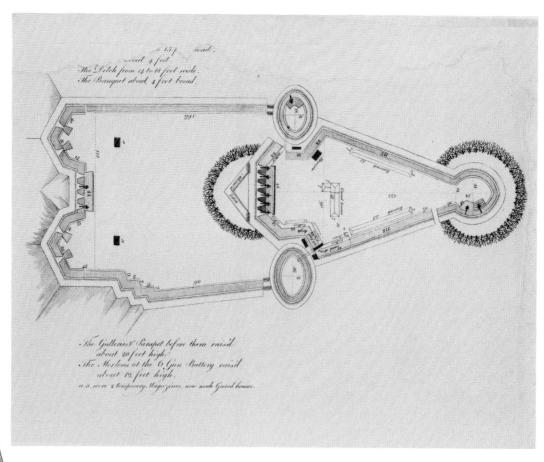

77.
Plan of the fort on Bunker's Hill as
published in William Carter's
*A Genuine Detail of Several En-
gagements*, London, 1784. Massachusetts Historical Society.

76.
Musket of the type ordered by
Committees of Safety to outfit
their militia in 1775. Division of
Military History. The National
Museum of History and Tech-
nology, Smithsonian Institution.
[Not in exhibition.]

The HON^{ble} Sr Wm HOWE.

78.
SIR WILLIAM HOWE. Unidentified engraver. Mezzotint, 1777. Anne S.K. Brown Military Collection, Brown University Library.

On the morning of June 17 generals Gage, Clinton, and Burgoyne met for breakfast to decide what would be done about the audacious rebels entrenched in Charlestown. As the British men-of-war pelted the redoubt, the generals argued on the proper course of action. Clinton suggested that the Americans be attacked from both the front and rear, thus blocking a retreat and assuring a British victory. His sound plan, which would have "shut . . . [the rebels] up in the Peninsula as in a bag"[53] was vetoed by Gage and Howe, who wanted to teach the Patriots a lesson about the strength and authority of the British army. A direct frontal assault and show of force was decided upon instead, and General Howe was chosen to lead the attack. If the rebels could be intimidated by the King's troops, their ragged army and thus the muscle of the revolutionary movement would disintegrate.

Sir William Howe
(1729-1814)

79.
ISRAEL PUTNAM. John Trumbull.
Pencil, 1790. The Putnam Phalanx,
Hartford.

On June 17 Howe gathered on Boston Common between 2,000 and 2,300 of his choicest troops dressed in brightly colored uniforms and burdened with packs of equipment weighing close to a hundred pounds each. Rowing to the Charlestown shore under the cover of heavy fire from the ships, they formed into three lines. Assigning Brigadier General Robert Pigot to the left flank against the breastwork and Major John Pitcairn, the intrepid commander of marines during the skirmishes at Lexington and Concord, to the center against the redoubt, he led the right flank against the rail fence. At 3 p.m. the scarlet-jacketed British regulars began the laborious climb up the steep hill. Immediately, townsmen from neighboring Charlestown began to fire on Pigot's troops from the rear, making the situation very uncomfortable for the attacking soldiers. Pigot and Pitcairn fell back, but Howe pressed forward.

Israel Putnam
(1718-1790)

Meanwhile, Israel Putnam had anxiously gone to Cambridge to request reinforcements from a reluctant General Ward. Returning empty-handed, Putnam detached some of his Connecticut troops and sent them forward to reinforce Prescott at the redoubt while he and others strengthened the contingent guarding the rail fence on the apron of the hill. With the self-possessed calmness of Prescott, Putnam encouraged his men to stand fast against the approaching enemy. Gradually, reinforcements dispatched by Ward began to trickle in across Charlestown Neck, but some never arrived at the scene of the battle and others came too late to be of use. The available troops

126

and one new detachment from New Hampshire under the command of John Stark, which brought the total of colonials to between 1,200 and 1,700 men and boys, would have to do their best to repulse the full-scale British attack. Because of the scarcity of powder, both Prescott at the redoubt and Putnam at the rail fence ordered the troops to hold their fire until—in Putnam's immortal words—they saw "the whites of their eyes." [54] The bright sea of red coats approaching in waves almost overwhelmed some of the men, unaccustomed to battle conditions. But, swearing he'd kill any man who fired without orders, Putnam patrolled the lines, kicking up leveled rifles and maintaining order until the British were within fifty yards. The simultaneous blast of fire from the fortifications was too much for the advancing line of redcoats; their ranks decimated, they fell back in droves to regroup.

The blood of the wily and intrepid Putnam ran fast through his veins at Bunker Hill. His previous career in the military, spanning the decade during and after the French and Indian War, had been punctuated by bold adventures, including a shipwreck off the Cuban coast and a narrow rescue from being burned at the stake by a group of frontier Indians. Returning to his farm in Pomfret, Connecticut, Putnam had joined the Sons of Liberty and served in the Provincial Assembly. Roused by the increasingly desperate plight of neighboring Boston after 1773, he was ready to go to Massachusetts's aid at a moment's notice. Thus, on hearing the news of the skirmish at Lexington and Concord, Putnam abandoned his plow in the field and hastened to Cambridge without even stopping to change his clothes, purportedly riding the sixty-eight miles in one day.

As New England armed against the invading British troops, Putnam was appointed brigadier general of the Connecticut forces. His men liked "Old Put," and he was popular throughout the colonies. Two days after Bunker Hill, on June 19, the Continental Congress would elect him fourth major general under Washington—the only officer to be unanimously elected by the quarrelsome delegates. "[H]is fame as a Warrior had been so far extended thro the Continent," Eliphalet Dyer wrote, "that it would be in Vain to urge any of our Gen[eral] officers in Competition with him and he Carried by Universal Voice." [55]

Now, on Bunker and Breed's hills, as Putnam's and Prescott's men watched the British retreat, they cheered at their unexpected victory. The officers had to restrain the men from chasing the soldiers all the way back to the river. Howe, undaunted, rallied his men once more to attempt another attack. Irritated by the constant gunfire from Charlestown, he sent word to Burgoyne to burn down the town. As Burgoyne's troops on Copp's Hill shelled the town, setting it ablaze, Howe and Pigot gathered their forces for another assault. Through his field glasses Burgoyne watched "one of the greatest scenes of war that can be conceived":

> *. . . straight before us a large and noble town in one great blaze . . . the hills*
> *round the country covered with spectators, the enemy all in anxious suspense;*
> *the roar of cannon, mortars, and musketry, the crush of churches, ships upon*
> *the stocks, and whole streets falling together in ruin to fill the ear . . . and*
> *the reflection that perhaps a defeat was the final loss to the British Empire in*
> *America, to fill the mind, made the whole a . . . complication of horror and*
> *importance beyond anything that ever came my lot to be witness to. . . .*[56]

80.
The Death of General Warren at the Battle of Bunker's Hill, 17 June, 1775. John Trumbull, 1832-34. Wadsworth Atheneum.

Once again, by holding their fire until the last possible moment, the Americans rained musketballs down on the attackers, strewing even more British bodies over ground already littered with dead and wounded. Both Pigot's and Howe's men fell back to the beach. Resolving to try once more rather than suffer an embarrassing defeat by a provincial army of rabble, Howe was helped by Clinton, who had just arrived on the scene declaring that he had never seen "so great a want of order." With their supply of powder almost gone, and Putnam vainly trying to organize reinforcements to join the front lines, the Americans could not hold off their attackers any longer. Their fire had "gone out like a candle." Even the presence of Joseph Warren, now commissioned general, failed to rally the men. Helpless before the bayonets of the enemy, who climbed over the redoubt on the third assault, they beat a hasty retreat. Warren was the last to leave, and it was just as he turned to go that he was felled by a British bullet. As the men escaped toward the neck over Bunker Hill, Putnam tried to rally them to stand and fight, but to no avail. The British gained possession of the peninsula.[57]

When the French foreign minister, Vergennes, received news of the battle, he was heard to remark, "two more such victories and England will have no army left in America."[58]

It was a "dear bought Victory" for the British.[59] Over forty percent of Howe's men, or 1,054 British troops, were killed or wounded, including a great number of officers—among them Major Pitcairn. American casualties, which exceeded four hundred, were "trifling in comparison with ours," a British soldier wrote home.[60] An indefatigable and unhurt Colonel Prescott, in a coat tattered by shot and torn by bayonets, begged General Ward after the battle for more troops and a chance to retake the peninsula, but Ward wisely refused. Clinton urged Howe to attack the undefended headquarters at Cambridge and thus demolish what was left of the American army, but Howe complained that the men were "too much harassed and fatigued to give pursuit to the rebels. . . ."[61] If Howe had followed Clinton's advice, he could have delivered a crushing blow to the potential of the American army and nipped colonial military power in the bud. By the end of July, Earl Percy, General Gage's subordinate, was reporting:

> *here we are so cooped up, and now so surrounded with lines and works as not to be able to advance into the country without hazarding too much. For our army is so small, we cannot even afford a victory, if it is attended with any loss of men.*[62]

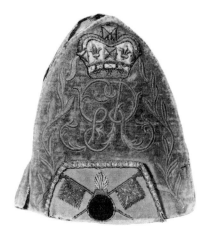

Through a series of military blunders on the part of both Americans and British, the bloodiest battle of the Revolution was fought on Bunker and Breed's hills before the Declaration of Independence was even written. The Americans were defeated, but they had shown the King not only that they were capable on the battlefield but that the conflict between America and Great Britain had become a contest that would ultimately be solved by soldiers rather than legislators.

THE SWORD AND THE OLIVE BRANCH

". . . [T]he decisive Day is come on which the fate of America depends . . .," Abigail Adams wrote in despair to her husband John in Philadelphia on June 18.

> *—Charlestown is laid in ashes. The Battle begun upon our intrenchments upon Bunkers Hill . . . has not ceased yet. . . . Almighty God, cover the heads of our Country men and be a shield to our Dear Friends. How [many ha]ve fallen we know not—the constant roar of the cannon is so [distre]ssing that we can not Eat, Drink or Sleep.*[63]

81.
British (top) and Providence grenadiers' hats said to have been worn at the Battle of Bunker Hill.

Not until the evening of June 24, after several days of maddening rumors, did the agitated Continental Congress receive definite news of the battle fought on Bunker and Breed's hills. Upon receipt of the news, the Congress accelerated its efforts to ready the colonies for war. All of the powder that could be spared from Philadelphia was sent immediately to Boston. On June 24 a committee consisting of Robert Treat Paine, Roger Sherman, Stephen Hopkins, Christopher Gadsden, John Dickinson, Benjamin Harrison, and William Floyd was appointed to devise ways and means of putting the "Militia of America in a proper state for the defense of America."[64]

The incremental movement toward independence was quickened, but not decided, by the new blood spilt in Massachusetts. Not everyone in the Congress was willing or anxious to plunge into war with Great Britain. "The Congress," Roger Sherman wrote to Joseph Trumbull, "are very diligent in making every needful provision in

BUNKERS HILL
or America's Head Dress

82.
Bunker's Hill or America's Head Dress satirized the popular coiffure of the day and the British soldiers' difficult uphill charge. Matthew Darly. Engraving, 1776. Colonial Williamsburg.

their power for the Support of the American Cause at the same time do not neglect any probable means for a reconciliation with great Britain. . . ."[65] Few delegates honestly believed that the ministry would submit to their demands and that reconciliation would be forthcoming, but the vigorous measures advocated by the radicals still remained unacceptable. Even fiery Whigs like John Adams realized that

> . . . *America is a great, unwieldy body. Its progress must be slow. It is like a large fleet sailing under convoy. The fleetest sailors must wait for the dullest and slowest. Like a coach and six, the swiftest horses must be slackened, and the slowest quickened, that all may keep an even pace. . . .*[66]

83.
BENJAMIN HARRISON. Unidentified
artist, date unknown. Virginia
Historical Society.

Benjamin Harrison, scion of an already old and established Virginia family, had busied himself with military affairs during the meetings of the Second Continental Congress. Thus, he seemed a particularly apt choice to serve on the committee to devise ways and means of putting the militia in a state of defense. His fellow Virginian, George Washington, depended on him to generate and promote support of military measures and guide them through the legislative processes of the Congress.

Benjamin Harrison
(1726?-1791)

Colonel Harrison, whom Silas Deane described as "an uncommonly large man . . . rather rough in his address and speech," was well known for his expansive good humor and firm adherence to Whig principles.[67] John Adams, however, reacted impatiently to his hesitancy to push extreme measures and criticized the corpulent man's indulgence in the frivolous and humorous side of life. The Virginian was, he wrote,

> *another Sir John Falstaff, excepting in his larcenies and robberies, his conver-*
> *sation disgusting to every man of delicacy or decorum, yet, as I saw he was*
> *to be often nominated with us in business, I took no notice of his vices or*
> *follies, but treated him, and Mr. Hancock too, with uniform politeness.*[68]

Benjamin Harrison may have offended the puritanical and self-righteous John Adams, but as a public servant he served with distinction, both in Philadelphia and Williamsburg. Reelected successively to the Virginia House of Burgesses from 1749 to 1775, the moderate Harrison was frequently chosen Speaker. Both during and after the war, his constituents continued to return him to public office, including three terms as Virginia's governor. In Philadelphia his close attention to military matters and work in helping to organize the militia for defense would earn him chairmanship of the Board of War.

When the question of independence was brought to a vote, Harrison did not hesitate to add his voice to the radicals'. Later, while watching his spare colleague from Massachusetts, Elbridge Gerry, follow him in affixing his name to the treasonous Declaration of Independence, the corpulent Harrison remarked:

> *Gerry, when the time of hanging comes, I shall have the advantage of you;*
> *it will be over with me in a minute, but you will be kicking in the air half an*
> *hour after I'm gone.*[69]

84.
WILLIAM FLOYD. Ralph Earl, 1793.
Independence National Historical
Park. [Original not in exhibition.]

*William Floyd
(1734-1821)*

Not as jovial or colorful as Harrison, William Floyd of New York was, nevertheless, a valuable member of the committee chosen to devise ways and means of putting the American militia in a state of defense. Floyd lacked the eloquence that brought many of his colleagues fame, but his sound judgment and equanimity earned him the respect of the other delegates and were responsible for the committee's success in producing an efficient militia organization.

As a member of both the first and second Congresses, William Floyd did not aggressively champion colonial rights; but he was not as conservative as other more visible members of the New York delegation. The son of a wealthy land proprietor, Floyd became the lord of his family manor at an early age and a leading citizen of his community. As he watched the quarrel with the mother country progress, he came to believe that the colonies had real grievances against Parliament and the Crown. Once he had decided that Great Britain was wrong in its treatment of America, he was willing, unlike so many other New Yorkers, to join with the other colonies in the fight against the Crown. His appointment to the committee to ready the colonial militia for defense was proof of a growing unanimity among the delegates and the colonies they represented.

Like many others who played an inconspicuous role in the coming of independence, Floyd, the first of the New York delegation to sign the Declaration of Independence, paid dearly for his support of the colonial cause. After leading a regiment against the first British attack on Long Island, he lost his entire estate to the depredations of the British army. Homeless and without means of support, Floyd remained in the Congress until 1783, supporting himself and his family solely from his salary as a delegate.

During the first months of 1775 Joseph Hewes, delegate from North Carolina, had battled with the teachings of his Quaker upbringing against war. Bloodshed in Massachusetts now portended extensive future fighting. Hewes's belief in colonial rights overcame his commitment to the Quaker doctrine, and he resigned from the Society of Friends. On June 14 Hewes was appointed to serve on the committee "to bring in a draught of Rules and Regulations for the government of the Army." [70]

Joseph Hewes (1730-1779)

85.
JOSEPH HEWES. Charles Willson Peale, 1776. United States Naval Academy Museum.

On June 30 Hewes's committee presented the Congress with sixty-nine Articles of War for its approval. Emphasizing moral rectitude, the rules and regulations reflected the prevalent fear among the colonists of military domination and discipline. One of the articles "earnestly recommended to all Officers and Soldiers, diligently to attend divine service. . . ." Another warned that if any ". . . Officer be thus guilty of profane cursing or swearing, he shall forfeit and pay for each and every such offense. . . ." The articles made a stab at providing for the welfare of the soldiers and the establishment of rules of conduct, but on the whole they formed an ineffective code that would have to be rewritten in a few months. The delegates were ready to establish an army for their defense, but they were still prey to a nagging hatred and distrust of standing armies and a military establishment. They also were hesitant to admit that a strong army would eventually be needed to fight Great Britain. [71]

Born in New Jersey and apprenticed in Philadelphia to a merchant, Hewes had moved to North Carolina when he was about thirty years old. Within the space of a few years, he had built up a thriving business in the still young colony. His agreeable manner and highly developed sense of moral integrity impressed the citizens of Edenton, where he settled, and he was chosen to represent them in the Provincial Assembly from 1766 to 1775, as well as in the Continental Congresses in Philadelphia.

During the first Congress Silas Deane wrote that both Hewes and his fellow delegate from North Carolina, Richard Caswell, were "of sedate and settled characters, well affected to the general Cause, but have not spoke as yet publicly." Quiet delegate that he was, Hewes pursued his work in the Congress with exhausting diligence. He served on many committees, and eventually made use of his experience in shipping as chairman of the Committee of Marine. Regardless of his hard work for colonial rights, however, Hewes continued to shrink from the idea of independence until he was finally persuaded by John Adams that his constituents in North Carolina desired it. Then he "started suddenly upright, and lifting up both of his hands to Heaven, as if he had been in a trance, cried out, 'It is done! and I will abide by it.' " [72]

133

KEEPING THE HATCHET BURIED

While preparing for a war against external enemies, the Congress did not ignore potential internal threats to their cause. If the Indians were persuaded to enter into an alliance with the British, they could pose a serious danger to Americans. On June 16 the Congress appointed a committee to decide what steps should be taken "for securing and preserving the friendship of the Indian Nations." Appointed to the committee were Philip Schuyler, Patrick Henry, James Duane, James Wilson, and Philip Livingston.[73]

Philip Livingston
(1716-1778)

Philip Livingston joined that large group of delegates to the Continental Congress who held moderate Whig views and distrusted democracy. A Patriot and, in his native New York, a liberal, Livingston maintained an active and dignified dissent from British policy despite the fact that he was to the manner born and a wealthy merchant in a conservative colony. His activities in support of colonial rights were as austere as his countenance. Livingston wanted a redress of grievances, not revolution.

During his years in public office—as an alderman of New York City for nine years, as a member of the Provincial Assembly from 1763 to 1769 and Speaker in 1768, and as a delegate to the Continental Congress from 1774 to 1778—Livingston always chose a mitigating tone and a conciliatory posture in the growing rift between the colonies and England. "Philip Livingston," wrote John Adams, complaining of the New Yorker's reluctance to approve extreme measures against the Crown, "is a great, rough rapid mortal. There is no holding any conversation with him. He blusters away; says if England should turn us adrift, we should instantly go to civil wars among ourselves."[74]

On July 12, 1775, the committee on Indian Affairs turned in a report that was accepted by the Congress detailing a plan to preserve the goodwill of the Indians through the creation of three Indian departments run by three different boards of commissioners. The northern department would include the Six Nations, the southern department would be devoted to the Cherokee, and the middle department would encompass all the Indian nations lying between the other two. The commissioners were to be responsible for seizing and keeping in "safe custody" any agent of the King found to be "active in stirring up or inciting the Indians," and $17,000 was voted for rum and gifts.[75] The following day the Congress approved a Speech to the Six Nations, written in the dramatic language of Indian diplomacy and urging neutrality. "Brothers and Friends!" the speech asked,

> *We desire you will hear and receive what we have now told you. . . . This is a family quarrel between us and Old England. You Indians are not concerned in it. We don't wish to take up the hatchet against the King's Troops. We desire you to remain at home, and not join on either side, but keep the hatchet buried deep.*[76]

If the Congress hoped to spare the frontier the terrorizing warfare that characterized former Indian alliances with their enemies, their plan did not completely suc-

86.
PHILIP LIVINGSTON. Thomas McIlworth, 1764 or 1766. The Long Island Historical Society.

ceed. Some Indians, notably the Oneidas and Tuscaroras of the Iroquois League, were won over to the American cause. Others continued their long alliance with the British and for the duration of the war constituted a serious threat to the southern, northern, and western frontiers.

On the same day that the Congress approved the establishment of three Indian departments to control the potential threat to the western frontier, it also turned its attention eastward to the seacoast and the problem of protecting the lifeline of the colonies— their trade and commerce. A committee consisting of John Jay, Benjamin Franklin, Silas Deane, Richard Henry Lee, and Christopher Gadsden was appointed on July 12 to "devise ways and means to protect the trade of these colonies."[77]

Christopher Gadsden (1724-1805)

135

87.
CHRISTOPHER GADSDEN. Rembrandt Peale, circa 1795-97. City
of Charleston, South Carolina.

The vital question of trade had emerged at an earlier meeting of the Congress on July 3, when, faced with the necessity to import goods and munitions, the delegates suddenly realized that their nonimportation rulings were victimizing Americans as much as the English. The nonexportation agreement was to go into effect on September 10, and the members of the Congress worried that they would be cutting off possible sources of military stores by the severe reduction of their markets.

Christopher Gadsden, a highly successful and wealthy merchant from Charleston, South Carolina, whom historians have called the "Sam Adams of the South," was fully in favor of taking extreme steps against Great Britain in the form of economic coercion. Gadsden had long embroiled himself in anti-British activities, and as the aristocratic leader of Charleston's artisans and port workers, he had become the acknowledged spokesman for the radicals of South Carolina. This zeal for colonial rights had not abated over the years. He "leaves all New England Sons of Liberty far behind," wrote Silas Deane, "for he is for taking up his firelock and marching straight to Boston . . . were his wife and all his children in Boston, and they were there to perish by the sword, it would not alter his sentiments or proceeding for American Liberty. . . ."[78]

During the first Congress, Gadsden had been infuriated at those merchants who were concerned about the sacrifices they would be forced to make if the Association was adopted. He could not sympathize even with his fellow Carolinians who depended so heavily on the rice trade for their well-being. To his mind, unity of purpose was essential to the colonial cause. Political considerations transcended personal ones.

Gadsden was, however, a shrewd businessman who possessed foresight as well as political acumen. While most merchants feared the results of the loss of parliamentary controls over colonial commerce, Gadsden realized that unrestricted trade would result in expanded markets and increased profits, not chaos and ruin. Even more important was the principle involved. "[A] right to regulating trade," John Adams recalled Gadsden as saying, "is a right of legislation, and a right of legislation in one case is a right in all; this I deny."[79]

On July 15 the Congress decided to bend the rules of the Association to allow the importation of military stores, but to keep the news of its decision secret. A week later the committee to protect colonial trade brought in a report that reflected Gadsden's opinions on free trade. John Adams also realized the benefits that would be derived by adopting "a Resolution to invite all Nations to bring their Commodities to Market here," but the Congress "like Fools" tabled the recommendation.[80]

Independence Postponed:
The Mecklenburg Resolutions, May—July, 1775

While minutemen and regulars were fighting in Massachusetts, and the Continental Congress was appointing committees and debating policy, the Anglo-American quarrel was escalating just as decisively, if more quietly, throughout the colonies. By the spring of 1775 Americans were beginning to feel that Great Britain had pushed them to the wall. In Massachusetts that feeling had led to bloodshed; in North Carolina, it led to almost as significant an indicator of the state of relations between the colonies and the mother country, the Mecklenburg Resolutions.

ſeſſed, but that the Country People in open Boats had boarded and taken the Tender, and retaken the Prize. The Lieutenant loſt an Arm, the Gunner wounded in the Head, and the Doctor's Mate in his Legs. The Seamen were ſent Priſoners into the Country.

That an Expreſs was arrived to the Congreſs at Philadelphia, with a particular Account of the taking of Tyconderoga, which important Paſs they ſtrongly recommended to their Wiſdom to ſufficiently ſecure, to prevent any Incurſions from Canada.

By a Gentleman from Saliſbury, we have an Account, that the famous Joſeph Pettaway had been tried at the Court of Oyer and Terminer lately held there, for a Robbery, had been convicted, received Sentence of Death, and was to be executed. This is the Perſon who, in Company with Jacob Odam, robbed Mr. John Foy, as mentioned in this Paper ſometime ago. Odam ſurrendered himſelf to Government, and is now in this Gaol. He has impeached Pettaway, and many others, ſome of whom, we hear, have been taken, and bailed, though it appeared by Odam's Confeſſion that they were acceſſary to Foy's Robbery. The Father of Odam accompanied his Son here, and on Suſpicion of his being acceſſary to the many Felonies committed by him, has been committed to Gaol. This public Notice is therefore given, that if any Thing is alledged againſt him he may be brought to Juſtice.

Charlotte Town, Mecklenburg County, May 31.
This Day the COMMITTEE *met, and paſſed the following*
RESOLVES:

WHEREAS by an Addreſs preſented to his Majeſty by both Houſes of Parliament in *February* laſt, the *American* Colonies are declared to be in a State of actual Rebellion, we conceive that all Laws and Commiſſions confirmed by, or derived from the Authority of the King or Parliament, are annulled and vacated, and the former civil Conſtitution of these Colonies for the preſent wholly ſuſpended. To provide in ſome Degree for the Exigencies of the County in the preſent alarming Period, we deem it proper and neceſſary to paſs the following RESOLVES, viz.

1. That all Commiſſions, civil and military, heretofore granted by the Crown, to be exerciſed in theſe Colonies, are null and void, and the Conſtitution of each particular Colony wholly ſuſpended.

2. That the Provincial Congreſs of each Province, under the Direction of the Great Continental Congreſs, is inveſted with all legiſlative and executive Powers within their reſpective Provinces; and that no other Legiſlative or Executive does or can exiſt, at this Time, in any of theſe Colonies.

3. As all former Laws are now ſuſpended in this Province, and the Congreſs have not yet provided others, we judge it neceſſary, for the better Preſervation of good Order, to form certain Rules and Regulations for the internal Government of this County, until Laws ſhall be provided for us by the Congreſs.

4. That the Inhabitants of this County do meet on a certain Day appointed by this Committee, and having formed themſelves into nine Companies, *to wit*, eight for the County, and one for the Town of *Charlotte*, do chooſe a Colonel, and other military Officers, who ſhall hold and exerciſe their ſeveral Powers by Virtue of this Choice, and independent of *Great-Britain*, and former Conſtitution of this Province.

5. That for the better Preſervation of the Peace, and Adminiſtration of Juſtice, each of theſe Companies do chooſe from their own Body two diſcreet Freeholders, who ſhall be impowered each by himſelf, and ſingly, to decide and determine all Matters of Controverſy ariſing within the ſaid Company under the Sum of Twenty Shillings, and jointly and together all Controverſies under the Sum of Forty Shillings, yet ſo as their Deciſions may admit of Appeals to the Convention of the Select Men of the whole County; and alſo, that any one of theſe ſhall have Power to examine, and commit to Confinement, Perſons accuſed of Petit Larceny.

6. That thoſe two Select Men, thus choſen, do, jointly and together, chooſe from the Body of their particular Company two Perſons, properly qualified to ſerve as Conſtables, who may aſſiſt them in the Execution of their Office.

7. That upon the Complaint of any Perſon to either of theſe Select Men, he do iſſue his Warrant, directed to the Conſtable, commanding him to bring the Aggreſſor before him or them to anſwer to the ſaid Complaint.

8. That theſe eighteen Select Men, thus appointed, do meet every third *Tueſday* in *January*, *April*, *July*, and *October*, at the Court-Houſe in *Charlotte*, to hear and determine all Matters of Controverſy for Sums exceeding Forty Shillings; alſo Appeals: And in Caſes of Felony, to commit the Perſon or Perſons convicted thereof to cloſe Confinement, until the Provincial Congreſs ſhall provide and eſtabliſh Laws and Modes of Proceeding in ſuch Caſes.

9. That theſe Eighteen Select Men, thus convened, do chooſe a Clerk to record the Tranſactions of the ſaid Convention; and that the ſaid Clerk, upon the Application of any Perſon or Perſons aggrieved, do iſſue his Warrant to one of the Conſtables, to ſummons and warn the ſaid Offender to appear before the Convention at their next ſitting, to anſwer the aforeſaid Complaint.

10. That any Perſon making Complaint upon Oath to the Clerk, or any Member of the Convention, that he has Reaſon to ſuſpect that any Perſon or Perſons indebted to him in a Sum above Forty Shillings, do intend clandeſtinely to withdraw from the County without paying ſuch Debt, the Clerk, or ſuch Member, ſhall iſſue his Warrant to the Conſtable, commanding him to take the ſaid Perſon or Perſons into ſafe Cuſtody, until the next ſitting of the Convention.

11. That when a Debtor for a Sum below Forty Shillings ſhall abſcond and leave the County, the Warrant granted as aforeſaid ſhall extend to any Goods or Chattels of the ſaid Debtor as may be found, and ſuch Goods or Chattels be ſeized and held in Cuſtody by the Conſtable for the Space of Thirty *Days*, in which Term if the Debtor fails to return and diſcharge the Debt, the Conſtable ſhall return the Warrant to one of the Select Men of the Company where the Goods and Chattels are found, who ſhall iſſue Orders to the Conſtable to ſell ſuch a Part of the ſaid Goods as ſhall amount to the Sum due; that when the Debt exceeds Forty Shillings, the Return ſhall be made to the Convention, who ſhall iſſue the Orders for Sale.

12. That Receivers and Collectors for Quitrents, Public and County Taxes, do pay the ſame into the Hands of the Chairman of this Committee, to be by them diſburſed as the public Exigencies may require. And that ſuch Receivers and Collectors proceed no farther in their Office until they be approved of by, and have given to this Committee good and ſufficient Security for a faithful Return of ſuch Monies when collected.

13. That the Committee be accountable to the County for the Application of all Monies received from ſuch Officers.

14. That all theſe Officers hold their Commiſſions during the Pleaſure of their reſpective Conſtituents.

15. That this Committee will ſuſtain all Damages that may ever hereafter accrue to all or any of theſe Officers thus appointed, and thus acting, on Account of their Obedience and Conformity to theſe Reſolves.

16. That whatever Perſon ſhall hereafter receive a Commiſſion from the Crown, or attempt to exerciſe any ſuch Commiſſion heretofore received, ſhall be deemed an Enemy to his Country; and upon Information being made to the Captain of the Company where he reſides, the ſaid Captain ſhall cauſe him to be apprehended, and conveyed before the two Select Men of the ſaid Company, who, upon Proof of the Fact, ſhall commit him the ſaid Offender into ſafe Cuſtody, until the next ſitting of the Convention, who ſhall deal with him as Prudence may direct.

17. That any Perſon refuſing to yield Obedience to the above Reſolves ſhall be deemed equally criminal, and liable to the ſame Puniſhments as the Offenders above laſt mentioned.

18. That theſe Reſolves be in full Force and Virtue, until Inſtructions from the General Congreſs of this Province, regulating the Juriſprudence of this Province, ſhall provide otherwiſe, or the legiſlative Body of *Great-Britain* reſign its unjuſt and arbitrary Pretenſions with Reſpect to *America*.

19. That the ſeveral Militia Companies in this county do provide themſelves with proper Arms and Accoutrements, and hold themſelves in conſtant Readineſs to execute the commands and Directions of the Provincial Congreſs, and of this committee.

20. That this committee do appoint Colonel *Thomas Polk*, and Doctor *Joſeph Kennedy*, to purchaſe 300 lb. of Powder, 600 lb. of Lead, and 1000 Flints; and depoſit the ſame in ſome ſafe Place, hereafter to be appointed by the committee.

Signed by Order of the Committee.
EPH. BREVARD, *Clerk of the Committee.*

WILLIAMSBURG, MAY 13.
FREDERICKSBURG, Committee Chamber, *Saturday the 29th of April*, 1775.

AT a Council of one hundred and two members, Delegates of the Provincial Convention, officers and ſpecial deputies of fourteen companies of light horſe, conſiſting of upwards of ſix hundred well armed and diſciplined men, friends of conſtitutional liberty and America, now rendezvouſed here in conſequence of an alarm occaſioned by the powder being removed from the country magazine in the city of Williamſburg in the night of Thurſday the 21ſt inſtant, and depoſited on board an armed ſchooner by order of his Excellency the Governor.

The Council having before them the ſeveral matters of intelligence reſpecting this tranſaction, and particularly a letter from the Hon. PEYTON RANDOLPH, Eſq; Speaker of the late Houſe of Burgeſſes of Virginia, received here laſt night by an expreſs diſpatched to Williamſburg for the purpoſe of gaining intelligence, informing that the Gentlemen of the city of Williamſburg and neighbood have had full aſſurances from his Excellency that this affair ſhall be accommodated, and adviſing that the Gentlemen aſſembled here ſhould proceed no further at this time, this Council came to the following determination, and offer the ſame as their advice to thoſe public ſpirited Gentlemen, friends to BRITISH LIBERTY and AMERICA, who have honoured them by this appointment. Highly condemning the conduct of the Governor on this occaſion, as impolitic, and juſtly alarming to the good people of this colony, tending to deſtroy all confidence in Government, and to widen the unhappy breach between Great Britain and her colonies, ill timed and totally unneceſſary, conſider this inſtance as a full proof that no opinion which may be formed of the good intentions of a Governor in private life can afford ſecurity to our injured and oppreſſed country, but that obedience to arbitrary, miniſterial mandate, and the moſt oppreſſive and tyrannical ſyſtem of Government, muſt be the fatal line of conduct to all his Majeſty's preſent ſervants in America; at the ſame time juſtly dreading the horrors of a civil war, influenced by motives of the ſtrongeſt affection to our fellow ſubjects of Great Britain, moſt ardently wiſhing to heal our mutual wounds, and therefore preferring peaceable meaſures whilſt the leaſt hope of reconciliation remains, do adviſe that the ſeveral companies now rendezvouſed here do return to their reſpective homes. But conſidering the juſt rights and Liberty of America to be greatly endangered by the violent and hoſtile proceedings of an arbitrary Miniſtry, and being firmly reſolved to reſiſt ſuch attempts at the utmoſt hazard of our lives and fortunes, do now pledge ourſelves to each other to be in readineſs, at a moment's warning, to re aſſemble, and, by force of arms to defend the laws, the liberty, and rights of this, or any ſiſter colony, from unjuſt and wicked invaſion. Ordered that expreſſes be diſpatched to the troops aſſembled at the Bowling Green, and alſo to the companies from Frederick, Berkeley, Dunmore, and ſuch other counties as are now on their march, to return them thanks for their cheerful offers of ſervice, and to acquaint them with the determination now taken.

GOD SAVE THE LIBERTIES OF AMERICA.

The foregoing determination of Council having been read at the head of each company, was cordially and unanimouſly approved.

At a Committee appointed and held for Hanover County, at the Courthouſe, on Tueſday the 9th of May, 1775.

PRESENT,

John Syme, Samuel Overton, William Craghead, Meriwether Skelton, Richard Morris, Benjamin Anderſon, John Pendleton, John Robinſon, Nelſon Berkeley, and George Dabney, junior.

AGREEABLE to a Reſolution of the Committee held at Newcaſtle the 2d Inſtant, ſetting forth, that they being fully informed of the violent Hoſtilities committed by the King's Troops in America, and of the Danger ariſing to the Colony by the Loſs of the Public Powder, and of the Conduct of the Governor, which threatens altogether Calamities of the greateſt Magnitude, and moſt fatal Conſequences to this Colony, and therefore recommending Repriſals to be made upon the King's Property, ſufficient to replace the Gunpowder taken out of the Magazine, it appears to this Committee, that the Volunteers who marched from Newcaſtle, to obtain Satisfaction for the Public Powder, by Repriſal, or otherwiſe, proceeded on that Buſineſs as follows, to wit, "That an Officer with 16 Men was detached to ſeize the King's Receiver General, with Orders to detain him; and this, it was ſuppoſed, might be done without impeding the Progreſs of the main Body. The ſaid Receiver General not being apprehended, owing to his Abſence from home, the ſaid Detachment, according to Orders, proceeded to join the main Body on its March to Williamſburg; and the Junction happened the 3d Inſtant, at Doncaſtle's Ordinary, about Sunſet. A little after Sunriſe next Morning, the commanding Officer being aſſured that proper Satisfaction, in Money, ſhould be inſtantly made, the Volunteers halted, and the Propoſal being conſidered by them, was judged ſatisfactory as to that Point; and the following Receipt was given, to wit, "Doncaſtle's Ordinary, New "Kent, May 4, 1775, received from the Hon. "Richard Corbin, Eſq; his Majeſty's Receiver General, 330l. as a Compenſation for the Gunpowder lately taken out of the Public Magazine "by the Governor's Order; which Money I promiſe to convey to the Virginia Delegates at the "General Congreſs, to be, under their Direction, "laid out in Gunpowder for the Colony's Uſe, and "to be ſtored as they ſhall direct, until the next "Colony Convention, or General Aſſembly, unleſs "it ſhall be neceſſary, in the mean Time, to uſe "the ſame in Defence of this Colony. It is agreed, "that in Caſe the next Convention ſhall determine "that any Part of the ſaid Money ought to be returned to his Majeſty's ſaid Receiver General, "that the ſame ſhall be done accordingly.

Teſt, PATRICK HENRY, Jun."
SAMUEL MERIDITH. (A true Copy)
PARKE GOODALL.

It was then conſidered, as that a General Congreſs would meet in a few Days, and perhaps a Colony Convention would ſhortly aſſemble, and that the Repriſal now made would amply replace the Powder, with the Charges of Tranſportation, the commanding Officer wrote the following Letter, and ſent it by Expreſs.

SIR, MAY 4, 1775.

The Affair of the Powder is now ſettled, ſo as to produce Satisfaction to me, and I earneſtly wiſh to the Colony in general. The People here have it in Charge from Hanover Committee to tender their Service to you, as a Public Officer, for the Purpoſe of eſcorting the Public Treaſury to any Place in this Colony where the Money would be judged more ſafe than in the City of Williamſburg. The Repriſal now made by the Hanover Volunteers, though accompliſhed in a Manner leaſt liable to the Imputation of violent Extremity, may poſſibly be the Cauſe of future Injury to the Treaſury. If therefore you apprehend the leaſt Danger, a ſufficient Guard is at your Service. I beg the Return of the Bearer may be inſtant, becauſe the Men wiſh to know their Deſtination. With great Regard, I am,

Sir, *Your moſt humble Servant,*
PATRICK HENRY, Jun.

To ROBERT CARTER NICHOLAS, *Eſq; Treaſurer.*

Teſt, SAMUEL MEREDITH. (A true Copy)
GARLAND ANDERSON.

To which an Anſwer was received from the ſaid Mr. Nicholas, importing, that he had no Apprehenſions of the Neceſſity or Propriety of the proffered Service. For which Reaſons, and underſtanding, moreover, from others, that the private Citizens of Williamſburg were in a great Meaſure quieted from their late Apprehenſions for their Perſons and Property, the Volunteers judged it beſt to return home, and did ſo accordingly, in order to wait the further Directions of the General Congreſs, or Colony Convention. It appears alſo to this Committee, that before, and on the March, ſtrict Orders were repeatedly given to the Volunteers to avoid all Violence, Injury and Inſult, towards the Perſons and Property of every private Individual; and that in executing the Plan of Repriſal on the Perſons of the King's Servants, and his Property, Bloodſhed ſhould be

88.
The Mecklenburg Resolutions, adopted by the North Carolina Provincial Congress May 31, 1775. *The North Carolina Gazette*, New Bern, June 16, 1775. Mrs. John G. Wood, Sr. [Original not in exhibition.]

In ratifying the Association of the previous autumn, the Congress had recommended that every county in the colonies establish a Committee of Safety. In Mecklenburg County, the committee, like every other radical activity, was dominated by Colonel Thomas Polk. For twenty years Polk had been one of Mecklenburg's leading citizens. By May 1775 his staunch advocacy of colonial rights had rendered him a terror to Loyalists. That month, acting in his capacity as colonel of the country militia, Polk requested that every militia company elect two delegates to a convention to consider the state of Anglo-American relations. In doing so, he rose, as Samuel Johnston, president of North Carolina's Provincial Congress, wrote to Joseph Hewes in Philadelphia, "a very pretty spirit in the back country (see the newspapers). He has gone a little farther than I would choose to have gone," Johnston concluded, "but perhaps no further than necessary." [81]

Thomas Polk (1732-1794)

The "very pretty spirit" that Tom Polk was raising embodied itself in a set of resolutions, adopted by the convention on May 31, 1775, in Charlotte, the county seat. The resolutions were directed against the Declaration of the King and Parliament of February 1775 that the colonies were in a state of rebellion and that the leaders of the Continental Congress were traitors. The main premise of the Mecklenburg Resolutions was that since Parliament had taken the patently unjust step of declaring the Americans rebels, then "all laws and Commissions confirmed by, or derived from the Authority of the King or Parliament, are annulled and vacated, and the former civil Constitution of these colonies for the present wholly suspended." The resolutions invested the Provincial Congress of each colony with all executive and legislative power within the colony and provided some basic rules for the good order of Mecklenburg County, specifically to remain in force until the Congress should provide new laws. This was a drastic step, but it was not yet a declaration of independence. The Mecklenburg men were no more willing than were most other Americans at the time to take responsibility for severing permanently the connection with Great Britain. The resolves contained the notable proviso:

> *That these resolves be in full Force and Virtue, until Instructions from the General Congress of this Province, regulating the Jurisprudence of this Province, shall provide otherwise,* or the legislative body of Great Britain *resign its unjust and arbitrary Pretentions with Respect to* America.[82]

To the British, who were not prepared to accept the idea that the key to reconciliation rested solely in their hands, the Mecklenburg Resolutions were still another sign of treasonable intent on the part of Americans. Josiah Martin, the royal governor of North Carolina, claimed in a letter to Dartmouth that

> *The Resolves of the Committee of Mecklenburg which Your Lordship will find in the enclosed News Paper, surpass all the horrid and treasonable publications that the inflamatory spirits of this Continent have yet produced.... A Copy of these Resolves I am informed were sent off by express to the Congress at Philadelphia, as soon as they were passed in the Committee.*[83]

The resolves were indeed carried to Philadelphia by the express rider Captain James Jack, but they never appeared in the journals of the Continental Congress. The Congress was not quite ready to take the steps outlined in the Mecklenburg document.

Captain Jack, according to one contemporary witness in Mecklenburg, "brought back to the county the thanks of Congress for their zeal, and the advice of Congress to be a little more patient until Congress shold take the measures thought to be best."[84]

THE DEFENSE OF ARMAMENTS AND A GESTURE FOR PEACE

From the opening days of the Second Continental Congress in May into the hot days of July 1775, John Dickinson had seen most of his plans for reconciliation put into effect or adopted by the delegates. John Adams, Dickinson's main adversary on the radical side of the political spectrum, did not approve of his opponent's proposals for achieving reconciliation with Great Britain. But the majority of the other delegates were more determined than Adams "not to dissolve that union [with Great Britain] which has so long and so happily subsisted between us, and which we sincerely wish to see restored."[85]

John Dickinson (1732-1808)

Innately conservative, John Dickinson feared revolution but not resistance. He found that many of his colleagues shared his views, and that his ability to articulate a firm but nonviolent response to British policies made him the leader of the large moderate faction in the Congress. Dickinson wanted to remain within the Empire, but he also wanted the King and Parliament to accede to the colonists' wishes and redress all grievances that had arisen since 1763. In order to achieve a reconciliation, Dickinson proposed that the Congress send another "humble and dutiful" petition to the King and open up negotiations with the ministry. Meanwhile, he urged and supported preparations for war within the colonies. Military readiness was essential, Dickinson believed, to prove and reinforce the firmness of the colonies in their demands, as well as to prepare for the possibility of a defensive war against the King's troops.

On June 23 the Congress appointed a committee of John Rutledge, William Livingston, Benjamin Franklin, John Jay, and Thomas Johnson to draft a declaration in defense of the creation of the Continental Army, which would be read by General Washington to the troops assembled in Boston and made public both in America and abroad. Three days later, dissatisfied with the committee's results, the Congress selected two more members, both renowned for their literary and intellectual abilities. The "Pennsylvania farmer," John Dickinson, and the newly arrived delegate from Virginia, Thomas Jefferson, were both appointed to lend their facile pens to the composition of the declaration setting forth the causes and necessity of taking up arms.

Jefferson submitted a draft to the committee that Dickinson protested as being "too harsh" and in need of "softening." According to Jefferson, Dickinson

> *was so honest a man, & so able a one that he was greatly indulged even by those who could not feel his scruples. We therefore requested him to take the paper and put it into a form he could approve.*[86]

Dickinson rewrote Jefferson's draft, preserving only the last few paragraphs as Jefferson had written them. The document that Dickinson finally presented to the Congress was not a soft statement, but rather a ringing indictment of British wrongdoing and a rallying cry to Americans to defend their liberties against an "unconditional submission" to "tyranny." Although Dickinson's declaration did not incite the colonists

89.
JOHN DICKINSON. Benoît Louis
Prévost after Pierre Eugène Du
Simitière. Engraving, 1779. The
Metropolitan Museum of Art.

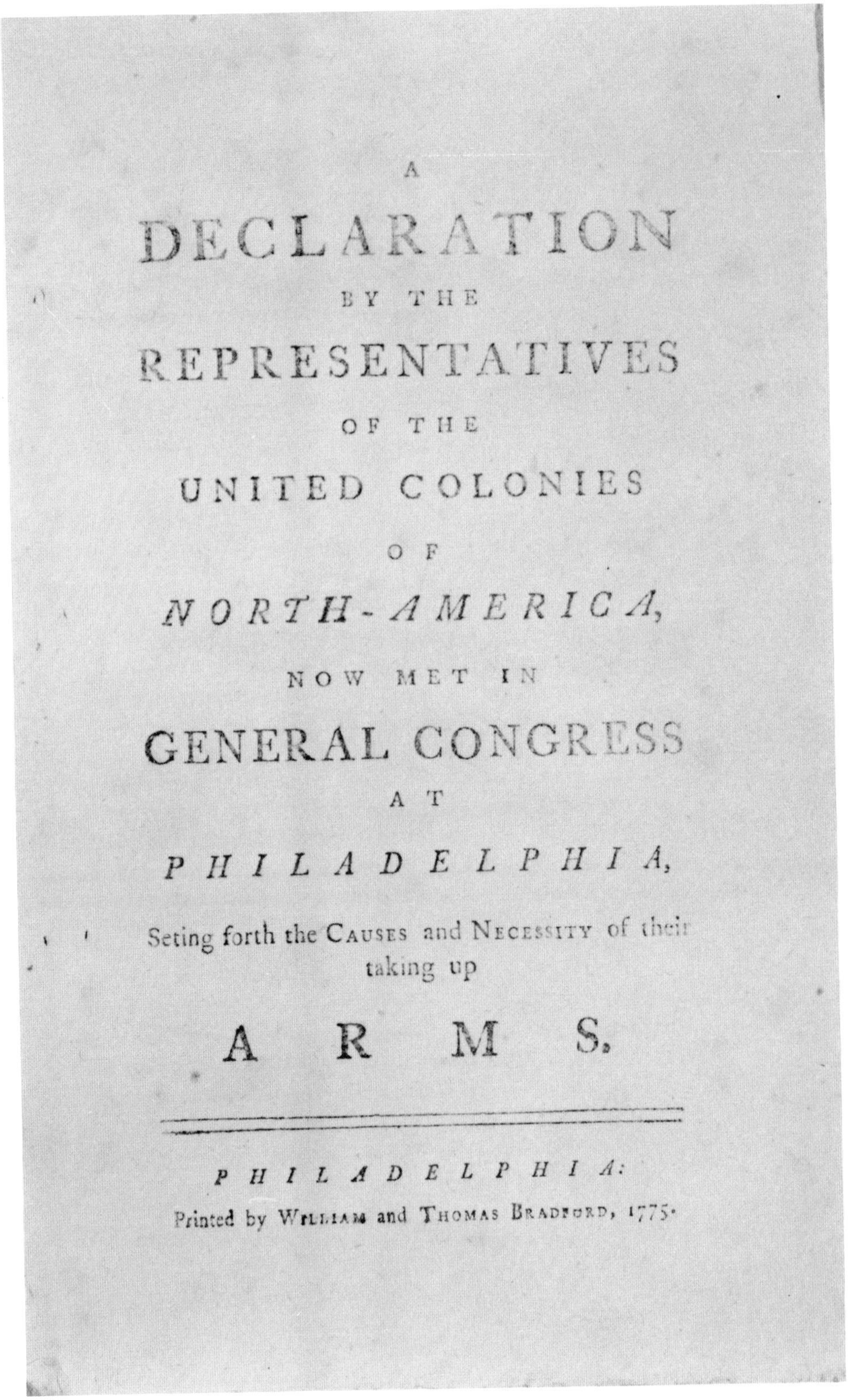

A

DECLARATION

BY THE

REPRESENTATIVES

OF THE

UNITED COLONIES

OF

NORTH-AMERICA,

NOW MET IN

GENERAL CONGRESS

AT

PHILADELPHIA,

Seting forth the CAUSES and NECESSITY of their
taking up

A R M S,

PHILADELPHIA:

Printed By WILLIAM and THOMAS BRADFORD, 1775.

90.
A Declaration By The Representa-
tives Of The United Colonies of
North America, . . . Seting forth the
Causes and Necessity of their taking
up Arms. Philadelphia, 1775.
Massachusetts Historical Society.

142

to violence, it did speak in the firmest tones possible of the readiness of America to resist the British with force:

> *Our cause is just. Our union is perfect. Our internal resources are great, and, if necessary, foreign assistance is undoubtedly attainable . . . the arms we have been compelled by our enemies to assume, we will, in defiance of every hazard, with unabating firmness and perserverance, employ for the preservation of our liberties; being, with one mind, resolved to die freemen rather than live slaves.*[87]

Then, assuring Great Britain that the colonies did not intend to dissolve their ties with the parent state, the "Spirited Manifesto," as John Adams called it, was approved by the Congress on July 6.

Two days after approving the Declaration on the Causes and Necessity of Taking Up Arms, the Congress adopted Dickinson's Petition to the King. Dickinson did not see any contradiction or inconsistency in forcefully stating the readiness of the colonies to resist Great Britain with arms while pleading with the King for permanent recon-

91.
Excerpt from William Knox's copy of the Olive Branch Petition, approved by the Continental Congress July 8, 1775, with Knox's "observations." William L. Clements Library, University of Michigan.

ciliation. He was prepared to defend the colonies, but not ready to give up hope that the King might come to his senses before the outbreak of war.

Although Adams had liked John Dickinson when he first met him in Philadelphia during the second Congress, he was not as impressed by this tall shadow of a man, who was "slender as a Reed, pale as ashes." It was a waste of time, Adams declared, ". . . to sit with a half dozen Witts, deliberating upon a Petition, Address, or Memorial . . ." when the Congress could be devoting its precious time to preparations for military defense. Adams sympathized with Dickinson's hesitancy to approve extreme measures when he learned that Dickinson was being badgered by his Quaker wife and family to desist. Presumably they complained, "Johnny you will be hanged, your Estate will be forfeited and confiscated, you will leave your Excellent Wife a Widow and your charming Children Orphans, Beggars, and infamous." But the continuing irresolution of the Congress distressed Adams, and the decision to petition the King on May 26, and the subsequent approval of Dickinson's draft on July 8, finally pushed Adams's temper to the exploding point. All of Mr. Dickinson's committees, "Petitions, Declarations, and Addresses," were, he believed, just so many "Prettynesses, Juvenilities, and . . . Puerilities." [88]

When Dickinson's petition to the King was introduced in the Congress in July, Thomas Jefferson reported that "the disgust against this humility was general." Adams became so upset over it that he wrote to James Warren in Massachusetts that "A certain great Fortune and piddling Genius, who Fame has been trumpeted so loudly, has given a silly Cast to our whole Doings. We are between Hawk and Buzzard." Unfortunately, Adams's letter fell into the hands of the British, who published it, John Adams insisted, "with a little garbling." Dickinson was quick to show his displeasure at the insult. The next time Adams encountered the Pennsylvania delegate, "He [Dickinson] passed hautily by. We are not to be upon Speaking Terms, nor bowing Terms, for the time to come," Adams decided. "Adams and Dickinson," wrote one observer, "now look ascance at each other and are not upon speaking terms, except in the language in which Cats talk together." [89]

The Olive Branch Petition, or "measure of imbecility" as John Adams termed it, was Dickinson's last-gasp attempt at reconciliation. In a heartfelt and eloquent plea, Dickinson affirmed the affection of the colonies for Great Britain and implored the King, in his "royal magnanimity and benevolence," to repeal the statutes that distressed the colonies so that harmony could be re-established. [90]

But John Dickinson had more in mind than an obsequious solicitation for reconciliation when he drafted the petition to the King. An astute politician and a firm believer in the justness of the colonies' complaints, he believed that "If they [the Crown] reject this application with contempt, . . . such treatment will confirm the minds of our countrymen to endure all the misfortunes that may attend the contest." The petition and its ultimate rejection by the King would force upon those colonists who still hoped for reconciliation the realization that war was inevitable. Had the Congress failed to supplicate the King for a redress of grievances, many colonists would have remained unconvinced that war was the only alternative left to them. Even the fiery radical Charles Thomson admitted that "Whatever hand Dickinson had in the promoting of [the petition] ought to have redounded to his credit as a politician." When the petition was approved on July 8, Dickinson sincerely hoped that if it should prove unacceptable to the King, it would at least defer further violence until the colonies had time to prepare adequately for the bloodshed that was sure to follow.[91]

Richard Penn, a rare combination of colonial sympathizer and member of the proprietary family of Pennsylvania, was entrusted by the Congress to carry the Olive Branch Petition to England. The weary Congress turned back to its chores and duties with reluctance. "We are all exhausted sitting so long at this place and being so long confined together that we feel pretty much as a Number of passangers confined togeather on board ship in a long Voyage," Eliphalet Dyer wrote at the end of July. Not until August 2 did the Congress complete its immediate business. Realizing that its work was only just beginning, it adjourned for a short recess, resolving to reassemble on "Tuesday, the fifth of September next."[92]

92.
GEORGE III. Benjamin West, circa 1779.
Cleveland Museum of Art.

V.

"The British Lion...Rouzed"

When Richard Penn, grandson of the peace-loving founder of Penn-sylvania, William Penn, came riding into London on a stagecoach from Bristol in the middle of August 1775, bearing the Olive Branch Petition of the Continental Congress, he found no minister in town prepared to receive him or accept his document. That August the King and members of Parliament were scattered to the country for summer holidays, and the government was left in the hands of various subministers and clerks. Lord Dartmouth, secretary of state for the American department, exhausted by his struggle to hold off the war party, which wished to declare the American rebellion a foreign war and treat it vigorously as such, had also gone to the country to rest.

On August 21 Richard Penn delivered the Congress's petition to Dartmouth's office in the minister's absence. On the twenty-third the Crown issued its proclamation declaring the government's determination to crush the "open and avowed rebellion" in America. The following day Dartmouth received the plea of his "Majesty's faithful subjects" to resume their former harmony with the mother country and obtain "some mode" of reconciliation and repeal of the statutes causing their distress.[1] The petition had come too late; with the publication of the proclamation, the war party in England was now in the saddle and the events that followed developed inexorably from the hard-line policy it espoused.

Richard Penn (1735-1811)

93.
RICHARD PENN. Joseph Highmore, date unknown. The Historical Society of Pennsylvania.

STRENGTHENING THE FORCES: AUGUST—DECEMBER, 1774

Since August 1774 the war party and its opposition had waged a battle within the Closet of the King and later in Parliament over American policy. The King's pride, and in some cases obstinacy, his commitment to Empire, and his belief in the righteous-ness of his position had prevailed over the liberal urgings of the minority. The fate of the colonies was determined not by the late arrival of the Olive Branch Petition or the King's refusal to receive it, but by George's resolution to maintain his Empire and by a Parliament that was influenced by events both at home and in the colonies to sup-port his decision.

George III
(1738-1820)

On the subject of America the King of England was adamant: "the dye is now cast," he wrote to Lord North just six days after the delegates assembled in Philadelphia for the first Continental Congress, "the Colonies must either submit or triumph. I do not wish to come to severer measures, but we must not retreat; by coolness and an unremitted pursuit of the measures that have been adopted I trust they will come to submit."[2]

The King's sentiments clearly indicated the strength of the forces aligned against the American Congress. George had grown resolute and tough since his accession to the throne of England in 1760. The political turbulence of the early years of his reign had passed. Now the King could enjoy the system of personal rule he had formerly sought to establish and realize his ambition "to be King" (as his mother had instructed him). With the appointment of the affable and devoted Lord North as Chancellor of the Exchequer, George found a civilized and pliable man who shared his ideas and was ready to carry out his wishes. Even Lord Chatham, hardly a friend of the North ministry, believed that North served the Crown "more successfully and more efficiently upon the whole than any other man could be found to do."[3] By the fall of 1774 Lord North had created a formidable conservative government in which George III played an active and determined role.

George III expected obedience in colonial matters. It was "unnatural," he believed, for Americans to enter into disputes with "their mother country." Like most Englishmen, George believed that the parent country was superior to the colonies, and that all that was necessary on his part—as a strict father—was to bring the "deluded colonists" to a "sense of their duty." The Continental Congress, he believed, presented an evil and terrifying challenge to British sovereignty and had to be destroyed. To do so, however, required substantial support in Parliament. Accordingly, in late summer 1774, George decided to dissolve Parliament and call for a new election to take place before the one scheduled by law for March 1775. He hoped that a new Parliament would strengthen the hand of the government against what he already conceived was an American rebellion. "The general Congress now assembling in America," he wrote on August 24 to Lord North, "the peace of Russia with the Turks, and unsettled state of the French ministry, are very additional reasons to show the propriety of the measure [the election]. Besides, I trust it will fill the House with more gentlemen of landed property, as the Nabobs, Planters, and other Volunteers are not ready for the battle."[4]

The King had a number of trump cards at his command. He could brand his opposition as unpatriotic, since no "patriots" could avow "the unnatural doctrine of encouraging the American colonies in their disputes with their mother country."[5] When one self-proclaimed "patriot"—Charles James Fox—did protest the government's policies, he was dismissed from his place on the Treasury Board. It was obvious that the King would not countenance opposition.

The King also knew he could count on the apathy of the British public toward the American issue. "Any remarkable highway robbery on Hunslow Heath," declared Edmund Burke earlier in 1774, "would make more conversation than all the disturbances in America."[6] In September that year Burke again remarked on the disposition of the public to ignore "the disorder and discontent of all America."[7] Thus, the King's sudden dissolution of Parliament and the results of the surprise election in the fall of

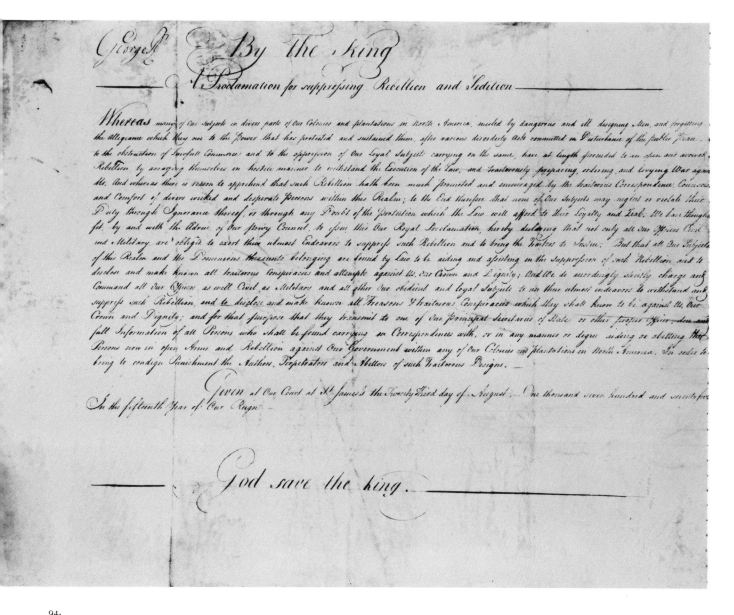

94.
George III's Proclamation for suppressing Rebellion and Sedition,
issued August 23, 1775. Public Record Office, London.

1774 did not stir the English people to protest. Rather, they returned to the House of Commons a nominal majority in support of the ministry, giving Lord North control of the Parliament, which the King dominated through him.

The King was "much pleased at the state of the supposed numbers in the new Parliament." In mid-November he was convinced that "the New England Governments are in a state of rebellion" and that "blows must decide whether they are to be subject to this country or independent." The American people, he wrote, "are ripe for mischief . . . we must either master them or totally leave them to themselves and treat them as Aliens." [8]

These sentiments colored his address to the opening session of the newly elected Parliament in December 1774 in a speech that became, according to John Wilkes, the "American Death warrant." [9] Condemning the nonimportation movement decided upon by the American Congress and the "most daring spirit of resistance and disobedience to the law" in Massachusetts Bay, George III declared his "firm and steadfast resolution to withstand every atempt to weaken or impair the supreme authority of the Legislature over all dominions of the Crown." [10]

As news of colonial defiance continued to reach London, the King's determination to crush American resistance hardened. Conciliation was not part of his plan; "Though a thorough friend to holding out the Olive Branch," he wrote to Lord North on February 15, 1775, "I have not the smallest doubt that if it does not succeed that when once vigorous measures appear to be the only means left of bringing the Americans to a due Submission to the Mother Country that the Colonies will Submit." [11] In the winter of 1775 both the Government and the Opposition presented plans, but negotiations, as French ambassador DeGuines wrote home to Foreign Minister Vergennes, were "impossible. The parties differ on the form and on the substance as widely as white and black." [12]

CONCILIATION AND COERCION, JANUARY—MAY 1775

William Pitt, First Earl of Chatham (1708-1778)

The first attempt to effect a reconciliation came from Lord Chatham (William Pitt), whose genius had directed the defeat of the French in North America fifteen years earlier and whose continuing friendship for the American colonies had given him a permanent place in American affections ever since. Now Chatham emerged from retirement to defend once again the British settlers in America. "I trust," he wrote to a friend in December 1774, ". . . that it will be found impossible for freemen of England to wish to see three millions of Englishmen slaves in America." [13]

Plagued by illness and often in conflict with the Crown, which considered him "a trumpet of rebellion," Lord Chatham had not hesitated to utilize all the force of his personality to urge the repeal of the Stamp Act of 1765, declaring in the House of Commons, "I rejoice that America has resisted." [14] At the urging of the King, he had again taken over the ministry in 1766, but this time with less success. He lost support when he accepted a peerage with the ministerial post, for now the public accused him of selling out to monarchy for security within the nobility. His ministry was badly formed, consisting of a strange mixture of political positions. And unabating illness, which finally caused him to retire altogether, made it difficult for him to act with his

95.
WILLIAM PITT. Richard Brompton,
1772. National Portrait Gallery,
London.

151

former energy. Handing over the reins of power to his ill-suited associate, the Duke of Grafton, Chatham thereafter appeared infrequently in Parliament and then only when called by principle and strong emotion.

It was his great concern for the American question that drew him to the House of Lords on January 20, 1775, to introduce a motion designed to recall the troops from Boston and open the way toward "a happy settlement of the dangerous troubles in America." It was, he said, an attempt to "knock at the door of this sleeping and confounded Ministry and [to] rouse them to a sense of their important danger." "It is not repealing a *piece of parchment* that can restore America to our bosom," he warned Parliament; "You must repeal her fears and her resentments; and you may then hope for her love and gratitude." The men who constituted the American leadership deserved Parliament's respect for their "solidity of reasoning, force of sagacity, and wisdom of conclusion, under . . . a complication of difficult circumstances." Any attempt, then, "to impose servitude upon such men, to establish despotism over such a mighty continental *nation* must be vain, must be fatal. We shall be forced ultimately to retract; let us retract while we can, not when we must." Chatham warned the members that "France and Spain [are] watching your conduct, and waiting for the maturity of your errors, with a vigilant eye to America." If the ministers persisted in misadvising the King, he said, "I will not say that the King is betrayed; but I will pronounce *That the Kingdom is undone.*"[15]

Some days later Chatham introduced a "Provisional Act for Settling the Troubles in America," which revealed his recognition of the need for change in the basic imperial structure. Monetary contributions from the colonies, he insisted, should not be "considered as a condition of Redress, but as a Testimony of their Affection." In matters of taxation, therefore, Britain must defer to the colonies themselves. In all other areas, however, Britain was supreme.[16]

Like the King, North, and most other political leaders in Great Britain, Chatham had always insisted upon the prerogative of the home government.

Now, however, his defense of America was more practical than ideological. His bill called for annulment of all the parliamentary acts obnoxious to the Americans, promised that colonial charters would not be altered except by due process of law, and authorized the meeting of a general congress at Philadelphia through which the colonies would make a free grant of revenue to the King. Thus legitimizing the Continental Congress, he would integrate it more fully into the British system by granting it authority to negotiate for the united colonies with the government of Great Britain. The colonies would become in effect autonomous, although subordinate, states within the Empire.

Chatham's bill was rejected. His proposal by implication would have repealed the Declaratory Act of 1766, which had affirmed the right of the British Parliament to bind the colonies and people of America in all cases whatsoever. To Tories like the Earl of Sandwich, First Lord of the Admiralty, Chatham's bill "sanctified the traitorous proceeding of the congress" and encouraged Americans' "hostile intentions."[17] The more moderate Rockingham Whigs, although seeking conciliation, also could not accept any deviation from the principle of parliamentary supremacy. Chatham's willingness to qualify this principle was as much an affront to them as it was to the Tories.

Divided ideologically and suffering, in any case, from a minority status, the Whig Opposition could not rally against the King's friends. Having "neither information, nor policy, nor union," as the indefatigable wit Horace Walpole commented, they were helpless.[18] Their weakness meant the rejection of a measure that might have compromised the differences between the colonies and the mother country. At the very least, if adopted, it would have been recognized as "a manifesto of peace and good will" by those Americans who were not so adamantly opposed to the principle of parliamentary supremacy.[19]

Benjamin Franklin, American agent for Massachusetts and Pennsylvania in London, watched the rejection of Chatham's "Provisional Act" with great disappointment. Although many members of the House of Lords believed that he was the real author of Chatham's bill—which does not seem to have been the case—Franklin approved Chatham's effort and hoped his bill would serve as the basis of a treaty and, meanwhile, delay the passage of further exacerbating acts. He had taken heart when Lord Dartmouth moved to place the bill on the table, to be considered more fully at a later date; and was dismayed when, after a short debate, Dartmouth changed his mind and indicated that he would vote to have the bill rejected immediately.

After eighteen years in England as agent for two of the largest American colonies

Benjamin Franklin
(1706-1790)

96.
BENJAMIN FRANKLIN. Jean-Baptiste Nini, after a profile sketch by Thomas Walpole. Terra cotta, 1777. National Portrait Gallery, Smithsonian Institution.

and as postmaster general of North America, Franklin had come to love English life, but he had also developed great distrust of British intentions and despised the corruption of the country's political system and the arrogance of its leadership. Removed from the emotionally charged atmosphere of Philadelphia, where he had started his career as a youth, Franklin had watched the proceedings in his native land apprehensively, concerned lest his fellow colonials, in their zeal for self-government, become too violent in their opposition to the mother country. For this reason, he had been disturbed by the news of the Boston Tea Party, for he feared that such extremism would stimulate extreme reactions. Given time, Great Britain would make peace with the colonies simply out of great need for their aid. In the meantime, violence except in self-defense, must be avoided at all costs short of abandoning American liberties. "If we are steady till another Session," he wrote to Joseph Galloway, "this Ministry must retire, & our Points will be gained." [20]

It was undoubtedly his hope for reconciliation that persuaded Franklin to enter into secret negotiations in December 1774 with two distinguished English Quakers, Dr. John Fothergill and David Barclay, Jr. The two men had asked Franklin to set down on paper the terms whereby Franklin believed the colonies could be reconciled. At first reluctant to commit himself, knowing that the First Continental Congress was in the process of composing a petition for redress of grievances, Franklin finally wrote a memorandum, "Hints for conversation upon the subject of terms that might probably produce a durable union between Great Britain and the colonies." [21] He was undoubtedly influenced to do so by the fact that he had known the young Barclay for years and that Fothergill was Lord Dartmouth's physician. Barclay was also a friend of Lord Hyde, who was working for peaceful settlement of the American problem. Whether the two men undertook the negotiations with Franklin on their own initiative, or were acting as intermediaries for Dartmouth, or Hyde, or possibly Lord North, is not known; but it is fairly clear that Dartmouth and Hyde saw the results of the negotiations, for one copy of the "Hints" contains "corrections and interlineations" in their handwriting. [22]

Thus, while Chatham's proposals were being voted down in the House of Lords, Franklin was busy composing seventeen "Hints" that went far beyond Chatham's measures. Franklin indicated the necessity to repeal the Coercive Acts, after which he promised that the tea destroyed in Boston Harbor would be paid for, and pledged his personal fortune to that end, a promise that the ministers happily accepted. Franklin then turned his attention to two sets of proposals—one involving mercantilist procedures and the other the question of taxation. The ministers were prepared to accept Franklin's suggestion that Americans be allowed to regulate their own customs, and that all duties be paid into the respective colonial treasuries for use within the colony from which the revenue was derived. Franklin's proposal for ending the dispute over taxation, however, was not so easily managed. Franklin had suggested that in times of peace Great Britain allow the colonies to pay their own governmental expenses and not make demands on them for financial support. The mother country, said Franklin, would be sufficiently compensated during such times by the profits from her monopoly of colonial commerce. In wartime, however, the King might impose requisitions on the colonies proportioned to the English land tax. Dartmouth and his colleagues would qualify this proposal by permitting the colonies to pay their own way in peacetime only if they established "a permanent fund for the support of [provincial government] after the precedents of the island of Jamaica." This involved maintenance of a permanent civil list—something which Massachusetts had resisted for a long time. The ministers believed that in time of war requisitions should be made "as heretofore, in mutual confidence that America will not furnish less, nor Great Britain expect more towards the general service than shall be justly proportioned to the abilities and circumstances of each colony." But as B. D. Bargar has pointed out, "it was precisely the lack of 'mutual confidence' which had precipitated the crisis in the first place." [23]

Franklin's other "Hints" also met with qualifying or equivocal answers. When Franklin suggested that British troops should not be allowed to enter or be quartered in a colony without the consent of its legislature, Dartmouth responded that it was unreasonable to require the consent of a municipal council for the stationing of regular troops in any English borough. Dartmouth would not accept Franklin's suggestion that the Quebec Act be repealed, indicating quite forcefully that that measure was not the business of "the colonies with whom the present contest is." As for Franklin's "Hint" that the Massachusetts Government Act be rescinded, Dartmouth could only promise to listen to any complaints that the people of Massachusetts might present about the "disadvantages and inconveniences" of the act altering their charter. The suggestion that Parliament formally disclaim the act originating in the reign of Henry VIII that made it possible for persons accused of treason to be transported to England for trial was also qualified; the ministers believed that before Parliament did so, the colonies would have to make provision for the impartial trial of traitors.[24]

Underlying the differences between the ministers and Franklin was a basic constitutional disagreement. All the individual subjects—quartering of troops, courts, judges' salaries, mercantilist provisions—could have been compromised if the British had been willing to accept Franklin's proposal that they repeal the Coercive Acts and surrender the right to tax in return for being granted the right to impose and benefit from commercial regulations. Alternatively, Franklin had suggested that America pay permanent grants of revenue to Britain in exchange for Britain's surrender of control over commerce. "The choice between free trade and freedom from taxation," according to Bargar, "was impossible for an Eighteenth-Century ministry to make." [25] While the ministers continued to clutch at straws, urging more meetings and negotiations, Franklin made plans for sailing home. In mid-March, convinced that further negotiations with North's government were futile, he was headed for America. While on the high seas, the battles of Lexington and Concord occurred, putting an end to whatever possibilities may still have existed for reconciliation.

With the defeat of Chatham's compromise proposal, Lord North took full command. Even while carrying on negotiations with Franklin, he had continued to press in Parliament for legislative coercion and military reinforcements. Petition after petition arrived in the House of Commons from London and Liverpool merchants, Manchester manufacturers, and Wolverhampton traders urging the government to avert the crisis that would surely disrupt England's economy. These were either voted down or ignored. Instead, Lord North proposed an address to the King in which Massachusetts would be called a rebellious colony and His Majesty would be asked to take immediate action to insure obedience there to the laws and sovereignty of Great Britain. In the

Frederick North, Second Earl of Guilford (1732-1792)

97.
LORD NORTH. Nathaniel Dance,
circa 1767-70. The Earl of Guilford.

meantime, 6,000 men were to be sent to join the armed forces already in the colonies, and New England would be restrained from all trade with Great Britain, Ireland, and the West Indies and excluded from the Newfoundland fisheries.

Then on the twentieth of February, Lord North did a turnabout. The King had agreed to North's offering one more—but final—gesture of reconciliation. North's plan offered each colony the opportunity to develop its own tax system for the support of civil government, the administration of justice, and the common defense, subject only to parliamentary approval. No other taxes would be required of the colonies except duties imposed for regulation of commerce. In time of war, however, the colonies would be expected "to contribute extraordinary supplies in a reasonable proportion to what is raised by Great Britain. . . ." The King and North hoped that the plan would unite the British and destroy colonial unity. "It shews what is expected," wrote the King, "and gives up no right." [26]

A storm greeted North's proposals. Militant members of Parliament believed it was too lenient; and opposition Whigs denounced it as "insincere and ambiguous." "To say, Give me as much money as I wish, till I say enough, or I will take it from you, and then to call such a proposition conciliatory for peace," David Hartley exclaimed, "is insult added to oppression." [27] Benjamin Franklin compared it to the method of a highwayman who expected his victims to pay until he decided they had paid enough. [28]

On February 27 North's motion was approved and copies were sent to each of the colonial governors along with a note from Dartmouth urging its acceptance. A few weeks later North introduced the second half of his policy—the New England Restraining Bill. "When the Americans are quiet and have respect for their mother country," North believed, "the mother country will be good natured to them." [29] Respect could come only through punishment and a display of strength. Since Massachusetts Bay was in a state of rebellion "it was just . . . to deprive that province of its fisheries." And since the Americans, through their Association agreements, had refused to trade with Great Britain, North insisted that "it was but just that we should not suffer them to trade with any other nation." [30]

With his two bills, Lord North revealed his lack of understanding of the nature of the colonial protest and his ignorance of the strength of colonial unity. The Conciliatory Resolution failed to tempt any of the colonies and, indeed, when it arrived in America, it convinced many that the British government did not really desire compromise. "Lord North's motion would be slavery," wrote a Philadelphian to Brigadier General Robertson.[31] The New York City Council stated that there was no hope for reconciliation on the terms stated in the proposal; and when all the colonies referred the matter to the Continental Congress, that body, on the thirty-first of July, voted that the "proposition is altogether unsatisfactory, because it imports only a suspencion of the mode, not a renunciation of the pretended right to tax us. . . ."[32]

In Parliament it was the voice of Edmund Burke, longtime secretary to the Whig leader Lord Rockingham and a key figure among the Rockingham Whigs, that protested most eloquently against Lord North's policy. For three hours, on March 22, Burke addressed the Commons, in a speech that has since come to be considered one of the finest pieces of eighteenth-century oratory. Tall and imposing, with a commanding presence that matched his lofty phrases, Burke insisted that "The proposition is peace." Such peace could only come about through the removal of the grounds for difference between the colonies and the mother country and by restoring colonial confidence in the British government. To effect this, concessions were necessary from Great Britain, concessions which would not weaken the nation since "The superior power may offer peace with honor and safety." American "strength and opulence," its "great and growing population" made America worth fighting for, but force was "a feeble instrument for preserving a people so numerous, so active, so growing, so spirited as this, in a profitable and subordinate connection with us." Force was but temporary—"a nation is not governed which is perpetually to be conquered"; it was uncertain in its outcome, and, worst of all, it impaired the object fought for: "I do not choose," said Burke, "wholly to break the American spirit, because it is the spirit that has made the country." [33]

America, said Burke, is marked by a "fierce spirit of liberty . . . stronger . . . probably than in any other people of the earth." The liberty to which Americans were devoted was English liberty, based on "the excellence of the English constitution." As with Englishmen, American love of liberty "fixed and attached on this specific point of taxing," a point that the colonial mode of government—"popular in an high degree"—strengthened.

Religious dissent had attached the colonists to the spirit of liberty as had colonial education in the law: "In no country, perhaps in the world is the law so general a study." "This study," he declared, "renders men acute, inquisitive, dexterous, prompt in attack, ready in defence, full of resources. . . . Here they anticipate the evil and judge of the pressure of the grievance by the badness of the principle. They awgur misgovernment at a distance, and snuff the approach of tyranny in every tainted breeze."

Edmund Burke
(1729-1797)

157

98.
EDMUND BURKE. James Barry,
1774. National Gallery of Ireland.

158

All of these factors—the English inheritance, their form of government, their religion, their education—together with their remoteness from the seat of government encouraged "a fierce spirit of liberty" in the colonies, according to Burke. Whether Englishmen liked it or not, they had to contend with this spirit and adjust their future conduct to its existence. "An Englishman," remarked Burke, "is the unfittest person on earth to argue another Englishman into slavery." [34]

What then was the solution? How, thought Burke, should Britain go about conciliating and conceding? Britain must *"admit the people of our colonies into an interest in the constitution,* and, by recording that admission in the journals of Parliament, give them as strong an assurance as the nature of the thing will admit that we mean forever to adhere to that solemn declaration of systematic indulgence. . . ."* Specifically, Burke hoped to bring about conciliation through the adoption by Parliament of thirteen resolutions that he hoped would meet the demands of the Americans and restore peace. Six of the resolves summarized previous taxation procedure which had deprived the colonists of their right to be taxed by their own representatives and pointed out the greater efficiency that had attended the collection of revenues when the colonial assemblies had been free to grant "large subsidies and public aids for his Majesty's service, according to their abilities." Five more resolutions continued to sound the practical note. Calling for repeal of the Tea Act and the Intolerable Acts, he attempted to remove these causes of colonial discontent; while in his two remaining resolutions he returned the courts to the colonists and made the courts of vice admiralty "convenient for those who would sue in them." [35]

"Mr. Burke may fail to convince," reported *Gentleman's Magazine,* "but he never fails to charm." Although "the attention of the House was rivitted to him" for three hours, and although his brilliant plea for conciliation "afforded the most exquisite entertainment [it] had no other effect." The members of Commons may have been moved to "the loudest, the most unanimous, and highest strains of applause," but they did not change their minds about America, and Burke's resolutions were defeated by a vote of 270 to 78.[36]

With the defeat of Burke's resolutions and the passage of the New England Restraining Act, parliamentary punishment of the dissident colonies moved into full swing. News had reached London that the colonies south of New England were also zealously applying the provisions of the Continental Association and promoting revolutionary activities. On March 9 Lord North asked permission to introduce a bill for restraining these colonies also—especially New Jersey, Pennsylvania, Maryland, Virginia, and South Carolina. Since New York, North Carolina, and Georgia seemed less aggressive in implementing the Association, North exempted them from the bill's provisions. But to David Hartley, North's measure could drive "the whole continent of America into despair." [37] Nevertheless, the bill was allowed to be introduced, and on March 30 it was read for the second time. The strength of the opposition was insufficient to stop its passage. Temple Luttrell could call it the work of "a banditti of robbers," and the Marquis of Granby, a supporter of Chatham, could exclaim in disgust:

> *In God's name, what Language are you now holding out to America!*

Thomas Howard,
Third Earl of Effingham
(1747-1791)

159

99.
THOMAS HOWARD, third Earl of
Effingham. Francesco Bartolozzi.
Pencil on paper, date unknown.
The Metropolitan Museum of Art.

*Resign your property, divest yourselves of your privileges and freedom,
denounce everything that can make life comfortable, or we will destroy your
commerce, we will involve your country in all the miseries of famine; and if
you express the sensations of men at such harsh treatment, we will then
declare you in a state of rebellion, and put yourselves and your families,
to fire and sword.*[38]

But to no avail: the bill was passed 192 to 46 and on April 13 received the royal
assent.

On May 15 Parliament again had the opportunity to display the strength of its
resolution to teach the colonists a lesson. That day Burke, who served as London
agent for the New York Assembly, presented a remonstrance from the colony to the
House of Commons supporting the stand of its sister colonies. Denying that New
Yorkers sought independence and assuring the Parliament of Great Britain that it
acknowledged its "supreme direction and government over the whole empire," the
New York Assembly nevertheless protested "the innovations which have been made
in the constitutional mode of government since the close of the last war"; these it held
responsible for American grievances.[39] The New York Remonstrance was rejected, as
was a similar memorial presented to the House of Lords three days later by the Duke
of Manchester, a Rockingham Whig.

While the Lords engaged in a lengthy but superficial debate on the question of the
New York memorial, the Earl of Effingham rose to call his peers' attention to the
more important meaning of its contents, for he believed that the Lords possessed the
power "of restoring harmony to this distracted Empire." Attempting to avoid the

argument over the right and power of taxation, Effingham explained that "whatever has been done by the *Americans* [was] the mere consequence of our unjust demands:

> *They have come to you with fair arguments, you have refused to hear them; they make the most respectful remonstrances; you answer them with bills of pains and penalties; they know they ought to be free you tell them they shall be slaves. Is it, then, a wonder if they say, in despair, 'for the short remainder of our lives, we will be free.'*[40]

The noble lord then drew a verbal picture of two armies facing each other—armies of brothers and countrymen—each dreading the event, yet each feeling that the "most trifling accident" could "cause the sword to be drawn." "In this dreadful moment," said Effingham, "a set of men more wise and moderate than the rest, exert themselves to bring us all to reason." The colonists, Effingham reminded his colleagues, were making "the first concessions." But Englishmen treated them "with contempt": "we prefer poverty, blood, and servitude, to wealth, happiness, and liberty." [41]

A captain in the Twenty-second Regiment of the British army, Effingham enjoyed the profession which "has been that of my ancestors for ages." [42] He had entered the army as a youth of fifteen. With the death of his father, the second Earl of Effingham, the young man had taken his place in the House of Lords. Here, his strong sense of justice and common sense had made him a prominent dissenter against the government's American policy. Now he would make his final, and most dramatic, dissent. Rather than go to America and "bear arms against my fellow-subjects . . . in what . . . is not a clear cause," he would resign his commission in the army. "Ever since I was of an age to have any ambition at all," declared Effingham, "my highest has been to serve my country in a military capacity." It was, therefore, "no small sacrifice" he was making; especially "when a predilection, strengthened by habit," had given him "so strong an attachment to his profession as I feel." Since his country had made his profession incompatible with his duty as a citizen, however, he felt bound to resign, as "the only method of avoiding the guilt of enslaving my country, and embruing my hands in the blood of her sons." [43]

Effingham's "sacrifice" had no effect. The Lords refused to hear New York's petition, just as the King and Commons had refused to heed similar memorials sent to them by New York at the same time. George III was grateful to the legislature: "You have maintained with a firm and steady resolution," he told Parliament as it brought its sessions to a close, "the rights of my crown and the authority of parliament, which I shall ever consider inseparable. . . . I am persuaded, that the most salutary effects must in the end result from measures formed and concluded on such principles." [44]

"THE AUTHORITY OF GOVERNMENT . . . MAINTAINED" AND DEBATED

While Lord North was offering conciliatory proposals with one hand and punitive programs with the other, he was also busily defending the policy of his government. For such a public defense, in the early spring of 1775 he turned to his friend, the Tory writer Samuel Johnson, who had come to his political aid before with defensive pamphlets.

100.
SAMUEL JOHNSON. Joseph
Nollekens. Plaster cast, after the
1776 original. Herman W. Liebert.

Samuel Johnson
(1709-1784)

By 1775 Samuel Johnson was a literary celebrity, having risen from a situation of
poverty to public acclaim as the author of the *Rambler*, a *Dictionary*, *Rasselas*, and
numerous polemics and reviews. In 1762 Johnson's achievement had been recognized
by the newly crowned King with the award of a pension of £300 a year, which
Johnson had accepted on the assurance that he would not become thereby a "state
hireling." Grateful for being spared "the shame of solicitation and the anxiety of
suspense," Johnson did not find it difficult after accepting the pension to write pamphlets at the administration's behest—especially since he usually agreed with the
ministry's position. [45]

Taxation No Tyranny was published early in March 1775. A trenchant critique of
the First Continental Congress's Address to the King—so devastating, indeed, that it
had to be edited by the government to allow room for diplomatic maneuvering—it

was criticized by Johnson's close friend and biographer James Boswell as being in its "extreme violence . . . unsuitable to the mildness of a Christian philosopher." [46] Johnson did not mind the editing; it was his employer's business, he told Boswell, much to the young man's dismay. Although privately Johnson had little respect for North's ministry, which was "feeble and timid, and cannot act with that authority and resolution which is necessary," he had no love for the Americans either.[47] They were hypocrites who cried for liberty while they would enslave Negroes, Indians, French Canadians, and Loyalists. Their "delirious dreams of Republican fanaticism" were "abortions of folly"; their arguments were "too foolish for buffoonery, too wild for madness." All they were being required to do was to pay the cost of their own safety, and Johnson belittled the idea that they ought to determine for themselves how much this ought to be. All the colonists' argument amounted to was "We do not like taxes, therefore we will not be taxed." If they had not been taxed before, then, Johnson retorted, "Very well, the longer they have been spared, the better they can pay." Surely they could afford to, argued Johnson, pointing out reports of their "greatness and their opulence, . . . the fertility of their land, and the splendor of their towns." Those who "thus flourish under the protection of our government should contribute something towards its expense," Johnson claimed. If it were true that the Americans were multiplying "with the fecundity of their own rattle-snakes, so that every quarter of a century doubles their numbers," then Johnson insisted that it was necessary to "attack a nation thus prolific while we may yet hope to prevail." [48]

The Englishman who went voluntarily to America, said Johnson, "cannot complain of losing what he leaves in Europe." Moreover, countless Englishmen were only "virtually represented" in Parliament—why not the Americans? But what really annoyed Johnson about the Americans was their patriotic "cant." Self-interest, he insisted, was at the heart of their outcry, just as it was in 1756 when the French and English fought. That war, he said, was "only the quarrel of two robbers for the spoils of a passenger"—the Indians to whom the land originally belonged. In the same way, he asked, why do we now hear "the loudest yelps for liberty among the drivers of negroes?" [49]

Johnson's anger was aimed also at American defenders in England; in fact, these he castigated even more than the colonists. They were "zealots of anarchy," "libertines of policy." They had no patriotism, no virtue, if they did not love England more than they seemed to love justice in America. English superiority and American obedience should be their foremost consideration. English power, English honor—these were what was important, not the obstinate and obdurate Americans who, as he told Boswell later, were "rascals, robbers, pirates." [50]

Johnson's diatribe might not have been so significant if it did not convey the view of the country gentlemen who made up North's majority in Parliament. Uninterested in ideas, essentially narrow in their interests and prejudiced against the Americans, the country squires could believe Johnson's accusation that the Americans were frauds, that they robbed their creditors, that they were lawless, and especially that they wouldn't pay their fair share of the Empire's taxes, the burden of which fell heavily upon themselves. The country squires were also immensely influenced by a pamphlet that followed soon on the heels of Johnson's, *A Calm Address to our American Colonies*, written by the leader of the Methodists, John Wesley.

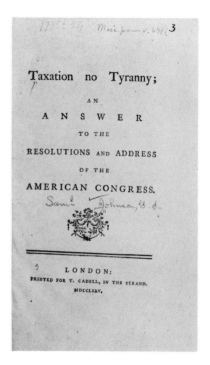

101.
Samuel Johnson's *Taxation no Tyranny*. London, 1775. Library of Congress.

103.
John Wesley's *A Calm Address to Our American Colonies*. London, 1775. Library of Congress.

102.
JOHN WESLEY. William Hamilton, 1788. National Portrait Gallery, London.

John Wesley (1703-1791)

Wesley's pamphlet was in effect a staid condensation of Johnson's *Taxation No Tyranny*. The American resistance to the mother country Wesley viewed as a conspiracy against monarchy; and since he was "bred up in the highest notions of passive obedience and non-resistance," it was perhaps inevitable that, as he wrote earlier, "all my prejudices are against the Americans." [51] But when Wesley had written this admission in a letter to Lord North early in June 1775, he was at that time urging North not to use force. The Americans, he believed then, were "an oppressed people, asking for nothing more than their legal rights, and in the most modest and inoffensive manner that the nature of the thing would allow." Moreover, Wesley had warned Lord North, "these men will not be frightened . . . they are as strong men as you; they are as valiant as you . . . for they are one and all enthusiasts—enthusiasts for liberty. . . . And we know how . . . men animated with this spirit will leap into a fire or rush into a cannon's mouth." [52]

After the publication of Johnson's fiery pamphlet, Wesley seems to have changed his mind. Now he was more intent upon warning the public against the attractions of American republicanism. "No Governments under heaven," he wrote, "are so despotic as the republican; no subjects are governed in so arbitrary a manner as those of a commonwealth. . . . Our sins will never be removed until we fear God and honour the King." Hoping to quench the flame which he saw raging over all the land, he urged Americans to "not bite and devour one another." They should put away their sins, he pleaded, by fearing God and honoring the King. [53]

Johnson's and Wesley's pamphlets raised a short but violent storm among American sympathizers in England. John Wilkes called Johnson "the pensioned advocate of despotism." Developing the same theme, another pamphleteer wrote that he expected to see "the philosophical doctor lolling in his carriage-and-four with an income equal to the revenue of a good bishopric." The poet Cowper cried, "Oh! I could thrash his old jacket until I made his pension jingle in his pocket." [54]

The pamphleteers of the Opposition were not any kinder to the clergyman. Wesley was compared to "a low and puny tadpole in divinity, which proudly seeks to disembowel a high and mighty whale in politicks." Some critics accused Wesley of seeking "lawn sleeves and a mitre"; what he deserved, they said, was "a hempen neckcloth." [55]

The most formidable opposition to the defenders of the government came from Catharine Macaulay, widow of the Scottish physician George Macaulay and author of an eight-volume history of England. Needless to say, Johnson did not care for Mrs. Macaulay. He found her sharp tongue little to his liking; and when she returned home from Paris in 1775, much taken with the current fashions, he remarked that it was better that she should "redden her own cheeks" than "blacken other peoples characters." [56] Her Whiggish principles were also distasteful to sardonic Samuel; on one occasion, he attempted to dramatize the foolishness of Mrs. Macaulay's democratic principles by inviting the footman to sit down to dine with them.

Catharine Macaulay (1731-1791)

Catharine Macaulay's intense enthusiasm for liberty grew out of her early absorption in Roman history. Encouraged in her libertarianism by close friendships with leading London Whigs and their American friends, notably Arthur and William Lee, who constituted the political circle of her brother John Sawbridge, a well-known liberal member of Parliament and Lord Mayor of London, Mrs. Macaulay soon lent her talented pen to the writing of radical pamphlets. During this period, she was particularly involved with the American question.

In 1775 Mrs. Macaulay's vigorous attack on George III's government, *Address to the People of England, Ireland, and Scotland on the present important crisis of affairs*, appeared. Here her purpose was to rouse her countrymen "from that guilty dissipation" which had permitted them to submit tamely to "oppressive taxes" and "corruption" from despots who are now extending "their venal course" to the American colonies. "With an entire supineness, England, Scotland, and Ireland, have seen the Americans year by year, stripped of the most valuable of their rights . . . to the eternal

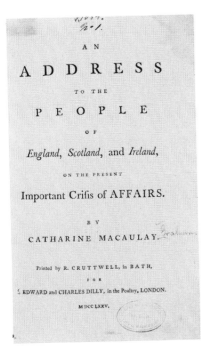

105.
Catharine Macaulay's *An Address To The People of England, Scotland, and Ireland, On The Present Important Crisis of Affairs.* London, 1775. Tracy W. McGregor Library, University of Virginia.

104.
CATHARINE MACAULAY. Jonathan Spilsbury after Catharine Read. Engraving, 1764. National Portrait Gallery, London.

shame of this country," she wrote. Now they were acquiescing to policies which if not challenged would sink the country "into the lowest abyss of national misery."

The British, warned Catharine Macaulay, have been misled by those who were "dazzled with the sunshine of a court." They were treated as if they were "ignorant and profligate," incapable of understanding the American situation or of reacting properly to it. Mrs. Macaulay had more faith in their capacity. Appealing to "that measure of understanding which the almighty has given in common to man," she explained the falsehoods being spread by those who wished to limit freedom. Especially was there no truth to the assertions of those who "by pensions taken from the public treasure . . . fancy that the times cannot be better." Pointing out the decline that had taken place in commerce—a decline testified to by "the starving mechanic" and the "half-famished poor"—and the rising cost of living that had been made even more unbearable by the "oppressive burden of our taxes," she exhorted Britons to "Rouse! and unite in one general effort; till, by your unanimous and repeated addresses to the

166

throne, and to both houses of parliament, you draw the attention of every part of the government to their own interests, and to the dangerous state of the British empire." If they did not, she warned, and if by their neglect "a civil war" broke out, "either the mother country, by one great exertion, may ruin both herself and America, or the Americans, by a lingering contest, will gain an independency." In the event of the latter consequence, not only would the British lose the advantages of colonial trade— "advantages which have hitherto preserved you from a national bankruptcy,"—but, "left to the bare possession of [their] foggy islands," the British would also lose the liberties and privileges which their ancestors had gained for them "as mitigations of that barbarous system of despotism imposed by the Norman tyrant on the inhabitants of this island." [57]

Despite the vigor of Mrs. Macaulay's attack, her pamphlet had little influence on the course of events. The masses she addressed had no voting power, while the country gentlemen were more absorbed by the problems of their estates and social affairs. The merchants were busy seeking markets elsewhere, once the American trade was closed, and as members of the substantial middle class they were alienated by the radicalism of colonial demands. "What is England now?" wrote the famous gadfly Horace Walpole; ". . . a sink of Indian wealth, filled by nabobs and emptied by maccaronis! A senate sold and dispised. . . . A gaming, robbing, wrangling, railing nation, without genius, character or allies." [58]

"THE BATTLE OF THE LEGISLATURE": AUGUST—DECEMBER, 1775

Lord Dartmouth was a friend and supporter of John Wesley and the Methodist church. A pious, peaceloving man, Dartmouth had assumed his office as secretary of state in 1772 with the hope of restoring harmonious colonial relations. The Americans put great faith in him, for across the Atlantic he was known as a man who was "in point of moral virtue . . . unexceptionable." [59] But just as Wesley was uncertain as to how he felt about the American resistance—on the one hand preaching toleration and on the other preaching strict discipline—so was Dartmouth. Perhaps Benjamin Franklin was accurate when he described Dartmouth as a weakling: he was "a truly good man," Franklin had written, "and wishes sincerely a good understanding with the colonies, but does not seem to have strength equal to his wishes." [60]

Wesley kept urging such strength on the secretary of state. When Dartmouth insisted upon dismissing the effectiveness of the Association embargo, by telling Wesley and the King that "trade [in Great Britain] was as plentiful and flourishing as ever and the people as well employed and well satisfied," Wesley contradicted him. "There cannot be a more notorious falsehood," he wrote, ". . . I aver that every part of England where I have been trade in general is exceedingly decayed and thousands of people are quite unemployed." Furthermore, Wesley tried to warn Dartmouth that the people were "dangerously dissatisfied," and their discontent was aimed primarily at "the King himself. He is the object," wrote Wesley, "of their anger, contempt and malice." [61]

Such information and warnings depressed Dartmouth during the summer of 1775, but did not stimulate him to action. Not as optimistic as the rest of the King's ministers

William Legge,
Second Earl of Dartmouth
(1731-1801)

106.
WILLIAM LEGGE, second Earl of
Dartmouth. Nathaniel Hone,
1777. Dartmouth College.

about the outcome of the rebellion and the chances of restoring peace without sacri-
ficing the principle of parliamentary supremacy, he was, as Arthur Lee commented,
"too moderate a character to attempt anything grand or decisive." [62]

Dartmouth hoped that the Continental Congress would disown the violence of Lexington, Concord, and Bunker Hill and thus placate an angry King who had already
warned him that England must "make her rebellious children rue the hours they cast
off obedience." [63] Upon receiving news of Bunker Hill, George III had quickly cast
about for a supply of mercenary troops to reinforce the army in America. Although
the King was turned down by Catherine the Great of Russia, Dartmouth knew that
George had successfully obtained the services of enough Hanoverians and Prussians to
emphasize the King's punitive policy. When General Gage was recalled from America
"that he may explain the various wants for carrying on the next campaign," and when
George III ordered the drafting of a proclamation announcing the government's intention of crushing the rebellion, then Dartmouth realized that his policy had failed.[64]
"Administration," Lord George Germain, leader of the war party, had said, must
"adopt real offensive measures or . . . resign their offices and leave the conciliatory plan
of meanness and submission to those who wish to be their successors upon such terms."
In the face of such hawklike utterances, even Lord North could only submit to the
demand that Americans be treated as an alien foe.

168

Yet, Dartmouth continued to hold out in the cabinet for peace. "Too old a *Whig* to approve such Measures," he hoped that the Proclamation of Rebellion would not be issued until the Continental Congress had been heard from. "I rather wish than expect," he wrote on August 6, 1775, to Undersecretary Knox, "a settlement of our differences upon the grounds of the terms stated in the [newspaper] article from Philadelphia. However, I see no reason why we may not set our feet upon . . . any ground that can be given, and though both sides will have a great way to go before they will be within the sound of each other's voice, it is not impossible that they may come near enough to shake hands at last. . . ." [65]

OLIVE BRANCH PETITION IGNORED

Dartmouth was to be disappointed again. When the Olive Branch Petition of the Continental Congress arrived in August 1775, it was ignored by King and Parliament alike. The King's proclamation of August 23 clarified the British determination to crush the rebellion, and by that time both the colonies and Great Britain were preparing for full-scale war.

"We have been seduced into a war," wrote Edmund Burke to Lord Rockingham in August. "War indeed is become a sort of substitute for commerce,

> . . . *the incredible increase of the Northern market . . . keeps up the spirits of the mercantile world and induces them to consider the American war not so much as their calamity as their resource in an inevitable distress. This is the state of most not all the merchants.*[66]

Burke's observations spelled the doom of the hopes of many Americans and their British supporters that the Association and consequent loss of the American trade would create sufficient economic pressure in England to force the merchants to come to the aid of the colonies once again as they had in 1766 and 1768. Although in January the British merchants had made such an effort by sending petitions to Parliament, they did not press to be heard when their petitions were ignored. Some merchants, alienated by the increasing radicalism that had come to characterize colonial politics, were strongly progovernment; and, as Burke pointed out, the demand for British goods on the continent more than balanced the interruption of commerce with America.

At the opening of Parliament on October 26, 1775, King George III was confident. Earlier, on September 10, he had written to Lord North, "If the Opposition is powerful next session it will much surprize me, for I am fighting the battle of the legislature, therefore have a right to expect an almost unanimous support." Not only did he have numbers on his side, but justice, also: "I know the uprightness of my intentions," he had said to North, "and therefore am ready to stand every attack of ever so dangerous a kind with the firmness that honesty and an attachment to the constitution will support." [67]

Now facing a legislature that he knew supported him, the King was at ease in a speech that reflected his sentiments. Making only veiled references to the Americans' Olive Branch Petition—"The authors and promoters of this desperate conspiracy have . . . meant only to amuse . . . whilst they were preparing for a general revolt"—

he again reiterated the necessity to maintain the Empire:

> *The object is too important, the spirit of the* British *nation too high, the resources with which* God *hath blessed her too numerous, to give up so many Colonies which she has planted with great industry, nursed with great tenderness, encouraged with many commercial advantages, and protected and defended at much expense of blood and treasure.*

Expressing disappointment that the Americans did not realize that "to be a subject of *Great Britain* . . . is to be the freest member of any civil society in the known world," the King concluded that "It is now become the better part of wisdom . . . to put a speedy end to these disorders by the most decisive exertions." In short, the King informed Parliament that he had increased his naval establishment and that he was considering "friendly offers of foreign assistance." "When the unhappy and deluded multitude . . . shall become sensible of their error," he concluded, he would be "ready to receive the misled with tenderness and mercy."[68]

Charles Watson-Wentworth, Second Marquess of Rockingham (1730-1782)

Despite their minority status, the Opposition would not allow the King's militant policy to go unchallenged. Again they rose to express their dissent. Long, brilliant, and bitter speeches followed the royal decision for war from members of the various Whig factions who nevertheless could not unite to command a majority in either house.

Heading the stalwarts in the Opposition was the Marquess of Rockingham, a man of great wealth and family position, whose career was grounded on a sense of duty rather than political ability. Horace Walpole described him as "ambitious, with excessive insolence, fond of talking business but dilatory in the execution."[69]

The course of Rockingham's career had been set in 1765 when he took over a new coalition ministry during the turbulent aftermath of the Stamp Act. Responsible for the repeal of that act and for the passage of the controversial Declaratory Act, he had by his advocacy of the latter measure produced a fatal division within the Whig party on the question of the extent of British supremacy over the colonies. The party split had weakened the effectiveness of the Whig Opposition during the crucial years that followed.

Early in January 1775 Rockingham's secretary, Edmund Burke, had suggested to Rockingham the expediency of joining Chatham in Parliament on the question of American policy "though you may never come to an understanding with him in other politics." But Rockingham could not agree with Chatham, who was ready to qualify the principle of British supremacy by admitting the existence of certain natural rights. His refusal to come to Chatham's aid spelled the failure of Chatham's conciliatory proposal. But Rockingham realized the validity of his secretary's warning that the Whigs must exert every effort to prevent the "full and decided engagement of parliament in this war."[70] On October 26, then, Rockingham made the effort.

The Whig leader did not disguise his contempt for the royal decision to make war on the colonies. "The measures recommended from the Throne," he said, "were big with the most portentous and ruinous consequences." Because Parliament had not been truly informed "of the true state and conditions of the Colonies," "injudicious and inefficacious" measures had been effected from which "no salutary end was reasonably to be expected." Parliament must review the proceedings if it were to bring

107.
CHARLES WATSON-WENTWORTH,
second Marquess of Rockingham.
Studio of Joshua Reynolds, date
unknown. National Portrait Gallery, London.

order to the "distracted affairs" of the British Empire and avoid resorting "to the alarming and dangerous expedient of calling in foreign forces . . . and the still more dreadful calamity of shedding *British* blood by *British* hands." To this end, he offered an amendment to the proposed response of the House of Lords to the King's speech that would indicate that "the disorders and discontents in the *British* Colonies rather increased than diminished by the means which have been used to suppress and allay them" and that these means, "not originally well-considered, or properly adapted to answer the ends to which they were directed," required reexamination.[71]

Among the supporters of Rockingham's amendment in the House of Lords were two distinguished peers of a liberal cast of mind who were offended by "the madness and absurdity" of those who expected to reduce the colonies by coercive measures.

George William Coventry was described by Horace Walpole as "a grave young Lord" when he succeeded his father to the earldom in 1751. A member of a Tory family, he was surprisingly independent in his views, although like most members of the British nobility he would never relinquish the principle of parliamentary supremacy. Nevertheless, he found the idea that the colonies could be conquered "wild and extravagant." Even if they were conquered, he told Parliament, they would be of "little value";

George William Coventry, Sixth Earl of Coventry (1722-1809)

171

108.
GEORGE WILLIAM, sixth Earl of
Coventry. Allan Ramsay, 1764.
Earl's Croome Court. [Not in
exhibition.]

Great Britain would be unable to maintain "for any considerable time, such a species
of dominion." [72] His reasons he gave at fuller length in another debate in March 1776.
"If you look on the map of the globe, and view Great Britain and North-America,
and compared the extent of both," he argued; "if you consider the soil, the harbours,
rivers, climate, and increasing population of the latter, nothing but the most obstinate
blindness and partiality can prevail on any man to entertain a serious opinion that such
a country will long continue under subjection to this." Instead of planning for war,
then, "we should vote a thanksgiving, and . . . leave America to itself, and . . . avail
ourselves of the only substantial benefit we can ever expect to derive from it, the
profits of an extensive commerce, and the strong support of a firm and friendly alliance for mutual defence and assistance." [73]

172

109.
CHARLES LENNOX. George
Romney, circa 1776. National
Portrait Gallery, London.

Charles Lennox, the Duke of Richmond, addressed himself to constitutional as well as practical aspects of the King's policy. Questioning the legality of the Crown's hiring Hanoverians without the consent of Parliament, he also pointed out the present weakness of British land and sea forces for such an enterprise as subjugating the Americans by force, and he reminded the Lords of the proven bravery of New Englanders.

An intimate adviser to Lord Rockingham, Richmond was a man of great influence, who had long been active as a friend of America. An "intrepid and tender" man, "inflexible and humane beyond example," according to Walpole, he had attempted to unite the two opposing factions in the Whig party—the Chathamites and Rockinghamites—but Chatham's caustic criticism of the Rockingham group's support of the Declaratory Act and his general unwillingness to cooperate made such a union impossible.

Richmond himself was ready to abandon the principle of the Declaratory Act. In the parliamentary debate of January 1775 he openly criticized it as anachronistic and impractical: "My own feelings and the bad use that has been made of that act," he told his fellow peers, "have convinced me that it is indefensible." [74]

With his failure to unite his party, however, and to stop the Tories from proceeding with their "ruinous" measures, Richmond gave up. When asked at the end of the year to come down to London from the country in order to oppose the government's bill prohibiting trade with the colonies, Richmond was reluctant to leave his dutchess alone "to do the Honours to 20 people in the House." Confessing to Rockingham that he felt "very languid about this American Business," he went on to insist that it was not opposition to one bill or another that would settle the matter, but "the whole System must be opposed." "The only thing that can restore common sense to this Country," he concluded, "is feeling the dreadfull consequences which must soon follow such diabolical measures." [75]

*Charles Lennox,
Third Duke of Richmond
and Lennox
(1735-1806)*

110.
JOHN MONTAGU, fourth Earl of
Sandwich. Joseph Highmore, 1740.
National Portrait Gallery, London.

John Montagu,
Fourth Earl of Sandwich
(1718-1792)

To the defense of the King's Address on October 26 rose the Earl of Sandwich, First Lord of the Admiralty and one of three top officers in the British cabinet. His record in that post was not glorious, or at least he had many detractors who insisted that he was to blame for the deterioration of the British navy during the first seven years he held his post (1771-78). Although the Admiralty was, as Sandwich once wrote, "the single object of my views," according to a member of his own party, Charles Middleton, such loyalty was not enough. Middleton complained in 1775 of Sandwich's "sad management" and asked, "Is it possible, my lord, that gentlemen who are at an office one day, and following their amusements or private concerns another, can carry on a line of business that requires not only great practical knowledge, but the closest application and attention?"[76]

Whatever his professional inefficiency, Sandwich was more than "zealous in [the] cause against the American rebels," a "pusillanimous" lot, as far as he was concerned, and a people with "the most traitorous and hostile intentions." Quite convinced that the Americans wanted "to free themselves from the restrictions laid on their commerce," he was determined to "render it impossible for the Americans either to resist, keep together, or subsist." To this end, once hostilities were underway, he worked hard to augment the navy's forces.[77]

On October 26 Sandwich was irate against his colleagues, who he believed were encouraging "the disorders in America" by their open and avowed support of the American rebels. Once force was brought against the colonists, he was confident that their "cowardice and want of spirit" would be revealed; and he was astonished that the power of the King on the aid of foreign troops should be even questioned.[78]

III.
AUGUSTUS HENRY FITZROY, third
Duke of Grafton. Nathaniel
Dance, date unknown. The Duke
of Grafton.

One more voice had to be heard against the King's Address before the majority would have its way and vote its acceptance and praise of it. This was the voice of Augustus Henry Fitzroy, third Duke of Grafton, a timid man but a longtime sympathetic friend of the colonies. Rising to the front ranks of politics more rapidly than his experience or talents warranted, he had been persuaded in 1766 to head the ministry dominated by William Pitt, the Earl of Chatham. Grafton had held the feeble government together after Pitt's retirement in 1767 until the North ministry was formed in 1770. Hoping to prevent extreme problems from arising with respect to the American colonies, he had then assumed the office of privy seal. But by the summer of 1775, administration measures had alienated him. He was especially alarmed to learn that

Augustus Henry Fitzroy,
Third Duke of Grafton
(1735-1811)

175

"no notice would be taken" of the Olive Branch Petition from the American Congress to the King. "It was evident to all considerate men," Grafton wrote in his *Autobiography*, "that the connection of the two countries hung on the decision." Unable to accept "the present desperate state of things," he wrote to Lord North in August asking him if there were not "sufficient matter in the contents" of the petition to warrant opening "some intercourse between [the] two parties."[79]

North's response left "no room for doubt" about the administration's stand: "Till the provinces have made some submission," he wrote, "it will be in vain to hope that they will come to any reasonable terms." The apprehensive minister then obtained an audience with the King to warn him that his ministers were not only impractical, but had "deluded themselves" and "were deluding his Majesty." But the King would not heed Grafton's warning. Instead, he informed him that a large body of German troops would soon join forces with Great Britain. Grafton could only reply to the astonished King that "twice that number would only increase the disgrace: and never effect his purpose."[80]

Thus, on the first day of the new Parliament, Grafton was in no mood to accept the King's Address. Overcoming his habitual reserve, he rose to condemn the measures recommended by the King and the conduct of the administration as well. The proposed Rockingham amendment was inadequate, he insisted, and he suggested in its place a bill to repeal all the acts passed in Parliament relative to America. "This," he claimed, ". . . will answer every end; and nothing less will accomplish any effectual purpose. . . ."

Although he suffered from "an indifferent state of health," Grafton vowed that he would "come down to this House in a litter" if necessary, "in order to express my full and hearty disapprobation of the matters now pursuing. . . .

> *Were I to lose my fortune and every other thing I esteem; were I to be*
> *reduced to beggary itself, the strong conviction and compulsion at once*
> *operating on my mind and conscience would not permit me to take any other*
> *part on the present occasion than that I now mean to adopt.*"[81]

Such a public expression of opposition no king in the eighteenth century could countenance. "I am curious to know whether the D. of Grafton, as his speeches in Parliament daily become more hostile, does not yet feel that it is at least most to his own credit to resign his employment," wrote the King to Lord North. "If not . . . I cannot let many days more elapse before I send for his seal."[82] The King gave Grafton one more "patient hearing," and then asked him on November 9 to relinquish his seal.

Charles James Fox
(1749-1806)

On October 26 the House of Lords gave its support to the King's Address by a vote of seventy-six to thirty-three. The victory of the majority was aided, some claimed, by Lord North's "slipping . . . bribes so elegantly under [the member's] ruffles."[83] When Rockingham's amendment failed, nineteen members of the opposition united to sign a formal protest against the rejection of the proposal, indicating in no uncertain terms that the signers could not

> *consent to an Address, which may deceive his Majesty and the publick into a*
> *belief of the confidence of this House in the present Ministers, who have*

R.ᵗHonᵇˡᵉ C.J. FOX.

112.
CHARLES JAMES FOX. Joshua
Reynolds, 1784. Lady Teresa
Agnew.

> *deceived Parliament, disgraced the nation, lost the Colonies, and involved
> us in a civil war, against our clearest interests, and upon the most unjustifiable
> grounds, wantonly spilling the blood of thousands of our fellow subjects.*[84]

In the House of Commons a similar protest was made, and an amendment identical to Rockingham's was submitted. One of the strongest independent leaders of the Whig Opposition in Commons, and one of the most fearless spokesmen for colonial rights— Charles James Fox—supported it. Condemning Lord North as the "blundering pilot" who had brought the nation to its present difficulties, he remarked that "Lord Chatham, the King of Prussia, nay, Alexander the Great never gained more in one campaign than the noble Lord has lost—he has lost a whole Continent." [85]

Fox was a wealthy young man with the reputation of being a "precocious rake," reared, like his father before him, "without the least regard to morality." [86] He was, however, richly endowed with natural abilities, including a good nature and cultivated tastes. Entering Parliament in 1768, by 1774 he was being singled out by the King, who found it necessary to give "the young Cub . . . a severe rap on the paws" for his outspoken criticism of administration policies.[87] Soon, he was dismissed from his government post for insubordination, thus beginning his lifelong battle against the excessive power of the Crown. He entered the camp of the Opposition with the object of destroying that power, which he saw as the source of the country's ills.

In the debate in the House of Commons on October 26, Fox justified American resistance to the "tryannical acts of a *British* Parliament." Lord North, claimed Fox, had spent as large a sum to acquire a "national disgrace" as Lord Chatham had expended "in gaining that glorious lustre with which he had encircled the British name." The administration, concluded Fox, should "place America where she stood in 1763, and . . . repeal every act passed since that period, which affected either her freedom or her commerce." [88]

Fox's philippic was to no avail. That day the Opposition was defeated in the Commons by a vote of 278 to 108. Spokesmen for the administration asserted the government's concern for "our unhappy fellow-subjects in America" who had been made "the instruments of the ambition and traitorous designs of those dangerous Men who have led them . . . to the standard of rebellion, and who have now assumed the powers of sovereign authority, which they exercise in the most despotick and arbitrary manner. . . ." Insisting that it had become "the part of wisdom . . . to put a speedy end to these disorders, by the most decisive exertions," the majority in Commons indicated its approval of the King's measures to quell the rebellion in America. Fox was impatient with such foolishness; he would not consent, he said, to "the bloody consequences of so silly a contest about so silly an object, conducted in the silliest manner that history, or observation, had ever furnished an instance of; and from which we were likely to derive nothing, but poverty, misery, disgrace, defeat, and ruin." [89]

A New Cabinet

With Grafton's resignation from the privy seal and his defection to the Opposition, Lord North was able to make cabinet changes that he had long seen as necessary. Lord Dartmouth, whose indecisive and ambivalent feelings about the administration's

113.
GEORGE SACKVILLE GERMAIN.
George Romney, 1778. L.G.
Stopford Sackville.

American policy had made him sullen and unhappy and—even more important— obnoxious to the war party, was given Grafton's privy seal, an office that he assumed happily since it removed him from cabinet decision-making. In Dartmouth's place as secretary of state for the colonies was placed Lord George Germain, one of the most hawklike members of the House of Lords.

The North wartime cabinet pleased the King. "I think the present arrangement will in every light greatly strengthen our hands," he wrote North on November 7. In the sense that Sandwich and Germain were hardline administration supporters, he was quite right. There was no question that stern measures would now be applied to the colonial rebellion.

Lord Germain was a talented administrator, whose cold and obstinate personality alienated him from "even . . . his political allies."[90] At the time of his appointment, the prime minister's brother wrote that he was "not without fears that Ld. George may be an unpleasant partner for Lord North. He is not a popular man and is reckoned impracticable and ambitious." A contemporary Whig historian put it less kindly: "The most odious of tasks was assigned to the most odious of instruments."[91]

Germain was a wealthy aristocrat who had ruined his distinguished military career during the Seven Years' War through sheer disobedience of orders at the Battle of Minden in 1759. Promptly dismissed from the service by King George II, who hated him because of his friendship with his grandson, the young heir-apparent Prince George, as well as because of his unsavory military record, Germain determinedly

*George Sackville Germain,
First Viscount Sackville
(1716-1785)*

179

114.
WILLIAM WILDMAN BARRINGTON,
second viscount. W. A. Rainger
after Joshua Reynolds. Mezzotint,
1865. Lewis Walpole Collection.

worked to redeem himself from the accusation of the court-martial that deemed him "unfit to serve his Majesty in any military capacity."[92]

By 1775 Horace Walpole, who was accustomed to view hardline Tories caustically, had to admit that Lord George had "persisted to act in public till the uncommon excellence of his abilities had surmounted the load of contempt under which he had lain." Moreover, Germain's dedication to "a plan of coercion" toward the colonies convinced George III to abandon any scruples he might have held about Germain's participation in his government. Germain's return to favor and office proved as complete as his former disgrace had been; now he commanded the same army that he once had been forbidden to serve. As Walpole remarked, quoting lines written by Lord Lansdowne, "Some fall so hard, they bound and rise again."[93]

Lord Germain brought a new forcefulness to the American department with his policy of "bringing the rebels to their knees."[94] Constantly trying to live down "the Ghost of Minden," who was always being "brought in neck and shoulders to frighten him with," he was determined to achieve a brilliant military victory over the rebels. His appointment came as a warning to the colonies that Great Britain intended to use force to bring them to their senses.[95]

William Wildman Barrington *(1717-1793)*

William Wildman Barrington, who headed the army as secretary of war in Germain's cabinet, did not share Germain's absolute commitment to a hardline policy or optimism with respect to its ultimate success. Troubled by the ministry's policies, the loyal Lord Barrington based his objections on military considerations as well as principle. "The contest will cost us more than we can ever gain by the success," he wrote to Dartmouth in 1774; ". . . experience has shown us that we have not strength in that part

180

of our dominions to levy such against an increased opinion prevailing there." Beyond expediency, Barrington believed "we have no right" to lay taxes on the colonies. He was persuaded that there were many Britons who "persuaded of the right, doubt at least the equity of such taxation." [96]

General Amherst and General Harvey supported Barrington in his assessment of the military difficulties inherent in a land war in America. Believing that such an undertaking would have "gloomy consequences," Barrington pressed for a blockade of American ports as being the only effective military action. [97]

After Bunker Hill, however, the King's determination to press ahead with recruitment and enlistments was strengthened, much to Barrington's discomfort. Again, the concerned war secretary wrote to George III and Lord Dartmouth opposing the raising of large numbers of land troops: ". . . my own opinion always has been and still is," he wrote to Lord North on August 8, "that the Americans may be reduced by a fleet, but never can be by the army." [98] Barrington's advice was not heeded. Without consulting him, Lord North moved forward with his coercive policy.

By the fall of 1775 Barrington's opinions became an embarrassment to the administration. Writing to Lord North, William Eden suggested that Barrington be removed from his office, a measure that "would be . . . wise & popular . . . pregnant with good consequences." North rejected the suggestion, although he admitted that Barrington "has certainly talked too much about his opinion & may perhaps not be so active in promoting measures as we could wish." Barrington himself repeatedly submitted his resignation, but when the King refused to accept it, he loyally continued to carry out a policy of which he did not approve. His release from office finally came in 1778 after what Horace Walpole called "forty years of servility." [99]

COMMITMENT TO WAR: THE PROHIBITORY BILL, NOVEMBER 20— DECEMBER 22, 1775

By mid-November North's wartime cabinet was securely established and ready to meet colonial threats to imperial unity. When news arrived in the fall that the Americans had invaded Canada, the British were convinced that the colonists were not only in rebellion, but even more, bent upon conquest. Any doubts that some of the country gentlemen may have held about the wisdom of the stern measures adopted were dispelled; they acquiesced without protest to the proposal of a land tax of four shillings to meet wartime expenses.

On November 20 Lord North issued what the Opposition called "a declaration of war" on America—the Prohibitory Bill. The Whig Opposition remained lethargic. But still there were legislators in both Houses ready to rise to battle.

In the House of Commons, one of the fiercest spokesmen for the Opposition was the gentle David Hartley, a dedicated liberal and tireless worker for reform and an intimate friend and correspondent of Benjamin Franklin. A man of eccentric habits and odd dress that gave him the appearance of an eighteenth-century Puritan, he impressed all whom he met as a man of "deep conviction and high principle." "Mr. Hartley is more for peace than any man in the kingdom," wrote John Adams. [100]

David Hartley (1732-1813)

181

DAVID HARTLEY ESQ.
Member of Parliament for Kingston upon Hull,
and His Britannic Majesty's Minister Plenipotentiary appointed to treat with the United States of America.

115.
DAVID HARTLEY THE YOUNGER.
James Walker after George
Romney. Mezzotint, 1784. The
British Museum.

182

On December 7 this "friend of mankind" introduced a series of motions designed "to establish a permanent Reconciliation between Great Britain and its Dependencies in North America."[101] Speaking with "unusual anxiety . . . from the greatness of the object . . . upon which not only the fate of our times, but of all future ages, both in this country and *America*, will depend," Hartley pleaded that his "treaty of pacification" be adopted. America, he pointed out, had assented to the King's "plan of contribution freely upon requisition" in the Continental Congress's "Petition to the King." That petition had been "ungraciously dismissed"; but now he wished "to point out some definite mode and terms of reconciliation in compliance with the prayer of that Petition." His intention, he informed the Lords, was "to support the dignity of *Great Britain* as the parent State, to afford redress of grievances to *America*, to restore peace to this distracted empire, and to reunite its common interests and exertions into one common cause."[102]

Hartley's proposals failed. When the Prohibitory Bill was returned for further parliamentary debate, he made one last effort to voice the protest of the battle-worn Whigs. Expressing the hope that the force of opposition to the bill "may remain as a memorial that some of us at least lament this final separation of America with an affectionate regret," he clarified to his fellow members the significance of what they had done:

> *The fate of America is cast. You may bruise its heel, but you cannot crush its head. It will revive again. The new world is before them. Liberty is theirs. They have possession of a free government, their birthright and inheritance, derived to them from their parent state, which the hand of violence cannot wrest from them. If you will cast them off, my last wish is to them; may they go and prosper! When the final period of this once happy country shall overtake ourselves either through tumult or tyranny, may another Phoenix rise out of our ashes!* [103]

On December 22 the Prohibitory Bill was signed into law. Its preamble stated that because of the "open rebellion and defiance to the just and legal authority of the king and parliament of Great Britain" in the colonies all trade and commerce with them was prohibited on pain of forfeiture of all vessels and cargoes "as if the same were the ships and effects of open enemies."[104]

To Americans the Prohibitory Bill was a "piratical Act, or plundering Act, or Act of Independency." John Adams believed the latter to be most appropriate, for by the measure the "King Lords and Commons have united in sundering this country from that I think forever. It is," said Adams to Horatio Gates, a "compleat Dismemberment of the British Empire. It throws thirteen Colonies out of the Royal Protection, levels all distinctions, and makes us independent in spight of our supplications and entreaties."[105]

116.
ABIGAIL ADAMS. Mather Brown,
1785. New York State Historical
Association, courtesy of the White
House.

VI.

Flaming Arguments

F ive days after the "dreadful Battle" of Bunker Hill, Abigail Adams once again
took up pen to write to her husband in Philadelphia. Forced to leave her
"peaceful abode in Boston" to take refuge in her husband's native town of
Braintree, "liable every hour of the day and of the night to be butchered in
cold blood, or taken and carried into Boston as hostages, by any foraging or marauding
detachment of men," she was called upon to be mother, father, tutor, and nurse to her
four young children; housekeeper; farmer; manufacturer of cloth, clothing, soap and
saltpeter, and other necessities; friend to suffering neighbors; nurse to afflicted relatives; and informed correspondent of her statesman husband.[1]

*Abigail Smith Adams
(1744-1818)*

THE SIEGE OF BOSTON

Enduring it all with "patience and fortitude," for ten months Abigail lived, as did
other Bostonians, "in continual expectation of Hostilities." By July 5, 1775, the situation was unbearable. "The most cruel and despotick of Tyrants" had turned the residents of the town into "the most abject slaves." Forbidden to leave their houses "upon
pain of death," they "dared not . . . bee heard or seen to ask a Question." When she
was informed by correspondents and friends of the condition of the prisoners taken at
Bunker Hill, she was aroused to fresh complaints against the British. With no nursing
care or resting place except the street pavements and jail, they had "no fresh provisions. Their Beaf . . . is all gone, and their own [the British] wounded men die very
fast, so that they have raised a report that the Bullets were poisoned. Fish they cannot
have," she reported, because they had "rendered it so difficult to procure. . . ." To add
to the anxiety, civilians were being imprisoned by the British, "we know not for what
in perticulier."[2]

As the siege continued, the distress of the town's inhabitants increased, affecting the
families who had fled to safety in the homes of friends and relatives in the outlying
towns. Food shortages and crowding led to epidemics of dysentry, small pox, and what
seems to have been diphtheria (canker of the throat). "Woe follows Woe," wrote
Abigail on September 25, "and one affliction treads upon the heal of an other. . . . The

185

117.
Flag of the United Train of Artillery of Providence, Rhode Island. This unit took an important part in the siege of Boston, where the Company contributed "four brass field pieces and twelve 18 and 24 pounders." Rhode Island Historical Society.

desolation of War is not so distressing as the Havock made by the pestilence. . . . Wherefore is it that we are thus contended with?"[3] The following week, Abigail's suffering was increased by the death of her beloved mother, Elizabeth Quincy Smith, after sixteen days of severe illness. "Have pity upon me," she cried to her husband, "have pitty upon me o! thou my beloved for the Hand of God presseth me soar." Still able to view her tragedy in the perspective of the large one that encompassed the country, she reported, "Tis a dreadful time with this whole province. Sickness and death are in almost every family. I have no more shocking and terible Idea of any Distemper except the Plague than this."[4]

By October, "no language [could] paint the distress of the inhabitants, most of them destitute of wood and of provision of every kind." The townspeople were "desperate and contriveing means of escape." The starving, the accidental firings that killed civilians as well as soldiers and drove "men, women and children screaming" in distress, hardened Bostonians' hearts against the British and made them determined to send "some of them to Heaven for mercy."[5] The worse the situation grew, the more outspoken did the people become about the necessity for independence. "Let us separate," wrote Abigail angrily on November 12; "they are unworthy to be our Breathren. Let us renounce them and instead of supplications as formerly for their prosperity and happiness, Let us beseach the almighty to blast their counsels and bring to Naught all their devices."⁶ Abigail was not alone. Earlier, in October, on visiting the American camp in Boston, a Dr. Belknap found that "the plan of independence was fast become a favorite point in the army and that it was offensive to pray for the king."⁷

On July 2, 1775, General George Washington, newly appointed commander in chief of the American forces, took over his command in Boston. Abigail reported that his appointment gave "universal satisfaction." She was particularly "struck" with the Virginia general: "Dignity with ease, and complacency, the Gentleman and Soldier look agreably blended in him. Modesty marks every line and feature of his face."⁸

Washington's job was to bring order to a motley group of militia that had streamed into Massachusetts following the Provincial Congress's appeal for help, and mold them into an effective defense force. New England militia were already in control of the town. Although they had lost Bunker Hill to the British—at staggering costs for the victors—they had successfully thrown a ring around the town, isolating General Howe in Charlestown on the now-fortified hill, and Gage at Boston Neck, looking to his scattered defenses on the points, hills, and wharves of Boston. Colonial militia held Winter Hill and Prospect Hill, and had strengthened the important posts around to Roxbury. "They have fortified all the Passes and Heights round this Town from Dorchester to Medford or Mystick, and it's not impossible for them to annoy the Town," Gage had written home pessimistically on June 23. Gage's pessimism was well-founded. The major problem facing the Americans now was to obtain enough large guns to cause the annoyance, he predicted. This became the assignment, and the achievement, of Henry Knox, one of the ablest military leaders to emerge during the Revolutionary War.⁹

Professionally, Henry Knox was a bookseller, the owner of a successful shop on Cornhill in Boston that was "a great resort for the British officers and Tory ladies."¹⁰ Son of a shipmaster who had died when Henry was twelve, leaving him the sole support of his mother, the young man early had revealed his capacity for enterprise and his interest in military affairs. While still a youth, he had joined the militia corps called "The Train," which later captured the three brass three-pounder guns that rendered such excellent service on the nineteenth of April. When "The Train" gave way to the "Boston Grenadier Corps," Lieutenant Knox was made second in command. Continuing to study military science, he maintained his men in good training, poised for the day when they would prove serviceable to the "patriot" cause.

Knox's romantic courtship of Lucy Flucker, daughter of the royal secretary of the province, gave a storybook cast to his career. In 1774 the couple were married despite the opposition of her Tory parents; and a year later, soon after Lexington and Concord, they were forced to flee Boston because of Gage's close surveillance of Knox's activities in helping the militia set up fortifications around the city. Legend has it that Lucy had sewn into her petticoats Henry's militia sword to avoid creating suspicions among the sentries at the various check points between Boston and Worcester.

Once Knox had settled Lucy safely in Worcester, he returned to the army in Bos-

Henry Knox
(1750-1806)

118.
HENRY KNOX. Charles Peale Polk
after Charles Willson Peale, date
unknown. National Portrait
Gallery, Smithsonian Institution.

ton to help establish two fortresses at Roxbury and fortifications for anticipated military action at Bunker Hill. In the fall of 1775 General Washington, appreciating Knox's engineering skills and special talent for organizing men and materiel, asked him to take over command of the artillery—and obtain artillery to command. Knox suggested that the British artillery captured at Fort Ticonderoga through the exertions of Allen and Arnold would provide just the relief the town required. Immediately, the commander in chief directed the "bulky young Bostonian" to organize an expedition for the purpose. The "want" of guns, said Washington in his instructions, "is so great that no trouble or expense must be spared to obtain them."[11]

Three hundred miles stretched between Boston and the storehouse of weapons at Fort Ticonderoga in New York. But Washington had chosen his man well. Knox possessed resiliency, courage, and a robust exuberance that quickly impressed the men he led. Making his way first to New York City to survey the army's artillery there and secure supplies and men, he then—late in November—set out for Albany, Saratoga, and Lake George northward to the fort, collecting men and supplies along the way. At Ticonderoga, Knox was able to assemble sixty tons of heavy artillery. Proceeding "down the w. bank of the Hudson as far as Albany, then to cross the river and down the e. Bank as far as Kinderhook, from whence to turn due e. across the Berkshires, through Great Barrington, Monterey, Otis, Blandford, Westfield, Springfield, and so to Cambridge," Knox soon discovered that what had at first seemed like an easy plan was not so easily implemented.[12] His heavy load constantly had to be rescued from sinking into Lake George, which had become unfrozen as a result of unseasonably warm weather. It took a whole week to traverse the thirty-three-mile length of the lake. But this was merely the beginning. Blizzards assaulted the hardy group as they pulled their load through the vicious terrain of the Berkshires, where roads turned unexpectedly into chasms and gorges, and steep grades ended in swamps and rivers. Even the ebullient Knox was forced to admit that it was "almost a miracle that people with heavy loads should be able to get up and down such hills as are here."[13]

At Westfield, Massachusetts, the worst of the trip was over. By then, Knox and his "noble train of Artillery" had become a curiosity show.[14] People crowded throughout the countryside to view Knox and his cannon, and the event turned into a festive occasion, with Knox not denying himself any of the celebration. At Springfield, some of Knox's men quit, but by enlisting local men, he was able to make the final trek to Framingham. On January 24, 1776, Knox greeted Washington and presented him with the fifty-nine cannon and mortars he had so arduously but persistently heaved from Ticonderoga.

While Henry Knox and his small band of militia laboriously made their way northwestward to Ticonderoga, Washington was restlessly surveying the Boston scene, seeking an opportunity to drive the British out of the town. Washington disliked inactivity, especially since he feared that the British would soon strike out again at the American forces surrounding them. Unknown to Washington, Howe and Gage had no such intention: the British were as fearful of the Americans as the Americans were of them. Only Sir Henry Clinton among the British military leaders called for immediate attack upon the Americans ensconced on Dorchester Heights. Clinton had guessed accurately that the Americans could not withstand such an attack so soon after Bunker

John Thomas
(1724-1776)

119.
JOHN THOMAS. Benjamin Blyth.
Pastel, 1777. Massachusetts
Historical Society.

Hill. But his advice was not heeded, and as the days passed into weeks, Washington was able to take advantage of British delays to refortify his positions around Boston.

How to maintain the extensive American line without sufficient ammunition or supplies and without a well-molded, disciplined army was Washington's problem. Marching, drilling, disciplining, sanitizing, and pulling 17,000 men into cohesive units was a fulltime job, made even more difficult by the fact that the army was constantly vanishing under his eyes as terms of enlistment came to an end. To bring order into the situation, Washington came to depend on a few trusted officers, the most faithful of whom was Brigadier General John Thomas of Kingston, Massachusetts.

A trained surgeon, Dr. John Thomas had joined the colonial forces during the French and Indian War, serving bravely in Nova Scotia and in Amherst's expedition to Canada. Retiring to a practice in Kingston, he was honored in 1770 by the appointment of justice of the peace. Soon, civilian duties gave way to renewed military activity when he joined the Sons of Liberty and raised a volunteer regiment. In February 1775 the Provincial Congress of Massachusetts chose him as one of the five general officers of the province's troops, and soon after, he was elected brigadier general by the Continental Congress.

General Thomas was a man of strong principles, who maintained high standards of patriotism and expected the same from others. When, early in April 1775, panic broke out in several New England harbor towns which feared attack from a hovering British navy, Thomas chastised the people for not possessing "a Greater Firmness and Resolution which the Times we Live in Requires." "Be not Terrefyed at Every Shadow and the Chat of Every Timerious Person," he warned his wife when she expressed concern at the possibility of British vessels raiding Plymouth.[15]

The YANKEY's return from CAMP.

FATHER and I went down to camp,
  Along with Captain Gooding,
There we fee the men and boys,
  As thick as hafty pudding.
        Yankey doodle keep it up.
Chorus.   Yankey doodle, dandy,
    Mind the mufic and the ftep,
    And with the girls be handy.
And there we fee a thoufand men,
  As rich as 'Squire David ;
And what they wafted every day,
  I wifh it could be faved.
        Yankey doodle, &c.
The 'laffes they eat every day,
  Would keep a houfe a winter :
They have as much that I'll be bound
  They eat it when they're a mind to.
        Yankey doodle, &c.
And there we fee a fwamping gun,
  Large as a log of maple,
Upon a ducid little cart,
  A load for father's cattle.
        Yankey doodle. &c.
And every time they fhoot it off,
  It takes a horn of powder—
It makes a noife like father's gun,
  Only a nation louder.
        Yankey doodle, &c.
I went as nigh to one myfelf,
  As 'Siah's underpining ;
And father went as nigh again,
  I tho't the deuce was in him.
        Yankey doodle, &c.
Coufin Simon grew fo bold,
  I tho't he would have cock'd it :
It fcar'd me fo, I fhrink'd it off,
  And hung by father's pocket.
        Yankey doodle, &c.
And captain Davis had a gun,
  He kind of clapt his hand on't,

And fluck a crooked ftabbing iron
  Upon the little end on't.
        Yankey doodle, &c.
And there I fee a pumpkin fhell
  As big as mother's bafon,
And ev'ry time they touch'd it off,
  They fcamper'd like the nation.
        Yankey doodle, &c.
I fee a little barrel too,
  The heads were made of leather,
They knock'd upon't with little clubs,
  And call'd the folks together.
        Yankey doodle, &c.
And there was captain Wafhington,
  And gentlefolks about him,
They fay he's grown fo tarnal proud,
  He will not ride without 'em.
        Yankey doodle, &c.
He got him on his meeting clothes,
  Upon a flapping ftallion,
He fet the world along in rows,
  In hundreds and in millions.
        Yankey doodle, &c.
The flaming ribbons in their hats,
  They look'd fo taring fine, ah,
wanted pockily to get,
  To give to my Jemimah.
        Yankey doodle, &c.
I fee another fnarl of men
  A digging graves, they told me,
So tarnal long, fo tarnal deep,
  They 'tended they fhould hold me.
        Yankey doodle, &c.
It fcar'd me fo, I hook'd it off,
  Nor ftop'd, as I remember
Nor turn'd about 'till I got home,
  Lock'd up in mother's chamber.
        Yankey doodle, &c.

120.
The lyrics of "The Yankey's
return from Camp," sung to the
tune of "Yankee Doodle."
American Antiquarian Society.

Thomas's sense of personal honor was as steadfast as his courage. When the Continental Congress named two brigadier generals as his seniors, both of whom had previously served under Thomas, the slighted general found it impossible to submit to their command and decided to resign. Immediately, Washington and Charles Lee protested his decision, reminding him that "when the liberties of your country, the fate of posterity, the rights of mankind are at stake, to indulge our resentments for any ill treatment we may have received as individuals" was ill-timed.[16] "For the sake of your bleeding country, your devoted province, your charter rights, and by the memory of those brave men who have already fell in this great cause," wrote Washington to the sensitive but patriotic Thomas, "I conjure you to banish from your mind every suggestion of anger and disappointment. . . ."[17] The generals' entreaties made an impact on Thomas and he consented to remain. Eventually, he was restored to command, and on March 4, 1776, it was General Thomas who was responsible for the speedy fortifications of Dorchester Heights that resulted in the evacuation of the British two weeks later.

General William Howe
(1729-1814)

BY HIS EXCELLENCY

WILLIAM HOWE,

MAJOR GENERAL, &c. &c. &c.

AS Linnen and Woolen Goods are Articles much wanted by the Rebels, and would aid and affist them in their Rebellion, the Commander in Chief expects that all good fubjects will ufe their utmoft Endeavors to have all fuch Articles convey'd from this Place: Any who have not Opportunity to convey their Goods under their own Care, may deliver them on Board the Minerva at Hubbard's Wharf, to *Crean Bruſh,* Eſq; mark'd with their Names, who will give a Certificate of the Delivery, and will oblige himſelf to return them to the Owners, all unavoidable Accidents accepted.

If after this Notice any Perſon ſecretes or keeps in his Poffeffion ſuch Articles, he will be treated as a Favourer of Rebels.

Bofton, March 10th, 1776.

121.
Broadside issued by General
William Howe ordering Bostonians
to deliver up their linen and woolen
goods or be "treated as a Favourer
of Rebels." March 10, 1776.
Massachusetts Historical Society.

On the morning of March 5—the fifth anniversary of the Boston Massacre—General William Howe awoke to a threatening sight. Facing his encampment on Dorchester Heights were two American forts, a line of artillery, and more than three thousand men. The effort of the Americans stunned him. Writing to Lord Dartmouth later of the miraculous feat, he insisted that "The rebels have done more in one night than my whole army would have done in a month. . . . It must have been the employment of at least twelve thousand men." One of his officers corroborated Howe's report: the fortifications, he wrote, "were raised with an expedition equal to that of Genii belonging to Aladden's Wonderful Lamp."[18] The British might have been even more fearful had they realized that General George Washington had joined his men on the Heights and was eagerly awaiting a confrontation.

On October 10, 1775, William Howe had succeeded Gage as commander of the British forces in North America. Without question superior to Gage in ability, Howe was only slightly better informed than his predecessor as to the temper of the people he had come to intimidate. He did, however, respect New England courage, and he was a realist. When he realized how much it had cost the British to maintain Charlestown Heights in the battle of Bunker Hill, he dreaded the possibility of having to storm lines made even more formidable by months of hard labor and hard-won heavy artillery. He also realized that if he took one of the fortified hills surrounding Boston Harbor, the Americans would simply fortify another. "The intrenched positions the rebels had taken" promised a hazardous campaign, he wrote to Dartmouth, suggesting that he be allowed to evacuate his troops after reinforcements arrived. Further south, he believed, the British would be in a better position to penetrate the country.[19]

Forced to remain in Boston at least through the winter, Howe set his men to work enlarging the fortifications at Bunker Hill and Boston Neck. Issuing proclamations that not only frightened but antagonized the people he was sent to subdue, he otherwise maintained a curious inactivity that convinced later historians that Bunker Hill had seriously weakened his fighting spirit and rendered him incapable of taking advantage of some great opportunities to crush the rebellion. Charles Lee called Howe "indolent, badly educated, and a poor thinker": "He shut his eyes, fought his battles, drank his bottle, had his little whore, advised with his consellors, received his orders from North and Germain (one more absurd than the other), took Galloway's opinion, shut his eyes, fought again. . . ." [20]

Whatever the reasons for his paralysis, there is no question that Howe refused to take the "Bull by the horns," and when confronted by Washington's frighteningly quick fortification of the heights, chose to fight another day. He did attempt—futilely— to fire on the forts, but they were too high for his cannonade to reach. He also decided to attack with 2,200 men under Brigadier General Jones, but the troops who, it is reported, looked "pale and dejected and told each other 'It will be another Bunker's Hill affair or worse'," were spared. That night a gale arose that made any expedition or landing impossible. The storm served as a convenient excuse. By time it had passed over, the American forts were impregnable. So well, indeed, had Washington's men done their job that Washington "could not forbear lamenting his disappointment at not meeting the enemy." [21]

With attack rendered impossible, Howe's only alternative was to save the army and evacuate the city, an unpleasant decision because it was an admission of his incapacity to judge his enemy adequately. Having written some rather bold letters home scorning the idea that he was endangered by the "rebels," he now had to admit that his whole army was not strong enough to face their attack. Moreover, in his effort to secure reinforcements from England, he had advised the ministry that his army should be retained at Boston until more troops arrived. Now, just as he was sailing from the harbor, he received the reply of the ministry approving his earlier resolution to remain at Boston and confirming his belief that evacuation "under such circumstances, would be an unadvisable measure." [22]

To the Tories who had remained in Boston secure in the protection of the British army, Howe's decision to evacuate came as a complete surprise. They did not delay packing, however, in preparation for exile at Halifax, Nova Scotia, perhaps eventually London.

Throughout the evacuation of Boston, an implicit understanding arose between Washington and Howe. If Washington did not attack the British, Howe would refrain from burning the city. When the process of evacuation seemed to slow down, Washington hastened the British exit on March 16 by taking Nook's Hill. His message was heeded: the following day the British sailed out of Boston, carrying with them "every thing they could [po]ssibly take," according to Abigail Adams, "and what they could not they have burnt, broke, or hove into the water." Boston was "once more the Habitations of Americans" and Massachusetts was free of British interference for the remainder of the war.[23]

By Washington's side in the triumphal entry into Boston of the Continental Army rode Henry Knox. The honor shown him was highly deserved, since it was the artillery he had so laboriously hauled from Ticonderoga that played such a significant part in ending the siege. John Thomas was promoted to major general and was immediately called to command the American forces around Quebec. Arriving on May 1 to assume command he contracted small pox a month later and died, June 2, at Sorel, Canada. Knox, however, lived to contribute his invaluable service to the country throughout the years of war and peace that followed the siege and liberation of Boston.

Washington's Navy

As General Washington assessed his position in Boston during the eleven months that the town lay under siege, he came to realize the importance of organizing a navy. The royal fleet guarding the entrance to Boston Harbor offered protection to the supply ships that sailed in and out of the port bearing replenishments of food, war materiel, and ammunition to the besieged troops. If some of these ships could be captured, the hardpressed American army would be the beneficiary. Moreover, some effort had to be made, he realized, to prevent the British fleet—powerful in 1775 with its 270 vessels—from invading the American colonies whose shores, marked by estuaries and navigable rivers, were easily accessible by water. Even a small flotilla of six schooners and a brigantine would be useful, Washington decided. Since the Congress had not yet taken formal steps toward establishing a navy, however, he was forced to rely on his own resourcefulness. For help in devising a plan for creating an informal navy, Washington turned to John Glover, colonel of the Twenty-First Marblehead Regiment.

John Glover (1732-1797)

John Glover had spent his life dealing with men whose living depended on the ocean. Born in Salem, Massachusetts, he had moved at a young age with his widowed mother and three brothers to Marblehead where he made his reputation. By the 1760s the young man had earned enough money as a cobbler and dealer in liquors and rum to become a merchant shipowner engaged in trade with the West Indies, the Iberian peninsula, and the southern colonies. Occasionally, he had assumed command of his own ships, an experience that served him well when Washington approached him requesting aid.

As a prosperous merchant, Glover was considered an important member of his community in 1775. He had already demonstrated his political sympathies by serving on the local committee of correspondence from 1772 to 1774 and by joining the province's militia. Starting as an ensign in the Third Military Foot Company of Marblehead, he had earned the rank of captain in the militia by 1773. When hostilities between the Whig and Tory factions within Massachusetts increased to the point that the provincial government decided to demand the resignation of Tory officers, Glover was commissioned second lieutenant colonel, third in command. Three weeks after Lexington and Concord, he was made commander of the unit. By the end of May the Provincial Congress was ready to vote him a colonel's rank in the emerging Massachusetts army.

With customary vigor, Glover recruited for his new regiment, calling upon the local fishermen whom he had previously trained as minutemen and whose skills were equally effective on land and on sea. His regiment was run "with the quarter-deck efficiency of a sea captain," an efficiency which was noted when his unit was incorporated in June 1775 into the American army as the Twenty-First Regiment.[24] Attracted by the sturdiness of Glover's men, General Washington favored them as guards for his headquarters; but their test as military men was to come when they were called upon for their naval skills.

When Washington approached John Glover with his plan to harass the British navy, he had decided to outfit a single ship for a trial run. Glover, an experienced

B.·Gen Glover
marblehead, 1794,
        nov. 13

122.
JOHN GLOVER. John Trumbull.
Pencil, 1794. Park McCullough
House Association, North Ben-
nington, Vermont. [Original not in
exhibition.]

merchant and seaman, was to furnish the vessel, oversee its transformation from a
trading ship to an armed warship, and provide it with a trained crew. Glover's merchant ship the *Hannah* was selected for the experiment, and Glover's old friend and
trusted business associate, Nicholson Broughton, was chosen to serve as captain. The
ship was outfitted at Glover's wharf in Beverly, Massachusetts, and instructions were
given on September 2, 1775. Broughton and his men were ordered to capture British
ships bound in and out of Boston and seize all men and supplies. For pay, they would
receive a division of the prize money, and the captured vessels were to be sent to ports
near Washington's encampment.

The career of the *Hannah* was not successful. On its first run, the crew recaptured from the British a ship which turned out to be an American vessel, the *Unity*; and although the results were useful to the American cause, the crew received no bounty from the exploit. A few days later, the dissatisfied men mutinied, and a new crew had to be provided. On October 10, while fleeing from a British warship, the *Hannah* ran aground outside Beverly, where townsmen disarmed her in order to prevent her artillery from falling into British hands. By the end of the month, the *Hannah* was retired.

But she had served her purpose. Washington was convinced that his naval idea was valid and decided to ask for two more vessels. His request coincided with the decision of the Continental Congress on October 5 to build and equip an American fleet.

A Continental Navy, October 5—November 5, 1775

The first official suggestion for the Continental Navy came from the Rhode Island Assembly on August 26, 1775, when it instructed its delegates to the Congress "to use their whole influence . . . for building at the Continental expense a fleet of sufficient force for the protection of these colonies." [25] The suggestion created some dissension within the halls of the Pennsylvania State House. New Englanders, who had already outfitted and commissioned armed vessels to patrol their coastal areas, favored Rhode Island's proposal. Southerners were more reluctant to enter into such an expense, while conservatives from all the colonies opposed any action that would make reconciliation with Great Britain more difficult. A few believed it would be "sheer madness to send ships out upon the sea to meet the overwhelming naval force of England." [26]

In early October news reached the Congress almost at the same time as it reached Washington that two unarmed and unescorted British military supply ships were on the high seas bound for Quebec. The situation was too tempting to be ignored, especially by those who, like John Adams, ardently favored the creation of an American navy. On October 19 Adams wrote to James Warren, "What think you of an American Fleet? I don't mean 100 ships of the Line," he hastened to add, but a small force capable of limited action.[27] Debating the issue in the Congress, the New Englander won his point. By the end of the month the Congress had authorized four armed vessels and appointed Adams and six others to a naval committee. Three weeks later, Adams was ready with a draft of "rules for the government of the American navy." On November 5 Congress appointed Esek Hopkins of Rhode Island commander in chief, and on the twenty-fifth passed resolutions establishing a continental fleet.

Esek Hopkins (1718-1802)

Esek Hopkins's appointment as commander in chief of the new American navy reflected not only his reputation as a capable seaman and captain during the French and Indian War but also the influence of geography and politics in decision-making that frequently characterized eighteenth-century governmental bodies. Hopkins's brother, Stephen, formerly governor of Rhode Island and now one of that colony's distinguished representatives in the Continental Congress, was a member of Adams's naval committee and had contributed to the new navy one of the ships as well as a considerable number of men for the crew. Rhode Island's eagerness for a navy, as we have seen, was the first step toward the creation of a continental navy, and in recognition of that colony's interest, the Congress had determined that it would receive first choice of the com-

ADMIRAL HOPKINS
Commandeur en Chef de Flotte Americaine des XIII.
Provinces unies.
Se vend a Londres chez Thom. Hart.

123.
ESEK HOPKINS. Unidentified engraver. Mezzotint, 1776. Anne S. K. Brown Military Collection, Brown University Library.

manding officers, a plum that fell to the fifty-seven-year-old Esek. The other commands were also distributed on the basis of geography and as a result of the wielding of political influence by delegates from those colonies that took a special interest in the enterprise.

"A most experienced and venerable officer," Esek Hopkins was also fiercely independent. Arriving in Philadelphia on January 5, 1776, he received orders from the Naval Committee to proceed directly to the Chesapeake Bay, there to attack and destroy all enemy naval forces if they were not too strong. He was also presented with Adams's rules outlining discipline, management, and care of crews; procedures for captured vessels; and methods of carrying on communication with the Congress and Washington. Once the Chesapeake Bay area was secured, he was to continue south, eliminating the British forces in the waters of the Carolinas. Then he was to proceed north to Rhode Island on a similar mission. He also was to take command of all supply vessels captured in the name of the Continental Navy, and once the prisoners and cargo had been disposed of, he was empowered to appoint new officers for the captured ships. His orders ended with a clause granting him independent judgment in the case of bad weather, "unfortunate accident, or disaster," just so long as the ends were "useful to the American cause" and would "distress the enemy." [28]

Immediately, the Yankee captain took advantage of the clause in his orders and designed his own action. Setting sail from Delaware on February 17, 1766, the fleet headed not for the Chesapeake Bay, but for New Providence in the Bahamas where a supply of artillery and powder was known to be stored. The fleet arrived on March 1. Two days later a landing party of two hundred marines and fifty sailors under the command of Captain Samuel Nicholas was organized and with very little effort captured Fort Montague, halfway between the shore and the town. Inside the fort were seventeen cannon.

Meanwhile, Captain Hopkins had heard that in the main fort at Nassau more than two hundred men were stationed, guarding another supply of powder and military equipment. To avoid confrontation, he issued a statement to the islanders stating that his purpose was merely

> *To take possession of the powder and warlike stores belonging to the crown and if I am not opposed in putting my design in execution, the persons and property of the inhabitants shall be safe, neither shall they be suffered to be hurt in case they make no resistance.*[29]

His promise was accepted. The governor surrendered the keys to Fort Nassau and permitted the men to enter. There they found seventy-one cannon, fifteen brass mortars, and four casks of powder.

On March 16-17 Hopkins and his fleet set sail for Rhode Island. Two weeks later, at Block Island, they captured several British vessels—a six-gun schooner, an eight-gun brig, and two merchant ships. That night, April 5, the fleet met the *Glascow*, a twenty-gun ship carrying 150 men. In the ensuing battle, Hopkins lost ten men, while eight were wounded; the *Glascow* suffered only one man lost, three wounded, but was so badly hit that she was forced to return to England for repairs. Hopkins failed to pursue her because, as he later reported,

> *it would have brought an Action with the whole of the fleet and as I had upwards of thirty of our best Seamen on board the Prizes, and some that were on board had got too much Liquor out of the Prizes to be fit for duty.*[30]

The failure of the Continental Navy to subdue the *Glascow* and Hopkins's hesitancy to pursue later earned him the censure of the Congress.

For the time being, however, Hopkins's expedition was deemed a success. Hopkins himself, as John Paul Jones, then a lieutenant on one of his ships, wrote, was "respected throughout the fleet and I verily believe that the officers and men in general would go

124.
Esek Hopkins's sword. Professor
John K. Latimer.

to any length to execute his orders."[31] The Marine Committee, in turn, suggested that a schooner be purchased and rechristened *Hopkins*.

Hopkins's success spread confidence throughout the land and undoubtedly contributed much to the people's willingness to risk their lives and fortunes for independence. Local incidents along the Atlantic coast also dramatized to reluctant Americans the need for separation. In particular, "flaming" Falmouth provided, as Washington himself predicted, a persuasive argument.[32]

FLAMING FALMOUTH, OCTOBER 18, 1775

On October 18, 1775, British gunships acting under orders from Admiral Samuel Graves opened fire on the coastal town of Falmouth, Massachusetts, now Portland, Maine. By evening, only ashes remained where once the small town had stood, and the townspeople were left to face the onslaught of a northern winter without shelter, food, or supplies. "Truly, 'their tender mercies are cruelties,' " wrote General Greene to Governor Ward, Rhode Island's delegate to the Continental Congress. As news of Falmouth reached other seaport towns, their inhabitants also gathered up their belongings and fled to the country, fearful of similar feats of retaliation directed against them by "commissioned pirates and licensed robbers."[33]

The devastation of Falmouth marked the culmination of Admiral Samuel Graves's career as commander in chief of the British navy in North American waters. Appointed in March 1774, with orders to patrol the 1,800-mile American coast and St. Lawrence Seaway and to enforce the Boston Port Bill, Graves had arrived in Boston in July 1774, but for some reason, he chose to remain in that port until September 1775. A passive and timid commander, called by some an admiral of the harbor, Graves was incapable of carrying out the great responsibility with which he was burdened. He was further hampered by the poor condition of his twenty-five to thirty vessels, most of which were badly outfitted and undermanned, a reflection of the low condition to which the British navy had fallen under the administration of the Earl of Sandwich.

Samuel Graves (1713-1787)

In Boston Graves did provide Gage's army with support when necessary, since the army's only access to supplies during the long siege was the sea. Beyond this, he refused to act, preferring to consider the navy neutral in the conflict between the Americans and the British despite Bunker Hill and the presence of American militia encircling the town. "Our Boats moving Guard have often been fired at home from the Shore," he wrote, "But I have given the Captains of his Majesty's Ships and Vessels Orders not to fire again upon any account unless they are absolutely attacked and someone wounded or killed."[34]

Americans appreciated Graves's inactivity. It allowed them to accelerate their raids on the British encampments along the inlets of Boston Harbor. Rebel whale boats would sneak into shore, steal needed supplies, and burn British hay and lighthouses— all under the nose of Samuel Graves. The admiral soon learned that untrained American men at sea were just as effective as untrained American soldiers on land. By the time Graves was replaced in December 1775, the whale fleet had grown to 300 ships, and it was feared that any one of these unarmed vessels might capture a British warship.

Instead of increasing his naval operations and extending them into the waters up

125.
ALEXANDER FRAZER. Unidentified
engraver, date unknown. Maine
Historical Society. [Not in
exhibition.]

and down the coast, Graves called for more men. Soon, his superiors in England began
to wonder what he was doing in America. General John Burgoyne wrote to Lord
Germain in August 1775 that he could "only say what he is not doing." And Burgoyne
went on to catalogue Graves's inactivities: he was not supplying the camp with fresh
meat, he was not protecting herds on the islands off Boston Harbor, he was not preventing rebel ships from disturbing the British army. In short, he was "not doing
anything he should." [35]

Eventually, Graves could not ignore the barbed criticism of his dismal command.
In September he drew up a plan of retaliation and presented it to Gage. Once assuming an aggressive stand, Graves became viciously bold. Unable to stop the Americans
at sea, or unwilling to take the risk, he proposed destroying all coastal towns that aided
the rebels and committed crimes against Britain. Falmouth was to be first. According
to General Greene, Portsmouth in New Hampshire, Newport and Bristol in Rhode
Island, and other ports further south were marked for destruction. Graves's plan and
its execution did not subdue the rebellion; instead, it created "a blaze of indignation"
that made people wish, as Greene reported, "a declaration of independence." [36]

Captain Henry Mowat
(?-?)
and
Alexander Frazer
(?-?)

It was British Captain Henry Mowat who actually executed Graves's plan to burn
and lay waste towns along the northeast coast and destroy their shipping. Graves had
assigned to Mowat the gunships *Canceaux* and *Halifax*, together bearing fourteen
guns and seventy-five men, and additional schooners carrying one hundred extra
troopers. Falmouth was his destination.

For years Falmouth's sturdy pine forests had supplied British men-of-war with their
tall masts. In mid-May 1775, however, the local residents had threatened to detain

a shipment of masts to England, and Mowat had been sent to protect the outgoing vessel. In the process, he was captured by the zealous patriots and held for several hours before being released on bond. Overhearing threats to his life, Mowat escaped to his ship; but the Falmouth rebels continued to detain the mast ship, and in doing so, incurred the wrath of Admiral Graves and ensured Mowat's return visit.

On October 16 Mowat anchored once again in Falmouth Harbor and immediately dispatched Lieutenant Alexander Frazer to shore to deliver to its inhabitants notice of the town's punishment: "you have been guilty of the most unpardonable Rebellion," Mowat told the townspeople, and "a just Punishment" would be executed on them.[37] In two hours, Mowat informed them, their town would be burned.

Observing the "general distress increase, among the women and children in the Streets," Frazer agreed to relay the town's counterproposals to Mowat. Two hours later, a committee from the town stepped on board ship to bargain for time. Mowat was ready to compromise: if hostages and the town's cannon and ammunition were conveyed to him, he would present Falmouth's case to the authorities in Boston. Indicating that the cannon had already been removed from the town, the committee asked for more time to secure the weapons. Mowat gave them until eight o'clock in the evening; and when at that time eight to ten weapons were delivered to him, he accepted them as a sign of "good faith," while insisting that the remainder be delivered by nine o'clock the following morning.[38]

The citizens of Falmouth did not take advantage of the night's reprieve. Families were not sent away, supplies were not gathered, nor a militia mustered. Yet, sometime during the night, the townspeople must have summoned up their courage, for at nine o'clock the following morning they refused to comply with Mowat's orders. One inhabitant of Falmouth summarized their position:

> *Mowat having stated to the committee his only condition on which the town could be spared, and that was for the inhabitants to deliver up their arms and swear allegiance to his majesty the King George the third; this condition being inadmissable the town was sacrificed to the cause of Liberty and Patriotism as there was no other alternative.*[39]

Henry Mowat had no alternative either; at 9:40 he ordered firing to begin.

The firing continued all day. Dodging the "horrible shower of balls, from three to nine pound weights, bombs, carcasses, live shells, grape shot and musket balls," the townspeople attempted to secure their worldly goods. During the day, a party of British seamen and marines, led by Frazer, landed to set fire to the wharf, vessels, storehouses, and those parts of town not yet engulfed in flame. Frazer did his job well; he was later cited for his "spirited conduct, and activity in the execution of that duty." By six in the evening, Falmouth was entirely in flames, its storehouses, distilleries, and cargo ships destroyed, and four of its vessels captured. Only two of Mowat's men were wounded, and one man was lost.[40]

The burning of Falmouth was contrary to eighteenth-century standards of acceptable warfare. According to an unwritten code, military action was not to be taken against civilians or against enemy property. Falmouth, then, was "the sort of blunder which approaches a crime against one's cause," according to historian Allen French.[41] To the Americans, it symbolized British cruelty and terrorism. Instead of deterring

American privateering, it encouraged such plundering expeditions on a greater scale than ever. Later, the Continental Congress would appeal to "world opinion" and recommend to its own citizens that "cruelty should find no admission among a free people." Americans, warned the Continental Congress, should

> *take care that no pages in [their] annals . . . be stained by a recital of any action which justice or Christianity may condemn, and rest assured that whatever retaliation may be necessary or tend to their security, this Congress will undertake the disagreeable task.*[42]

THE BURNING OF NORFOLK, JANUARY 1, 1776

At four o'clock in the morning of New Year's Day, 1776, guns from British ships anchored in Norfolk harbor bombarded the town and landing parties set fire to warehouses on the waterfront. In town, American riflemen from North Carolina and Virginia retaliated by putting to the torch the luxurious homes of prominent Norfolk Tories. By the end of the day, most of Virginia's largest seaport had gone up in flames, and one more "flaming argument" was added to the expanding list of complaints the colonists were accumulating against "the best of Kings."

John Murray,
Earl of Dunmore
(1732-1809)

The firing of Norfolk had its origins in Virginia's earliest efforts to achieve colonial unity against what some of its leading radicals considered British tyranny. John Murray, Earl of Dunmore, had come to Virginia as governor in 1771 after serving for eleven months as governor of New York. In honor of his new assignment, he had named his daughter Virginia; and the colony had responded by naming two counties after him. Mutual admiration and affection, however, were short-lived. As the revolutionary spirit spread and relations with the mother country worsened, Dunmore increasingly alienated himself from the Virginians he governed. Called "a man of little force; irritable, changeable, and hasty . . .," Dunmore vacillated between indecisiveness and aggressiveness, boldly attacking the Virginian rebels when opportunities presented themselves, and meekly withdrawing when challenged.[43] Dunmore constantly made strategic errors. When on May 25, 1774, for instance, the House of Burgesses passed a resolution calling for a day of fast to protest the Boston Port Bill, Dunmore unwittingly drove the more conservative members of the assembly into the camp of the radicals by dissolving the House.

Not quite a year later—on the twentieth of April, 1775—after a period of calm inactivity, Dunmore again blundered when he decided to raid the Williamsburg magazine and transfer the colony's powder to the king's ship *Magdalen,* lying in the James River. Attempting to appease the wrath of the citizens of Williamsburg, Dunmore explained that the powder was removed for fear of a slave uprising and would be returned when needed. Although his transparent lie was finally accepted by the excited townsfolk, it was not by those who lived further inland. These gathered by the hundreds at Fredericksburg ready to descend on Dunmore.

Alarmed by the excitement he had created, the governor issued another proclamation repeating his lame excuse of a possible slave insurrection. Dunmore's confidence van-

126.
JOHN MURRAY, Earl of Dunmore.
Joshua Reynolds, 1765. Mrs.
Elizabeth Murray.

By *his Excellency the Right Honourable* JOHN *Earl of* DUNMORE, *his Majesty's Lieutenant and Governour-General of the Colony and Dominion of* Virginia, *and Vice-Admiral of the same:*

A PROCLAMATION.

AS I have ever entertained Hopes that an Accommodation might have taken Place between *Great Britain* and this Colony, without being compelled, by my Duty, to this most disagreeable, but now absolutely necessary Step, rendered so by a Body of armed Men, unlawfully assembled, firing on his Majesty's Tenders, and the Formation of an Army, and that Army now on their March to attack his Majesty's Troops, and destroy the well-disposed Subjects of this Colony: To defeat such treasonable Purposes, and that all such Traitors, and their Abetters, may be brought to Justice, and that the Peace and good Order of this Colony may be again restored, which the ordinary Course of the civil Law is unable to effect, I have thought fit to issue this my Proclamation, hereby declaring, that until the aforesaid good Purposes can be obtained, I do, in Virtue of the Power and Authority to me given, by his Majesty, determine to execute martial Law, and cause the same to be executed throughout this Colony; and to the End that Peace and good Order may the sooner be restored, I do require every Person capable of bearing Arms to resort to his Majesty's S T A N-DARD, or be looked upon as Traitors to his Majesty's Crown and Government, and thereby become liable to the Penalty the Law inflicts upon such Offences, such as Forfeiture of Life, Confiscation of Lands, *&c. &c.* And I do hereby farther declare all indented Servants, Negroes, or others (appertaining to Rebels) free, that are able and willing to bear Arms, they joining his Majesty's Troops, as soon as may be, for the more speedily reducing this Colony to a proper Sense of their Duty, to his Majesty's Crown and Dignity. I do farther order, and require, all his Majesty's liege Subjects to retain their Quitrents, or any other Taxes due, or that may become due, in their own Custody, till such Time as Peace may be again restored to this at present most unhappy Country, or demanded of them for their former salutary Purposes, by Officers properly authorised to receive the same.

GIVEN under my Hand, on Board the Ship William, *off* Norfolk, *the* 7th *Day of* November, *in the* 16th *Year of his Majesty's Reign.*

D U N M O R E.

G O D SAVE THE K I N G.

127.
Shipboard proclamation of martial law issued by John Murray, Earl of Dunmore, ordering all persons "capable of bearing Arms, to resort to His Majesty's STANDARD, or be looked upon as Traitors." November 7, 1775. Tracy W. McGregor Library, University of Virginia.

ished, however, when Patrick Henry descended upon the capital at the head of the Hanover militia and an ever-growing mob of armed men. Panicking, he offered payment for the powder, which Henry was forced by the more conservative leaders to accept. Prevented from carrying out what was probably his real intention of seizing the government and beginning the Revolution immediately, Henry returned home, while Dunmore remained in occupation of the governor's "palace."

Dunmore continued to overplay his hand. As soon as Henry's force was dispersed, he issued a proclamation declaring Henry an outlaw and warning the people against giving him aid. Feeling against Dunmore rose so high that he was forced to flee for safety to the British vessel *Fowey* floating in Yorktown Harbor. From the safety of his ship he attempted to govern, reconvening the old House of Burgesses on June 1, 1775, only to have it adjourn three weeks later. With its adjournment, the extralegal convention ruled in its place. The governor, now a fugitive, sought refuge with the British fleet.

Attempting to use the fleet to force Virginians to remain loyal to the crown, Dunmore found a stronghold of loyal supporters in the seaport town of Norfolk, among the Scots merchants whose dependence on British trade and hatred of colonial economic sanctions and boycotts had kept them loyal to the mother country. In October 1775, much to the dismay of the few rebels who remained within the town, these merchants invited Dunmore to Norfolk; and it was from this port of safety that Dunmore committed his final folly—the issuing on November 7 of a proclamation declaring martial law and granting freedom to all slaves belonging to rebels who joined the royal standard. The proclamation cemented the uneasy alliance of more moderate Virginians with the radicals and forced many conservatives to abandon hope for reconciliation. It also made Dunmore "the best hated man in the colony and settled all the colonists' scruples about making war on him." [44]

Once having begun, Dunmore continued to proceed aggressively against the rebels. Learning that there were some militia in the area, he gathered together 200 of his men, made his way to Kemps, a village a few miles southeast of Norfolk, and won an easy victory over the frightened Americans, who, "after firing one volley, fled from the field, their leaders whipping up their horses as they streamed through Kemps." His victory made him, according to George Washington, "the most formidable enemy America has." Washington feared that "his strength will increase as a snowball by rolling; and faster, if some expedient cannot be hit upon to convince the slaves and servants of the impotency of his designs. . . ." [45]

The Virginia Convention agreed. Seeing no alternative, the newly appointed Committee of Safety, executive body of the convention, sent to Norfolk Virginia's Second Regiment commanded by William Woodford.

The choice of William Woodford as commander of the Virginia militia represented the triumph of the conservatives within the Virginia governing body. It eliminated from active service the popular radical lawyer Patrick Henry, who commanded the First Regiment and served as ranking officer in Virginia. By not sending activity reports to Henry, or asking Henry for commands, Woodford continued to uphold conservative authority. When Henry made his objections known to the Committee of Safety, it was finally decided that Woodford should report to Henry but continue to receive his orders from the committee.

William Woodford (1734-1780)

205

128.
WILLIAM WOODFORD. Charles
Willson Peale, 1778. Whereabouts
unknown; reproduced in *Pennsylvania Magazine of History and
Biography*, 1900. [Not in exhibition.]

The choice of William Woodford to command the Virginia troops was not, however, entirely politically motivated. Woodford was a veteran of the French and
Indian War, a Patriot who had served on the Caroline County committee to enforce
the Association, and a member of the Committee of Correspondence. He was not an
extremist—he refused to hang captured Tories as traitors as his troops demanded
and, instead, sent them and runaway slaves back to Willamsburg to stand trial. He
was also a fervent Patriot: when, later, news came to him that some rebels had been
wounded by citizens of Norfolk, he was ready to see that "the town of Norfolk" received "no favor." [46]

On December 1 Woodford confronted Dunmore at Great Bridge, on the road
leading to Norfolk. Stirred by a slave's report that Woodford was advancing with only
300 men, Dunmore had decided to take the initiative and meet him outside the city,
which was not easy to fortify. But Woodford had 700 men with him, all well prepared
for Dunmore's force of 500 regulars, Loyalists, and slaves. A clash resulted in Dunmore's retreating to his ships in Norfolk harbor, accompanied by his ragged band and
the town's Tories. According to Wertenbaker, "many a dainty lady, who had been
accustomed to every luxury, now found herself crowded into some dark hold, intended
only for hogshead of tobacco or barrels of rum or molasses." [47].

Back in the safety of his ships, Dunmore gave way to the rage and despair that, in
taking possession of him, now ruled his behavior. "When he learned of the defeat of
his troops, he raved like a madman, actually threatening to hang the boy who brought
the news," according to an account given by T. J. Wertenbaker.[48] Meanwhile,
Woodford's army had been reinforced by Patriot troops from North Carolina under
the command of Colonel Robert Howe. On December 14 1,000 American militia
marched into Norfolk and took over the harbor and the town's defenses. Dunmore,
his anger increased by his predicament and the terrible conditions on board the
crowded ship, which was spawning hunger, disease, and death, made one last move
for revenge. Thus it was that on the first of January he ordered his guns to fire on
the city that had once offered him protection and hospitality. He had hoped to use
Norfolk as a base for British operations in the south and as a central rallying point for
Loyalists. His hopes went up with the flames that consumed the town.

The rebels added their share to the town's destruction. For three days the provincial troops rampaged through the town, plundering, burning, and destroying private
property, until Woodford finally ordered a halt. By that time, it was too late; two-
thirds of Norfolk had been destroyed. The job was completed in February when the
Virginia Convention ordered the remainder of the town burned.

Gathering together his fleet, Dunmore fled from Norfolk, to make his last stand
at Gwynns Island off the shore of Gloucester, Massachusetts. From there, he eventually made his way back to England, leaving behind in his deserted camp disease-
stricken corpses—victims of hunger, crowding, and the perils of civil war.

129.
British document box of the Revolutionary period. Guthman Collection.

MOORE'S CREEK BRIDGE, NORTH CAROLINA:

JANUARY— FEBRUARY 28, 1776

Josiah Martin (1737-1786)

In North Carolina, also, an overzealous governor, underestimating the strength of revolutionary fervor, precipitated an armed encounter that placed Americans even further on the road to independence. Josiah Martin, a Crown-appointed governor, had come to North Carolina in August 1771 during a period of increasing discontent. After only two months in office, he and the popularly elected assembly had clashed over the imposition of a shilling tax for the sinking fund. In 1772 a survey depriving North Carolina of territory brought on another conflict between the royal governors and the legislature. The following year, arguments over judicial procedure influenced Governor Martin to dissolve the assembly and allow North Carolina's court system virtually to collapse. Citizens who were impressed by the sense that "something must be done to save the country from anarchy" organized North Carolina's first independent Provincial Congress at New Bern on August 25, 1774, and no proclamations or accusations of rebellion or illegality could deter them from asserting their right "to assemble and remonstrate against grievances." [49]

When the Provincial Congress passed the Mecklenburg Resolutions in May 1774, Martin was convinced of his impotency and, indeed, of his danger. Sending his family on to New York, he joined his fellow southern governors in seaborne exile on a British sloop-of-war, the *Cruizer*, anchored in Wilmington Harbor.

One last hope remained for Governor Martin for a restoration of British control: the presence of loyal Scots Highlanders in the interior counties and of slaves who might rally to the Crown under British leadership, support, and promise of freedom. In March 1775 Martin wrote confidently to Lord Dunmore, assuring him of the help of 20,000 men. In October plans were drawn up by the British to send troops down from Boston under the command of Sir Henry Clinton to rendezvous with Sir Peter Parker and the British fleet at Cape Fear. The expedition was designed to secure the entire South for the British.

Early in January Martin summoned all loyal subjects to the royal standard and pardoned them for all past offenses. Eighty-year-old Donald McDonald was sent into Highlander country to recruit MacDonalds, McLeods, McLeans, Stuarts, Campbells, McArthurs, and others "not bearing Celtic names." By February 15, 1776, marching "with a quick step to the piper" and raising their "bonnets in a huzzah for the King," 3,500 Scots and Loyalists arrived at Cross Creek to rally around Martin. Upon learning that Martin was not there to greet them and that they would have to make their own way to Wilmington and Brunswick, where Martin awaited them on shipboard, many of the men immediately deserted. Eventually, the force whittled down to 1,300 Highlanders and 300 Loyalists.

James Moore (1737-1777)

North Carolina rebels were not unprepared to meet this challenge. By February 1776 a fairly stable government had been established in the colony to substitute for the collapsed royal structure. A colonial governor had been elected, a provincial council formed, and district and town committees of safety set up. Almost immediately, the Provincial Congress turned its thoughts to raising military units for the defense of its people and on behalf of the Continental Army. Two colonial regiments of 500 men were ordered, and each district was instructed to raise a battalion of fifty minutemen. James Moore was chosen colonel of the First North Carolina Regiment by a margin of one vote.

James Moore was a wise choice. An experienced veteran of the French and Indian War, Moore was also involved in revolutionary politics and was a member of the Provincial Congress that elected him colonel. Josiah Martin hoped that Moore's narrow victory over John Ashe would create dissension and cause Ashe and his followers to take the British side. Instead Ashe, who was Moore's brother-in-law, led his independent ranger group into the Patriot fold where they worked furiously for the revolutionary cause.

The British had not been too careful to maintain secrecy. As early as December 18, 1775, when the Provincial Congress met, news of their planned invasion of North Carolina had seeped out, forcing the Carolinians to prepare a defense strategy. In February the New Bern Committee of Safety was aware that the Loyalists had begun their march to Cross Creek and were preparing to join Martin at Brunswick. After eighty hours of "unremitting service, night and day, making preparations," Colonel Moore and his regiment headed toward Cross Creek to confront them.[50] At Rockfish, seven miles below the Creek, where Moore anticipated the Tory group would have to cross, he made camp and waited for reinforcements. On February 19 these arrived, bringing his force up to 1,100. Here at Rockfish, too, Moore received a message from McDonald urging him "to join the royal standard." Moore sent back a copy of the patriots' Test Oath, as an invitation for McDonald's men to join the Continental Army.[51]

Undoubtedly hesitant at meeting Moore's army face-to-face, McDonald unexpectedly withdrew to Campbellton and crossed to the east side of Cape Fear. Quickly and brilliantly, Moore responded. Dispatching additional troops to Cross Creek, the Loyalist base, he and his men moved to Elizabeth Town where they remained until February 25, delayed by supply problems. Meanwhile, his trusted colleague, Colonel

Richard Caswell, head of the New Bern regiment, was sent to Corbetts Ferry to prevent a crossing there, while additional troops were sent to Moore's Creek Bridge, still another possible route.

James Moore knew that he could count on Richard Caswell, who has been called "perhaps the most versatile man of his day." [52] Surveyor, lawyer, orator, statesman, and soldier, he had distinguished himself in all his activities. One of the first Whig leaders in North Carolina to foresee that the conflict between Great Britain and her colonies would undoubtedly conclude in war, he had actively joined the revolutionary group and been elected a member of the Continental Congress. When the Provincial Government formed its army, he resigned in order to return home to "raise, arm, equip and drill his regiment." [53] Now he would put his well-trained army to the test.

Richard Caswell (1729-1789)

Caswell had hardly arrived at Corbetts Ferry when he realized that the Tory army had bypassed him and was on its way to Moore's Creek Bridge. Informing Moore of the event, he proceeded on Moore's orders to join the other forces at the bridge and await the enemy. By the time he arrived, the soldiers sent earlier to the bridge had succeeded in raising breastworks and entrenchments on the east and west sides of the river and in removing the planks from the bridge, leaving only slick, rounded beams.

On February 26 the Highlanders arrived, led by the elderly Donald McDonald. Too ill to lead the fight, McDonald relinquished command to the young Colonel McLeod, who had literally left his wife at the altar to fight for the King's cause. The next morning, to "the shrill notes of their pilbroch," the Scots were summoned to battle—only to encounter the remnants of a recently deserted American camp and a dismantled bridge.[54] Caswell's men had craftily left their campfires burning while crossing the creek to join the Patriot forces on the other side.

"Drums beat, bagpipes skirled," and with the sound of the battle cry, "King George and Broadsides," the hapless Loyalists began their attack. As the Scots attempted to cross the beams of the bridge, many fell into the water and drowned. Those who managed the perilous crossing encountered the murderous fire of Caswell's well-concealed men. In a few moments, between thirty and seventy Tories were either killed or wounded, including the loyal McLeod. The rebels suffered only two wounded, one of whom later died.[55] Ninety-nine Loyalists, including Donald McDonald, were taken prisoner; and the Tory cause in North Carolina was checked for the next four years.

The "three-minute ambush at Moore's Creek" brought encouragement and hope not only to North Carolinian Patriots, but throughout the colonies. "Theretofore," as Samuel Ashe reported, "reconciliation had been desired, now as if by magic the watchword became independence." [56]

Josiah Martin, awaiting the arrival of his reinforcements on board ship at Brunswick, could not, however, accept the reality of the defeat. "The little check the Loyalists have received will not have any extensive consequences," he wrote home. But Sir Henry Clinton, arriving finally at Cape Fear, immediately recognized the meaning implicit in the disaster. Waiting only until Sir Peter Parker joined him from England, he abandoned the project of uniting the Loyalists of North Carolina and sailed off to Charleston, turning British attention to the deep South.

FORT MOULTRIE, CHARLESTON, JUNE 28, 1776

Before sailing for Charleston, South Carolina, in May 1776, Sir Henry Clinton had to endure two months of privation and discomfort sitting in Cape Fear Harbor awaiting the arrival of Sir Peter Parker with the main fleet. Parker's squadron was to bring to Clinton and his army the naval forces needed to fulfill the plan for a southern campaign that had been hatched by London officials during the summer and fall of 1775. That plan depended on cooperation between the British army and navy forces and colonial Loyalists. It called for the penetration of the South to scotch the rebellion therein and secure it once and for all for the British.

Timing was essential to the success of the British plan. Loyalist uprisings had to be staged to coincide with the arrival of reinforcements before the rebels could muster the strength to endure the attack. But, before the Loyalists could be tempted to rise, they had to be assured that the British would be successful. Alhough governors like Josiah Martin were optimistic about the extent of Loyalist sympathy in the South, realistic military leaders like Sir Henry Clinton were not. Martin and other colonial governors, Clinton believed, were "too sanguine," and he decided not to wait for indeterminate help to come from uncertain numbers of Loyalists in the back country.[57]

Sir Henry Clinton (1738?-1795)

When Sir Henry Clinton took over the southern campaign he was second in command of the British troops in North America, Generals Howe and Carleton sharing the first command. He had come to Boston in May 1775 to participate bravely in the disasters of Bunker Hill and eventual evacuation of the city. Clinton was not a stranger to the colonies: he had grown up in New York while his father was governor from 1741 to 1751, and, in fact, had been commissioned at the age of thirteen as captain lieutenant in the New York militia. Continuing his military pursuits upon his return to London, he had served in many of the German campaigns before retiring for ten years to sit in Parliament and establish political connections. Back in America, he believed that he understood Americans better than did his superiors, and throughout his career in the colonies he continued to make suggestions—which went unheeded—criticize authority, and initiate frequent quarrels with his colleagues. His biographer has also indicated that although Clinton was "greedy for authority," he was "afraid of exercising it because it represented an area, the paternal, where a part of himself insisted he did not belong. Trespassing here produced a sense of guilt, with which he was threatened whenever he attempted to grasp the reins. Grasping and drawing back alternated throughout his career."[58]

When appointed to head the southern expedition, Clinton both embraced and feared the assignment. His force of 1,200 to 1,500 "boys" seemed too small for the task, his orders were not specific enough, and the royal governors' reports were not trustworthy. His worst fears had been confirmed at Cape Fear, and the long and uncomfortable two-month wait did not help his indecisiveness. Finally, however, he had to take action. Sir Peter's ships were straggling into the harbor and he would have to take up a joint command with the naval officer. Parker had also brought Clinton new orders: he was to "begin a winter campaign, to re-establish order in the four provinces, and afterwards to join the Commander-in-Chief early in spring at five thousand miles distance!"[59]

130.
Sir Henry Clinton. Attributed
to Andrea Soldi, circa 1762. The
American Museum in Britain,
Bath.

131.
PETER PARKER. Valentine Green
after Lemuel Francis Abbott.
Mezzotint, 1800. The Metropolitan Museum of Art.

Sir Peter Parker, like Clinton and so many other British military leaders, began his military career at an early age, presumably serving as a young boy under his father, Rear Admiral Christopher Parker. Appointed a Knight in 1772, after years of little activity, he was at last given command in October 1775 of the small squadron being sent to North America.

Parker's assignment went awry from the beginning. Scheduled to set sail from Cork in December, he was delayed in port until February. Finally departing with ten gunships that acted as convoy for a fleet of thirty transports bearing 2,500 men under the command of Lord Cornwallis, he sailed head on into a gale. The fleet was forced to separate, and not until eighty days later did the main group wander into Cape Fear.

Until Parker's arrival, Clinton had been mulling over a plan to attack the Chesapeake Bay area. But when two junior officers reported, after a quick scouting expedition, that Charleston, South Carolina, remained undefended, guarded only by an unfinished fort on Sullivan's Island, Clinton agreed, somewhat reluctantly, to turn the fleet southward.

The joint force anchored in Charleston Harbor on June 8. Clinton immediately issued a proclamation to the townspeople declaring the existence of "a most unprovoked and wicked rebellion within South Carolina" and offering in the King's name "free pardon to such as should lay down their arms and submit to the laws."[60] In the meantime, he landed four to five hundred of his men on Long Island, an unattended strip of land north of Sullivan's Island and separated from it only by a supposedly shallow breach of water. While Parker continued to maneuver his ships and wait for perfect weather and favorable tides, and while Clinton fretted, the Carolinians continued to work on the incompleted fort and, under the orders of the newly arrived General Charles Lee of the Continental Army, to erect bridges capable of carrying retreating soldiers.

Charles Lee had arrived in Charleston early in June on orders from the Continental Congress. The Congress had been aware from early January that Charleston might be attacked and had taken the precaution of increasing the number of continental regiments in South Carolina from twelve to fourteen. To ensure the safety of the southern theater, however, they had decided to send the general to the scene.

Charles Lee had joined the American cause in 1775 after a successful, but unrewarded, career in the British army. Dissatisfied with the lack of recognition, after the French and Indian War he had become a soldier of fortune, wandering through central and eastern Europe and offering his services to whatever nation paid the highest price. Finally returning to England in 1771, he began writing bitter attacks on the Tory party and King George III. As he became more deeply involved in liberal causes, he resigned his position in the British army and sailed to America.

Lee's reputation as a military man of broad experience and innovative tactical ideas, and as a widely read and well educated thinker, spread throughout the colonies as he traveled around meeting political leaders and taking up his pen again in favor of revolution and liberty. Even John Adams had to admit that Lee was the only American officer who had read more on the history and art of warfare than he.[61] Thus, when the Congress came to appoint military leaders, Charles Lee's name headed the list of candidates. Because the Congress could not ignore Artemas Ward's service at Boston,

132.
CHARLES LEE. Unidentified en-
graver, probably English.
Mezzotint, 1775. National Portrait
Gallery, Smithsonian Institution.

CHARLES LEE, Esqr.
MAJOR GENERAL of the CONTINENTAL-ARMY in AMERICA.
Publish'd as the Act directs 31 Octr. 1775. by C. Shepherd, London.

Lee was appointed second in command; but upon Ward's resignation the following
year, he was promoted to be first in command under Washington. Even more important, the Congress felt confidence in him, and in troublesome situations turned to him
for advice and assistance.

In February, when the Congress learned of the British plan to invade the South,
Lee's original orders to travel to Canada and rescue the American forces bogged down
in front of Quebec were countermanded. Soon, accompanied by his customary following of devoted dogs, he was on his way to Charleston at a leisurely pace with orders to

help the Carolinians stave off the "rod of correction which the King had directed to be prepared for his recalcitrant subjects in the southern provinces."[62]

On June 9 Lee inspected the unfinished American defenses on Sullivan's Island. Lee's presence, wrote William Moultrie, commander of the fort, "gave us great spirits, as he was known to be an able, brave and experienced officer, though hasty and rough in his manner. . . ."[63] Lee was not as complimentary about Moultrie's unfinished fort constructed of palmetto logs. He did not "like that post," he declared; "it could not hold out half an hour; there was no way to retreat and the garrison would be sacrificed."[64]

Lee's criticism encountered the steadfast resistance of the fort's commander. Colonel William Moultrie, a native South Carolinian and a veteran of the colony's military and political battles, had been working on his fort for several months and refused to give it up. Local sentiment was with him; and despite Lee's insistence that the fort should be abandoned, Governor John Rutledge ordered work on it to continue.

William Moultrie (1731-1805)

Moultrie and Lee were cast from different molds. Moultrie's "easy manner" bordered on incompetence to the tersely disciplined general. Moultrie was willing to shift work when convenient; he allowed vital laborers to leave and then was forced to request Lee's help in retrieving them. Lee urged Moultrie to exert himself and to issue firm orders, ending his admonition, however, with the excuse that his harshness of tone arose from "an anxiety for the public" and "in some measure from my concern for the reputation of a Gentleman of so responsible a Character as Col. Moultrie. . . ."[65]

Moultrie possessed positive characteristics that did much to counter Lee's natural pessimism. He was confident about the strength of his fort and the ability of his men to withstand a siege, an optimism that maintained morale even while it increased Lee's suspicions of Moultrie's capacity. "We shall beat them," Moultrie continually asserted; and when one fellow officer expressed his fears that the British men-of-war would crumble their fort "in half an hour," Moultrie is said to have replied, "Then we will lie behind the ruins and prevent their men from landing."[66]

But Moultrie couldn't convince his superior officer, and finally Lee persuaded the governor to withdraw half the men and powder from the fort, leaving Moultrie with only 435 men and less than 500 pounds of powder. He then fortified other points, sending 780 men to the east end of the island to prevent Clinton's landing and stationing another contingent of troops on Heddrals Point, north of Sullivan's Island.

Lee's adversary, Sir Henry Clinton, was also having his difficulties. Having landed some three thousand troops on mosquito-infested Long Island on June 16, he discovered to his amazement that instead of the breach separating Long Island from Sullivan's Island measuring an expected eighteen inches deep, it measured seven feet. Sir Peter immediately sent ships to rescue the hapless troops, but sharpshooters on the north end of Sullivan's Island prevented the vessels from landing and Clinton and his men remained marooned and ineffectual.

As Clinton brooded, Parker continued optimistic. Soon he was drilling his men in the art of scaling forts and carrying on a siege, secure in the belief that he could take the fort without Clinton's help. By this time, it had become a matter of "honour" that he and the navy act unaided. The weather was the only obstacle to his contemplated heroic achievements.

133.
WILLIAM MOULTRIE. Charles
Willson Peale, 1782. National
Portrait Gallery, Smithsonian
Institution.

June 28 brought the desired conditions. While Lee was still attempting to persuade Moultrie to finish a bridge suitable to maintain a retreat, Moultrie had gone to visit the east end of the island. Witnessing the movements of the British fleet, he immediately rushed back to his fort and ordered the men to their posts. The ensuing battle was a surprise to all except the indefatigable Moultrie and his confident Carolinians.

Barrages of fire and broadsides from eight gunships bearing over one hundred artillery pieces did not move Moultrie's men from their defenses. The men held fast, and, surprisingly enough, so did the fort. The spongy palmetto logs simply absorbed the fire, instead of shattering under impact. At first, the Carolinians responded with a nervous rapid fire that wasted their precious powder; but as they gained confidence and experience (Moultrie is supposed to have nonchalantly smoked his pipe while issuing orders), they stuck to their guns and improved on their precision—in a way devastating to the British ships and crew.[67]

As the Carolinians' supply of powder began to dwindle in the afternoon, Moultrie was forced to reduce the firing. General Lee refused to send more shot and ordered a retreat if necessary. But luckily, Governor Rutledge was prevailed upon to send 700 pounds. At five in the evening, vigorous firing was renewed.

The Patriots concentrated their fire on two fifty-gun ships, the *Experiment* and, particularly, the *Bristol*, which carried the green and overly optimistic commander Sir Peter Parker. The entire crew of the *Bristol* were casualties. Sir Peter himself suffered the humiliation of having his pants blown off while standing alone on the quarterdeck watching his ships being destroyed.

"I wish I was master of language," reported the amazed Lee, "to paint . . . their [the Carolinians'] unequaled heroism."[68] After meeting Moultrie, the general is reported to have simply said, "Colonel, I see you are doing well here; you have no occasion for me; I will go to town again."[69]

By nine in the evening, the battle was over. General Clinton believed that the British would have retired even earlier if the tide had permitted a safe withdrawal. It took the British two weeks to repair some of the vessels sufficiently so that they could return with the troops to New York; the rest of the battered fleet remained in Charleston for more extensive repairs.

Clinton had obviously failed in his first independent command. Having passively submitted to Parker's idea to attack Charleston, even though he had originally held to another plan, he had foolishly landed on Long Island without first surveying the depth of the breach or the safety of the position. As a result, he had stranded himself and his troops just when they were needed for battle.

Soon the event was ridiculed in a ballad, presumably sung by Sir Peter Parker:

> *Bold Clinton by land*
> *Did quietly stand*
> *While I made a thundering clatter;*
>
> *But the channel was deep,*
> *So he only could peep,*
> *And not venture over the water.*
>
> *De'el take 'em their shot*
> *Came so swift and so hot,*

134.
*Sir Peter Parker's Attack Against
Fort Moultrie.* James Peale, circa
1782. Colonial Williamsburg.

And the cowardly dogs stood so stiff, sirs!
　　That I put ship about,
　　And was glad to get out,
Or they would not have left me a skiff, sirs!

　　Now bold as a Turk
　　I proceed to New York,
Where with Clinton and Howe you may find me.
　　I've wind in my tail
　　And am hoisting my sail,
To leave Sullivan's Island behind me.[70]

Charles Lee generously credited Moultrie and his men for the victory. On July 30 he reviewed the troops and again offered his praises. Later he told Moultrie: "I should have thanked you and your Garrison . . . *viva voce* at the Fort . . . only a great deal of busyness prevented. I do most heartily thank you, and shall do you justice in my letters to the Congress. . . ."[71] Lee was as good as his word. "The behavior of the garrison, both men and officers, with Colonel Moultrie at their head, I confess astonished me," he wrote; "It was brave to the last degree. I had no idea that so much

218

coolness and intrepidity could be displayed by a collection of raw recruits."[72] On July 4 Moultrie received even more honor. Governor John Rutledge visited the fort and proclaimed that it was to be named Fort Moultrie in honor of its valiant defender.

The Carolinians' victory at Fort Moultrie was of great significance for the early success of the American Revolution. As George Bancroft has written:

> [it] *saved not a post, but the state. It kept seven regiments away from N.Y. for two months, it gave security to Georgia, and three years peace to Carolina; it dispelled throughout the South the dread of British superiority; it drove the loyalists into obscurity. To the other colonies it was a message of brotherhood and union from South Carolina as a self directing republic. . . . The victory at Fort Moultrie was the bright morning star that harbingered American independence.*[73]

The Continental Congress was particularly jubilant over Moultrie's victory in Charleston Harbor, even to the point of voting General Lee a $30,000 advance in salary to help him pay for his Virginia plantation. Congress had particular need of a victory, for just six weeks earlier it had received word that the Americans had withdrawn their siege of Quebec and abandoned Canada. With that abandonment, the Congress had to relinquish its dream of winning the Canadians to the American cause and achieving political and military unity throughout the North American continent.

EXPEDITION TO CANADA, JUNE 27, 1775—MAY 5, 1776

The dream of winning Canada had begun early in 1774, when the First Continental Congress had sent a message to the Canadians urging them to join the colonial cause. Later, Canadians were invited to send representatives to the Second Continental Congress. Neither of these invitations had been answered, largely because they had been suppressed by Canada's royal governor, Sir Guy Carleton. From then on the colonials had resorted to propaganda emanating from individuals like Ethan Allen or from provincial congresses denouncing the Quebec Act as "a form of tyranny" and identifying the American fight with Canadian dissatisfactions.

In February 1775 the Boston Committee of Correspondence secretly sent John Brown, a lawyer from Pittsfield, to Montreal to make contact with the group called "old subjects"—men of British birth or from the original thirteen colonies, who disliked the Quebec Act because they believed it favored the "papist" French and offered no protection to the English in the form of English law and institutions. Brown found encouragement for the Americans among this group. A month later he reported back that the Canadians were sympathetic and had assured him of the neutrality of the French population as well as of the Canadian Indians. Brown recommended the capture of the weakly defended British garrison at Ticonderoga and the even weaker post at Crown Point. These would provide an opening wedge into Canada. Brown's recommendation, together with the decisions taken by Ethan Allen and Benedict Arnold among others, led to the capture of Ticonderoga and its priceless artillery in May 1775. His prediction was correct. By winning control of Lake Champlain, the Americans were able to open the way for invasion into Canada from the south.

135.
SIR GUY CARLETON. Unidentified
artist, date unknown. The Earl
and Countess of Malmesbury.

Sir Guy Carleton
(1724-1808)

The task of protecting Canada fell on Guy Carleton, whose name has been inextricably interwoven with Canadian history as the architect of the British policy incorporated into the Quebec Act of 1774. A strict and dour Ulsterman, "distant and reserved in manner, rather arrogant in temper," [74] Carleton was not the benevolent liberal that the provisions of the Quebec Act suggest. As governor of Quebec, he ruled in an arbitrary and narrow way, ruthlessly disposing of those whom he distrusted or who thwarted his will.

Carleton had risen to his eminent post through military service. Skillful as an engineer, he had been sent, on Pitt's and Wolfe's insistence, to help in the conquest of Canada in 1759. With Wolfe, he had participated in the storming of Quebec and had been badly wounded during that heroic battle. In 1766 Carleton had returned to Quebec by way of New York to become lieutenant governor of the province, but in 1774 he was back in England to help draw up the act for the governing of Quebec. In 1775 he was formally appointed governor, and when General Gage was recalled that year, the command of the British army in America was divided between him and William Howe, he being placed in charge of the Canadian troops.

Carleton's views on how to meet the rebellion were well known by 1775. As early as 1767 he had sent a letter to General Gage in New York outlining his strategy. The colonies, Carleton firmly believed, must learn to obey. Long years of military service had convinced him that respect for existing authority was essential to civilization, and

220

Carleton was willing to use force to insure that respect. Carleton had opposed an elected legislature in Quebec because, as he said, Canada should not follow the example of the rebellious colonies to the south who had been encouraged in their insolence by too much freedom. He himself would rule in Canada, with the help only of "men of Good Sense, Truth, Candor, and Impartial Justice; persons who prefer their duty to the King and the Tranquillity of His Subjects, to unjustifiable Attachments, Party Zeal, and to all selfish mercenary views." [75] Carleton's was the philosophy of the Enlightened Despot, and he had complete confidence in his capacity to carry off that role.

Carleton also foresaw in 1767 the coming of the American Revolution. In his memorandum to Gage, he suggested that the British secure New York and Quebec and establish a line of communication between the two garrisons. Such a line would isolate the New England colonies and make their subjugation easier. Carleton urged Gage to make the fort at Ticonderoga impregnable, because this would be the first objective of the revolutionaries and, consequently, the first British stronghold to fall under attack. The British, insisted Carleton, must not spare money or effort in rooting out dissidents and impressing those who "might not be ready to do their Duty." [76]

Carleton had hardly returned to Quebec from his English visit when his worst fears were realized. In September 1774 he received a letter from Gage asking Canada to send reinforcements to rebellious Boston and inquiring into the possibility of forming "a body of Canadians and Indians." [77] But Carleton now was out of touch with Canadian sentiment. When he had left for England in 1770, he had carried with him the belief that 18,000 French Canadians could be aroused to help in the event of a colonial uprising. This belief was reinforced by the favorable reaction of the French settlers to the Quebec Act. Carleton did not realize, however, that the majority of "habitants" resented the restored clerical and seignorial privileges which suppressed their own, and that their seeming "loyalty" was in reality a kind of passive resistance that would result, at the least, in neutrality.

The fall of Ticonderoga and Crown Point rudely awakened Carleton to the reality of French Canadian neutrality. Turning to the Catholic Church for support, he asked the friendly bishop Msgr. Briand to issue a proclamation denouncing the American rebels. Briand obliged; but again, Carleton seems to have overemphasized the influence of the Church on the common people and underestimated the people's resentment of the privileged clergy class. Briand's proclamation fell on deaf ears, and recruitment of a Canadian army continued to pose difficulties.

Confusion developed between Carleton and the British authorities in London that also made it difficult for him to organize a military force. Misled by his earlier optimistic projections and by the expectation that Carleton would be able to make use of the more than two thousand Indians who, according to Indian Superintendent Guy Johnson, stood ready to fight, the English war ministery did not send reinforcements to help the governor hold off an American invasion.

Carleton was unwilling to make use of the Indians in his military plans. Complaining that they were undependable and difficult to mobilize at the appropriate moment, he continued to mislead the home government as to their eventual use. Without Indian help, therefore, and with an inadequate militia force, Carleton faced the Americans in a truly weakened condition. Only the irresolution of the Continental Congress about the proposed expedition to Canada and American errors in planning saved Canada for the British Empire. By the time the invasion occurred, Carleton was able to muster a sufficient number of parish companies to take advantage of the severity of the northern winter and the perils of the wilderness to repel the invaders.

Richard Montgomery
(1738-1776)

In May 1775, when the Continental Congress received news of the capture of Ticonderoga and Crown Point by Ethan Allen and Benedict Arnold, it could do nothing else but approve the *fait accompli*. Aware of the importance of bringing Canada to their side, the delegates saw in the bold and unauthorized act the prevention of their greatest fear: an invasion from Canada of British regulars accompanied by fierce Indian tribes which, once loosed on the frontier, would devastate the New York and New England countryside.

Thus, a month later, on June 27, when the Continental Army was created, one of the first theaters of war to be designated was Canada. General Philip Schuyler was ordered to invade that colony; with him was Richard Montgomery, a newly commissioned brigadier general in the Continental Army. Schuyler's orders were to seize Montreal and other parts of Canada if it were not "disagreeable to the Canadians."[78]

A former officer in the British army, who had fought with Amherst in 1759 in the successful operation against Ticonderoga, Crown Point, and Montreal, Richard Montgomery had returned to America in 1772 in the belief that there was no future for him in the highly stratified British establishment. The tall, pock-marked, but splendid-looking Montgomery had prospered in the new land since his arrival. He had taken up farming in New York, married the daughter of Robert R. Livingston, and had been elected to the New York Provincial Congress. Reluctantly, he accepted his new position in the Continental Army:

> *The Congress having done me the honor of electing me a brigadier-general in their service* [he wrote] *is an event which must put an end for a while,* perhaps for ever, *to the quiet scheme of life I had prescribed for myself; for, though entirely unexpected and undesired by me,* the will of an oppressed people compelled to choose between liberty and slavery must be heard.[79]

Meticulous—often fussy—in his attention to details, General Schuyler was slow in getting his expedition underway. To the energetic Montgomery and impatient Washington, the delay was unbearable. Finally, Montgomery could wait no longer. Without orders from Schuyler, on August 28 he led a contingent of the American forces up Lake Champlain toward Montreal. Stirred by Montgomery's departure, Schuyler immediately set out to meet him, and the two forces joined at Champlain and proceeded together to Ile aux Nois. At this point, Schuyler fell ill and was forced to return to Albany, leaving Montgomery in sole command.

Despite the poor quality of his troops—they were, Montgomery is said to have reported, the "worst stuff imaginable for soldiers"—and logistical problems, Montgomery immediately laid siege to Fort St. Johns on the Richelieu River southwest of Montreal, which the Americans under Ethan Allen had captured in May, but which an embarrassed Congress had returned to the British soon after. Now Carleton had strengthened the fort with a limited force under the command of Colonel Preston, and had anchored two schooners in the river nearby, one of which carried twelve brass four- and six-pound cannon. Unwilling or unable to avail themselves of the boats,

An East View of MONTREAL, *in Canada*   *Vue Orientale de* MONTREAL, *en Canada*

Drawn on the SPOT by Thomas Patten   Engraved by P. Canot

136.
*An East View of Montreal, in
Canada.* Pierre-Charles Canot
after Thomas Patten. Engraving,
1768. The Public Archives of
Canada.

Preston and his men remained within the fort. The Americans captured the two vessels, and a contingent of the force, under Major Brown and James Livingston, proceeded down the river to Chambly, halfway between St. Johns and Montreal, which Carleton had fortified with additional troops. Chambly's strong walls housed only eighty men, but had guns and ammunition enough to delay the progress of the Americans. But the commander at Chambly made no effort either to use or destroy his gunpowder and cannon, and after a day and a half surrendered. With replenished stores, the Americans returned to St. Johns to continue their siege.

From September 5 to November 2 the British soldiers occupying the fort at St. Johns resisted the Americans and waited for reinforcements from Carleton. They never came. Finally, with his men sick and his supplies gone, Preston was forced to surrender. He had lost over seven hundred men during the fifty-five day siege. Now the area was open to an American invasion; the cry was "To Montreal!"

For the second time in his career, Montgomery approached Montreal, closing in from all sides exactly as the British had done under Amherst. Strategy, however, was unnecessary: the city that the British had taken "with the utmost sacrifice" fifteen years before refused to fight. Montgomery was welcomed with joy, and Carleton was forced to abandon Montreal and sneak away by boat to Quebec. He later justified his procedure to Dartmouth: there was, he wrote, a "want of Hands." "The lower orders will not act, and there are not means to defend the place," he explained.[80] On November 12, eleven vessels loaded with powder and supplies carried him and 130 men downstream. What should have been a routine trip turned into a perilous adventure. Below Montreal, the fleet was halted and the last of the Redcoats sent to oppose Montgomery fell to Montgomery's forces. "I blush for his Majesty's troops!" Montgomery declared; but the Americans were not as superior as they thought they were, for they had lost their prize catch.[81] Carleton managed to slip through the Americans in a whaleboat, and later, disguised as a peasant, supposedly walked right past the rebels. On November 19 Carleton arrived in Quebec in time to confront Benedict Arnold and his men who had been camped outside the city since November 5.

Benedict Arnold
(1741-1801)

Benedict Arnold had returned to his home in Connecticut in May 1775, humiliated and unhappy about the way his services at Ticonderoga and Fort St. Johns had gone unrewarded by a suspicious Congress. Quarrels that had taken place between him, Ethan Allen, and Colonel Hinman of Connecticut, who had been sent with troops to reinforce him, ended in his being "investigated" and forced to resign. Hot-tempered and impatient, Arnold was also a shrewd and intelligent military strategist, and it was difficult for him to accept an order to turn over his command to individuals whose expertise he questioned. Barnabas Deane, who was present at Champlain when the change of command was ordered, insisted that Arnold had been "greatly abused and misrepresented by designing persons."[82] Some of this could not be helped. Arnold had taken his employment from the Massachusetts Provincial Congress, and when that colony relinquished to Connecticut its claim to Lake Champlain, it in effect abandoned Arnold. This, however, was an insult he could not endure; he left the scene and the command and returned home.

Also hastening Arnold's return home was the news of his wife's illness. What must have truly inflicted pain was the discovery that he was too late: his wife had died and was already buried when he arrived, and his three sons were being cared for by a sister. To add to his difficulties, he fell sick with gout just when he had to present his accounts to Massachusetts for reimbursement. Massachusetts refused half of his claims, which added to his humiliation, and he was forced to seek the help of Silas Deane in the Continental Congress. Eventually, the Congress refunded the balance of Arnold's expenditures.

Despite all these personal affronts, Arnold persevered. During the summer of 1775 he developed a careful plan for a Canadian expedition and traveled to Cambridge to present it to General Washington. Washington was sympathetic, especially since Arnold's plan coincided with his own hope of finding a new route for an attack on Quebec. Thus, Washington proposed to the Congress that Arnold be commissioned colonel in the Continental Army in charge of an expedition to Quebec.

Two expeditions to Canada were planned. The first, involving Schuyler and Montgomery, would end with the capture of Montreal. The other, under Arnold, would take a new route through the Maine wilderness by way of three rivers—the Kennebec, Dead, and Chaudière—to Quebec. The hope was that Arnold would force Carleton to withdraw from Montreal to defend Quebec, thus easing the capture of the former city by Montgomery. If Carleton chose to make his stand at Montreal, then the capture of Quebec would be facilitated.

COLONEL ARNOLD.

Who commanded the Provincial Troops sent against QUEBEC, through the Wilderness of Canada, and was Wounded in Storming that City, under General Montgomery.

137.
BENEDICT ARNOLD. Unidentified
engraver, probably English.
Mezzotint, 1776. Anne S.K.
Brown Military Collection, Brown
University Library.

138.
A Bird's Eye View of the Lower town of Quebec taken from the Bishop's Palace, showing the Citadel & Chateau. J. Hunter. Watercolor, circa 1780. The Public Archives of Canada.

Arnold's expedition represented a remarkable feat. Consisting of three rifle companies from Pennsylvania and Virginia and ten companies of New England musketmen, it was divided into four divisions, the leading one under the command of the rugged Virginian rifleman, Captain Daniel Morgan, and the rearguard under Lieutenant Colonel Roger Enos of Vermont. On September 29 all divisions set off from Gardiner, Maine, into the forested wilderness.

Hurrying his men along to escape the perils of Maine's early winter, Arnold encountered many obstacles: his bateaux built of green lumber fell apart, many of his provisions were ruined, and his men suffered raw and blistered shoulders from carrying the 400-pound boats. Heavy rains turned the shallow river into yellow mud, and when the men drank the water, they immediately fell ill with nausea and diarrhea. To remain cheerful was impossible. As rations ran out, men deserted—the most serious desertion being that of Captain Enos, who took with him the division he headed and most of what was left of the food. The weather and the intrusion of such a large army into the woods frightened the wild game into hiding, and many meals consisted of boiled moccasins and soup made of shaving soap. Arnold was everywhere, trying to help his men, save provisions, and distribute whatever supplies he had to the various divisions. He personally saved the life of one young soldier, and most of the men spoke of his "firmness and zeal" in inspiring the troops "with resolution." [83]

On November 8 Arnold and more than six hundred men finally reached the St. Lawrence River opposite the walls of Quebec. "It is not in the power of any man to command success," wrote Washington, "but you have done more—you have deserved it. My thanks are due, and sincerely offered to you for your enterprizing and persevering spirit."[84] The Canadian garrison was weak, but Arnold's men were weaker. Even more important, Arnold did not possess canoes or equipment necessary to attack the citadel. By the time he had assembled canoes to cross the river, a storm prevented a crossing. Meanwhile, word had reached the British of his arrival, and reinforcements were rushed from Montreal to Quebec. Before hazarding an assault under such circumstances, Arnold decided to wait for Montgomery to join him.

On December 2, Montgomery arrived. By this time, Quebec held about 1,200 men, while the combined American troops numbered less than a thousand. Some of Montgomery's soldiers had departed during the long wait, their enlistments having expired; an epidemic of smallpox had carried away others. Arnold, too, faced the loss of much of his army through the expiration of enlistments on the last day of the year. Therefore, the two leaders decided to attack at the first storm, and before the end of the year. On the evening of December 30 and the early morning of the thirty-first, therefore, the Americans launched their assault, Montgomery leading a force against the lower town from Wolfe's Cove, and Arnold from St. Roque.

Through a blinding snowstorm in the early hours of December 31, Aaron Burr marched behind General Montgomery as a member of the 300-man force invading lower Quebec. It was a strange place for a young law student to find himself. A descendant of the famous theologian, Jonathan Edwards, and son of the second president of the College of New Jersey (Princeton), Aaron Burr had been raised by his uncle, Timothy Edwards, according to the religious and educational values of the day. Rebellious and restless, however, Aaron had found the discipline of tutors and home responsibilities irksome, and at a young age he ran away to sea. By thirteen, however, he seems to have settled into the expected mold and was enrolled at Princeton, graduating in September 1772. Theological school was the next step, but, again, the independent youth found the confinement of such studies unpleasant, and turned his attention instead to the study of the law.

Aaron Burr (1756-1836)

News of Lexington and Concord aroused Burr to dreams of military glory. Immediately determining "to risk his life for his country's freedom," he set out for Cambridge, stopping on the way, however, in Philadelphia to pick up letters of recommendation to General Washington from John Hancock and Lewis Morris.[85] Washington received the brash volunteer cooly. The camp was in a state of disarray, and, for a while, Burr could do little to help with the war effort. Talk of the impending expedition to Canada once again stirred him to action. Determined to join it, Burr recruited some companions and marched sixty miles to Newburyport, where the expedition was to be launched. There he met Arnold, who accepted him as a volunteer, and soon Burr and his friends, dressed in the garments of the frontier and carrying tomahawk, gun, and bayonet, were braving the rigorous march through Maine to Canada.

Sent by Arnold to Montgomery to seek reinforcements, Burr, according to legend disguised as a Catholic priest, thus came to Montgomery's attention. Arnold had given him a letter of introduction, recommending Burr to Montgomery's "favor." Impressed

with the young man's bearing, Montgomery made Burr a captain and took him on his staff as aide-de-camp.

Accompanying Montgomery back to Quebec, Burr became witness to the disaster that struck the American forces as they entered Lower Quebec. Unopposed at first, they came to a private dwelling, at which point Montgomery assured him that "We shall be in the fort in two minutes."[86] The British, however, had been alerted to the invasion by an American deserter, and were prepared. As Montgomery approached, shots rang out from the house. Immediately, the popular general fell. Panic overwhelmed the troops. Burr tried to rally the scattering men, but when the rear command ordered a retreat, his effort was thwarted. One witness noted that he attempted to return to the scene and "amidst a shower of musquetry, to bring off on his shoulder the body [of Montgomery]."[87] But the general's size and weight were too much for the small youth, and the deep snow made it impossible.

Montgomery's body was recognized by the British, and in his burial he was accorded all the honors of war. Burr returned to Arnold's staff, now commissioned major.

228

140.
Letter from Benedict Arnold to
Richard Montgomery introducing
Aaron Burr, November 30, 1775.
Maine Historical Society. [Original
not in exhibition.]

Daniel Morgan
(1736-1802)

142.
Sword carried by General Richard
Montgomery when he was killed at
Quebec. Division of Military
History, The National Museum of
History and Technology, Smith-
sonian Institution.

The invasion had not gone well for Arnold, either. Badly wounded with a musket
ball in his leg, he was forced to give up his command to Daniel Morgan, who lacked
his knowledge of the Quebec streets and, more seriously, lacked the rank and status
that would force Arnold's officers to respect his decisions.

Daniel Morgan personified the flamboyance and rugged self-assertiveness of the
frontier. More comfortably at home in the backwoods and small towns of the southern
piedmont than in the drawing room, he was, however, a well-seasoned and natural
leader who won the respect of his sharpshooting colleagues by his skills with the rifle,
his efficiency, and his courage. Having raised himself by his bootstraps as an independent wagoner and a frontier fighter well-schooled with the tomahawk and the knife as
well as the rifle, he had earned something of a reputation when the Congress went
about raising troops in June 1775, after Lexington and Concord. Morgan was immediately commissioned a captain, and placed in charge of an infantry company of men
known for their "amazing hardihood" gained through "living so long in the woods."[88]
No man was more suited to head one of the two Virginia regiments than this six-foot,
200-pound veteran of the French and Indian War and subsequent frontier warfare.

Recruiting ninety-six men, and not waiting to be called, Morgan hastened to Washington's camp in Cambridge. In an amazing three weeks he had covered the distance
of 600 miles. When his men marched into Boston, they astonished the staid citizenry
with their moccasins, Indian leggings, and leaf-colored tunics clutched at the waist
with a belt holding a fierce-looking tomahawk and knife. But while their sharpshooters gleefully attempted to pick off British sentries, causing Edmund Burke to exclaim
in Parliament, "Your officers are swept off by the rifles if they but show their noses!",
Morgan's men wearied their officers with their exuberance and affronted Bostonians
with their brawling, drinking, and occasional nude swims in the Charles River.[89]

It was natural that Morgan's rifle company should have been selected to accompany
Arnold on his expedition to Canada. In the first place, Washington had a special affection for these rough frontiersmen who came from his own colony and even the region
he had once represented in the Virginia Assembly. More important, their skills were
specially suitable for the kind of terrain Arnold had to encounter, as they later proved
when exhausting portages, angry and swollen rivers, and deep swamps threatened the
expedition with disaster. Morgan thought nothing of stripping to the waist and joining
his men in the rough work of clearing a trail for the troops following behind. His
strength and endurance were amazing, even to the New England farmers and fishermen who had grown hardy from conquering the rough ground and seas of the Atlantic coast. As one Pennsylvania rifleman wrote home, the problems posed by the wilderness were "left to the energy of Morgan's mind, and he conquered."[90]

Morgan continued to play an important role when Arnold's expedition reached
Quebec and a plan for capturing the stronghold was required. It was he who led
Arnold's men in the early hours of December 31 into the blinding snowstorm, around
the ice cakes floating in the river, and into the Lower Town. When Arnold fell,
Captain Morgan, the only one among Arnold's officers who had seen important military service, took charge. Yelling for the rest of the company to follow, he dashed
toward the barrier set up to prevent entry into the town. Hurling a ladder against the
wall, he was the first to reach the top; and undeterred by a ball through his hat and
a second creasing his cheek, he rose from where he fell and again mounted the ladder

141.
The Death of General Montgomery in the Attack on Quebec, 31 December 1775. John Trumbull, 1832-34. Wadsworth Atheneum.

and jumped over the wall. After him came his trusty riflemen who overcame the troops stationed at the barrier and saved him from the enemy's bayonets.

Entering Sault au Matelot where he was to await Montgomery's force so that the two groups could push into the Upper Town together, Morgan decided against delaying. Noting the lack of defenses, he advised that the troops push on immediately. Unfortunately, he was prevailed upon by the other officers, who were contemptuous of this rough frontiersman, to wait for the hapless commander, who unknown to the group, had been shot down after leading his men through two undefended palisades. Montgomery's fearful subordinate, Lieutenant Colonel Donald Campbell, ordered a retreat. When the Americans withdrew, Carleton sent units to the upper end of Sault au Matelot and to the Palace Gate, which lay behind Arnold's troops. Thus, Morgan and his men were trapped; and despite brave fighting and a plea to Arnold's officers that he be allowed to fight a way out, he was forced to surrender. When the Americans threw down their arms, Morgan would not yield his sword until his men pleaded with him to give it up. Finally, he handed it to a priest, angrily remarking "not a scoundrel of these cowards shall take it out of my hand." [91]

If Morgan's advice had been followed when the group entered Sault au Matelot, he might have been successful and the city might have fallen. Later, he learned that he had correctly gauged the British confusion at the moment. An immediate thrust forward would have avoided the trap; and once the troops reached the Upper Town,

231

A U X
H A B I T A N T S
DE LA PROVINCE DU CANADA.

AMIS ET COMPATRIOTES;

NOTRE Précédente Adreſſe vous a démontré nos Droits , nos Griefs & les Moyens que nous avons en notre pouvoir , & dont nous ſommes autoriſés par les CONSTITU-TIONS BRITANNIQUES , à faire uſage pour maintenir les uns , & obtenir juſtice des autres.

NOUS vous avons auſſi expliqué , que votre Liberté , votre Honneur & votre Bonheur , ſont eſſentiellement & néceſſairement liés à l'Affaire malheureuſe que nous avons été forcé d'entreprendre , pour le ſoutien de nos Priviléges.

NOUS voyons avec joie , combien vous avez été touché , par les remontrances juſtes & équitables de vos Amis & Compatriotes , qui n'ont d'autres vues que celles de fortifier & d'établir la cauſe de la Liberté : les ſervices que vous avez déjà rendus à cette cauſe commune , méritent notre reconnoiſſance ; & nous ſentons l'obligation où nous ſommes , de vous rendre le reciproque.

LES meilleures cauſes ſont ſujettes aux événements , les contre-temps ſont inévi-tables , tel eſt le ſort de l'humanité ; mais les ames génereuſes , qui ſont éclairées & échauffées par le feu ſacré de la Liberté , ne ſeront pas découragées par de tels échecs , & ſurmonteront tous les obſtacles qui pourront ſe trouver entr'eux & l'objet prétieux de leurs vœux.

NOUS ne vous laiſſerons pas expoſé à la fureur de vos ennemis & des nôtres ; deux Bataillons ont reçu ordre de marcher au Canada , dont une partie eſt déjà en route ; on leve ſix autres Bataillons dans les Colonies unies pour le même ſervice , qui partiront pour votre Province auſſi-tôt qu'il ſera poſſible ; & probablement ils arriveront en Canada , avant que les Troupes du Miniſtere , ſous le Général Carleton , puiſſent recevoir des ſecours : en outre , nous avons fait expédier les ordres néceſſaires pour faire lever deux Bataillons chez vous. Votre aſſiſtance pour le ſoutien & la conſervation de la Liberté Amériquaine , nous cauſera la plus grande ſatisfaction ; & nous nous flattons que vous ſaiſirez avec zèle & empreſſement , l'inſtant favorable de co-opérer au ſuccès d'une entrepriſe auſſi glorieuſe. Si des forces plus conſidérables ſont requiſes , elles vous ſeront envoyées.

APRÉSENT , vous devez être convaincus , que rien n'eſt plus propre à aſſurer nos intérêts & nos libertés , que de prendre des méſures efficaces , pour combiner nos forces mutuelles , afin que par cette réunion de ſecours & de conſeils , nous puiſſions éviter les efforts & l'artifice d'un ennemi qui cherche à nous affoiblir en nous diviſant ; pour cet effet , nous vous conſeillons & vous exhortons , d'établir chez vous des Aſſociations en vos différentes Paroiſſes , de la même nature que celles qui ont été ſi ſalutaires aux Colonies unies ; d'élire des Députés pour former une Aſſemblée Provin-ciale chez vous , & que cette Aſſemblée nomme des Délegués , pour vous repréſenter en ce Congrès.

NOUS nous flattons de toucher à l'heureux moment , de voir diſparoître de deſſus cette terre , l'Etendard de la Tyrannie , & nous eſpérons qu'il ne trouvera aucune place en l'Amérique Septentrionale.

Signé au Nom & par l'Ordre du Congrès : JOHN HANCOCK , *Préſident.*

A Philadelphie , le 24 *Janvier* 1776.

143.
Aux Habitants De La Province Du Canada, broadside issued by
John Hancock, January 24, 1776.
The Library Company of Philadelphia.

144.
DANIEL MORGAN. Attributed to
Charles Willson Peale, date
unknown. Virginia Historical
Society.

Quebec would have been an American victory. The knowledge gave Morgan little
satisfaction in the light of the fact that in the fighting approximately one hundred
Americans were casualties, and over four hundred had been taken prisoner.

Badly injured, Arnold took command of the decimated army, issuing orders from
his hospital bed. On January 10, 1776, the Congress commissioned him a brigadier
general. But Morgan was not released from prison until August 1776. Once he
reached American lines, he was recognized for his courageous behavior and promoted
to colonel.

In Montreal, meanwhile, General David Wooster had assumed command and was
ignoring Arnold's pleas for reinforcements. Instead, Wooster concentrated on securing
Montreal and left Arnold to his own devices.

David Wooster had known Benedict Arnold when the two were fellow Masons in

David Wooster
(1711-1777)

233

New Haven, Connecticut. There, Wooster was known as "a conservative and law-abiding man by instinct and reputation."[92] Although he deplored the necessity to break with Great Britain, when the time for decision arrived he gave his support to the Patriots. But he was sixty-four years old in 1775, and the years had made him somewhat petty and fussy about the details and propriety of rank. When he was appointed brigadier general by the Continental Congress in June—the only general officer in the colonies not promoted to full rank—he was naturally vexed that his long and distinguished military record in the French and Indian War had not been properly rewarded. He particularly fretted about the fact that he had been placed under younger men. Soon he was picking a quarrel with General Philip Schuyler, who was also prone to respond sensitively to real or imagined insults. Ordered north by Schuyler in September, Wooster wrote that his appointment in the Continental Army was "not very agreeable to me." Schuyler was outraged by such an improper attitude; "these insults from a General Officer," he wrote to the Congress, he felt keenly, as "a man of honor ought." He would, he declared, have sent Wooster's regiment on without its commander if he had not been informed bluntly that it would not go. Continuing to protest loudly and constantly to whomever would listen that Richard Montgomery had no right to outrank him, Wooster made his way to Montreal and Quebec, where he finally found himself in command.[93]

"The old pettifogger from New Haven" did not abate his quarrelsome complaining. Now it was Arnold who provided grist for his mill. Distrustful of Canadians, without tact, (he closed all Catholic churches on Christmas Eve), surrounded by enemies, unable to discipline his troops, and unable to muster sufficient cash or provisions for their maintenance, he was truly, as J. H. Smith has called him, "A general . . . of a hayfield."[94]

Needless to say, Arnold was not happy with Wooster's arrival in Quebec. Surely he must have smarted when Wooster, ignorant of the facts and of Arnold's and Montgomery's immense efforts, boasted, "I'll scale those walls if there's enough space between them and the heavens."[95] Fortunately, perhaps, Arnold managed a heroic exit. Soon after Wooster arrived, and while his leg was still weak from its earlier wound, his horse fell upon him, putting him out of commission. A week later Arnold requested and received permission to return to Montreal.

Wooster's course of action closely followed Arnold's plan. He mounted guns on the far side of the St. Lawrence river and in mid-April proceeded to bombard the city—with little effect. By April 27 he had exhausted almost all his cannon powder. He continued to remain confident and unperturbed, however, until April 29 when a commission arrived in Montreal from the Congress to investigate the situation and to persuade the Canadians to join in the struggle against Great Britain.

Samuel Chase, Benjamin Franklin, Charles Carroll, and John Carroll, who constituted the congressional committee, were appalled at what they found: a sickly and unpaid army, an officer who, in their words, was "unfit—totally unfit—to command your army and to conduct the war" and whose presence was "prejudicial to our affairs"; and an alienated people. Washington was as critical: "I have no opinion at all of [Wooster's] enterprising genius," he wrote. On May 1, on the commission's recommendation, General John Thomas replaced David Wooster in command.[96]

It was not General Wooster, however, who was responsible for the loss of Quebec.

DAVID WOOSTER, Esq.
Commander in Chief of the Provincial Army against QUEBEC.

145.
DAVID WOOSTER. Johann Martin
Will. Engraving, 1776-78. Anne
S.K. Brown Military Collection,
Brown University Library.

The situation was lost before he even arrived on the scene. Later, the Congress acquitted him of the charge of incapacity and continued his commission—but without assignment. During the border raids of 1776 and 1777, he served in the Connecticut militia and on April 27, 1777, while rallying his men in Danbury to meet Tryon's raiders, he was mortally wounded.

On May 5, 1776, the siege of Quebec formally ended. General Thomas ordered a retreat, which turned into a rout when the Americans learned that Carleton's reinforcements from Great Britain had just arrived. At Sorel, General Thomas died, leaving preparation of the retreat once again to Benedict Arnold. Arnold persuaded the new American commanding officer, John Sullivan, to bring order to the evacuation by destroying bridges behind them, plundering useful provisions, and blocking roads. As the British army closed in, Arnold and Sullivan led their "dead and dying men" to the ships awaiting to evacuate them at Fort St. Johns.[97]

The last man off the mainland of Canada was Benedict Arnold. Once all the soldiers were safely in the canoes, he shot his horse and, carrying his saddle and bridle, climbed in the last canoe and shoved off. With Arnold and the American expedition went the last hope of a united American front and a fourteenth state.

235

COMMON SENSE;

ADDRESSED TO THE

INHABITANTS

OF

AMERICA,

On the following interesting

SUBJECTS.

I. Of the Origin and Design of Government in general, with concise Remarks on the English Constitution.

II. Of Monarchy and Hereditary Succession.

III. Thoughts on the present State of American Affairs.

IV. Of the present Ability of America, with some miscellaneous Reflections.

Man knows no Master save creating HEAVEN,
Or those whom choice and common good ordain.

THOMSON.

PHILADELPHIA;

Printed, and Sold, by R. BELL, in Third-Street.

MDCCLXXVI.

147.
George Washington's copy of
Thomas Paine's *Common Sense*.
Philadelphia, 1776. The Boston
Athenaeum.

VII.

The Road to Independence

Reconciliation . . . like an agreeable dream, has passed away and left us," wrote Thomas Paine in January 1776.[1] So obvious was this conclusion that it is surprising it took so long to be articulated in print. During 1775 and 1776, the minds of many Americans had moved in this direction. But perhaps it required a newcomer to the American scene to realize this truth with clear objectivity, and to state it at once simply and cogently to the American people.

Thomas Paine had not been long in Philadelphia when he wrote *Common Sense*. In the time between his arrival in November 1774, and its publication January 10, 1776, he had keenly assessed the situation of his adopted land and had drawn conclusions about the dilemma it faced. As early as January 1775, in the first issue of the *Pennsylvania Magazine*, which he later edited, he had expressed his feelings about "the present perplexities of affairs" in an imaginary "Dialogue between General Wolfe and General Gage in a Wood Near Boston." Paine had Wolfe, speaking from Elysian Fields, warn Gage to resign his commission if he had "any regard for the glory of the British name" or for his future life. But, like many other Americans in January 1775, Paine still hoped for reconciliation.[2]

By the middle of April, all realistic expectations that peaceful relations could be restored had been dashed. Lexington and Concord had aroused the colonists to the need for defense, the British to the need for punishment. In May the colonial Congress met again, to whose deliberations Paine—living and writing in Philadelphia—must have been privy. In June Bunker Hill set the scene of still another battle. The Olive Branch Petition was signed and sent in July, and in August was coldly received by Lord Dartmouth. By October it was rejected and George III was calling for military efforts to end the disorders and "put down the revolt" in America. With General Gage given permission to use force and with the colonies closed to all commerce by royal proclamation on December 23, Britain's policy was clear. It was now up to the colonies to determine themselves whether indeed they intended to establish "an independent Empire" or whether they would answer force with force only to reassert their old dependency. The latter course could not possibly be expected; and it was only a matter of time before independence would be proclaimed and force utilized to secure the establishment of a new nation.

Hastening the inevitable was the appearance of Paine's rousing pamphlet. Here, anonymously, Paine argued against the tyrannies of a government "so exceedingly complex" that it was impossible for it to govern wisely. Inveighing against England and her King, he urged Americans to cease their partnership so that every man would become "a virtuous supporter of the rights of mankind and of the free and independent states of America."[3]

Thomas Paine (1737-1809)

Thomas Paine was the son of a poor Quaker staymaker. He had grown up in poverty in England, enjoying only the rudiments of an education. His early experiences and sufferings had, however, sensitized him to social issues and ideas. As his first biographer, Moncure Conway wrote:

> *There was no dreg in the poverty of his people that he had not tasted, no humiliation in their dependence, no outlook of their hopelessness, he had not known....*[4]

Paine emigrated to America on the advice of Benjamin Franklin, who found him "an ingenious worthy young man." Once arrived, Paine continued to impress such influential colonial leaders as President John Witherspoon of the College of New Jersey (later Princeton), the scientist David Rittenhouse, and the physician Dr. Benjamin Rush. It was Rush who encouraged Paine to publish *Common Sense*, which, as the physician asserted, "burst from the press with an effect which has rarely been produced by types and paper in any age or country."[5]

Logically pointing out the failure of American efforts—particularly the Association boycott—to effect a reconciliation with Great Britain, Paine argued in his pamphlet that America must now look to her own devices to guarantee her liberties. America needed money to buy munitions for the war she had been forced to wage by British tyranny. To obtain funds, the resumption of trade was a necessity. "Our plan is commerce," he wrote; "and that, well attended to, will secure us the peace and friendship of all Europe." Only an independent nation could achieve commercial greatness, because independence would allow America to trade with the whole world.[6]

Common Sense was more than merely another recitation of American grievances, however. What was new in Paine's pamphlet was not its rebellious spirit or its forceful language, but its association of the American cause with "the cause of all mankind." By extending the significance of the colonial cause from the local to the universal, Paine legitimized revolutionary action for many who still conceived of revolution as an act against nature. "This sun never shined on a cause of greater worth," wrote Paine.

> *Tis not the affair of a city, a country, a province, or a kingdom, but of a continent—of at least one-eighth part of the habitable globe. Tis not the concern of a day, a year, or an age; posterity are virtually involved in the contest, and will be more or less affected even to the end of time by the proceedings now. Now is the seedtime of continental union, faith, and honor.*[7]

Paine also attempted to destroy the image many Americans held of England as "the parent country." Europe, not England, he proclaimed, gave birth to America, by sending to the New World "the persecuted lovers of civil and religious liberty. Hither have they fled, not from the tender embraces of the mother, but from the cruelty of the monster."[8]

146.
THOMAS PAINE. John Wesley
Jarvis, circa 1805. National Gallery
of Art, Washington.

The size of the American continent itself justified an extension of America's meaning for the world: "we claim brotherhood," wrote Paine, "with every European Christian." Because of this, Americans should reject arguments that tied their country's future to Great Britain for imperial reasons or for the sake of military protection. In fact, added this newly arrived American, stating what was to become an American tradition for over a century to come, "It is the true interest of America to steer clear of European contentions, which she never can do while, by her dependence on Britain, she is made the makeweight in the scale of British politics." [9]

Appealing to the people's manhood—"if you have and can still shake hands with the murderers, then . . . you have the heart of a coward and the spirit of a sycophant"; reason—"the universal order of things"; and nature—"never can true reconcilement grow where wounds of deadly hate have pierced so deep," Paine presented a blueprint for a government that answered his definition of a proper republic: simple, equal, and free, a government that would contain "the greatest sum of individual happiness, with the least national expense." [10] His resounding call to liberty must have echoed in every colonial mind that studied his pamphlet, as it has to oppressed peoples everywhere since:

> *O ye that love mankind! Ye that dare oppose not only tyranny but the tyrant, stand forth! Every spot of the Old World is overrun with oppression. Freedom has been hunted round the globe. Asia and Africa have long expelled her. Europe regards her like a stranger, and England has given her warning to depart. O! receive the fugitive, and prepare in time an asylum for mankind.*[11]

By the end of the pamphlet, Paine had elevated the American struggle above the level of economic and political self-interest that had characterized it up to that time to the moralistic level of a movement for humanity. The colonists were now fighting for an idea.

Common Sense placed Paine in the colonial limelight and made its way into people's minds with little opposition. For many Americans who, like General George Washington, still toasted the King at dinners and public gatherings, it cut the Gordian knot. After *Common Sense,* such toasts underwent modification, with the addition of phrases like, "May the crowns of tyrants be crowns of thorns," or "The downfall of Tyrants and Tyranny." [12] By January 31, 1776, Washington was writing to his aide, Joseph Reed of Pennsylvania, that "the sound doctrine and unanswerable reasoning contained in the pamphlet *Common Sense,*" along with "a few more of such flaming arguments, as were exhibited at Falmouth and Norfolk," would soon convince most Americans of "the propriety of a separation." [13]

A few replies to Paine's pamphlet were attempted—two pamphlets denouncing its sentiments and its author and some magazine articles. Most Loyalists were silenced by now as a result of the fast movement of events that put their cause increasingly in a bad light. Some were awaiting the arrival of the British peace commissioners, hopeful that there lay the promise of reconciliation. Two men, however, shocked at the possibility of "revolution and the chaos it promised," were unwilling to sit back quietly and wait. One of these, the Maryland landowner James Chalmers, signing himself "Candidus," published *Plain Truth.* The other, "Cato," published in the *Pennsylvania Ledger* a series of skillfully composed letters identified as the work of the Reverend William Smith, provost of the College of Philadelphia.[14]

William Smith was born and educated in Scotland. In 1751 he emigrated to America to assume the role of tutor in New York City. Almost immediately, he published views on education that were well received and brought him an invitation from Benjamin Franklin to take charge of the newly chartered academy in Philadelphia. After returning to England to be ordained an Anglican priest, he assumed the office of provost of the College, Academy, and Charitable School of Philadelphia, which, operating under an enlarged "Plan of Education" drawn up by the provost, was renamed the College of Philadelphia. Soon Smith was a dominant figure in the intellectual life of Philadelphia. He helped found schools for the Germans in the western settlements of Pennsylvania and, always hopeful that he would be appointed the first American bishop, maintained active communication with church officials in England. Through a large effort, he made the college a progressive and prominent educational institution.

Smith's ardent support of proprietary interests and of strong military measures during the French and Indian War won him many enemies among the Quaker pacifists in

William Smith (1727-1803)

148.
WILLIAM SMITH. Thomas Sully after Gilbert Stuart, 1855. Robert H. Hicks.

241

Philadelphia. In 1757, for political as well as literary reasons, Smith established the *American Magazine and Monthly Chronicle of the British Colonies*, one of the first of such periodicals in America. The magazine was notable for its encouragement of poetry as well as for its scientific and religious articles.

As a result of difficulties with the Pennsylvania Assembly, Smith was jailed in 1758 for publishing "seditious libels," and in order to appeal his case to the King, he sailed to England. There he was warmly received as a result of his writings, and when he returned to Philadelphia in 1759, he carried with him several honorary degrees from British institutions and encouragement from English educators.

During the crises of the 1760s and 1770s this energetic and influential clergyman often found himself agreeing with the colonists. He opposed the Stamp Act as "contrary to the faith of charters and the inherent rights of Englishmen"; but he never contemplated revolution. To Smith, the answer to the colonial question lay in the complete reorganization of the Empire, not in a renovation of taxation policies and certainly not in independence. Thus, when Paine's *Common Sense* made its explosive appearance, Smith unabashedly picked up his pen to challenge Paine's assumptions and conclusions. Under the pseudonym "Cato," he wrote his eight letters arguing against Paine's proposal that the colonies seek ties with other European nations and break their connection with Great Britain. To substitute an unknown foreign power for the benevolent English, under whose control the colonies had prospered for more than a hundred years, seemed foolhardy to Smith. Since Great Britain had always heeded colonial complaints and was attempting to bring about peaceful conciliation, the colonists would not, he believed, rush precipitously into unknown dangers.

The debate between the two did not stop here. Paine had been visiting the American troops mustered in New York under General Charles Lee. When his friends in Philadelphia informed him of Smith's challenges to *Common Sense*, he rushed home to reply. Under the nomenclature "Forester," Paine denied that Britain had America's best interests at heart: "conquest, and not reconciliation" was her goal. To accept "foreign assistance" did not mean that America would surrender its land or control to France or Spain; it meant simply the acceptance of guns and ammunition. "It is the true interest of America," reiterated Paine, "to steer clear of all European contentions." [15]

After his encounter with Paine's venomous pen, Smith never ventured into politics again. His outspoken defense of the British connection aroused great hostility among his contemporaries, as did what the Reverend Ezra Stiles called his "haughty, self-opinionated, Character." [16] When the Pennsylvania Assembly voided the charter of his college in Philadelphia in 1779, Smith moved to Chestertown, Maryland, where he served as rector of Chester Parish and founded Washington College (1782), of which he became president. In 1789 when the charter of Philadelphia College was restored, he returned to Philadelphia to resume his position as provost, but he never recovered his influence in the Philadelphia community.

FRANCE DECIDES TO AID AMERICA

One of Thomas Paine's most compelling arguments in *Common Sense* was that a declaration of independence would bring foreign assistance to America. It would be "unreasonable," he pointed out, to expect assistance from France or Spain "if we mean only to make use of that assistance for the purpose of repairing the breach and strengthening the connection between Britain and America, because these powers would be sufferers by the consequences." [17]

Paine was well aware of the rivalry that bitterly affected Anglo-French relations after the Peace of Paris in 1763, despite the fact that France had, seemingly, accepted the loss of her colonial interests on the North American continent. France, however, had not accepted the humiliation that accompanied defeat, nor her loss of prestige among the European powers. Now the diplomatic representative of His Britannic Majesty received precedence over His Most Christian Majesty's diplomats at various court receptions, and French influence was at its lowest ebb.

Almost immediately after peace was declared, therefore, the French government began to look for occasions "by which we could avenge ourselves on England and tear up the treaty of Paris." The Family Compact with Spain was a first step toward achieving this goal; a second step was to take advantage of "the tendency of the English colonies to revolt against their metropolis." [18] "Only the revolution which will occur some day in America," wrote France's minister of foreign affairs, Comte de Choiseul, to His Catholic Majesty, Charles III of Spain, "though we shall probably not see it, will put England back to that state of weakness in which Europe will have no more fear of her." [19]

Beginning in 1764 Choiseul began to send secret observers to the American colonies to report on England's military strength in America and the political sentiments of the colonists. Spies were also sent to England, and the French government waited eagerly to discover whether in truth Americans were sufficiently discontented with the mother country to engage in insurrection.

In 1767 the French foreign minister chose the Baron de Kalb to go to Amsterdam to inquire into the "rumors in circulation about the English colonies." If he discovered that the Americans had been stirred by British policy to the point of rebellion, then De Kalb was to "make preparations for a journey to America." [20] Obviously, the information that De Kalb picked up in the Dutch city was convincing; on October 4, 1767, he set sail for America.

Baron de Kalb (1721-1780)

Choiseul's spy was a middle-aged man of keen judgment and worldly experience. Born Hans Kalb, the son of a Bavarian peasant, he had made his own way in the world since the day he had, as a youth, changed his name to Jean de Kalb and joined the French army. A good horseman with unusual physical energy and health, he had seen action on many of Europe's battlefields. Later, he would prove his command of military discipline during the American Revolution at the Battle of Camden where he received a mortal wound while fighting for American independence. In 1768, however, it was his political as well as military shrewdness that was called upon for an assessment of the Anglo-American situation. Since De Kalb had learned to speak English fluently, and, of course, possessed a mastery of German, Choiseul believed he would be most welcome to both the English and the Americans, who were known to admire officers from the army of Frederick the Great and would be more likely to speak freely to a German than to a Frenchman who was still considered an enemy.

It did not take long for De Kalb to assess American loyalties. Landing in Philadelphia on January 12, 1768, while excitement still prevailed over the Stamp Act and its repeal,

149.
BARON JOHANN DE KALB. Charles
Willson Peale, circa 1781-82.
Independence National Historical
Park. [Not in exhibition.]

he almost immediately identified with the American cause. Agreeing with the principle
of "no taxation without representation," and full of admiration for the courage and
ingenuity of the Americans in mounting a program of nonimportation of British goods,
he also saw that England would attempt conciliation in order to "preserve this invaluable
magazine of raw products and this most profitable market for its manufactures." [21]
Americans were, he believed, "free and enterprising," but fundamentally "little inclined to shake off the English supremacy with the aid of foreign powers." An alliance
with France would "appear to them to be fraught with danger to their liberties." Therefore, the time was not yet propitious for French involvement in England's colonial difficulties. In fact, De Kalb reported, if England should go to war with France, the conflict
would "hasten their reconciliation" by throwing them into an alliance against a common
enemy.[22]

De Kalb foresaw "that if all the provinces can be united under a common representation, an independent state will certainly come forth in time." But after visiting Philadelphia, New York, and Boston and noting the "impulse" of Massachusetts to independence, he discouraged Choiseul's hopes in that direction. ". . . all, from the leaders down
to the humblest citizen," he wrote, "seem to be imbued with a heartfelt love of the
mother country . . . [and] have never contemplated the possibility of extreme
measures." [23]

De Kalb's message did not please the ambitious Choiseul. Accurate as these observations undoubtedly were, Choiseul believed them to be superficial and pronounced De

244

Kalb's work useless. Yet, Choiseul was forced to act upon De Kalb's advice. Temporarily abandoning the notion that his country could interfere directly in America, he began to formulate a plan whereby France and Spain would foment discontent in the colonies by opening the ports of French and Spanish possessions to North American trade. Since the British forbade direct trade with these foreign colonies, so the reasoning went, Americans would chafe even more at the commercial restraints of the mother country. Moreover, a diversion of American products from the mother country to France's and Spain's island possessions could only weaken England, who, it was believed, depended for her prosperity on colonial raw materials. In 1770, however, Choiseul fell from power, and his plan was never executed.

Some kindly fate must have been watching over America's interests when the newly crowned Louis XVI decided to appoint Charles Gravier, Comte de Vergennes, foreign minister in 1774. The French monarch would not by himself have become involved in American affairs. A sluggish youth, Louis was thoroughly imbued with monarchical principles; revolution against a king was not a measure he could view lightly, however much his court circle may have been charmed by sentimental pictures of the virtuous republican life. Moreover, on moral principles, Louis XVI did not wish to strike secretly at a nation with which France was at peace. Vergennes was also not an admirer of republican government; but he did not share Louis's scruples. As a practical politician, "a methodical thinker" and "a circumspect and prudent man," he was passionately committed, as was his predecessor Choiseul, to the recovery of France's honor at home and abroad. It was said of Vergennes that he could never hear of the Treaty of 1763 and not shudder.[24] National pride, then, dictated that he pursue a foreign policy for his country much in the spirit of Choiseul's—that is, to maintain France's alliances with Spain and Austria against England and Prussia and to plan for eventual war with England when France was in a position to be sure of success. Having at his disposal Choiseul's reports and memoranda on Britain's colonial difficulties, it was inevitable that he, too, should look to America to solve the problem of France's hurt pride. The prize would be larger than mere psychological gratification, important as that was; it involved the diversion of American trade to France and her possessions and the consequent weakening of the enormous maritime power of Great Britain.

When Vergennes took over the office of the secretary of foreign affairs toward the end of July 1774, he was fifty-five years old, a career diplomat from an old, but not particularly illustrious, Burgundian family. He had seen service in France's diplomatic corps since his twentieth birthday, working his way up from various minor posts to become minister at Trèves, minister to Turkey, and, finally, ambassador to Sweden. In all these positions, he had demonstrated cleverness as well as capacity to handle complex diplomatic maneuvers with the aim of salvaging France's waning power in Europe and raising it from the low point it had reached in 1772 when it had stood by passively and allowed Prussia, Russia, and Austria to divide Poland.

Like all new and young kings, on assuming the throne Louis XVI had immediately set to work to rid the court of the politicians and courtiers who had dallied about his grandfather and contributed to the unpopularity of his later years. Having watched Vergennes's career with admiration, and seeking to eliminate the frivolity that he believed had corrupted the former king's court, Louis XVI came to believe that Ver-

Louis XVI
(1754-1793)
and
Charles Gravier,
The Comte de Vergennes
(1719-1787)

245

151.
CHARLES GRAVIER, Comte de
Vergennes. Unidentified artist,
date unknown. Musée National
du Château de Versailles.

gennes's solid virtues would add a substantial element to the monarchy, and so, almost immediately recalled him from Sweden to assume an important position in his council.

If, to Louis XVI, the appointment of Vergennes seemed a good thing for France, it proved especially good for America. Even before Vergennes arrived in Paris, the French government had been maintaining a close watch on American affairs, especially on what was called the "insurrection of the Bostonnais,"[25] to see whether General Gage indeed possessed the "talent and . . . sagacity and patience to calm the spirit of insubordination which has possessed almost all the English colonies."[26] The Coercive and Quebec Acts had assured the French that there was no mending the breach between Britain and her American possessions. But the fear persisted throughout the first half of 1775 that Lord Chatham (William Pitt) would recover power, "become the conciliator and there is a man to dread,' as the French chargé d'affaires in London wrote to Vergennes in June: "what can be the conditions of the conciliation? Conditions little honorable to England, and then an audacious minister, accustomed to glory, will look upon our colonies as a necessary compensation."[27]

Uncertain as to the timing of his next move, Vergennes was happy to accept the suggestion of his London ambassador that a secret agent be sent to America to ascertain the state of affairs there "from the political and military standpoint." In July 1775 Achard de Bonvouloir was assigned this duty, with verbal instructions to listen and watch carefully what was being discussed and experienced in the British colonies and send home accurate reports. He also was to persuade the Americans that France was their friend, that the French admired their courageous efforts, and—to allay American fears—that France had no intention of attempting to recover Canada. He was not, however, to bind the French ministry to any commitments, nor was he to suggest that his arrival in America was prompted by official interest in the American cause. For this

246

150.
LOUIS XVI. Antoine François
Callet, 1775. Musée National du
Château de Versailles.

task, Bonvouloir was given 200 louis (equivalent to £200) and a preparation of milk, which could be used to write secret reports and presumably could be developed by a red-hot shovel. Sworn to secrecy, he was to travel as a private citizen; if anything went amiss, he was to expect to be disowned by the French government.[28]

Achard de Bonvouloir
(1749-1783)

On September 8, 1775, Bonvouloir set sail for America, arriving early in December after a "frightful passage . . . one hundred days at sea . . . reduced to two biscuits a day . . . a little salt beef and stale water."[29] While on the high seas, momentous news had been received in America that was to render his mission almost unnecessary. On August 23, 1775, King George III had issued his proclamation declaring the colonies in a state of rebellion and the members of the Continental Congress traitors. Vergennes received the news in Paris even before it arrived in the colonies—ten days after the proclamation was issued. Thus, before Bonvouloir had even boarded ship, Vergennes was convinced that this "chef-d'oeuvre of insanity on the part of the [British] Government" had "unanswerably" destroyed "all hopes of conciliation."[30]

On November 9 news of the proclamation reached the Congress in Philadelphia, which immediately went into secret session. Twenty days later, a Committee of Secret Correspondence was formed, consisting of Benjamin Harrison, Benjamin Franklin, John Dickinson, Robert Morris, and John Jay.

The Secret Committee almost immediately was approached by the newly arrived Bonvouloir, who insisted in his report home that he had "made them no offer . . . absolutely none. . . ." When the committee wished to ascertain whether France would come to the colonies' aid, he could only reply tentatively that she might and "all they could do was to submit their propositions to that country." Bonvouloir did admit, upon questioning, that France looked with favor upon their cause, that she would be able to send at least two good engineers to help, and that the Americans might attempt to institute commercial relations with France, but at their own risk.[31]

"These affairs are so delicate," Bonvouloir wrote home, "that with all the goodwill possible, I tremble as I advance." But "toiling day and night," he believed he had made "progress in their confidence"; certainly, he was "learning to talk English very prettily."[32]

Encouraging the French to intervene in the Anglo-American struggle was Bonvouloir's exaggerated report that "Every man here is a soldier, the troops are well clothed, well paid, and well commanded. They have about fifty thousand men under pay, and a still greater number of volunteers who wish no pay. Judge how this sort of men would fight."[33] Bonvouloir, however, reported that the Americans still hesitated at declaring their independence and seeking a French alliance. George III "had not as yet done them evil enough," he wrote. The Americans "still waited to have more of their towns destroyed and more of their homes burned before they would completely abhor the emblems of British power."[34]

Bonvouloir's report reached Vergennes March 3, 1776. Vergennes was already entertaining the idea of offering secret aid to the Americans. Such "secret favors" would maintain "the courage of the Americans" by providing them with "vague hopes, which would assist to develop ideas of independence." At the same time, it would keep the British occupied "in an active and costly campaign" that might eventuate in the humiliation of Great Britain in Europe. Now Vergennes was convinced that this would

152.
PIERRE AUGUSTIN DE
BEAUMARCHAIS. Jean Marc
Nattier. Guy de Beaumarchais.
[Original not in exhibition.]

be the best policy for France to pursue at the time. He had been brought to this conviction by the enthusiastic suggestion of Pierre-Augustin Caron de Beaumarchais.

Watchmaker, musician, playwright, businessman, and secret diplomatic envoy—these
were the occupations that engaged one of the most romantic and influential Frenchmen
to become involved in the American cause. Pierre-Augustin Caron was born in 1732
into the family of a Parisian clockmaker. By the age of twenty-two, he had perfected
an improvement to watches and been invited to demonstrate it at the court of Louis XV.
Not quite two years later, he obtained (for a sum) appointment as clerk controller in
the royal household, charged with the duty of escorting the royal meat to table with
drawn sword. That year—1755—he married a widow ten years his senior, who possessed property in the village of Beaumarchais; young Pierre Caron thereupon became
Caron de Beaumarchais, a name which he was to make famous throughout Europe.
Himself made a widower within ten months, he became a favorite of Louis XV's
daughters, and soon, through purchase of high offices, earned the status of nobility.

Adventures in Spain, France, and England followed Beaumarchais's rise to fame,
during which period he wrote plays, attempted to compose a musical comedy, and,
finally—in 1772-73—completed *The Barber of Seville*. Like his famous character
Figaro, Beaumarchais was "welcomed in one town, imprisoned in another, everywhere
rising above circumstances; praised by these people, blamed by those . . . mocking the
foolish, braving the wicked. . . ." [35]

When Louis XVI assumed the throne of France, Beaumarchais offered his services

Pierre-Augustin
Caron de Beaumarchais
(1732-1799)

249

"promptly, quickly, and secretly: . . . I have a head, a heart, and army, but no tongue."[36] In order to track down scurrilous libel against the throne, Louis immediately accepted his offer. But in 1775 a more important confidential mission was entrusted to Beaumarchais. That spring, to satisfy Vergennes's hopes of exploiting the deepening Anglo-American quarrel, Beaumarchais was sent to London to gather information on the state of English politics and finances.

Beaumarchais had many friends in London in both Government and Opposition circles. Especially useful to him were Lord Rochford, secretary of state for the Southern department, and John Wilkes, the radical publisher who was now Lord Mayor of London. Arthur Lee, agent for Massachusetts Bay after Franklin left England in 1775, also became a friendly informant, who seems to have convinced Beaumarchais that Americans were intent upon severing their political connection with Great Britain. The fighting at Lexington and Concord in April 1775 suggested to Beaumarchais, already sympathetic to the American cause, that the struggle between the colonists and the mother country was going to be long and costly and that here was the opportunity for which France had been waiting. At the beginning of December, then, he presumably wrote a long memorandum to King Louis to convince him to intervene in the Anglo-American situation. Emphasizing his belief that neither side of the colonial struggle should be allowed to win since, in the event of either victory, France's island possessions would be endangered, he informed the King that it was France's duty, if she wished to preserve peace in Europe, to prevent "at all costs the conclusion of peace between England and America, and in preventing the one from triumphing over the other." The one way in which France could achieve this purpose was by giving Americans "sufficient help to put their forces on an equal footing with those of England—but no more." If that help were given secretly, England would not be offended. Beaumarchais emphasized, too, that help should be given speedily in order to keep the pot boiling.[37]

In December 1775 the Secret Committee appointed by the Continental Congress the previous month to purchase guns and military supplies in Europe asked Arthur Lee to act as its agent in London. Lee's and Beaumarchais's mission from that time on took one direction: to obtain France's help in America's effort to resist England. Since the English had already arranged to send equipped and trained German mercenaries to the colonies to quell the rebellion, the situation was truly crucial.

On February 29, 1776, Beaumarchais offered the King of France on behalf of Lee and the American Congress a longlasting treaty of commerce that would secure for France "all the profits with which we [the Americans] have enriched England for a century." "Has France absolutely decided to refuse us all help," asked Beaumarchais in behalf of his American friends, "and thus become the victim of England and the laughingstock of Europe because of this incredible torpor?"[38]

Beaumarchais's and Lee's pleadings for help were in vain: King Louis believed that to take advantage of the English situation would be "un-Christian," while Vergennes, concerned about the course Prussia, an ally of England, would take, and whether Spain would join France in aiding the Americans, found it necessary to temporize. In April Beaumarchais was still pleading for "arms, gunpowder . . . above all . . . engineers" for America. "The Americans," he wrote to Vergennes, are in as good a situation as they can be. Army, fleet, food supplies, courage—everything is excellent. But without gunpowder and without engineers, how can they be victorious or even defend themselves? Are we going to let them perish rather than lend them one or two millions?"[39]

As Beaumarchais and Lee watched the British expeditionary force being prepared to sail, their urgings became even more strident. "Engineers and gunpowder!" was the constant note in Beaumarchais's reports.

In the spring of 1776 the situation slowly began to change. In April the Continental Congress declared American commerce to be free, except with Great Britain. When the English seized an American merchant vessel bound for Nantes and led it to Bristol, they aroused the pride of the French King by demanding that the French merchant to whom the ship's cargo was assigned be punished by the French government for entering into a trade deemed illegal by the British. Angry at this high-handed behavior, Louis XVI was more amenable to Beaumarchais's advice that France should intervene in the American conflict. In May 1776 Beaumarchais was ordered to return to Paris to prepare a plan for sending secret help to the Americans. Vergennes ruled out Beaumarchais's and Lee's plan for direct monetary aid in the fear that France's peaceful relations with Great Britain would be threatened. But since France's arsenals were filled with outmoded war materiel, as a result of the recent renovation and modernization of the French army, it was decided to send these antiquated supplies to America, not directly, but through an independent commercial firm (Roderigue Hortalez & Cie.) headed by Beaumarchais. The government of France, and later Spain, would loan the firm a million livres each (approximately $200,000) and with a similar amount of money that Beaumarchais would raise among his business acquaintances, the adventurer-turned-businessman would buy from the government the needed supplies—gunpowder, guns, muskets, blankets, shoes, clothing—and ship them to the Americans, receiving in return such products as tobacco and rice, which would be sold in France with the help of the French government. Vergennes insisted that Beaumarchais's firm be independent and self-supporting, with Beaumarchais either profiting from its success or bearing its losses.[40]

The subsequent history of Beaumarchais's career as an intermediary between the French government and the American Congress is a tangled affair and not as happily unraveled as the tangled plots spun out by Beaumarchais's imagination in his famous *Marriage of Figaro* (1778). With two American agents in Paris—Silas Deane and Arthur Lee—sending back to the Congress conflicting reports about the materials Beaumarchais's firm was supplying, Congress was confused as to whether they were a gift of the French government or a commercial venture. As a result, Beaumarchais's bills never got paid, and it was not until 1835 that his descendants, after much hard work and petitioning, collected from the United States Government 800,000 francs—a fraction of the three millions that Beaumarchais is said to have spent in his zeal for the American cause. As John Bigelow, the American minister to France in 1870 wrote:

> *To him more than any other person belongs*
> *the credit of making Louis XVI comprehend the*
> *political importance of aiding the colonies*
> *in their struggle with Great Britain; he*
> *planned and executed the ingenious scheme by*
> *which the aid was to be extended; he sent*

*the first munitions of war and supplies which
the colonists received from abroad and he sent
them, too, at a time when, humanly speaking, it
was reasonably certain that without such aid
from some quarter, the colonists must have
succumbed.*[41]

GEORGIA JOINS THE REVOLUTION

Throughout the year 1775 colonial unity gained strength under the galvanizing effect of Lexington and Concord and Bunker Hill. As military reports replaced political articles in the radical newspapers, American attitudes underwent subtle change and hopes for an accommodation receded.[42] The changes that took place were most apparent in the South, and especially in the colony of Georgia, which up to 1775 had maintained royal government and a seeming aloofness from the troubled life of its northern neighbors.

Founded in 1732, Georgia was the youngest of the British provinces along the Atlantic seaboard south of Halifax. Unlike the older colonies, it had been planted and developed under the supervision and financing of Parliament and owed its well-being to that body. Georgians could not argue, therefore, as could the inhabitants of the other colonies, that their enterprise had been founded by private effort and that Parliament was now trying to reap unearned benefits. Georgia, moreover, took a long time to develop; in 1770, possessing only 50,000 settlers, it still required British garrisons to protect it from the constant menace of the Creek confederation. Georgians, indeed, could and did accept the economic justification for the Stamp Act since they benefited so highly from the British military strength it was designed to support. In 1774, while the other colonies shook with righteous indignation over the Intolerable Acts, a few radicals in Georgia attempted to impose an embargo on trade, but most Georgians were occupied casting nervous glances toward the dark pine forests where the Indians were daubing themselves with war paint. Thus, at the beginning, Georgia temporized on the Anglo-American quarrel and ignored the First Continental Congress and its Association.

But not all Georgians were loyal to Great Britain. Early in 1766 a group of Sons of Liberty organized in Savannah and so disturbed the royal governor, James Wright, that he complained bitterly to the British authorities that he had suffered "the greatest Mortification to see the Reins of Government nearly hoisted out of my Hands, His Majesties authority Insulted, and the Civil power obstructed."[43] South Carolinian radicals, under the leadership of Christopher Gadsden, encouraged this solid core of Georgians who opposed British policy, and it was this group primarily, who, by exploiting every advantage which British restrictive policy provided, finally converted loyal Georgia to rebellion. One of the most active leaders of the Georgian radicals was a young lawyer, George Walton.

Born in Virginia, George Walton was orphaned as a small child and left to the care of an uncle, who apprenticed him to a carpenter. Unwilling to accept the lowly position that fate had thrust upon him, the young boy studied during the night by the "light of fat fagots which he collected and husbanded for that purpose." [44] So favorably did his diligence impress his master that once his apprenticeship was concluded, he was permitted to retain his earnings. By the age of twenty, he was prepared to leave Virginia and seek his fortune in the new colony of Georgia.

In Savannah he studied for the bar, and soon enjoyed success as a lawyer in the small but prospering metropolis. Almost immediately, he identified with the radical cause, and by July 1774 he was ready to move his activities into the open. On the twenty-seventh of that month, a "respectable number of the freeholders and inhabitants of the Province" met at Tondee's tavern and elected a committee to prepare resolutions declaring Georgia's opposition to the "alarming and arbitrary impositions of the late acts of the British parliament, respecting the town of Boston." Messages were sent to distant parishes inviting their cooperation and another meeting was scheduled for August 10.[45]

Alarmed at these "revolutionary" proceedings, Governor Wright issued a proclamation pronouncing the meeting "unconstitutional, illegal, and punishable by law." But the radicals ignored Wright's threat and met again as they had earlier determined, to frame and adopt resolutions condemning parliamentary legislation and offering aid to the "suffering poor in Boston." [46]

Most Georgians were indifferent to the radicals' efforts, and the motion they presented to the August meeting to "send six deputies to the General Congress of the American Colonies" was voted down. For another year Georgia remained outside the main course of colonial events. Only one parish—St. John's—composed mainly of transplanted New Englanders, ignored the threats of the royal governor and on its own initiative sent Dr. Lyman Hall in the spring as a special delegate to the Continental Congress.

The following June Walton and his fellow radicals attempted once again to "bring about a union of Georgia with her sister Colonies in the cause of freedom." [47] Exploiting to the full the shock experienced by most Georgians at the news of Concord and Lexington, they pushed their advantage. On June 1, under their prompting, Savannah sent supplies to the army beseiging Boston. On June 5 the radicals erected the town's first Liberty Pole; and on the twenty-second they organized a Council of Safety—of which Walton was a member—to correspond with the Continental Congress and the other parishes of Georgia.

Radical sentiment, growing prodigiously as Georgia traversed in weeks ground that had taken the other colonies months, reached a peak with the calling of a Provincial Congress to meet in Savannah on July 4, 1775. Walton was one of the primary organizers of the meeting and was elected secretary of the Congress, serving on the committee of intelligence and helping to draft addresses to the King and the people of Georgia. On July 5 the Provincial Congress passed its key resolution: "That this Congress do put this Province upon the same footing with our sister Colonies." [48] The next day the delegates implemented the resolution by resolving, in sixteen motions, to align Georgia with the Continental Association adopted so many months ago by the other colonies. On July 10 the Congress endorsed a declaration of rights, based upon

George Walton (1741-1804)

154.
GEORGE WALTON. Charles Willson Peale, circa 1781. Yale University Art Gallery.

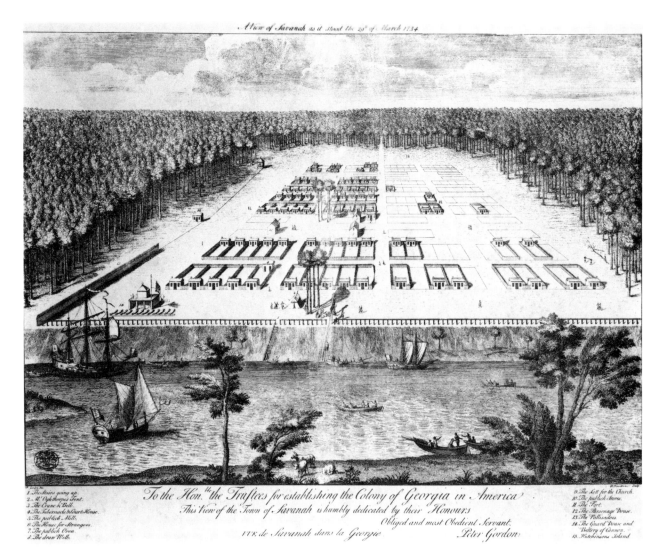

A View of Savannah as it stood the 29th of March 1734 . . . .

To the Honble the Trustees for establishing the Colony of Georgia in America
This View of the Town of Savanah is humbly dedicated by their Honours
Obliged and most Obedient Servant.
VUE de Savanah dans la Georgie
Peter Gordon.

153.
A View of Savannah as it stood the 29th of March 1734. Pierre Fourdrinier after Peter Gordon. Engraving, 1734. Library of Congress.

the argument that Americans were free-born and should enjoy all the rights of Englishmen. It also embraced the new radical idea, just beginning to enjoy widespread credence, that the only legitimate link between America and Great Britain was through the Crown.

Having now gone as far as any other colony had gone without violence, the Georgians on July 12 proved that they were not unwilling to use force to defend their rights. Word had come that a vessel, heavily laden with powder for the Indians and Loyalists, had left England for Georgia. Determined to intercept the vessel, South Carolina sent an armed contingent to the mouth of the Savannah River. The Provincial Congress of Georgia could not ignore the threat or the challenge. It commissioned a schooner, which, on July 10, captured the powder transport off the Georgian coast. Not only had Georgia proven itself to the other colonies, but it became the first province to commission a vessel for naval use in the Revolutionary War, and the capture of the transport was the first to be made under orders of a provincial congress.

The Georgian Congress grew stronger as 1775 came to an end. It organized a Provincial Council of Safety, of which Walton was elected president in December. By the beginning of 1776 the radicals were completely in control and the royal governor had fled. On January 20, 1776, the Congress of Georgia elected its first delegation to the Continental Congress, consisting of John Houstoun, Lyman Hall, Button Gwinnett, and, of course, George Walton. Instructing them to keep in mind Georgia's particular danger and needs, it adjured the delegates to remember "that the great and righteous cause in which we are engaged is not provincial, but continental." [49]

"A TIDE IN THE AFFAIRS OF MEN"

Since the first meeting of the Continental Congress in September 1774, Richard Henry Lee of Virginia, a leader of the radical faction within the Congress, had taken pains to avoid the appearance that he sought independence. Not as certain of his goals as his fellow radicals John and Sam Adams, who had no doubt from the beginning of the controversy that England and the colonies must part company, he had maintained a discreet silence when the actual question was posed. But from the conclusion of the First Continental Congress, frequently in response to specific situations that called for bold decisions, Lee had become increasingly outspoken. Each proposal and each resolution, although responded to pragmatically, reflected Lee's militancy; and each committed America more to independence.

Richard Henry Lee (1732-1794)

Lee had hardly returned home from the first Congress when he found himself in attendance at the Virginia convention that met from March 20 to March 27, 1775. Here, debating a resolution of Patrick Henry's calling for Virginia to arm herself, Lee followed Henry's bold proclamation, "give me liberty or give me death!" with an oration that according to Edmund Randolph, "fanned and refreshed with a gale of pleasure." [50] He whose quarrel was just was "thrice armed," quoted Lee, drawing on the Bible to assert that the "race is not to the swift, nor the battle to the strong." Lee also urged Virginia to draw up a plan to encourage manufacturing in the colony in order to give practical meaning to the Association agreement to stop imports. He argued against the acceptance by the colony of Lord North's peace proposal, and he continued to encourage the colony to maintain its freedom when the royal governor Lord Dunmore attempted to remove the military supplies in the Williamsburg arsenal.

When Lee returned to Philadelphia in May 1775, his militancy was strengthened by the realization that war had already broken out in Massachusetts. The conflict was an American conflict, he declared, not one limited to New England. Thus, he actively participated in the decision to raise a Continental Army to aid the Massachusetts minutemen and, as chairman of the committee to draft Washington's commission and instructions, he revealed a deeper commitment to the use of force.

On June 3, 1775, Lee was appointed chairman of a committee to prepare an Address to the Inhabitants of Great Britain. In his boldest statement up to now, he informed the British of the grievances sustained by the colonists at the hands of their ministry. The colonists had been denied, he wrote, trial by jury; their charters had been annulled, their commerce destroyed, and a despotic government had been established on their northern border. Now the British attack on Massachusetts was destroying all

155.
RICHARD HENRY LEE. Peter
Maverick and James Barton
Longacre after an unlocated
miniature. Engraving, 1827.
National Portrait Gallery,
Smithsonian Institution.

hopes for a peaceful settlement: "Can Men deliberate with the Bayonet at their Breast?
Can they treat with Freedom, while their towns are sacked . . . ?" The effect of this
on the British people was clear. If the Americans lost their freedom, Lee warned, then
the British would lose theirs soon after. "Soldiers who have sheathed their Swords in
the Bowels of their *American* Brethren, will not draw them with more reluctance
against you. Your liberty will be the price of your victory; your ruin, of your defeat." [51]

Although Lee—on paper, at least—continued to express peaceful goals, wishing, as
he wrote in July in a letter from the Congress to the Lord Mayor of London, "for a
lasting connection with G. Britain on terms of just and equal liberty," he undoubtedly
realized by now that such letters were futile. [52] When the King refused to recognize
the Congress's petition, Lee realized that independence was but a short distance ahead.
Proposing a resolution to create an independent American postal service, Lee persuaded
the Congress to cut one of the first ties binding the colonies to Great Britain. On July
26, 1775, the Congress approved the resolution, and an independent postal service
became another milestone on the road to political independence.

As a member of a committee of five to devise ways to protect colonial trade, Lee also
revealed a pragmatism that continued to place the colonies on an independent course.
In retaliation for the recent parliamentary acts restraining colonial trade, Lee proposed
that the Congress close all customs-houses in the colonies and allow unrestricted trade
with foreign countries in defiance of the British navigation acts. Although the Congress was not willing to go so far and declare openly their independence of Britain's

256

trade laws, it did decide to encourage exports to the foreign West Indies in exchange for certain necessities and war supplies. Lee, however, saw the need for foreign trade to maintain a successful resistance to Great Britain. Eventually, the only way foreign trade could be permitted would be through separation.

In October 1775 Lee participated in the committee decision to establish a continental navy—another step in the direction of separation. The infant American navy, he wrote in November to Catharine Macaulay in England, was "as Hercules was once in his cradle." By the spring, he was certain that it would be ready "to annoy our enemies greatly, and to afford such protection to the Trade of North America." [53]

Lee's biographer suggests that a great influence in converting Lee to the idea of independence was Thomas Paine's *Common Sense*, of which he was "a prodigious admirer, if not partly a writer." [54] Certainly, by the beginning of February, Lee had made up his mind. Writing to Landon Carter April 1, he explained, "As well, dear Sir, might a person expect to wash an Ethiopian white as to remove the taint of despotism from the British court." [55] On April 20 he wrote to Patrick Henry that the declaration by Parliament and the King that the colonies were in a state of rebellion had "to every intent and purpose dissolved our government, uncommissioned every magistrate, and placed us in the high road to Anarchy." It was therefore necessary for Virginia to declare her independence and form a government; other colonies would follow her example. "There is," he quoted from Shakespeare, his favorite author, "a tide in the affairs of men." That tide had now arrived for America. Without foreign commerce, we could not win the war we were engaged in, and no foreign country would give aid "until we take rank as an independent people." "Ages yet unborn," he concluded, "and millions existing at present, may rue or bless that assembly on which their happiness or misery will so eminently depend." [56]

In May Lee cosponsored with John Adams a resolution in the Continental Congress that advised all provinces that had not already done so to set up their own governments. The passage of the resolution prompted John Adams to remark that "This day the Congress has passed the most important resolution that was ever taken in America." [57] That month, also, Lee persuaded the Virginia Convention to instruct its delegates in the Congress to "propose to that respectable body to declare the United Colonies free & independent states." [58]

The Virginia Convention responded. Its delegates had already heard from their counties that the people favored separation and were prepared to take the bold step. When the resolution instructing Virginia delegates to propose a declaration of independence was unanimously adopted, "the exultation [in Richmond] was extreme," according to Thomas Ludwell Lee; "the british flag was immediately struck on the Capitol, and a continental hoisted in its room. The troops were drawn out, and we had a discharge of Artillery and small arms." [59]

Now, as John Adams wrote, independence "rolls in upon us like a torrent." [60] A month before the Virginia Convention met, North Carolina had instructed her delegates "to concur with the delegates of the other Colonies in declaring Independency." [61] Later in May Thomas Nelson, Jr. arrived in Philadelphia with the Virginia resolutions in hand; on the twenty-seventh they were presented to and read by the Congress. On June 7 Lee rose in Congress and moved

> *That these United Colonies are, and of right ought*

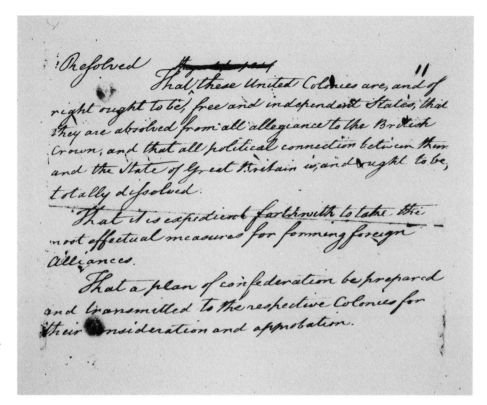

156.
Lee's Resolution of Independence,
June 7, 1776. National Archives.
[Original not in exhibition.]

*to be, free and independent States, that they are
absolved from all allegiance to the British Crown,
and that all political connection between them and the
State of Great Britain is, and ought to be, totally
dissolved.*

*That it is expedient forthwith to take the most effec-
tual measures for forming foreign Alliances.*

*That a plan of confederation be prepared and trans-
mitted to the respective Colonies for their consideration and approbation.*[62]

*George Mason
(1725-1792)*

When the Virginia Convention voted to instruct its delegates in the Continental Congress to move for separation from England, they took one more step on the road to
the establishment of independent government: they appointed a committee to prepare
a declaration of rights and a constitution for the Old Dominion. The idea that a
society could exist without formal government was alien to Americans, who believed
that to avoid the chaos of anarchy a provincial government must quickly be substituted
for the deposed King. In this situation, a new kind of man was required. The talents
of men like Patrick Henry and Samuel Adams were better suited to tearing down than
creating political systems. Virginia, which had initiated the movement toward a declaration of independence, now was to lead the way in state building. To do so, it
turned to the constructive genius of one of its greatest political architects, George Mason.

157.
GEORGE MASON. Dominic W.
Boudet after John Hesselius, 1811.
S. Cooper Dawson, Jr.

A successful planter, Mason had received his education at home in his uncle's large library. He never received formal legal training, but his reading was extensive enough to make him one of Virginia's most trusted authorities on public law. A leading citizen of Fairfax County, Mason served as trustee of the town of Alexandria, justice of the county court, and vestryman of the local Anglican church. In 1759, together with his good friend and neighbor George Washington, Mason represented Fairfax County in the House of Burgesses.

Not interested in public acclaim, Mason managed to remain in the background during the turbulent prerevolutionary decade as a quiet but effective supporter of American rights. He gave advice to those who sought legal ways of conveying property without paying the stamp tax and he wrote the resolves for nonexportation that were rejected in Williamsburg in 1769 during the Townshend Act crisis. During the following years Mason began to associate more prominently with the Virginians known as the "Movement Party." These—including Washington, Jefferson, and Madison—came to rely on the learned planter for arguments on behalf of colonial rights. Together they worked, as Jefferson wrote later, for "unanimity among our constituents" so that by the "harmony of the bold with the cautious, we advance with our constituents in undivided mass, and with fewer examples of separation than, perhaps, existed in any other part of the Union." [63]

In July 1774, with the closing of the port of Boston, Mason appeared more boldly on the public stage. At a county meeting on the eighteenth, he read a series of resolutions of his own composition which were adopted and came to be known as the Fairfax Resolves. Of great significance in the document, beyond the clear assertion of the right of a people to be governed by laws of their own consent, was the call for a continental congress "to concert a general and uniform plan for the defence and preservation of our common rights" and to develop "a solemn covenant or association" designed to stop trade with Great Britain until redress was obtained. The ideas contained in the Fairfax Resolves, together with Thomas Jefferson's *A Summary View of the Rights of British America* and James Wilson's *Considerations*, were of great influence during the deliberations of the First Continental Congress, and became the theoretical as well as practical basis of the first Congress's decisions. [64]

It was Mason who proposed the plan adopted by his county called the Fairfax Independent Company of volunteers, which was in effect a militia group designed to provide "strength . . . & stable security" to a free government so that "those sacred rights to which ourselves were born" would be transmitted "to our children & posterity." [65] Annual elections of officers were an important aspect of the militia's organization, justified by Mason by his doctrine of innate equality. [66]

By the following July Mason was not only deeply committed to his militia regiment, but he was emerging even more prominently into Virginia politics. Elected to the Provincial Convention and then to its Committee of Safety (after he had refused appointment as a delegate to the Continental Congress), he gave all his energies, when not troubled by sickness or the gout, to building up the military defense he believed would be required on the Potomac River.

In early 1776, as all minds turned to the possibility of declaring independence, Mason once again ran for a seat in the convention—but this time he narrowly made it, to such extreme positions had men been pushed. Arriving in Williamsburg the day after the convention voted to instruct its delegates in the Congress to move for independence —a somber day of fast and solemn religious services—he was immediately drafted to aid in the task of constructing a new government.

The task was not easy. Although there had been general unanimity for independence, large differences prevailed to affect the establishment of a new system—differences of class, economic condition, sectional interest, religious belief, and social organization. Between the aristocracy of the eastern—or Tidewater—plantations and the frontier settlers of the western—or Piedmont—farms were to be found the moderate group led by Mason and Thomas Jefferson. It would be the responsibility of these men to strike the balance between liberty and order, between aristocracy and democracy. Mason's contribution was the Virginia Declaration of Rights, one of the most notable documents of the revolutionary era and one that summarized America's revolutionary ideology.

Mason was given virtually a free hand to prepare the draft of the declaration, in recognition of his genius as well as his general impatience with men who did not share his sharp perceptions. Drawing upon the Enlightenment concept of natural law and rights and the English common law tradition of personal freedom, he composed a rational and dignified document to which Jefferson's Declaration of Independence, the various state constitutions, and the French Declaration of the Rights of Man were all obligated. Its basic premise was that "all men are created equally free and independent, and have certain inherent natural rights" that were inalienable. These included "the enjoyment of life and liberty, with the means of acquiring and possessing property." Political power had been instituted for the common good; therefore, no individual or group was entitled to special privileges. The right to vote, however, should be limited to those who owned sufficient property to ensure a genuine concern for the welfare of the community. Only elected representatives of the people could exercise executive or legislative power over them. Certain basic English rights were reiterated: fair trial by a jury of peers; prohibition of excessive or unjust punishments; freedom of the press and religion.

The Virginia Convention adopted the declaration on June 5, almost as Mason had written it. Defenders of slavery, objecting to the phrase "all men are created equally free and independent," circumvented the problem by providing that men's rights were guaranteed only "when they enter into a state of society" and slaves were not "in society." The convention also added prohibitions against general warrants and included statements providing for the territorial integrity of the new state.

The Declaration of Rights provided the theoretical underpinning of Virginia's new constitution. To compose this, the members turned once again to George Mason. Mason's plan of government was based upon strict separation of powers. It provided for a bicameral legislature; an elected governor invested with executive power; and a property qualification on the franchise. To some Virginians, the new constitution appeared to turn Virginia toward a new direction. To Richard Henry Lee, for instance, it was "democratic." To Carter Braxton, it was too democratic, and in his *An Address to the Convention of the Colony and Ancient Dominion of Virginia on the Subject of Government,* he proposed an aristocratic plan of government that Lee believed was so contrary to the trend of the times that it was in little "danger of doing harm." [67]

Neither man's assessment was right. Virginia's constitution was not entirely democratic, but a beginning had been made—and that beginning owed much to George Mason.

Carter Braxton (1736-1797)

158.
CARTER BRAXTON. Unidentified artist, date unknown. Donald M. Braxton, on loan to the National Portrait Gallery, Smithsonian Institution.

Not all Americans—not even all Virginians—were happy about Lee's resolutions for independence. About the same time that Lee was deciding that independence was necessary, Carter Braxton, also a member of the Virginia delegation to Philadelphia, was protesting the interest in "Independency and total separation from Great Britain" that agitated the Continental Congress.

A member of the Tidewater aristocracy and a leader of the second rank in his colony, Braxton had proved himself an able, though far from brilliant, delegate to the House of Burgesses. "He was a decent, agreeable and sensible speaker," Benjamin Rush reported, "and in private life an accomplished gentleman." Despite an innate political and social conservatism, he had supported Virginia and the colonies in their quarrel with the mother country. In 1769 Braxton had signed the Virginia Resolutions, contending that only the House of Burgesses had the right to lay taxes on Virginians; he also had supported nonimportation as a response to the Townshend Acts. From 1774 to 1776 Braxton served in the Provincial Convention that replaced the dissolved House of Burgesses, and in 1775 the convention appointed him to the colonial Committee of Safety. To win the good will of Virginia's moderates and conservatives, the convention named Braxton in February 1776 to fill the place in the Congress vacated by the death of Peyton Randolph.

Braxton was a decidedly reluctant revolutionary. Rush believed that he "was suspected of being less detached than he should be from his British prejudices." Perhaps Rush knew that earlier, in 1775, Braxton had mortgaged his estates in order to invest heavily in a British mercantile venture, an act of faith that would have been severely tried if war broke out between Virginia and the mother country. Certainly, Braxton made every effort to avert such a conflict. When Lord Dunmore seized Virginia's supplies and ammunition, it was Braxton who had worked out the compromise with Patrick Henry, through his father-in-law, Colonel Corbin, in which the governor retained the munitions upon agreement to pay the colonial treasury their full value.

It is likely that Braxton sought compromise for social and political reasons as well as out of self-interest. Fearing that separation would shake the rigidly stratified social and political structure that his class now controlled, he feared the coming of democracy with independence. Braxton's strong anti-New England prejudices were based on that fear. In his letter to his uncle, Landon Carter, he accused the northern colonies of not wishing reconciliation. They were too far committed to democracy, according to Braxton, to wish to continue to be ruled by a monarch.

Braxton was not entirely opposed to separation—some day. Independence was an object to be wished for, he conceded to his uncle, but only when it could be obtained with safety and honor. At present, he believed, independence was a delusive bait that Americans snapped at without realizing it was attached to a very sharp hook. America was still defenseless and could not support the commerce necessary to prosecute a successful war against Britain. An alliance with France was not sufficient inducement to severing the ties that bound Americans to the mother country. Would the colonists be wise to throw off their connection with their kinsmen in England to rush into the arms of the ancient enemy, France? A nation as dedicated as the French to intrigue and deception would be certain to exact harsher terms from the Americans than the British. The reason there was so much talk of independence, Braxton informed his uncle, was that there were actually some members who were "afraid to await the Arrival of [Peace] Commissioners, lest the dispute should be accommodated much agt their Will even upon the Admission of our own terms."[68]

Commission for Peace

Braxton's suspicions that a declaration of independence was being hastened by the expectation of the arrival of Peace Commissioners was not unfounded. Joseph Reed, writing from Philadelphia to his commander in chief in Boston on March 15, reported that the possibility had "laid fast hold of some here and made its impression on the Congress." Reed himself was "more afraid of these commissioners, than their generals and armies. If their propositions are plausible," he believed, "and behaviour artful, I am apprehensive they will divide us."[69]

The British Peace Commission had been a long time in preparation, as a result of which Americans were alerted to its impending arrival months before Admiral Lord Richard Howe—half of the commission—actually set foot on American soil. From early autumn 1775 Lord North had considered the possibility of negotiating with Americans for peace, but he faced a divided and discontented cabinet. Warned by his young undersecretary, William Eden, that his ministers were "surly in their Language, sulky in their Conduct, and ill-disposed to your Administration," he vacillated between sending more troops and making overtures of reconciliation. Finally, however, he was able to take vigorous action by recalling the ineffectual General Gage and Admiral Graves, sending five Irish regiments to Charleston, South Carolina, and, in January 1776, accepting into Britain's service some twenty-three thousand German mercenaries.

Having proved his militancy to the war party, the King, and the nation at large, which had become determined to take stern measures after receiving news of the Canadian invasion, North was ready to please the doves in the government who still hoped for a peaceful settlement. Thus, he turned his attention once again to the project of a peace commission that would "supersede governors . . . call assemblies, and . . . settle a form of taxation on easy terms with the Conciliatory Proposition."

Until early in 1776 Lord North's plan for such a peace commission was frustrated by the refusal of the militant Lord Germain to support it. Germain, hoping to redeem his reputation for cowardice by pursuing a vigorous policy of coercion against the colonies, disapproved of the plan and particularly of the individuals whose names were suggested as possible commissioners. But Lord North had left the establishment of the plan up to his ingenious undersecretary, William Eden, and it was by his efforts that the commission finally was launched in May.

159.
WILLIAM EDEN. Henry Edridge.
Watercolor, 1809. National
Portrait Gallery, London.

William Eden
(1744-1814)
William Eden had been educated at Eton and Christ Church, Oxford, where he had proved himself a brilliant student. Going on to become one of England's most promising young lawyers, in 1772 he published a notable legal treatise, *Principles of Penal Law*, and was appointed undersecretary of state. Two years later, he was elected to the Commons, where his brilliance manifested itself in questions of law and economics. It was, however, his talent for behind-the-scenes maneuvering that attracted Lord North's attention and presented the ambitious Eden with an opportunity to be helpful to the powerful minister.

In October 1775, at Lord North's request, Eden wrote to Lord Germain suggesting that since the rebellion was well on the way to being crushed, it was time to consider sending a commissioner to America with power to settle everything in dispute. The power of the commission, as Eden conceived it, would be extensive, including the capacity to grant pardons, open ports, and "make corrections" in some of the governments. Eden suggested that Germain accept the post; but Germain refused and his later appointment to the cabinet removed him permanently from any list of possible candidates. Nothing daunted, early in 1776 Eden put forth a shrewd suggestion that he thought would win the approval of the militants: he proposed that Admiral Lord Howe be appointed peace commissioner.

264

Richard Howe had joined His Majesty's Navy in 1740. By 1762 he had become a lord of the Admiralty and by 1775 a vice admiral. Although he had never commanded a fleet in combat, the swarthy "Black Dick" had proved himself an able administrator, a fine sailor, and a perceptive student of naval tactics and strategy, respected by his peers and popular with his men.

Admiral Lord Richard Howe (1726-1799)

Howe had already shown an interest in helping to settle the quarrel with the colonies. Both he and his brother William were grateful for the way Massachusetts had honored the memory of their brother George, who had fallen at Ticonderoga during the French and Indian War. Moreover, the admiral was on friendly terms with prominent American residents in London, including Benjamin Franklin. The last thing Great Britain should do, he believed, was to undertake an internecine war with the American colonies. Not that he thought the home government should yield to the colonists on the points in dispute; rather, he fatuously imagined that the colonists needed no more than to be calmed down and that he was the person to do it.

Eden found the militants receptive to a peace commission headed by Howe since Howe had let it be known that he would be willing to go to America as commander in chief as well as peace commissioner. Dartmouth was happy with the selection because he knew how well disposed Howe was toward the colonies. The only unhappy person was Eden. With his eye always on the main chance, Eden had suggested that Howe be accompanied by a civilian colleague in the hope that he would be appointed himself. Howe, however, convinced that he alone could salve American feelings and thus preserve the empire, did not want anybody for a colleague. It was with great reluctance that he finally accepted as a second member of the commission his own brother, General William Howe, who was already commanding British troops in America.

With all parties agreed on the suitability of Admiral Howe as a commissioner, the dispute between Dartmouth and the militants shifted to the question of Howe's instructions. The militants, fully aware of Howe's inclination to be lenient with the rebels, imagined that he would get on with the war if his instructions left him no room to do anything but accept an American surrender. Concerned to avoid damaging the principle of parliamentary supremacy, the militants, along with North, believed that as necessary conditions for negotiations the Americans must lay down their arms, dissolve the Continental Congress, and restore the royal governments. Germain and the extremists also insisted that each colony declare unequivocally its submission to the will of Parliament. On this point, Dartmouth disagreed vehemently. Germain threatened to resign from the cabinet if the point did not carry, and Dartmouth threatened to resign if it did. Unwilling to lose either of his ministers, North turned to the celebrated Chief Justice of the King's Bench, Lord Mansfield, to work out a compromise. Mansfield's efforts were successful, and both sides accepted his proposal that the commissioners wait to see what the colonies offered before demanding submission. Any colony that did not make some sort of offer could not expect to be included in the negotiations and would continue to feel Britain's armed wrath. The commissioners might deal with such colonies only under the explicit direction of Parliament.

Howe himself raised further difficulties by demanding that he be given wider latitude. He was finally convinced by Germain, who had succeeded Dartmouth as colonial secretary, to accept the terms of the commission's instructions, but by the time the admiral was ready to depart for America months had been wasted—months in

160.
RICHARD EARL HOWE.
Thomas Gainsborough, circa 1765.
The Earl Howe.

which congressional moderates, hoping desperately for the appearance of a British peace commission, were losing their fight to stave off a declaration of independence. By the time Howe sailed into New York Harbor on July 12, 1776, it was too late.

THE DECLARATION OF INDEPENDENCE

The commission for restoring peace was, in any case, "a delusion."[70] The Howe brothers' instructions were based upon the parliamentary resolution of February 20, 1775—Lord North's olive branch—and the colonies had already declared its inadequacy. So much had intervened between then and the day of the commissioners' arrival that it would have taken a complete concession—never mind a firm order to submit—for the colonists to have turned from their separatist path and once more accept the control and protection of the mother country.

The news that France was ready to come to the aid of the colonies—albeit secretly—convinced some reluctant delegates like John Dickinson, William Livingston of New Jersey, and Henry Laurens of South Carolina that independence was now possible. Other moderate delegates, like Carter Braxton and Edward Rutledge, tried to postpone a decision on Lee's resolution of June 7, meanwhile writing to conservatives at home for help in preventing the rash act. Rutledge, for instance, wrote to John Jay on June 29, urging him to hasten to Philadelphia lest the delegates declare America independent and place it thereby in the hands of impudent New Englanders. Men of good sense, wrote Rutledge, must keep the staff of power in their own hands, or the democratic factions would make pernicious use of it. Defenders of the proprietary interests in Pennsylvania and Maryland, fearing that independence would rob the Penns and Calverts of control, also tried to dam the rising tide. Elbridge Gerry of Massachusetts wrote to James Warren on June 25 that since he had arrived in Philadelphia, he had witnessed a continual conflict between the New England delegates and the proprietary interests. And yet, Gerry acknowledged, as did all those who favored independence, that they would have their way, that independence was inevitable.

On July 2 the Continental Congress unanimously adopted Richard Henry Lee's motions of June 7. Only the New York delegations, lacking enabling instructions from its provincial convention, abstained. Writing to his wife the following day, John Adams declared that July 2, 1776, would be remembered as the most significant day in American history. Although he regretted the delay, he believed it served important purposes: "The hopes of reconciliation which were fondly entertained by multitudes of honest and well-meaning, though weak and mistaken people, have been gradually, and at last totally extinguished." The time given for discussion had helped "cement the union." Aware as he was "of the toil and blood and treasure that it will cost us to maintain this Declaration and support and defend these States," he saw "through all the gloom . . . the rays of ravishing light and glory."[71]

In another communication of the same date, Adams mentioned casually that Abigail would see "in a few days, a Declaration setting forth the causes which have impelled us to this mighty revolution, and the reasons which will justify it in the sight of God and man."[72] Here he was referring to the work of a committee appointed on June 10 to draw up a declaration that would serve as an effective apologia for rebellion. The

161.
THOMAS JEFFERSON.
Mather Brown, 1786.
Charles Francis Adams.

268

committee included Robert Livingston, a moderate; the venerable Benjamin Franklin; two long-time radicals, Roger Sherman and John Adams; and a sandy-haired young newcomer from Virginia, Thomas Jefferson, who had taken his seat only the summer before and had been absent from Philadelphia half that time.

The same set of circumstances that helped make a Virginian commander in chief of the Continental Army helped make another Virginian, Thomas Jefferson, the most important member of the committee. The presence of a southerner on the committee was required to steady the nerves of those colonies still wavering over independence. A delegate from the middle colonies, where the commitment to independence was weakest, could not make a credible apologia for separation from the mother country. At the same time, it would be unseemly for a New Englander to take the lead in justifying publicly an act that many believed New England had been trying to bring about for years. Moreover, since Virginia's resources were important for a successful prosecution of the war effort, the province's pride had to be satisfied. The Congress was fortunate that the available Virginian was also the best possible person for the job.

Thomas Jefferson (1743-1826)

Born in 1743 in Goochland (now Albemarle) County, on what was then the western edge of civilization in Virginia, Jefferson had received a sound early training in the classics and had gone on to study at the College of William and Mary. In Williamsburg, the range of his intellectual interests, broad by nature, was expanded even further by acquaintance with the urbane royal governor, Francis Fauquier, and the lawyer, George Wythe, under whom Jefferson undertook the study of law.

Young Jefferson had inherited from his father a position of distinction in his community, which he used in 1769 to win a seat in the House of Burgesses. Here, Jefferson first gave evidence of the conduct that would always mark his participation in

162.
Portable desk on which Thomas Jefferson wrote the Declaration of Independence. Division of Political History, The National Museum of History and Technology, Smithsonian Institution. [Not in exhibition.]

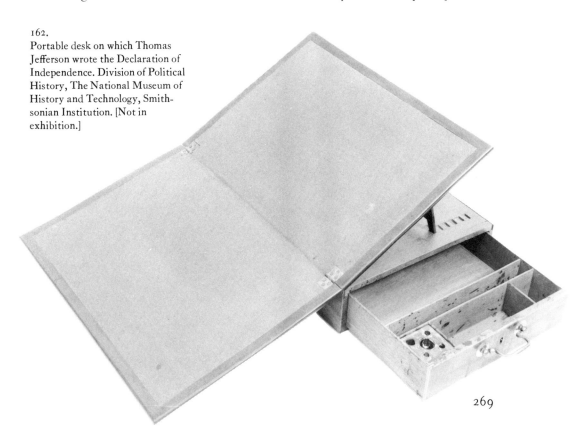

A N.W. VIEW OF THE STATE HOUSE IN PHILADELPHIA *taken 1778*

163.
A Northwest View of the State House in Philadelphia. James Trenchard after a 1778 drawing by Charles Willson Peale. Engraving in *The Columbian Magazine*, July 1787. The Watkinson Library, Trinity College.

legislative bodies; he was silent in general sessions, rarely making a notable speech from the floor; but he was active, articulate, and extremely effective in committee.

From his first days as a burgess, Jefferson was identified with the radical, anti-British group. In 1774, traveling more quickly down the road to revolution than most of his fellow Virginians, Jefferson wrote *A Summary View of the Rights of British America*, which his friends presented to the Virginia Convention during the illness that prevented him from attending the meeting. The pamphlet revealed for the first time the foundation in natural rights of Jefferson's political philosophy and foreshadowed the arguments that he would use to justify American independence. Too advanced for the Convention to accept in 1774, the work spread Jefferson's name as a talented political writer and marked him as a rising radical luminary. In the summer of 1775 the Virginia Convention recognized Jefferson's importance by sending him to Philadelphia to fill the place of Peyton Randolph in the Continental Congress.

Jefferson and Adams differed later concerning how the drafting of the committee's declaration came to be assigned to the young Virginian; but, however it came about, Jefferson was soon at work preparing a document that consisted of two basic parts. The first was a statement of political philosophy, setting forth the principles upon which

270

Americans believed their liberties were based. The second part detailed how the King of England had violated those liberties, not unintentionally but with obvious and habitual malice, and thereby lost the right to command American allegiance.

In the short but powerful philosophical segment, Jefferson drew upon the political theories of John Locke, whose ideas on liberty and social compact were common intellectual currency among Jefferson's contemporaries. He may have also been influenced by George Mason's recent distillation of Locke's principles in his *Declaration of Rights.* Jefferson declared it to be self-evident that all men were created equal and that they were, by virtue of being born human, entitled to certain rights, including life, liberty, property, and the pursuit of happiness. Using Locke's concept of government as a compact, he explained that it was to preserve these rights that governments were instituted; when, therefore, a government became destructive of those rights, the people were justified in overthrowing it and in establishing a new government.

In the second part of the declaration, Jefferson undertook to prove that the government of the colonies, under the King, deprived Americans of their natural rights and that the attitude of the King, as revealed in his actions, rendered American rights insecure under his rule. The declaration censured the King rather than Parliament because all Americans had by now accepted Jefferson's argument of 1774 that the only valid link between England and America was through the throne.

The King, Jefferson declared, had refused to allow laws necessary for the "public good," and had forced laws to be "suspended in their operation till his Assent should be obtained." In other cases he had refused to pass laws unless the people gave up their right to be represented in the legislature, "a right inestimable to them and formidable to tyrants only." Legislative bodies had been assembled at inconvenient and distant places "for the sole purpose of fatiging them into compliance with his measures." Moreover, he had dissolved such legislative assemblies repeatedly and had refused to allow others to be elected in their place, exposing the "State . . . to all the dangers of invasion from without, and convulsions from within." Through laws making it difficult for foreigners to obtain citizenship and discouraging immigration to America, he had obstructed population growth.[73]

Then, Jefferson listed specific complaints reaching all the way back to 1765, and rehearsed every grievance that the Americans claimed against the home government during the prerevolutionary decade. Americans, claimed Jefferson, had been patient. "In every stage of these oppressions," he wrote, "We have Petitioned for Redress in the most humble terms." But these petitions had been "answered only by repeated injury." "A Prince," the Declaration commented, "whose character is thus marked by every act which may define a Tyrant, is unfit to be the ruler of a free People."[74]

Now that George III had failed them, and their "British brethren" had remained "deaf to the voice of justice and of consanguinity," Americans, Jefferson argued, had no choice but to "acquiesce in the necessity, which denounces our Separation, and hold them as we hold the rest of mankind, 'Enemies in War, in Peace Friends'."

> *We therefore, the Representatives of the united States of America, in General Congress, Assembled, appealing to the Supreme Judge of the world for the rectitude of our intentions, do, in the Name, and by*

164.
The Meeting Chamber in
Independence Hall, Philadelphia,
in which the Declaration of
Independence was adopted.

*Authority of the good People of these Colonies, solemnly publish and
declare, that these United Colonies are and of Right ought to be Free
and Independent States, . . . And for the Support of this Declaration,
with a firm reliance on the Protection of Divine Providence, we mutually
pledge to each other our Lives, our Fortunes, and our sacred Honor.*[75]

Jefferson submitted his work to Adams and Franklin for criticism, but they contented themselves with only a few stylistic changes. On June 28 the committee submitted the declaration to the whole Congress; but still not sure as to whether Lee's motions should be adopted, the Congress put the declaration aside until July 2. While Jefferson fidgeted and Franklin tried to calm him with homely parables, the Congress went over the Virginian's declaration, word by word, for the better part of three days. Out of deference to the delegates from South Carolina and Georgia, the Congress eliminated Jefferson's denunciation of the slave trade and incorporated Lee's original resolution for independence into the final draft of the declaration.

On what was for Philadelphia a mild summer day—Jefferson, ever the meticulous observer, noted that it was 76 degrees at one o'clock—the Congress formally adopted the declaration. There was no great stir. Only John Hancock, the president of the Congress, and Charles Thomson, the secretary, signed their names to the document on July 4. The Congress ordered a parchment copy engrossed and most of the other members added their signatures on August 2.

Not until July 8 was the declaration made public, when it was read by order of the local Committee of Safety to a cheering crowd outside the State House in Philadelphia. Jefferson was not identified as the author. The significance of Jefferson's work would not be clear, either to him or to his contemporaries, for a number of years. Yet Thomas Jefferson, in writing what was intended to be a piece of propaganda, enshrined at the heart of American political philosophy the great principle of equality and human dignity. Abraham Lincoln, who did so much himself to perpetuate these

principles, summarized Jefferson's achievement when he declared, thirty-three years after the Virginian's death:

> *All honor to Jefferson—to the man who in the concrete pressure*
> *of a struggle for national independence by a single people, had the*
> *coolness, forecast, and sagacity to introduce into a merely revolutionary*
> *document an abstract truth, applicable to all men and all times, and*
> *so to embalm it there that to-day and in all coming days it shall be*
> *a rebuke and a stumbling-block to the very harbingers of reappearing*
> *tyranny and oppression.*[76]

165.
Congress Voting Independence.
Edward Savage, after 1796.
National Portrait Gallery, Smithsonian Institution.

IN CONGRESS, JULY 4, 1776.

The unanimous Declaration of the thirteen united States of America.

166.
The 1823 facsimile of the Declaration of Independence engraved by
W.J. Stone. University of Indiana.

Notes

PROLOGUE

[1]Peter Oliver, *Peter Oliver's Origin and Progress of the American Rebellion: A Tory View*, Douglass Adair and John A. Schutz, eds., San Marino, California, 1961, pp. 113-114.

[2]*Ibid.*, p. 114.

[3]*Ibid.*, p. 115.

[4]*Ibid.*

[5]*Ibid.*, pp. 115-116.

CHAPTER I

[1]John Adams to William Tudor, September 29, 1774, in Edmund Cody Burnett, ed., *Letters of Members of the Continental Congress*, vol. 1, Washington, 1921, p. 260.

[2]The Connecticut delegates to the Governor of Connecticut (Jonathan Trumbull), October 10, 1774, *ibid.*, vol. 1, p. 69.

[3]Quoted in Ernest H. Baldwin, "Joseph Galloway, the Loyalist Politician," *Pennsylvania Magazine of History and Biography*, vol. 26 (July—December, 1902), p. 424.

[4]Joseph Galloway, *Historical and Political Reflections on the Rise and Progress of the American Rebellion*, London, 1780, pp. 66-67.

[5]Cornelia Meigs, *The Violent Men: A Study of Human Relations in the First American Congress*, New York, 1949, p. 41.

[6]Joseph Galloway to the Governor of New Jersey (William Franklin), September 5, 1774, in Burnett, ed., *Letters*, vol. 1, p. 9.

[7]" 'I have Deduced Your Rights' . . . Joseph Galloway's Concept of his Role, 1774-1775," Robert M. Calhoon, *Pennsylvania History*, vol. 35, no. 4, October 1968, p. 358.

[8]Quoted in Baldwin, "Joseph Galloway," *Pennsylvania Magazine of History and Biography*, vol. 26 (1902), p. 312.

[9]Letter to Governor William Franklin, September 3, 1774, quoted in *ibid.*, p. 309.

[10]John Adams, "Diary," August 30, 1774, in L. H. Butterfield, ed., *The Diary and Autobiography of John Adams*, vol. 2, Cambridge, Massachusetts, 1962, p. 115.

[11]Quoted in Baldwin, "Joseph Galloway," p. 310.

[12]Galloway to William Franklin, September 6, 1774, in Burnett, ed., *Letters*, vol. 1, p. 9.

[13]Thomson to Benjamin Franklin, quoted in John J. Zimmerman, "Charles Thomson, the Sam Adams of Philadelphia," *Mississippi Valley Historical Review*, vol. 45 (December 1958), p. 468.

[14]John Adams, "Diary," September 5, 1774, in Butterfield, ed., *Diary and Autobiography*, vol. 2, p. 123.

[15]Burnett, ed., *Letters*, vol. 1, p. 54.

[16]John Adams, "Diary," September 6, 1774, in Butterfield, ed., *Diary and Autobiography*, vol. 2, p. 125.

[17]*Ibid.*, p. 126.

[18]Silas Deane to Mrs. Deane, September 7, 1774, in Burnett, ed., *Letters*, vol. 1, p. 18.

[19]John Adams to Mrs. Adams, September 28, 1774, *ibid.*, vol. 1, p. 34.

[20]John Adams to Mrs. Adams, September 16, 1774, *ibid.*, vol. 1, p. 32.

[21]Samuel Adams to Joseph Warren, September 9, 1774, *ibid.*, vol. 1, p. 27.

[22]John Adams, "Diary," September 10, 1774, in Butterfield, ed., *Diary and Autobiography*, vol. 2, p. 131.

[23]Quoted in The Rev. Edward D. Neill, "Rev. Jacob Duché, the First Chaplain of Congress," *Pennsylvania Magazine of History and Biography*, vol. 2 (1878), p. 63.

[24]John Adams to Mrs. Adams, September 16, 1775, in Burnett, ed., *Letters*, vol. 1, p. 33.

[25]Silas Deane to Mrs. Deane, September 7, 1774, in Burnett, ed., *Letters*, vol. 1, p. 18.

[26]Quoted in Neill, "Rev. Jacob Duché . . . ," p. 70.

[27]Letter sent to other towns in Massachusetts by Boston Committee of Correspondence, June 8, 1774, quoted in L. H. Gipson, *The Triumphant Empire: Britain Sails Into the Storm*, New York, 1965, p. 139n.

[28]*Boston Gazette*, June 20, 1774, quoted in Richard Frothingham, *The Life and Times of Joseph Warren*, Boston 1865; reprinted New York, 1971, p. 333.

[29]General Gage to Dartmouth, September 2, 1774, quoted in Gipson, *The Triumphant Empire*, p. 163.

[30]Peter Force, ed., *American Archives*, "Proceedings of the Continental Congress," 4th series, vol. 1, Washington, 1837; reprinted New York, 1972, p. 776.

[31]Quoted in Richard M. Ketchum, "Men of the Revolution—I," *American Heritage* (August 1971), vol. 22, no. 5, p. 21; John Cary, *Joseph Warren, Physician, Politician, Patriot*, Urbana, Illinois, 1961, p. 124.

[32]Quoted in *Appleton's Encyclopedia*, vol. 6, p. 364.

[33]Letter, early September, 1774, quoted in Frothingham, *Joseph Warren*, p. 355.

[34]Force, ed., *American Archives*, vol. 1, p. 776f.

[35]Quoted in Ketchum, *American Heritage*, p. 21.

[36]Cary, *Joseph Warren*, p. 203.

[37]Caesar Rodney to Thomas Rodney, September 9, 1774, in Burnett, ed., *Letters*, vol. 1, p. 27.

[38]John Adams to Mrs. Adams, September 25, 1774, in *ibid.*, p. 47; and John Adams to Thomas Jefferson, November 12, 1813, quoted in Merrill Jensen, *The Founding of a Nation*, New York, 1968, p. 487.

[39]Joseph Galloway, *History and Political Reflections on the Rise and Progress of the American Rebellion*, London, 1790, p. 49.

[40]Richard Henry Lee, *Memoir*, vol. 1, pp. 109-110, quoted in Oliver P. Chitwood, *Richard Henry Lee: Statesman of the Revolution*, Morgantown, West Virginia, 1967, p. 65.

[41]Force, ed., *American Archives*, vol. 1, p. 904.

[42]John Adams, "Diary," September 17, 1774, in Butterfield, ed., *Diary and Autobiography*, vol. 2, pp. 134-135.

[43]Quoted in John C. Miller, *Sam Adams, Pioneer in Propaganda*, Palo Alto, California, 1936, p. 234.

[44]Quoted in Gipson, *The Triumphant Empire*, p. 251.

[45]John Adams to Abigail Adams, September 18, 1774, in L. H. Butterfield, ed., *The Adams Family Correspondence*, vol. 1, Cambridge, Massachusetts, 1963, p. 157.

[46]Quoted in Baldwin, "Joseph Galloway," p. 314.

[47]"Mr. Galloway's Plan for a Proposed Union between Great Britain and the Colonies," in Force, ed., *American Archives*, vol. 1, p. 906.

[48]Burnett, ed., *Letters*, vol. 1 (James Duane to Samuel Chase), December 29, 1774, p. 88.

[49]John Adams, "Notes on Debates," *ibid.*, p. 53.

[50]*New York Gazette and Mercury*, April 23, 1770. Quoted in Edward P. Alexander, *A Revolutionary Conservative*, New York, 1938, p. 97.

[51]James Duane in Poughkeepsie, *New York Journal*, December 20, 1779, quoted in *ibid*, p. 121.

[52]John Adams, "Notes on Debates," in Burnett, ed., *Letters*, vol. 1, p. 54.

[53]Joseph Galloway to William Franklin, September 3, 1774, quoted in Baldwin, "Joseph Galloway," p. 309.

[54]Edward Rutledge to Judge Bee, October 1774, quoted in John Sanderson, *Biography of Signers of the Declaration of Independence*, vol. 3. Philadelphia, 1823, p. 17.

[55]John Adams, "Diary," October 24, 1774, in Butterfield, ed., *Diary and Autobiography*, vol. 2, p. 156.

[56]Edward Rutledge to John Jay, June 29, 1776, in Burnett, ed., *Letters*, vol. 1, p. 17.

[57]Quoted in Chitwood, *Richard Henry Lee*, p. 66.

[58]Quoted in Baldwin, "Joseph Galloway," p. 420.

[59]Quoted in *ibid.*, p. 424.

[60]John Adams to Joseph Palmer, September 26, 1774, in Burnett, ed., *Letters*, vol. 1, p. 48.

[61]Letter from Boston Committee of Corespondence to the Continental Congress, September 29, 1774, in Force, ed., *American Archives*, vol. 1, p. 908.

[62]*Ibid.*

[63]*Ibid.*

[64]Quoted in Margaret Vowell Smith, *Virginia, 1492-1892, with a History of the Executives*, Washington, 1893, p. 211.

[65]Quoted in David H. Strother, "Edmund Pendleton of Virginia," *Pennsylvania Magazine of History and Biography*, vol. 3 (1879), p. 178.

[66]Quoted in Hugh Blair Grigsby, *The Virginia Convention of 1776*, Richmond, 1855; reprinted New York, 1969, p. 46.

[67]Quoted in John C. Miller, *Sam Adams*, p. 328; and Sam Adams, "Proposed Letter to General Gage," in Burnett, ed., *Letters*, vol. 1, p. 69.

[68]Force, ed., *American Archives*, vol. 1, p. 899.

[69]Stephen Hopkins, *The Rights of Colonies Examined*, Providence, Rhode Island, 1765, p.19.

[70]Silas Deane to Mrs. Deane, September 7, 1774, in Burnett, ed., *Letters*, vol. 1, p. 18.

[71]*Ibid.*

[72]John Adams, "Diary," in Butterfield, ed., *Diary and Autobiography*, vol. 2, p. 85.

[73]*Ibid.*, p. 114.

[74]*Ibid.*, p. 129.

[75]Adams to Mrs. Adams, September 29, 1774, in Burnett, ed., *Letters*, vol. 1, pp. 60-61.

[76]Adams to William Tudor, September 29, 1774, in Burnett, ed., *Letters*, vol. 1, p. 60.

[77]Quoted in *ibid.*, p. 46.

[78]Joseph Galloway, "Statement to a Committee of the House of Commons," in *ibid.*, p. 76.

[79]Force, ed., *American Archives*, vol. 1, pp. 911, 912.

[80]John Sullivan to John Langdon, September [October] 5, 1774, in Burnett, ed., *Letters*, vol. 1, p. 63.

[81]*Ibid.*

[82]Charles Park Whittemore, *A General of the Revolution: John Sullivan of New Hampshire*, New York, 1961, p. 3.

[83]Quoted in *ibid.*, p. 7.

[84]Quoted in *ibid.*, p. 8.

[85]"Proceedings of the Continental Congress," October 20, 1774, in Force, ed., *American Archives*, vol. 1, p. 914.

[86]*Ibid.*, pp. 913-915.

[87]Quoted in Arthur M. Schlesinger, *The Colonial Merchants, 1763-1776*, New York, 1939, p. 409n.

[88]Edward S. Delaplaine, *The Life of Thomas Johnson*, New York, 1927, p. 87.

[89]Francis Newton Thorpe, *The Constitutional History of the United States*, vol. 1, Chicago, 1901, pp. 82-94; and C. F. Adams, ed., *The Works of John Adams*, vol. 2. pp. 395-6, quoted in Delaplaine, *Thomas Johnson*, pp. 97, 98.

[90]Quoted from C. F. Adams, ed., *Works of John Adams*, vol. 2, p. 506. Quoted in *Dictionary of American Biography*, vol. 5, p. 121.

[91]Quoted in Delaplaine, *Thomas Johnson*, p. 98.

[92]Quoted from C. F. Adams, ed., *Familiar Letters of John Adams and his Wife . . .*, p. 59. Quoted in *Dictionary of American Biography*, vol. 6, p. 607.

[93]Quoted in Kenneth R. Rossman, *Thomas Mifflin and the Politics of the American Revolution*, Chapel Hill, North Carolina, 1952, p. 6.

[94]Quoted in *ibid.*, p. 13.

[95]Quoted in *ibid.*, p. 15.

[96]Quoted in *ibid.*, p. 21-22.

[97]Quoted in Schlesinger, *The Colonial Merchants*, p. 437.

CHAPTER II

[1]"Remonstrance to Gage" in H. A. Cushing, ed., *The Writings of Samuel Adams*, vol. 3, New York, 1904-08, p. 161.

[2]Peter Force, ed., *American Archives*, 4th series, vol. 1, Washington, 1837; reprinted New York, 1972, pp. 917-21, 929-37.

[3]Edmund Cody Burnett, ed., *Letters of Members of the Continental Congress*, vol. 1, Washington, 1921, pp. 28-9; quoted in Oliver P. Chitwood, *Richard Henry Lee: Statesman of the Revolution*, Morgantown, West Virginia, 1967, p. 62.

[4]Quoted in Chitwood, *ibid.*, p. 13.

[5]Quoted in *ibid.*, p. 18.

[6]*Ibid.*, chapt. 3.

[7]Force, ed., *American Archives*, vol. 1, pp. 923-924.

[8]*Ibid.*, p. 927.

[9]*Ibid.*

[10]*Ibid.*, p. 928.

[11]Quoted in Chitwood, *Richard Henry Lee*, p. 72.

[12]Quoted in *ibid.*, pp. 72-74.

[13]Force, ed., *American Archives*, vol. I, p. 921.

[14]Quoted in George Pellew, *John Jay*, Boston and New York, 1890, pp. 15-16; *Dictionary of American Biography*, vol. 5, p. 5; Herbert Alan Johnson, *John Jay, 1745-1829*, Albany, New York, 1970, p. 9; Frank Monaghan, *John Jay, Defender of Liberty Against Kings and Peoples*, New York, 1935, p. 56.

[15]Quoted in Pellew, *John Jay*, p. 40.

[16]Quoted in *ibid.*, p. 41.

[17]Quoted in Richard B. Morris, *John Jay, the Nation and the Court*, Boston, 1967, pp. 6-7; Pellew, *John Jay*, p. 40.

[18]Quoted in Clifford K. Shipton, *Sibley's Harvard Graduates*, vol. 11, Boston, 1937-1970, p. 386-7.

[19]Burnett, ed., *Letters*, vol. I, p. 50.

[20]Force, ed., *American Archives*, vol. I, p. 930.

[21]*Ibid.*, p. 933.

[22]Dickinson to Logan, September 14, 1804, in Charles J. Stille, *The Life and Times of John Dickinson, 1732-1808*, Philadelphia, 1891, p. 145n. For Adams's participation, see L. H. Butterfield, ed., *The Diary and Autobiography of John Adams*, vol. 2, 1961.

[23]Quoted in George F. Willison, *Patrick Henry and His World*, New York, 1969, p. 123.

[24]Force, ed., *American Archives*, vol. I, pp. 934-938.

[25]Quoted in Willison, *Patrick Henry*, pp. 258-259.

[26]Quoted in Thomas J. Wertenbaker, *Give Me Liberty: The Struggle for Self-Government in Virginia*, Philadelphia, 1958, p. 241.

[27]Myles Cooper to Sir William Johnson, November 6, 1767, in *Letters of a Westchester Farmer*, C. H. Vance, ed., White Plains, New York, 1930, p. 12f.

[28]Samuel Seabury, *Free Thoughts on the Proceedings of the Continental Congress*, quoted in Moses Coit Tyler, *The Literary History of the American Revolution*, vol. 1, New York and London, 1897, pp. 338, 339, 341.

[29]Quoted in *ibid.*, p. 340.

[30]Samuel Seabury, *The Congress Canvassed*, quoted in Vance, ed., *Letters of A Westchester Farmer*, p. 88.

[31]Quoted in W. A. Benton, *Whig Loyalism*, Rutherford, New Jersey, 1969, p. 125.

[32]Quoted in Tyler, *Literary History*, vol. 1, p. 359.

[33]Quoted in *ibid.*, p. 360.

[34]Quoted in *ibid.*, p. 363.

[35]Quoted in *ibid.*, p. 365.

[36]Quoted in *ibid.*, p. 367.

[37]Myles Cooper, *A Friendly Address to All Reasonable Americans*, quoted in Alexander Clarence Flick, *Loyalism in New York During the American Revolution*, New York, 1969, p. 11n.

[38]Quoted in *ibid.*

[39]Quoted in *ibid.*, p. 12n. Tyler, *Literary History*, vol. 1, p. 395.

[40]Flick, *Loyalism in New York*, pp. 24, 26.

[41]Myles Cooper, *The Patriots of North America*, quoted in Philip Davidson, *Propaganda and the American Revolution, 1763-1783*, Chapel Hill, North Carolina, 1941, p. 294.

[42]Letter to William Bradford, Jr., January 20, 1775, in William T. Hutchinson and William M. E. Rachel, eds., *Papers of James Madison*, vol. 1, Chicago, 1962, p. 135.

[43]Quoted in Arthur M. Schlesinger, *Prelude to Independence, The Newspaper War on Britain, 1764-1776*, New York, 1966, pp. 210-11.

[44]January 29, 1776, in V. H. Paltsits, "John Holt—Printer and Postmaster," New York Public Library *Bulletin*, vol. XXIV (1902), p. 494.

[45]Quoted in Nathan Schachner, *Alexander Hamilton*, New York, 1957, p. 38.

[46]Alexander Hamilton, *A Full Vindication of the Measures of the Congress*, quoted in Harold C. Syrett, ed., in *The Papers of Alexander Hamilton*, vol. 1, New York, 1961, pp. 46-7.

[47]*Ibid.*, p. 56.

[48]*Ibid.*

[49]*Ibid.*, p. 54.

[50]*Ibid.*, p. 78.

[51]Alexander Hamilton, *The Farmer Refuted*, in *ibid.*, p. 82.

[52]Hamilton, *The Farmer Refuted*, quoted in Tyler, *Literary History*, vol. 1, p. 386f.

[53]Quoted in *ibid.*, p. 387.

[54]Quoted in John A. Stevens, Jr., *Colonial Records of the New York Chamber of Commerce, 1768-1784*, New York, 1971, pp. 94-95.

CHAPTER III

[1]Douglass Adair and John A. Schutz, eds., *Peter Oliver's Origin and Progress of the American Rebellion*, San Marino, California, 1961, p. 115.

[2]Joseph Warren to Josiah Quincy, Jr., November 21, 1774, in Josiah Quincy, *Memoir of the Life of Josiah Quincy, Junior*, Boston, 1875, p. 178f.

[3]John Adams, "Diary," August 25, 1774, in L. H. Butterfield, ed., *The Diary and Autobiography of John Adams*, Cambridge, Massachusetts, vol. 2, 1961, p. 110.

[4]Gage Correspondence, letter to Viscount Barrington, February 10, 1775, quoted in John Richard Alden, "Why the March to Concord?" *American Historical Review*, vol. 49 (April 1944), p. 447.

[5]C. E. Carter, ed., *The Correspondence of General Thomas Gage, with the Secretaries of State, 1763-1775*, vol. 2, New Haven, Connecticut, 1931, p. 394.

[6]Quoted in Alden, "Why the March to Concord?" p. 450-451.

[7]Lieutenant William Sutherland to Gage's secretary, April 27, 1774, quoted in Allen French, *General Gage's Informers*, Ann Arbor, Michigan, 1932, p. 42.

[8]Lieutenant John Barker, "A British Officer in America," *Atlantic Monthly*, vol. 39, p. 389.

[9]Ezra Stiles, in F. B. Dexter, ed., *The Literary Diary of Ezra Stiles*, New York, 1901, p. 604.

[10]Revere to Jeremy Belknap, January 1, 1798, in E. H. Goss, *The Life of Colonel Paul Revere*, vol. 1, Boston, 1891, p. 187f.

[11]*Ibid.*, pp. 188-190.

[12]Quoted in Allen French, *The Day of Lexington and Concord*, Boston, 1925, pp. 109-110n.

[13]Harold Murdock, *The Nineteenth of April, 1775*, Boston, 1923. Arthur Tourtellot made the same suggestion in 1959 in, *William Diamond's Drum; The Beginning of the War of the American Revolution*, Garden City, New York, 1959.

[14]Pitcairn to Gage, April 26, 1775, in French, *Gage's Informers*, p. 53.

[15]Lexington Historical Society, *Proceedings*, vol. 4, pp. 91-92; quoted in Clifford K. Shipton, *Sibley's Harvard Graduates*, vol. 13, Boston, 1933-1970, p.214.

[16]Quoted in French, *Gage's Informers*, p. 14.

[17]Massachusetts Historical Society *Proceedings*, vol. 55, p. 18; quoted in Shipton, *Sibley's*, vol. 15, p. 41.

[18]Amos Barrett, "An Account of the Battle of Concord, April 19, 1775," in Henry True, ed., *Journal and Letters of Rev. Henry True*, Marion, Ohio, 1900, p. 31.

[19]William Emerson, "Diary," quoted in Shipton, *Sibley's*, vol. 15, p. 42.

[20]Barrett, "An Account," in *Journal and Letters*, p. 31.

[21]*Ibid.*, p. 33.

[22]Barker, quoted in French, *Gage's Informers*, p. 83.

[23]Massachusetts Historical Society *Proceedings*, vol. 56, p. 89; quoted in Shipton, *Sibley's*, vol. 15, p. 42.

[24]Quoted in French, *The Day of Lexington*, p. 217.

[25]Barrett, "An Account," in *Journal and Letters*, p. 33.

[26]Barker, "A British Officer," p. 400.

[27]Quoted in French, *The Day of Lexington*, p. 224.

[28]Barker, "A British Officer," p. 400.

[29]Frederick Mackenzie, *Diary of Frederick Mackenzie*, vol. 1, Cambridge, Massachusetts, 1903, p. 19.

[30]Percy to the Duke of Northumberland, April 20, 1775, in C. K. Bolton, ed., *Letters of Hugh, Earl Percy, from Boston and New York, 1774-1776*, Boston, 1902, p. 54.

[31]Mackenzie, *Diary*, p. 26f.

[32]Percy to General Harvey, April 20, 1775, in Bolton, ed., *Letters of Hugh, Earl Percy*, p. 53.

[33]Mackenzie, *Diary*, p. 27.

[34]William Heath, *Heath's Memoirs of the American War*, Boston, 1798; reprinted Freeport, New York, 1904, p. 15.

[35]*Ibid.*, p. 19, 20.

[36]*Ibid.*, p. 21

[37]Quoted in French, *The Day of Lexington*, p. 261.

[38]Heath, *Memoirs*, p. 23.

[39]Quoted in Arthur Tourtellot, *William Diamond's Drum; The Beginning of the War of the American Revolution*, Garden City, New York, 1959, p. 202.

[40]Heath, *Memoirs*, p. 23.

[41]Percy to General Harvey, April 20, 1775, in Bolton, ed., *Letters of Hugh, Earl Percy*, p. 53.

[42]Paul Revere to Jeremy Belknap, January 1, 1798, quoted in Goss, *Paul Revere*, vol. 1, p. 184.

[43]Quoted in *ibid.*, p. 208.

[44]Quoted in *ibid.*

[45]Quoted in Tourtellot, *William Diamond's Drum*, p. 229.

[46]Quoted in *ibid.*

CHAPTER IV

[1]Quoted in Lynn Montross, *The Reluctant Rebels; The Story of the Continental Congress, 1774-1789*, New York, 1950, p.64.

[2]Quoted in Edmund Cody Burnett, *The Continental Congress*, New York, 1941, p. 64.

[3]Quoted in *ibid.*, p. 64.

[4]Edmund Cody Burnett, ed., *Letters of Members of the Continental Congress 1774-1776*, vol. 1, Washington, 1921, p. 118.

[5]Quoted in *National Cyclopedia of American Biography*, vol. 1, p. 103.

[6]Quoted in Clifford K. Shipton, *Sibley's Harvard Graduates*, vol. 12, Boston, 1933-1970, p. 423.

⁷Peter Force, ed., *American Archives*, 4th series, vol. 2, Washington, 1836; reprinted New York, 1972, p. 1840.

⁸*Ibid.*

⁹*Ibid.*, p. 1900.

¹⁰*Ibid.*, pp. 1845, 1842.

¹¹*Ibid.*, p. 1845.

¹²Burnett, ed., *Letters*, vol. 2, p. 101.

¹³Quoted in Shipton, *Sibley's*, vol. 12, p. 468.

¹⁴Quoted in Justin H. Smith, *Our Struggle for the Fourteenth Colony: Canada and the American Revolution*, vol. 1, New York and London, 1907, p. 118.

¹⁵Quoted in George L. Clark, *Silas Deane, A Connecticut Leader in the American Revolution*, New York, 1913, p. 29.

¹⁶Quoted in Burnett, *Letters*, p. 68.

¹⁷Quoted in Clarence W. Rife, "Ethan Allen, An Interpretation," *The New England Quarterly*, vol. 2 (1929), p. 568.

¹⁸Quoted in Allen French, *The Taking of Ticonderoga in 1775: The British Story*, Cambridge, Massachusetts, 1928, p. 27.

¹⁹*Ibid.*, p. 28.

²⁰Force, ed., *American Archives*, p. 606.

²¹Quoted in French, *Taking of Ticonderoga*, p. 84; and Charles A. Jellison, *Ethan Allen, Frontier Rebel*, Syracuse, New York, 1969, p. 118.

²²Ethan Allen, "A Narrative of Col. Ethan Allen's Captivity, and Treatment by the British, from 1775 to 1778," in Richard M. Dorson, ed., *America Rebels: Narratives of the Patriots*, New York, 1953, p. 38. Allen's "Narrative" also failed to include Benedict Arnold as having entered the fort with him "side by side." Later, Allen's widow was quoted as saying, "this narrative . . . shows more of his true character than all else ever written by him." (Rife, "Ethan Allen," p. 570n.)

²³Quoted in Smith, *Our Struggle*, p. 140; Dartmouth to Gage, July 1, 1775, in Jellison, *Ethan Allen*, p. 120.

²⁴"Allen's Narrative" in Dorson, ed., *America Rebels*, p. 38.

²⁵Quoted in Smith, *Our Struggle*, p. 144.

²⁶"Lieutenant Feltham's Reports," in French, *Taking of Ticonderoga*, p. 51; and Jellison, *Ethan Allen*, p. 122.

²⁷Quoted in Merrill Jensen, *The Founding of a Nation*, New York, 1968, p. 608.

²⁸Force, ed., *American Archives*, p. 1841.

²⁹*Ibid.*, p. 1847.

³⁰*Ibid.*, p. 1848.

³¹L. H. Butterfield, ed., *The Diary and Autobiography of John Adams*, vol. 3, Cambridge, Massachusetts, 1962, p. 323.

³²*Ibid.*,

³³Burnett, ed., *Letters*, vol. 1, pp. 126, 128. Quoted in Herbert Sanford Allan, *John Hancock; Patriot in Purple*, New York, 1948, p. 196.

³⁴Butterfield, ed., *Diary and Autobiography*, vol .3, p. 323.

³⁵Quoted in James Thomas Flexner, *George Washington in the American Revolution (1775-1783)*, Boston and Toronto, 1967, p. 9.

³⁶Quoted in Curtis P. Nettels, *George Washington and American Independence*, Boston, 1951,

p. 122; James Thomas Flexner, *George Washington; the Forge of Experience, 1732-1775*, Boston and Toronto, 1965, p. 312.

[37]Force, ed., *American Archives*, p. 1848.

[38]Quoted in Flexner, *George Washington in the American Revolution*, p. 16; Willard M. Wallace, *Appeal to Arms: A Military History of the American Revolution*, New York, 1951, p. 55; Burnett, ed., *Letters*, vol. 1, p. 138.

[39]Burnett, ed., *Letters*, vol. 1, p. 136.

[40]Quoted in Nettels, *George Washington*, p. 152.

[41]Quoted in George H. Billias, ed., *George Washington's Generals*, New York, 1964, p. 90.

[42]Quoted in Don R. Gerlach, "Philip Schuyler and 'The Road to Glory': A Question of Loyalty and Competence," *New-York Historical Society Quarterly*, vol. 49 (October 1965), p. 346.

[43]Butterfield, ed., *Diary and Autobiography*, vol. 3, p. 324.

[44]Quoted in John F. Roche, *Joseph Reed, a Moderate in the American Revolution*, New York, 1957, pp. 37, 48, 39.

[45]Quoted in *ibid.*, pp. 65, 66, 77.

[46]Burnett, ed., *Letters*, vol. 1, p. 142.

[47]Quoted in Wallace, *Appeal to Arms*, p. 32.

[48]Quoted in Charles Martyn, *The Life of Artemas Ward*, New York, 1921, p. 117.

[49]Quoted in Shipton, *Sibley's*, vol. 12, p. 335.

[50]Quoted in *ibid.*, p. 333.

[51]Quoted in Harold Murdock, *Bunker Hill; Notes and Queries on a Famous Battle*, Boston, 1927, p. 56.

[52]Quoted in Allen French, *The First Year of the American Revolution*, Cambridge, Massachusetts, 1934, pp. 217, 219.

[53]Quoted in Wallace, *Appeal to Arms*, p. 36.

[54]Quoted in Richard Frothingham, *History of the Siege of Boston*, Boston, 1873, p. 140.

[55]Burnett, ed., *Letters*, vol. 1, p. 137.

[56]Quoted in Wallace, *Appeal to Arms*, p. 42.

[57]Quoted in *ibid.*; French, *The First Year*, p. 249.

[58]Quoted in George Bancroft, *History of the United States*, vol. 4, New York, 1883-1885, p. 260.

[59]Quoted in French, *The First Year*, p. 253.

[60]Quoted in Margaret Wheeler Willard, ed., *Letters on the American Revolution, 1774-1776*, Port Washington, New York, 1925; reissued 1968, p. 136.

[61]Quoted in Wallace, *Appeal to Arms*, p. 46.

[62]Quoted in Jensen, *Founding of a Nation*, p. 616.

[63]L. H. Butterfield, ed., *The Adams Family Correspondence*, vol. 1, Cambridge, Massachusetts, 1963, p. 222.

[64]Force, ed., *American Archives*, p. 1854.

[65]Burnett, ed., *Letters*, vol. 1, p. 154.

[66]*Ibid.*, p. 132.

[67]*Ibid.*, p. 28.

[68]*Ibid.*, p. 394n.

[69]Quoted in Hugh Blair Grigsby, *The Virginia Convention of 1776*, Richmond, Virginia, 1855; reprinted New York, 1969, p. 96.

[70]Force, ed., *American Archives*, p. 1847.

[71]*Ibid.*, p. 1857.

[72] Burnett, ed., *Letters*, vol. 1, p. 45; quoted in Memory F. Mitchell, *North Carolina's Signers,* Raleigh, North Carolina, 1964, p. 7.

[73]Force, ed., *American Archives*, p. 1849.

[74]Quoted in *Dictionary of American Biography*, vol. 6, p. 351.

[75]Force, ed., *American Archives*, p. 1879.

[76]*Ibid.*, p. 1882.

[77]*Ibid.*, p. 1880.

[78]Burnett, ed., *Letters*, vol. 1, p. 18.

[79]*Ibid.*, p. 30.

[80]*Ibid.*, p. 174.

[81]Quoted in W. H. Hoyt, *The Mecklenburg Declaration of Independence*, New York and London, 1908, p. 62.

[82]Quoted in A. S. Salley, Jr., "The Mecklenburg Declaration: The Present Status of the Question," *American Historical Review*, vol. 13 (October 1907), pp. 1, 17.

[83]Quoted in *ibid.*, p. 68.

[84]Quoted in Hoyt, *The Mecklenburg Declaration*, p. 68. In later years a considerable controversy arose over the Mecklenburg Resolutions. The records of the committee that passed the resolves were destroyed in a fire in 1800. John McKnitt Alexander, whose father, Abraham Alexander, had been chairman of the Mecklenburg County Committee of Safety, tried to reconstruct the resolutions from memory. In so doing, he unconsciously incorporated into the resolves phrases from Thomas Jefferson's Declaration of Independence. He also confused the date the resolves were passed, making it May 20 rather than May 31, and he included a reference to the shedding of Patriot blood at Lexington. There was no mention of Lexington in the original resolutions, as reported in contemporary newspapers, and they would probably have passed had there never been such a confrontation. Others who, like John Alexander, had been contemporaries but not participants in the passage of the resolves dredged up similar confused memories. This gave rise to the legend that Mecklenburg County had declared its independence a year in advance of the rest of the colonies and that Jefferson had copied key passages in his Declaration from the Mecklenburg original. It took the better part of a century for historians to sort the problem out and assign Mecklenburg its true place in the revolution of an independent American nation.

[85]Force, ed., *American Archives*, p. 1869.

[86]Quoted in Julian P. Boyd, "The Disputed Authorship of the Declaration on the Causes and Necessity of Taking Up Arms," *The Pennsylvania Magazine of History and Biography*, vol. 74 (January 1950), pp. 57, 58.

[87]Force, ed., *American Archives*, p. 1869.

[88]Quoted in Bernhard Knollenberg, "John Dickinson v. John Adams, 1774-1776," American Philosophical Society *Proceedings*, vol. 107 (April 15, 1963), pp. 139, 140; Butterfield, ed., *Diary and Autobiography*, vol. 3, p. 316; Burnett, ed., *Letters*, vol. 1, p. 161-2.

[89]Burnett, ed., *Letters*, vol. 1, pp. 158, 176; Butterfield, ed., *Diary and Autobiography*, vol. 3, p. 319, vol. 2, p. 173; quoted in James Truslow Adams, *Revolutionary New England, 1691-1776*, New York, 1968, p. 428.

[90]Burnett, ed., *Letters*, vol. 1, p. 130n; Force, *American Archives*, p. 1871.

[91]Quoted in Lawrence Henry Gipson, *The Triumphant Empire: Britain Sails Into the Storm, 1770-1776*, New York, 1965, p. 338n; David L. Jacobson, *John Dickinson and the Revolution in Pennsylvania 1764-1776*, Berkeley and Los Angles, California, 1965, p. 100.

[92]Burnett, ed., *Letters*, vol. 1, p. 181; Force. ed., *American Archives*, p. 1904.

CHAPTER V

[1]Quoted in John R. Alden, *The American Revolution, 1775-1783*, New York, 1954, p. 62; Peter Force, ed., *American Archives*, 4th series, vol. 2, Washington, 1839; reprinted New York, 1972, p. 1870.

[2]W. Bodham Donne, ed., *The Correspondence of King George the Third with Lord North from 1768 to 1783*, vol. 2, London, 1867, p. 202.

[3]Quoted in Stanley Ayling, *George the Third*, New York, 1972, p. 240.

[4]Donne, ed., *Correspondence with Lord North*, vol. 1, p. 201.

[5]Quoted in Ayling, *George the Third*, p. 244.

[6]Quoted in Bernard Donoughue, *British Politics and the American Revolution, the Path to War 1773-75*, London, 1964, p. 199.

[7]Quoted in *ibid*.

[8]Donne, ed., *Correspondence with Lord North*, vol. 1, pp. 214-15, 216.

[9]Quoted in Pauline Maier, *From Resistance to Revolution, Colonial Radicals and the Development of American Opposition to Britain, 1765-1776*, London, 1972, p. 236.

[10]Quoted in *ibid*., p. 236.

[11]Sir John Fortescue, ed., *The Correspondence of King George the Third*, vol. 3, London, 1928, p.175.

[12]Quoted in George Bancroft, *History of the United States*, vol. 4, New York, 1883-1885, p. 271·

[13]Quoted in Alan Valentine, *Lord George Germain*, Oxford, England, 1962, p. 341.

[14]Quoted in Lawrence Henry Gipson, *The British Empire: Thunder-Clouds Gather in the West, 1763-1766*, New York, 1961, p. 378.

[15]*Old South Leaflets*, vol. 8, Directors of the Old South Work, Old South Meeting House, Boston, Massachusetts, 1883, pp. 15, 16, 21, 22.

[16]Hubert Hall, "Chatham's Colonial Policy," *The American Historical Review*, vol. 5, New York, 1900, p. 674.

[17]Quoted in Lawrence Henry Gipson, *The Triumphant Empire: Britain Sails Into the Storm, 1770-1776*, New York, 1965, pp. 283, 284.

[18]Quoted in Alan Valentine, *Lord North*, vol. 1, Norman, Oklahoma, 1967, p. 354.

[19]B. D. Bargar, *Lord Dartmouth and the American Revolution*, Columbia, South Carolina, 1965, p. 132.

[20]Franklin-Galloway correspondence, quoted in Cecil B. Currey, *Road to Revolution: Benjamin Franklin in England 1765-1775*, New York, 1968, pp. 376-77.

[21]Albert Henry Smyth, ed., *The Writings of Benjamin Franklin*, vol. 6, New York, 1906, pp. 328-330.

[22]See B. F. Stevens, Hist., ed., Hist. Mss. Comm., *14th Report, App. Part X*, p. 236; quoted in Bargar, *Lord Dartmouth*, p. 134.

[23]Bargar, *Lord Dartmouth*, p. 136.

[24]Quoted in *ibid*.

[25]*Ibid*., p. 138.

[26]*Ibid*., p. 139; John Brooke, *King George III*, New York, 1972, p. 178.

[27]Quoted in Weldon A. Brown, *Empire or Independence, A Study in the Failure of Reconciliation, 1774-1783*, Port Washington, New York, 1941, p. 51.

[28]See Albert Henry Smyth, ed., *The Writings of Benjamin Franklin*, vol. 6, p. 314.

[29]Quoted in Ayling, *George III*, p. 244.

[30]Quoted in Gipson, *Triumphant Empire*, p. 297.

[31]Quoted in Bargar, *Lord Dartmouth*, p. 143.

[32]Wilbur C. Abbott, *New York in the American Revolution*, New York, 1929, p. 134; Force, ed., *American Archives*, p. 1901.

[33]*Old South Leaflets*, vol. 8, Old South Meeting House—Burke's Speech on Reconciliation, pp. 1-20 *passim*.

[34]*Ibid.*

[35]Quoted in Gipson, *The Triumphant Empire*, p. 304.

[36]Quoted in Solomon Lutnick, *The American Revolution and the British Press, 1775-1783*, Columbia, Missouri, 1967, p. 55.

[37]Quoted in Gipson, *The Triumphant Empire*, p. 300.

[38]*Ibid.*; quoted in Gipson, *The Triumphant Empire*, pp. 300, 307.

[39]Quoted in Gipson, *ibid.*, p. 308.

[40]Force, ed., *American Archives*, vol. 1, p. 1840.

[41]*Ibid.*

[42]*Ibid.*, p. 1841n.

[43]Force, ed., *American Archives*, vol. 1, pp. 1841-42.

[44]Journals of the House of Commons XXXV, p. 395; quoted in Gipson, *Triumphant Empire*, p. 310.

[45]Quoted in *The Encyclopedia Brittanica*, vol. 13, p. 48.

[46]James Boswell, *Boswell's Life of Johnson*, London, 1904, p. 590.

[47]Quoted in Valentine, *Lord North*, p. 364.

[48]Samuel Johnson, *Taxation No Tyranny; an Answer to the Resolutions and Address of the American Congress*, 3d edition, London, 1775, *passim*.

[49]*Ibid.*

[50]Quoted in Claude H. Van Tyne, *The War of Independence, American Phase*, Boston, 1929, p. 168.

[51]Frederick C. Gill, ed., *Selected Letters of John Wesley*, London, 1956, p. 166.

[52]*Ibid.*

[53]John Wesley, *A Calm Address to Our American Colonies*, quoted in Van Tyne, *The War of Independence*, pp. 163-165.

[54]Quoted in Van Tyne, *The War of Independence*, p. 169.

[55]Quoted in C. E. Vulliamy, *John Wesley*, London, 1931, p. 326; Van Tyne, *The War of Independence*, p. 164.

[56]Quoted in *Dictionary of National Biography*, vol. 12, p. 407.

[57]Catharine Macaulay, "An Address to the People of England, Ireland, and Scotland on The Present Important Crisis of Affairs," in Paul H. Smith, comp., *English Defenders of American Freedoms 1774-1778*, Washington, 1972, pp. 107-122 *passim*.

[58]Quoted in Claude H. Van Tyne, *Causes of War of Independence: Being the First Volume of the Founding of the American Republic*, Boston and New York, 1922, p. 325.

[59]Quoted in Maier, *From Resistance to Revolution*, p. 229.

[60]Quoted in Sir Leslie Stephen and Sir Sidney Lee, eds., *Dictionary of National Biography*, London, 1921, vol. 5, p. 858.

[61]Frederick C. Gill, ed., *Selected Letters of John Wesley*, pp. 168, 169.

[62]Quoted in Maier, *From Resistance to Revolution*, p. 232.

[63]Quoted in Donoughue, *British Politics*, p. 275.

[64]Valentine, *Lord North*, pp. 373-74.

[65]Quoted in Charles Ritcheson, *British Politics and the American Revolution*, Norman, Oklahoma, 1954, p. 194; Bargar, *Lord Dartmouth*, p. 154.

[66]Quoted in Valentine, *Lord North*, p. 638; Donoughue, *British Politics*, pp. 153-154.

[67]Donne, ed., *Correspondence with Lord North*, p. 267.

[68]Force, ed., *American Archives*, vol. 6, p. 1.

[69]Quoted in Alan Valentine, *The British Establishment, 1760-1784*, vol. II, Norman, Oklahoma, 1970, p. 911.

[70]Quoted in G. H. Guttridge, *English Whiggism and the American Revolution*, Berkeley, California, 1942, p. 83.

[71]Force, ed., *American Archives*, vol. 6, p. 5.

[72]*Ibid.*, pp. 5-6.

[73]Quoted in Gipson, *The Triumphant Empire*, p. 351.

[74]Quoted in Alison Gilbert Olson, *The Radical Duke; Career and Correspondence of Charles Lennox, Third Duke of Richmond*, London, 1961, p. 37.

[75]Quoted in *ibid.*, p. 169.

[76]Quoted in Mark M. Boatner, *Encyclopedia of the American Revolution*, New York, 1966, p. 969; John Brooke, *The Chatham Administration, 1766-1768*, London and New York, 1956, p. 32; Allen French, *The First Year of the American Revolution*, New York, 1934, pp. 346-7.

[77]Quoted in Gipson, *The Triumphant Empire*, p. 283; and Force, ed., *American Archives*, vol. 6, p. 7.

[78]Force, *ibid.*

[79]Sir William R. Anson, ed., *Autobiography and Political Correspondence of Augustus Henry, Third Duke of Grafton*, London, 1898, pp. 270-271.

[80]*Ibid.*, p. 271.

[81]Force, ed., *American Archives*, vol. 6, p. 6.

[82]Donne, ed., *Correspondence*, p. 282.

[83]Quoted in Van Tyne, *War of Independence*, p. 142.

[84]Force, ed., *American Archives*, vol. 6, pp. 14-16.

[85]*Ibid.*, p. 44.

[86]Quoted in Boatner, *Encyclopedia of the American Revolution*, p. 390; *Dictionary of National Biography*, vol. 6, p. 535.

[87]Quoted in Loren Reid, *Charles James Fox*, London, 1969, p. 46.

[88]Force, ed., *American Archives*, vol. 6, pp. 44, 45.

[89]Quoted ib Force, ed., *American Archives*, vol. 6, pp. 46, 47; Reid, *Charles James Fox*, p. 60.

[90]Quoted in Michael Pearson, *Those Damned Rebels, The American Revolution as Seen Through British Eyes*, New York, 1972, p. 115.

[91]Quoted in Valentine, *Lord George Germain*, pp. 96, 100.

[92]Quoted in Alden, *American Revolution*, p. 68.

[93]Pearson, *Those Damned Rebels*, pp. 114-15; quoted in Valentine, *Lord George Germain*, p. 100; Gerald Saxon Brown, *The American Secretary, The Colonial Policy of Lord George Germain, 1775-1778*, Ann Arbor, Michigan, 1963, p. 37.

[94]Quoted in Valentine, *Lord North*, p. 390.

[95]Quoted in French, *First Year of the American Revolution*, p. 566; Ritcheson, *British Politics,* p. 200.

[96]Quoted in Valentine, *Lord North*, p. 340.

[97]Ritcheson, *British Politics*, p. 199; Pearson, *Those Damned Rebels*, p. 113.

[98]Quoted in Valentine, *Lord North*, p. 378.

[99]Quoted in *ibid.*, pp. 383-84; Valentine, *British Establishment*, vol. 1, p. 53.

[100]Quoted in George Herbert Guttridge, *David Hartley, M.P. An Advocate of Conciliation 1774-1783*, Berkeley, California, 1926, pp. 234, 242.

[101]Quoted in Gipson, *Triumphant Empire*, p. 348.

[102]Force, ed., *American Archives*, vol. 6, pp. 248-253.

[103]Quoted in Guttridge, *David Hartley*, pp. 270-71.

[104]Quoted in Gipson, *The Triumphant Empire*, p. 349.

[105]Quoted in French, *First Year of the American Revolution*, p. 568.

CHAPTER VI

[1]John Quincy Adams to Joseph Sturge, March 1846, in L. H. Butterfield, ed., *Adams Family Correspondence*, vol. 1, Cambridge, Massachusetts, 1963, pp. 223-224n.

[2]Abigail Adams to John Adams in *ibid.*, pp. 225, 231, 239, 248-9.

[3]*Ibid.*, p. 284.

[4]*Ibid.*, pp. 288-9.

[5]*Ibid.*, p. 306.

[6]*Ibid.*, p. 324.

[7]Quoted in Richard Frothingham, *History of the Siege of Boston*, Boston, 1873, p. 263.

[8]Butterfield, ed., *Adams Family Correspondence*, vol. 1, p. 246.

[9]Allen French, *The First Year of the American Revolution*, Boston and New York, 1934, p. 264.

[10]Quoted in North Callahan, *Henry Knox, General Washington's General*, New York and Toronto, 1958, p. 24.

[11]Quoted in *ibid.*, pp. 24, 32.

[12]Quoted in Donald B. Chidsey, *The Siege of Boston*, New York, 1966, p. 144.

[13]Quoted in Callahan, *Henry Knox*, p. 51.

[14]Chidsey, *The Siege of Boston*, p. 148.

[15]Thomas to his wife, quoted in French, *The First Year*, p. 162.

[16]Quoted in Charles Coffin, *The Life and Services of Major General John Thomas*, New York, 1844, p. 11.

[17]Quoted in *ibid.*, p. 13.

[18]Quoted in Frothingham, *History of the Siege of Boston*, p. 298.

[19]*Massachusetts Magazine*, January 1793, pp. 7-8; quoted in French, *The First Year*, p. 259.

[20]Quoted in Frothingham, *History of the Siege of Boston*, p. 20.

[21]Quoted in *ibid.*, p. 300.

[22]*Ibid.*

[23]Abigail Adams to John Adams, March 16, 1776, in Butterfield, ed., *Adams Family Correspondence*, vol. 1, p. 358; John Adams to Abigail, March 29, 1776, *ibid.*, p. 366.

[24]Quoted in George Athan Billias, ed., *George Washington's Opponents*, New York, 1969, p. 19.

[25]Quoted in Gardner Allen, *A Naval History of the American Revolution*, vol. 1, Boston and New York, 1913, p. 21.

[26]Quoted in *ibid.*, p. 22; Fletcher Pratt, *The Compact History of the United States Navy*, New York, 1957, p. 22.

[27]Edmund Cody Burnett, ed., *Letters of Members of the Continental Congress, 1774-1776*, vol. 1, Washington, 1921, p. 235.

[28]Quoted in Allen, *A Naval History*, vol. 1, p. 92.

[29]Quoted in *ibid.*, pp. 98-99.

[30]Quoted in *ibid.*, p. 102.

[31]Quoted in Dudley W. Knox, *A History of the United States Navy*, New York, 1948, p. 13.

[32]George Washington to Joseph Reed, January 31, 1776, in John C. Fitzpatrick, ed., *The Writings of George Washington*, vol. 4, Washington, 1931-44, p. 297.

[33]Peter Force, ed., *American Archives*, 4th series, vol. 3, Washington, 1840, p. 1145.

[34]Quoted in French, *The First Year*, p. 169.

[35]Quoted in Christopher Ward, *The War of the Revolution*, vol. 1, New York, 1952, p. 133.

[36]Force, ed., *American Archives*, p. 1146.

[37]William Bell Clarke, ed., *Naval Documents of the American Revolution*, vol. 2, Washington, 1966, p. 471.

[38]*Ibid.*, p. 515.

[39]Clarke, ed., *Naval Documents*, vol. 2, p. 489.

[40]Quoted in French, *The First Year*, p. 542.

[41]*Ibid.*, p. 543.

[42]Quoted in Lynn Montross, *The Reluctant Rebels*, New York, 1950, p. 112.

[43]Quoted in H. J. Eckenrode, *The Revolution in Virginia*, Hamden, Connecticut, 1964, p. 73.

[44]Thomas J. Wertenbaker, *Norfolk, Historic Southern Port*, Durham, North Carolina, 1931, p. 55.

[45]Quoted in French, *The First Year*, p. 578.

[46]Quoted in Wertenbaker, *Norfolk*, p. 60.

[47]Quoted in *ibid.*, p. 59.

[48]*Ibid.*

[49]Quoted in Samuel A'Court Ashe, *History of North Carolina, 1584-1783*, vol. 1, Spartanburg, South Carolina, 1971, p. 414; John Hill Wheeler, *Historical Sketches of North Carolina, 1584-1851*, Baltimore, 1964, p. 67.

[50]Ashe, *History of North Carolina*, p. 500.

[51]Quoted in Ward, *War of the Revolution*, vol. 2, New York, 1952, p. 663.

[52]Quoted in R. D. W. Connor, *Revolutionary Leaders of North Carolina*, Spartanburg, South Carolina, 1971, p. 80.

[53]Quoted in *ibid.*, p. 88.

[54]Quoted in Wheeler, *Historical Sketches*, p. 77.

[55]Ward, *War of the Revolution*, vol. 2, p. 52; Malcom Ross, *The Cape Fear*, New York, 1965, p. 125.

[56]Quoted in Ross, *Cape Fear*, p. 130.

[57]Quoted in Willard Mosher Wallace, *Appeal to Arms, A Military History of the American Revolution*, New York, 1951, p. 91.

[58]Frederick Wyatt and William B. Willcox, "Sir Henry Clinton: A Psychological Exploration in History," *William and Mary Quarterly*, 3d series, vol. 16 (January 1959), p. 19.

[59]Quoted in William B. Willcox, *Portrait of a General: Sir Henry Clinton in the War of Independence*, New York, 1964, p. 84.

[60]Quoted in George Bancroft, *History of the United States of America*, vol. 4, New York, 1887, p. 399.

[61]Billias, ed., *George Washington's Opponents*, p. 25.

[62]Quoted in Ward, *War of the Revolution*, vol. 2, p. 669.

[63]Quoted in *ibid.*, p. 670.

[64]Quoted in Bancroft, *History of the U.S.*, vol. 4, p. 339.

[65]Quoted in Samuel White Patterson, *Knight Errant of Liberty: The Triumph and Tragedy of General Charles Lee*, New York, 1958, p. 135.

[66]Quoted in Bancroft, *History of the U.S.*, vol. 4, p. 402.

[67]*Ibid.*, p. 406.

[68]Quoted in Patterson, *Knight Errant of Liberty*, p. 135.

[69]Quoted in Bancroft, *History of the U.S.*, vol. 4, p. 408.

[70]Quoted in Willcox, *Portrait of A General*. p. 90.

[71]Quoted in Patterson, *Knight Errant of Liberty*, p. 137.

[72]Quoted in Ward, *War of the Revolution*, vol. 2, p. 676

[73]Bancroft, *History of the U.S.*, vol. 4, pp. 409-410.

[74]Quoted in George M. Wrong, *Canada and the American Revolution*, New York, 1935, p. 223.

[75]Quoted in *ibid.*, pp. 229, 230.

[76]Quoted in *ibid.*

[77]Quoted in Billias, ed., *George Washington's Opponents*, p. 109.

[78]Quoted in John Richard Alden, *Canada and the American Revolution*, New York, 1954, p. 49.

[79]Quoted in Jared Sparks, *Lives of John Stark, Charles Brockden Brown, Richard Montgomery and Ethan Allen*, vol. 1, New York, 1834, p. 192.

[80]Billias, ed., *George Washington's Opponents*, pp. 116-117.

[81]Quoted in Wallace, *Appeal to Arms*, p. 72.

[82]Quoted in Willard M. Wallace, "Benedict Arnold: Traitorous Patriot," in *George Washington's Generals*, George Athan Billias, ed., New York, 1964, p. 168.

[83]Quoted in *ibid.*, p. 171.

[84]Quoted in *ibid.*, pp. 171-72.

[85]Matthew L. Davies, *Memoirs of Aaron Burr*, vol. 1, New York, 1971, p. 63.

[86]Quoted in Herbert S. Parmet and Marie B. Hecht, *Aaron Burr*, New York, 1967, p. 28.

[87]Quoted in *ibid.*, p. 29.

[88]Quoted in Billias, ed., *George Washington's Generals*, p. 294.

[89]Quoted in North Callahan, *Daniel Morgan, Ranger of the Revolution*, New York, 1961, p. 53.

[90]Quoted in Billias, ed., *George Washington's Generals*, p. 296.

[91]Quoted in Wallace, *Appeal to Arms*, p. 84.

[92]Willard M. Wallace, *Traitorous Hero: The Life and Fortunes of Benedict Arnold*, New York, 1954, p. 33.

[93]Quoted in Justin H. Smith, *Our Struggle for the Fourteenth Colony*, vol. 2, New York, 1907, pp. 45, 46; Lauran Paine, *Benedict Arnold, Hero and Traitor*, London, 1965, p. 64.

[94]Smith, *Our Struggle*, p. 230.

[95]Quoted in *ibid.*, p. 225.

[96]Quoted in Paine, *Benedict Arnold*, pp. 71, 72.

[97]Quoted in *ibid.*, p. 75.

CHAPTER VII

[1]*Common Sense*, in Nelson F. Adkins, ed., *Thomas Paine, Common Sense and Other Political Writings*, Indianapolis and New York, 1953, p. 19.

[2]Thomas Paine, "Dialogue Between Wolfe and Gage," in Moncure Daniel Conway, ed., *The Writings of Thomas Paine*, vol. 1, New York, 1969, pp. 12-13.

[3]Quoted in Adkins, ed., *Thomas Paine*, p. xxiii.

[4]Moncure Daniel Conway, *Life of Thomas Paine*, vol. 1, New York and London, 1892, p. 64.

[5]Quoted in *ibid.*, p. 61.

[6]Quoted in Adkins, ed., *Thomas Paine*, p. 22.

[7]Quoted in *ibid.*, pp. 3, 19.

[8]Quoted in *ibid.*, p. 21.

[9]Quoted in *ibid.*, p. 23.

[10]Quoted in *ibid.*, p. 32.

[11]Quoted in *ibid.*, p. 34.

[12]Quoted in Richard J. Hooker, "The American Revolution Seen Through a Wine Glass," *William and Mary Quarterly*, 3rd series, vol. 11 (January 1954), p. 58.

[13]Quoted in Christopher Ward, *The War of the Revolution*, vol. 2, New York, 1952, p. 849.

[14]Moses Coit Tyler, *The Literary History of the American Revolution*, vol. 1, New York and London, 1897, pp. 479-487.

[15]Quoted in Alfred O. Aldridge, *Man of Reason The Life of Thomas Paine*, Philadelphia and New York, 1959, p. 45.

[16]Quoted in Lorenzo Sabine, *Biographical Sketches of Loyalists of the American Revolution*, vol. 2, New York, 1966, pp. 316-17.

[17]Quoted in Adkins, ed., *Thomas Paine*, p. 43.

[18]Quoted in Samuel Flagg Bemis, *The Diplomacy of the American Revolution*, Bloomington, Indiana, 1957, p. 16n.

[19]Quoted in Edward S. Corwin, *French Policy and the Alliance of 1778*, Princeton, 1916, p. 40.

[20]Quoted in Friedrich Kapp, *The Life of John Kalb*, New York, 1884, pp. 45-51.

[21]Quoted in A. E. Zucker, *General De Kalb, Lafayette's Mentor*, Chapel Hill, North Carolina, 1966, p. 69.

[22]Quoted in Corwin, *French Policy*, p. 43.

[23]Quoted in Zucker, *General De Kalb*, pp. 75-6.

[24]Quoted in Bemis, *Diplomacy of the American Revolution*, pp. 17-18. James Breck Perkins, *France in the American Revolution*, Williamstown, Massachusetts, 1970, p. 27.

[25]Quoted in Elizabeth S. Kite, "French 'Secret Aid' Precursor to the French American Alliance 1776-1777," *The French American Review*, vol. 1 (April-June, 1948), p. 143.

[26]Quoted in Perkins, *France in the American Revolution*, p. 40.

[27]Quoted in *ibid.*, p. 44.

[28]*Ibid.*, p. 45.

[29]Quoted in *ibid.*, p. 46.

[30]Quoted in Kite, "French 'Secret Aid'," p. 144.

[31]Quoted in Perkins, *France in the American Revolution*, p. 47.

[32]Quoted in *ibid*.

[33]*Ibid.*, p. 48.

[34]Quoted in George Bancroft, *History of the United States of America*, vol. 4, New York, 1887, pp. 362-363.

[35]Quoted in Cynthia Cox, *The Real Figaro, The Extraordinary Career of Caron de Beaumarchais*, New York, 1962, p. 86.

[36]Quoted in *ibid.*, p. 75.

[37]Quoted in *ibid.*, p. 106. Charles J. Stillé claimed in 1837 that Controller-General Turgot was the author of this memorandum, which Beaumarchais claimed was his.

[38]Quoted in Georges Lemaitre, *Beaumarchais*, New York, 1949, p. 182.

[39]Quoted in *ibid.*, p. 184.

[40]A livre was approximately 20 cents in American money. John J. Meng, *The Comte de Vergennes, European Phases of his American Diplomacy 1774-1780*, Washington, 1932, p. 28n.

[41]Quoted in Cox, *The Real Figaro*, p. 123.

[42]Pauline Maier, *From Resistance to Revolution, Colonial Radicals and the Development of American Opposition to Britain, 1765-1776*, London, 1973, p. 267.

[43]Quoted in *ibid.*, pp. 84, 92.

[44]Charles C. Jones, Jr., *Biographical Sketches of the Delegates from Georgia to the Continental Congress*, Boston and New York, 1891, p. 169.

[45]*Ibid.*, p. 171; quoted in John Sanderson, *Biography of Signers of the Declaration of Independence*, vol. 4, Philadelphia, 1823, p. 155.

[46]Quoted in Jones, *Biographical Sketches . . . Georgia*, p. 172.

[47]Quoted in *ibid.*, p. 173.

[48]Quoted in *ibid.*, p. 184.

[49]Quoted in *ibid.*, p. 177.

[50]Quoted in Oliver Perry Chitwood, *Richard Henry Lee, Statesman of the Revolution*, Morgantown, West Virginia, 1967, p. 78.

[51]Worthington Chauncey Ford, ed., *Journals of the Continental Congress*, vol. 2, Washington, 1904, pp. 163-170.

[52]*Ibid.*, vol. 2, pp. 80, 157.

[53]Quoted in Chitwood, *Richard Henry Lee*, p. 90.

[54]Quoted in *ibid.*, p. 92.

[55]Quoted in *ibid.*

[56]Quoted in *ibid.*, pp. 92-3.

[57]Quoted in *ibid.*, p. 93.

[58]Quoted in Helen Hill Miller, *George Mason, Constitutionalist*, Cambridge, Massachusetts, 1938, p. 128.

[59]Quoted in Chitwood, *Richard Henry Lee*, p. 94.

[60]Quoted in *ibid.*, p. 94.

[61]Peter Force, ed., American Archives, 4th series, vol. 4, Washington, 1843; reprinted New York, 1972, p. 860.

[62]Ford, ed., *Journals of Continental Congress*, vol. 5, p. 425.

[63]Jefferson to William Wirt, August 14, 1814, quoted in Miller, *George Mason*, p. 112.

[64]Miller, *George Mason*, pp. 114-117.

[65]Quoted in *ibid.*, p. 118.

[66]*Ibid.*, pp. 118-19.

[67]Quoted in Chitwood, *Richard Henry Lee*, p. 98.

[68]Carter Braxton to Landon Carter, April 14, 1776, in Edmund Cody Burnett, ed., *Letters of Members of the Continental Congress*, vol. 1, Washington, 1921, p. 420.

[69]W. B. Reed, ed., *Life and Correspondence of Joseph Reed*, vol. 1, Philadelphia, 1847, p. 173.

[70]Quoted in Bancroft, *History of the United States*, vol. 4, p. 341.

[71]Charles Francis Adams, ed., *Familiar Letters of John Adams and His Wife Abigail Adams, During the Revolution*, New York, 1876, pp. 193-194.

[72]*Ibid.*, p. 191.

[73]Thomas Jefferson, "The Declaration of Independence," in Henry Steele Commager, ed., *Documents of American History*, vol. 1, New York, 1963, p. 101.

[74]*Ibid.*, p. 102.

[75]*Ibid.*

[76]Quoted in Dumas Malone, *Jefferson, The Virginian*, Boston, 1948, p. 226.

Bibliography

GENERAL

ADAMS, James Truslow. *Revolutionary New England, 1691-1776*. New York, 1968.

ALDEN, John Richard. *The American Revolution, 1775-1783*. New York, 1954.

BAKELESS, John & Katherine. *Signers of the Declaration*. Boston, 1969.

BANCROFT, George. *History of the United States*, vol. 4. New York, 1883-85.

BURNETT, Edmund Cody. *The Continental Congress*. New York, 1941.

BURNETT, Edmund Cody, ed. *Letters of Members of the Continental Congress*, vols. 1 & 2. Washington, 1921.

DORSON, Richard M. ed. *America Rebels: Narratives of the Patriots*. New York, 1953.

FEHRENBACH, T. R. *Greatness to Spare*. New York, 1968.

FORCE, Peter, ed. *American Archives*, 4th series, vols. 1-6. Washington, 1836-1846; reprinted New York, 1972.

FORD, Worthington Chauncey, ed. *Journals of the Continental Congress*, vols. 2 & 5. Washington, 1904.

FRENCH, Allen. *The First Year of the American Revolution*. Cambridge, Massachusetts, 1934.

GIPSON, Lawrence Henry. *The Coming of the Revolution, 1763-1775*. New York, 1954.
—— *The Triumphant Empire: Britain Sails Into the Storm, 1770-1776*, New York, 1965.

JENSEN, Merrill. *The Founding of a Nation. A History of the American Revolution, 1763-1776*. New York, 1968.

MAIER, Pauline. *From Resistance to Revolution, Colonial Radicals and the Development of American Opposition to Britain, 1765-1776*. London, 1972.

MILLER, John C. *Origins of the American Revolution*. Boston, 1943.

MONTROSS, Lynn. *The Reluctant Rebels; the Story of the Continental Congress, 1774-1789*. New York, 1950.

PECKHAM, Howard H. *The War for Independence*. Chicago, 1958.

VAN TYNE, Claude H. *The Causes of the War of Independence; Being the First Volume of the Founding of the American Republic*. Boston and New York, 1922.

—— *The War of Independence, American Phase*. Boston, 1929.

WARD, Christopher. *The War of the Revolution*, vols. 1 & 2. New York, 1952.

WRIGHT, Esmond. *Fabric of Freedom*. New York, 1961.

Bibliography

PROLOGUE

ADAIR, Douglass & John A. SCHUTZ, eds. *Peter Oliver's Origin and Progress of the American Revolution: A Tory View.* San Marino, California, 1961.

CHAPTER I

ALDEN, John Richard. *General Gage in America.* Baton Rouge, Louisiana, 1948.

ALEXANDER, Edward P. *A Revolutionary Conservative: James Duane of New York.* New York, 1938.

BALDWIN, Ernest H. "Joseph Galloway, the Loyalist Politician." *Pennsylvania Magazine of History and Biography,* vol. 26 (July-December 1902), pp. 161-191, 289-321, 417-442.

BISHOP, Joseph Bucklin. *A Chronicle of One Hundred and Fifty Years. The Chamber of Commerce of the State of New York, 1768-1918.* New York, 1918.

BOARDMAN, Roger Sherman. *Roger Sherman, Signer and Statesman.* Philadelphia, 1938.

BOYD, Julian P. "Joseph Galloway's Plans of Union for the British Empire, 1774-1780." *Pennsylvania Magazine of History and Biography,* vol. 64 (October 1940), pp. 492-515.

BUTTERFIELD, L. H., ed. *The Adams Family Correspondence,* vol. 1. Cambridge, Massachusetts, 1963.

—— *Diary and Autobiography of John Adams,* vol. 2. Cambridge, Massachusetts, 1962.

CALHOON, Robert M. "'I have deduced your rights'. . . Joseph Galloway's concept of his role, 1774-1775." *Pennsylvania History,* vol. 35 (October 1968), pp. 356-87.

CHINARD, Gilbert. *Honest John Adams.* Boston, 1933.

CHITWOOD, Oliver Perry. *Richard Henry Lee: Statesman of the Revolution.* Morgantown, West Virginia, 1967.

COLLIER, Christopher. *Roger Sherman's Connecticut.* Middletown, Connecticut, 1971.

CUSHING, H. A., ed. *The Writings of Samuel Adams,* vol. 3. New York and London, 1906.

DELAPLAINE, Edward S. *The Life of Thomas Johnson,* New York, 1927.

FROTHINGHAM, Richard. *The Life and Times of Joseph Warren.* Boston, 1865; reprinted New York, 1971.

GALLOWAY, Joseph. *History and Political Reflections on the Rise and Progress of the American Rebellion.* London, 1780.

GRIGSBY, Hugh Blair. *The Virginia Convention of 1776.* Richmond, Virginia, 1855; reprinted New York, 1969.

HOPKINS, Stephen. *The Rights of the Colonies Examined.* Providence, Rhode Island, 1765.

KETCHUM, Richard M. "Men of the Revolution—I," *American Heritage,* vol. 22 (August 1971), no. 5, p. 21.

KUNTZLEMAN, Oliver C. *Joseph Galloway, Loyalist.* Philadelphia, 1941.

MAYO, Lawrence S. "The Spirit of Massachusetts." *Commonwealth History of Massachusetts,* Albert B. Hart, ed., New York, 1966.

MEIGS, Cornelia. *The Violent Men: A Study of Human Relations in the First American Congress.* New York, 1949.

MILLER, John C. *Sam Adams, Pioneer in Propaganda.* Palo Alto, California, 1936.

NEILL, The Rev. Edward D. "Rev. Jacob Duché, the First Chaplain of Congress." *Pennsylvania Magazine of History and Biography,* vol. 2, 1878, pp. 58-73.

ROSSMAN, Kenneth R. *Thomas Mifflin and the Politics of the American Revolution.* Chapel Hill, North Carolina, 1952.

SALLEY, A. S., Jr. *Delegates to the Continental Congress from South Carolina, 1774-1789.* Columbia, South Carolina, 1927.

SCHLESINGER, Arthur M. *The Colonial Merchants and the American Revolution, 1763-1776.* New York, 1939.

SMEALL, J. F. S. "Revolutionary Process: The Publication of the Association, 1774-1775." *The North Dakota Quarterly* (Autumn 1962), vol. 30, pp. 89-98.

SMITH, Margaret Vowell. *Virginia, 1492-1892, with a History of the Executives.* Washington, 1893.

STROTHER, David H. "Edmund Pendleton of Virginia." *Pennsylvania Magazine of History and Biography,* vol. 3 (1879), pp. 177-179.

WHITTEMORE, Charles Park. *A General of the Revolution: John Sullivan of New Hampshire.* New York, 1961.

ZIMMERMAN, John J. "Charles Thomson, the Sam Adams of Philadelphia." *Mississippi Valley Historical Review,* vol. 45 (December 1958), pp. 464-480.

CHAPTER II

BENTON, W. A. *Whig Loyalism.* Rutherford, New Jersey, 1969.

CHITWOOD, Oliver P. *Richard Henry Lee: Statesman of the Revolution.* Morgantown, West Virginia, 1967.

DAVIDSON, Philip. *Propaganda and the American Revolution, 1763-1783.* Chapel Hill, North Carolina, 1941.

FLICK, Alexander Clarence. *Loyalism in New York During the American Revolution.* New York, 1969.

HUTCHINSON, William T. and William M. E. RACHEL, eds., *The Papers of James Madison,* vol. 1. Chicago, 1962.

JOHNSON, Herbert Alan. *John Jay, 1745-1829.* Albany, New York, 1970.

JONES, Thomas W. *History of New York in the American Revolution,* vol. 1. New York, 1879.

MINTZ, Max M. *Gouverneur Morris and the American Revolution.* Norman, Oklahoma, 1970.

MONAGHAN, Frank. *John Jay, Defender of Liberty Against Kings and Peoples.* New York, 1935.

MORRIS, Richard B. *John Jay, the Nation and the Court.* Boston, 1967.

PALTSITS, V. H. "John Holt—Printer and Postmaster." *New York Public Library Bulletin,* vol. 24, 1920.

PELLEW, George. *John Jay.* Boston and New York, 1890.

SCHACHNER, Nathan. *Alexander Hamilton.* New York, 1957.

SCHLESINGER, Arthur M. *Prelude to Independence, the Newspaper War on Britain, 1764-1776.* New York, 1966.

STEVENS, John A., Jr. *Colonial Records of the New York Chamber of Commerce, 1768-1784.* New York, 1971.

STILLE, Charles J. *The Life and Times of John Dickinson, 1732-1808.* Philadelphia, 1891.

SYRETT, Harold C., ed. *The Papers of Alexander Hamilton,* vol. 1. New York, 1961.

TYLER, Moses Coit. *The Literary History of the American Revolution,* vol. 1. New York and London, 1897.

VANCE, C. H., ed. *Letters of a Westchester Farmer.* White Plains, New York, 1930.

WERTENBAKER, Thomas J. *Give Me Liberty: The Struggle for Self-Government in Virginia.* Philadelphia, 1958.

WILLISON, George F. *Patrick Henry and His World.* New York, 1969.

WOLF, Edwin. "The Authorship of the 1774 Address to the King Restudied." *William and Mary Quarterly,* 3rd series, vol. 22 (April, 1965), pp. 189-224.

CHAPTER III

ADAIR, Douglass & John A. SCHUTZ, eds. *Peter Oliver's Origin and Progress of the American Revolution: A Tory View*. San Marino, California, 1961.

ALDEN, John Richard. *General Gage in America*. Baton Rouge, Louisiana, 1948.

——— "Why the March to Concord?" *American Historical Review*, vol. 49 (April 1944), pp. 446-454.

ALDERMAN, Clifford Lindsay. *The Royal Opposition; the Story of the British Generals in the American Revolution*. London, 1970.

BARKER, Lieutenant John. "A British Officer in America." *Atlantic Monthly*, vol. 39 (April and May, 1877).

BILLIAS, George Athan, ed. *George Washington's Opponents: British Generals and Admirals in the American Revolution*. New York, 1969.

BOLTON, Charles Knowles, ed. *Letters of Hugh Earl Percy from Boston and New York, 1774-1776*. Boston, 1902.

BUTTERFIELD, Lyman H., ed. *Diary and Autobiography of John Adams*, vol. 2. Cambridge, Massachusetts, 1961.

CARTER, C. E., ed. *The Correspondence of General Thomas Gage with the Secretaries of State, 1763-1775*, vol. 2. New Haven, Connecticut, 1931.

DEXTER, F. B., ed. *The Literary Diary of Ezra Stiles*. New York, 1901.

FRENCH, Allen. *The Day of Concord and Lexington*. Boston, 1925.

——— *General Gage's Informers*. Ann Arbor, Michigan, 1932.

FORBES, Esther. *Paul Revere and the World He Lived In*. Boston, 1942.

GOSS, Elbridge Henry. *The Life of Colonel Paul Revere*, vol. 1. Boston, 1891.

HEATH, William. *Heath's Memoirs of the American War*. Boston, 1798; reprinted Freeport, New York, 1904.

MACKENZIE, Frederick. *Diary of Frederick Mackenzie*, vol. 1. Cambridge, Massachusetts, 1930.

MURDOCK, Harold. *Earl Percy's Dinner Table*. Boston, 1907.

——— *The Nineteenth of April, 1775*. Boston, 1923.

QUINCY, Josiah. *Memoir of the Life of Josiah Quincy, Junior*. Boston, 1875.

TOURTELLOT, Athur B. *William Diamond's Drum; the Beginning of the War of the American Revolution*. Garden City, New York, 1959.

TRUE, Henry, ed. *Journal and Letters of Rev. Henry True; Also an Account of the Battle of Concord by Captain Amos Barrett*. Marion, Ohio, 1900.

CHAPTER IV

ADAMS, Charles F. "The Battle of Bunket Hill." *American Historical Review*, vol. 1 (April 1896), pp. 401-413.

ADAMS, James Truslow. "Portrait of An Empty Barrel." *Harper's Magazine*, vol. 161 (September 1930), pp. 425-434.

ALDEN, John Richard. *General Gage in America*. Baton Rouge, Louisiana, 1948.

ALLAN, Herbert Sanford. *John Hancock; Patriot in Purple*. New York, 1948.

ALLEN, Ethan. "Philip Livingston, New York Delegate in the Continental Congress, 1774-1777." *The Magazine of American History*, John Austin Stevens, ed., (May 1877), pp. 303-305.

BALCH, Thomas Willing. "Thomas Willing of Pennsylvania (1731-1821)." *Pennsylvania Magazine of History and Biography*, vol. 46 (1922), pp. 1-14.

BILLIAS, George A., ed. *George Washington's Generals*. New York, 1964.

Boyd, Julian P. "The Disputed Authorship of the Declaration on the Causes and Necessity of Taking Up Arms." *The Pennsylvania Magazine of History and Biography*, vol. 74 (January 1950), pp. 51-73.

——— "Silas Deane: Death by a Kindly Teacher of Treason?" *William and Mary Quarterly*, vol. 16 (April 1959), pp. 165-187.

Butterfield, Lyman H., ed. *Adams Family Correspondence*, vol. 1. Cambridge, Massachusetts, 1963.

——— *Diary and Autobiography of John Adams*, vols. 2 & 3. Cambridge, Massachusetts, 1962.

Chipman, Daniel. *Memoir of Colonel Seth Warner*. Middlebury, Vermont, 1948.

Clarke, George L. *Silas Deane, A Connecticut Leader in the American Revolution*. New York, 1913.

Cutter, William. *The Life of Israel Putnam*. New York, 1847.

Dorson, Richard M., ed. "A Narrative of Col. Ethan Allen's Captivity, and Treatment by the British, from 1775 to 1778," by Ethan Allen. In *America Rebels: Narratives of the Patriots*. New York, 1953.

Flexner, James Thomas. *George Washington; the Forge of Experience (1732-1775)*. Boston and Toronto, 1965.

——— *George Washington in the American Revolution (1775-1783)*. Boston and Toronto, 1967.

Freeman, Douglas Southall. *George Washington: Planter and Patriot*. New York, 1951.

French, Allen. *The Taking of Ticonderoga in 1775: the British Story*. Cambridge, Massachusetts, 1928.

Frost, John. *Lives of American Merchants*. New York, 1844.

Frothingham, Richard. *History of the Siege of Boston*. Boston, 1873.

Gerlach, Don R. *Philip Schuyler and the American Revolution in New York, 1733-1777*. Lincoln, Nebraska, 1964.

——— "Philip Schuyler and 'The Road to Glory': A Question Of Loyalty and Competence." *New York Historical Society Quarterly*, vol. 49 (October 1965), pp. 341-386.

Grigsby, Hugh Blair. *The Virginia Convention of 1776*. Richmond, Virginia, 1855; reprinted New York, 1969.

Hart, Albert Bushnell, ed. *American History Told by Contemporaries: Building the Republic, 1689-1783*, vol. 2. New York, 1898.

Hillard, George Stillman. "Christopher Gadsden." *Pennsylvania Magazine Of History and Biography*, vol. 3 (1879), pp. 186-189.

Hoyt, W. H. *The Mecklenburg Declaration of Independence*. New York and London, 1908.

Jacobson, David L. *John Dickinson and the Revolution in Pennsylvania, 1764-1776*. Berkeley and Los Angeles, California, 1965.

Jellison, Charles A. *Ethan Allen, Frontier Rebel*. Syracuse, New York, 1969.

Knollenberg, Bernhard. "John Dickinson v. John Adams, 1774-1776." American Philosophical Society *Proceedings*, vol. 107 (April 15, 1963), pp. 138-144.

——— *Washington and the Revolution, a Reappraisal*. New York, 1940.

Lossing, Benson J. *The Life and Times of Philip Schuyler*, vol. 1. New York, 1872.

Martyn, Charles. *The Life of Artemas Ward*. New York, 1921.

Mitchell, Memory F. *North Carolina's Signers*. Raleigh, North Carolina, 1964.

Murdock, Harold. *Bunker Hill; Notes and Queries on a Famous Battle*. Boston, 1927.

Nettels, Curtis P. *George Washington and American Independence*. Boston, 1951.

Partridge, Bellamy. *Sir Billy Howe*. New York, 1932.

Putnam, Alfred P. *A Sketch of General Israel Putnam*. Salem, Massachusetts, 1893.

RAMSAY, David. *The History of South Carolina*, vol. 2. Charleston, 1809.

RIFE, Clarence W. "Ethan Allen, An Interpretation." *The New England Quarterly*, vol. 2, 1929. pp. 561-584.

ROCHE, John F. *Joseph Reed, a Moderate in the American Revolution*. New York, 1957.

——— "Was Joseph Reed Disloyal?" *William and Mary Quarterly*, 3rd series, vol. 8, no. 3 (July 1951), pp. 406-417.

SALLEY, A. S., Jr. "The Mecklenburg Declaration: The Present Status of the Question." *American Historical Review*, vol. 13 (October 1907), pp. 16-43.

SEARS, Lorenzo. *John Hancock; the Picturesque Patriot*. Boston, 1912.

SMITH, Charles Page. *James Wilson, Founding Father 1742-1798*. Chapel Hill, North Carolina, 1956.

SMITH, Justin H. *Our Struggle for the Fourteenth Colony, Canada and the American Revolution*, vol. 1. New York and London, 1907.

SPARKS, Jared. "Life of Ethan Allen." *The Library of American Biography*, vol. 1. New York, 1834.

STILLE, Charles J. *The Life and Times of John Dickinson*. Originally published, 1891; reprinted New York, 1969.

TUCKERMAN, Bayard. *Life of General Philip Schuyler, 1733-1804*. Originally published, 1903; reprinted Freeport, New York, 1969.

WALLACE, Willard M. *Appeal to Arms: A Military History of the American Revolution*. New York, 1951.

WALSH, Richard. "Christopher Gadsden: Radical or Conservative Revolutionary?" *South Carolina Historical Magazine*, vol. 63 (October 1962), pp. 195-203.

WALSH, Richard, ed. *The Writings of Christopher Gadsden*. Columbia, South Carolina, 1966.

WILLARD, Margaret Wheeler, ed. *Letters on the American Revolution, 1774-1776*. Port Washington, New York, 1925; reissued 1968.

CHAPTER V

ABBOTT, Wilbur C. *New York in the American Revolution*. New York, 1929.

ADAMS, Randolph G. "The Olive Branch Petition." *The Magazine of History*, vol. 44, extra no. 176 (1931).

ANSON, William R., ed. *Autobiography and Political Correspondence of Augustus Henry, Third Duke of Grafton*. London, 1898; reprinted Millwood, New York, 1973.

AYLING, Stanley. *George the Third*. New York, 1972.

BARGAR, B. D. *Lord Dartmouth and the American Revolution*. Columbia, South Carolina, 1965.

BARNES, G. F. and J. H. OWEN, eds. *The Private Papers of John, Earl of Sandwich, first Lord of the Admiralty, 1771-1782*, vol. 1. London, 1932.

BOSWELL, James. *Boswell's Life of Johnson*. London, 1904.

BROOKE, John. *The Chatham Administration, 1766-1768*. New York, 1956.

——— *King George III*. New York, 1972.

BROWN, Gerald Saxon. *The American Secretary, the Colonial Policy of Lord George Germain, 1775-1778*. Ann Arbor, Michigan, 1963.

BROWN, Weldon A. *Empire or Independence, a Study in the Failure of Reconciliation, 1774-1783*. Port Washington, New York, 1941.

CONE, Carl B. *Burke and the Nature of Politics, the Age of the American Revolution*. Lexington, Kentucky, 1957.

CURREY, Cecil B. *Road to Revolution: Benjamin Franklin in England, 1765-1775.* New York, 1968.

DERRY, John W. *Charles James Fox.* London, 1972.

DONNE, W. Bodham, ed. *The Correspondence of King George the Third with Lord North from 1768 to 1783,* vols. 1 & 2. London, 1867.

DONOUGHUE, Bernard. *British Politics and the American Revolution, the Path to War, 1773-1775.* London, 1964.

FORTESCUE, Sir John, ed. *The Correspondence of King George the Third—From 1760 to December 1783.* London, 1967.

GILL, Frederich C., ed. *Selected Letters of John Wesley.* London, 1956.

GIPSON, Lawrence Henry. *The British Empire: Thunder-Clouds Gather in the West, 1763-1766.* New York, 1961.

GREEN, V. H. H. *The Hanoverians, 1714-1815.* London, 1948.

GREENE, Donald. *Samuel Johnson.* New York, 1970.

GUTTRIDGE, George Herbert. *David Hartley, M.P., and Advocate of Conciliation, 1774-1783.* Berkeley, California, 1926.

——— *English Whiggism and the American Revolution.* Berkeley, California, 1942.

HALL, Hubert. "Chatham's Colonial Policy." *The American Historical Review,* vol. 5 (1899-1900), pp. 659-675.

JOHNSON, Samuel. *Taxation No Tyranny; An Answer to the Resolutions and Address of the American Congress.* London, 1775.

KEPPEL, George Thomas, Sixth Earl of Albemarle. *Memoirs of the Marquis of Rockingham,* vols. 1 & 2. London, 1852.

LUTNICK, Soloman. *The American Revolution and the British Press, 1775-1783.* Columbia, Missouri, 1967.

Old South Leaflets, vol. 8. Directors of the Old South Work, Old South Meeting House, Boston, 1883.

OLSON, Alison Gilbert. *The Radical Duke; Career and Correspondence of Charles Lennox, Third Duke of Richmond.* London, 1961.

PEARSON, Michael. *Those Damned Rebels, the American Revolution as Seen Through British Eyes.* New York, 1972.

REID, Loren. *Charles James Fox: A Man for the People.* London, 1969.

RITCHESON, Charles. *British Politics and the American Revolution.* Norman, Oklahoma, 1954.

RUSSELL, Lord John, ed. *Memorials and Correspondence of Charles James Fox,* vol. 1. New York, 1859-66.

SMITH, Paul H., comp. *English Defenders of American Freedoms, 1774-1778.* Washington, 1972.

SMYTH, Albert Henry, ed. *The Writings of Benjamin Franklin,* vol. 6. New York, 1906.

VALENTINE, Alan. *The British Establishment, 1760-1784,* vols. 1 & 2. Norman, Oklahoma, 1970.

——— *Lord George Germain.* Oxford, England, 1962.

——— *Lord North,* vol. 1. Norman, Oklahoma, 1967.

VULLIAMY, C. E. *John Wesley.* London, 1931.

CHAPTER VI

ALLEN, Gardner W. *A Naval History of the American Revolution,* vols. 1 & 2. Boston and New York, 1913.

ASHE, Samuel A'Court. *History of North Carolina, 1584-1783.* Spartanburg, South Carolina, 1971.

BEIRNE, Francis. "Mission to Canada." *Maryland Historical Magazine*, vol. 60. (December 1965), pp. 404-420.

BILLIAS, George Athan. *General John Glover and His Marblehead Mariners.* New York, 1960·

—— *George Washington's Generals.* New York, 1964.

—— *George Washington's Opponents.* New York, 1969.

BUTTERFIELD, Lyman H., ed. *The Adams Family Correspondence*, vol. 1. Cambridge, Massachusetts, 1963.

CALLAHAN, North. *Daniel Morgan: Ranger of the Revolution.* New York, 1961.

—— "Henry Knox, General Washington's General." *New York Historical Society Quarterly*, vol. 44 (April 1960), pp. 150-165.

—— *Henry Knox, General Washington's General.* New York, 1958.

CHIDSEY, Donald B. *Siege of Boston.* New York, 1966.

CLARKE, William Bell, ed. *Naval Documents of the American Revolution*, vols. 2 & 3. Washington, 1966.

COFFIN, Charles. *The Life and Services of Major General John Thomas.* New York, 1844.

CONNOR, R. D. W. *Revolutionary Leaders of North Carolina.* Spartanburg, South Carolina, 1971.

DAVIS, Matthew L. *Memoirs of Aaron Burr*, vol. 1. New York, 1971.

DE MOND, Robert. *The Loyalists in North Carolina During the Revolution.* Durham, North Carolina, 1940.

ECKENRODE, H. J. *The Revolution in Virginia.* Hamden, Connecticut, 1964.

FITZPATRICK, J. C., ed. *The Writings of George Washington*, vol. 4. Washington, 1931-1944.

FRENCH, Allen. *The Siege of Boston.* New York, 1911.

FROTHINGHAM, Richard. *History of the Siege of Boston.* Boston, 1873.

HIGGINBOTHAM, Don. *Daniel Morgan.* Chapel Hill, North Carolina, 1961.

KNOX, Dudley W. *A History of the United States Navy.* New York, 1948.

LANCTOT, Gustave. *Canada and the American Revolution.* Cambridge, Massachusetts, 1967.

LEE, Lawrence. *The Lower Cape Fear in Colonial Days.* Chapel Hill, North Carolina, 1965.

MITCHELL, Lt. Col. Joseph B. *Decisive Battles of the American Revolution.* New York, 1962.

MOULTRIE, William. *Memoirs of the American Revolution*, vol. 1. New York, 1802.

PAINE, Lauran. *Benedict Arnold, Hero and Traitor.* London, 1965.

PARMET, Herbert S. and Marie B. Hecht. *Aaron Burr.* New York, 1967.

PATTERSON, Samuel. *Knight Errant of Liberty: the Triumph and Tragedy of General Charles Lee.* New York, 1958.

PEARSON, Michael. "The Siege of Quebec." *American Heritage*, vol. 23 (February 1972), pp. 9-15, 104-108.

—— *Those Damned Rebels, The American Revolution as Seen Through British Eyes.* New York, 1972.

PRATT, Fletcher. *The Compact History of the United States Navy.* New York, 1957.

RHETT, Robert. *Charleston.* Richmond, Virginia, 1940.

ROCHE, John F. "Quebec Under Siege." *Canadian Historical Review*, vol. 50 (March 1969), pp. 68-85.

ROSS, Malcolm. *The Cape Fear.* New York, 1965.

SCHACHNER, Nathan. *Aaron Burr.* New York, 1937.

SHY, John. *Toward Lexington.* Princeton, 1965.

SMITH, Justin H. *Our Struggle for the Fourteenth Colony*, vol. 2. New York, 1907.

SMITH, William Roy. *South Carolina as a Royal Province, 1719-1776*. Freeport, New York, 1970.

SPARKS, Jared. *Lives of Charles Lee and Joseph Reed*. Boston, 1846.

——— *Lives of John Stark, Charles Brockden Brown, Richard Montgomery, and Ethan Allen*, vol. 1. New York, 1834.

SPROUT, Harold and Margaret. *The Rise of American Naval Power*. Princeton, New Jersey, 1966.

WALLACE, Willard. *Appeal to Arms, A Military History of the American Revolution*. New York, 1951.

———*Traitorous Hero: The Life and Fortunes of Benedict Arnold*. New York, 1954.

WERTENBAKER, Thomas J. *Norfolk, Historic Southern Port*. Durham, North Carolina, 1931·

WHEELER, John Hill. *Historical Sketches of North Carolina, 1584-1851*. Baltimore, 1964.

———*Reminiscences and Memoirs of North Carolina and Eminent North Carolineans*. Baltimore, 1966.

WICKWIRE, Franklin and Mary. *Cornwallis and the American Adventure*. Boston, 1970.

WILLCOX, William B. *Portrait of a General: Sir Henry Clinton in the War of Independence*. New York, 1964.

WRONG, George M. *Canada and the American Revolution*. New York, 1935.

WYATT, Frederick and William B. Willcox. "Sir Henry Clinton: A Psychological Exploration in History. *William and Mary Quarterly*, 3d series, vol. 16 (January 1959), pp. 3-26.

CHAPTER VII

ADAMS, Charles Francis, ed. *Familiar Letters of John Adams and His Wife, During the Revolution*. New York, 1876.

ADKINS, Nelson F., ed. *Thomas Paine, Common Sense and Other Political Writings*. Indianapolis and New York, 1953.

ALDRIDGE, Alfred O. *Man of Reason, The Life of Thomas Paine*. Philadelphia and New York, 1959.

BECKER, Carl. *The Declaration of Independence; A Study in the History of Political Ideas*. New York, 1966.

BEMIS, Samuel Flagg. *The Diplomacy of the American Revolution*. Bloomington, Indiana, 1957.

BILLIAS, George Athan, ed. *George Washington's Opponents, British Generals and Admirals in the American Revolution*. New York, 1969.

CHITWOOD, Oliver Perry. *Richard Henry Lee, Statesman of the Revolution*. Morgantown, West Virginia, 1967.

CLARK, Dora Mae. "British Opinion of Franco-American Relations, 1775-1795." *William and Mary Quarterly*, 3d series, vol. 4 (July 1947), pp. 305-316.

CONWAY, Moncure Daniel. *Life of Thomas Paine*, vol. 1. New York and London, 1892.

CORWIN, Edward S. *French Policy and the Alliance of 1778*. Princeton, New Jersey, 1916.

COX, Cynthia. *The Real Figaro, the Extraordinary Career of Caron de Beaumarchais*. New York, 1962.

HOOKER, Richard J. "The American Revolution Seen Through a Wine Glass." *William and Mary Quarterly*, 3d series, vol. 11 (January 1954), pp. 52-77.

JONES, Charles C., Jr. *Biographical Sketches of the Delegates from Georgia to the Continental Congress*. Boston and New York, 1891.

KAPP, Friedrich. *The Life of John Kalb*. New York, 1884.

KITE, Elizabeth S. "French 'Secret Aid' Precursor to the French American Alliance, 1776-1777." *The French American Review*, vol. 1 (April-June 1948), pp. 143-152.

LEMAITRE, Georges. *Beaumarchais*. New York, 1949.

MALONE, Dumas. *Jefferson, The Virginian*. Boston, 1948.

MENG, John J. *The Comte de Vergennes, European Phases of his American Diplomacy, 1774-1780*. Washington, 1932.

MILLER, Helen Hill. *George Mason, Constitutionalist*. Cambridge, Massachusetts, 1938.

Palmer, Robert R. *The Age of the Democratic Revolution*. Princeton, New Jersey, 1959.

PEARSON, Hasketh. *Tom Paine: Friend of Mankind*. New York, 1937.

PERKINS, James Breck. *France in the American Revolution*. Williamstown, Massachusetts, 1970.

REED, W. B., ed. *The Life and Correspondence of Joseph Reed*, vol. 1. Philadelphia, 1847.

RITCHESON, Charles. *British Politics and the American Revolution*. Norman, Oklahoma, 1954.

RUTLAND, Robert A. *George Mason, Reluctant Statesman*. Williamsburg, Virginia, 1961.

RUTLAND, Robert A., ed. *The Papers of George Mason*, vol. 1. Chapel Hill, North Carolina, 1970.

SMITH, Horace W. *Life and Correspondence of the Rev. William Smith, D. D.*, vols. 1 & 2. New York, 1972.

SMYTH, Albert H. *The Philadelphia Magazines and Their Contributors, 1741-1850*. Philadelphia, 1892.

STILLE, Charles J. "Beaumarchais and 'The Lost Million'." *Pennsylvania Magazine of History and Biography*, vol. 11 (1887), pp. 1-36.

VALENTINE, Alan. *The British Establishment, 1760-1784*, vol. 1. Norman, Oklahoma, 1970.

VAN TYNE, Claude H. "French Aid Before the Alliance of 1778." *The American Historical Review*, vol. 31 (October 1925), pp. 20-40.

ZUCKER, A. E. *General De Kalb, Lafayette's Mentor*. Chapel Hill, North Carolina, 1966.

ENCYCLOPEDIAS

BOATNER, Mark Mayo. *Encyclopedia of the American Revolution*. New York, 1966.

DEXTER, Franklin B. *Biographical Sketches of the Graduates of Yale College*, vols. 1 & 2. New York, 1885-1919.

JOHNSON, Allan, ed. *Dictionary of American Biography*, vols. 1-10. New York, 1927.

JOHNSON, Rossiter, ed. *The Twentieth Century Biographical Dictionary of Notable Americans*, vols. 1-10. Boston, 1904.

LOSSING, B. J. *Biographical Sketches of the Signers of the Declaration of American Independence*. Glendale, New York, 1970.

The National Cyclopedia of American Biography, vols. 1-53. New York, 1898.

SABINE, Lorenzo. *Biographical Sketches of Loyalists of the American Revolution*, 2 vols. Port Washington, New York, 1966.

SANDERSON, John. *Biography of the Signers of the Declaration of Independence*, vols. 1-9. Philadelphia, 1823.

SHIPTON, Clifford K. *Sibley's Harvard Graduates*, vols. 5-15. Boston, 1937-1970.

STEPHEN, Sir Leslie and Sir Sidney LEE, eds. *The Dictionary of National Biography*, vols. 1-21. London, 1964.

WILSON, James G. and John FISKE, eds. *Appleton's Cyclopedia of American Biography*, vols. 1-6. New York, 1887.

Checklist of the Exhibition

Dimensions are in inches and height precedes width except where otherwise specified.

1. Letter from George III to Lord North, September 11, 1774, in which the King writes, "The dye is now cast, the Colonies must either submit or triumph. I do not wish to come to severer measures, but we must not retreat."
Her Majesty Queen Elizabeth II

2. Letter from Abigail Adams to Mercy Otis Warren, February 2 or 3, 1775, in which she writes, "The die is cast. . . . Heaven only knows what is next to take place but it seems to me the Sword is now our only, yet dreadful alternative. . . ."
Massachusetts Historical Society, Boston

3. Broadside. "An Act to discontinue, in such manner, for such time as is therein mentioned, the landing and discharging, lading or shipping of goods, wares, and merchandise, at the town, and within the harbour of Boston. . . ." [The Boston Port Bill.]
Providence: John Carter, 1774
The Library Company of Philadelphia

4. PETER OLIVER 1713–1791
William Williams 1727-1791
Oil on panel, 1781
11½ x 15¾
This portrait was painted in England where Oliver was living on a Loyalist pension. The artist had returned there in 1776 from the Americas where he had lived since 1747. It depicts Oliver mourning for his wife, Mary Clarke. The inscription on her tomb is translated: "Ah Mary holiest of wives never to be forgotten/ Great virtue has gone to heaven."
Andrew Oliver
Figure 2

5. FREDERICK NORTH, SECOND EARL OF GUILFORD 1732–1792, Prime Minister 1770–1782

John Singleton Copley 1738-1815
Crayon on paper, circa 1779
27½ x 21½
This is a study for Copley's painting *The Death of the Earl of Chatham*, 1779.
The Boston Athenaeum
Figure 1

6. *The Bostonians in Distress*
Johann Martin Will 1727-1806
Mezzotint, 1774
15⅞ x 11¼
Inscribed: "The Bostonians in Distress./ Joh. Martin Will excudit Aug. Vind /London Printed for R. Sayer, & J. Bennett, Map & Printsellers, Nº 53 Fleet Street, as the Act directs, 19 Novʳ 1774."
The Colonial Williamsburg Foundation
Figure 3

7. *The Able Doctor, or America Swallowing the Bitter Draught.*
Unidentified engraver, English version
Engraving, published in the *London Magazine*, April 1774, with a report on the Boston Port Bill
5 x 8¼
Assisted by politicians who favored colonial coercion, Lord North forces tea down America's throat. Britannia turns away in distress while France and Spain look on with interest.
The Colonial Williamsburg Foundation

8. *A Plan of the City and Environs of Philadelphia*
William Fadden, dates unknown
Engraving, 1777
24 x 18

Inscribed: "A Plan of the City and Environs of Philadelphia Survey'd by N. Scull and G. Heap/ Engraved by Willm Faden./ 1777"

Library of Congress, Map Division

Figure 4

9. North Elevation of Carpenters' Hall from the *Articles Of The Carpenters Company Of Philadelphia: And Their Rules For Measuring And Valuing House-Carpenters Work.*

Philadelphia: Hall and Sellers, 1786

The Carpenters' Company of the City and County of Philadelphia

Figure 6

10. Original copperplate engraving for the North Elevation of Carpenters' Hall.

Possibly by Thomas Bedwell from design of Robert Smith

The Carpenters' Company of the City and County of Philadelphia

11. *Instructions for the Deputies appointed to meet in General Congress on the Part of this Colony.* Publisher unknown, 1774.

Thomas Jefferson's copy, bearing his docket on the first page and notes on the fourth page.

Library of Congress, Manuscript Division

Figure 5

12. Broadside. "To the Inhabitants of ( ) at a Meeting of A Respectable Body of the Freeholders Inhabitants of the County of Chester, on the 18th of June, 1774 ... The Following Propositions were Deliberated and Unanimously Agreed To. . ." [approving a Congress of the Colonies and announcing the appointment of a Committee of Correspondence].

Philadelphia: James Humphreys, Junior, 1774

The Library Company of Philadelphia

13. PEYTON RANDOLPH circa 1721–1775

John Wollaston circa 1710–circa 1767

Oil on canvas, date unknown

36 x 29

Virginia Historical Society, Richmond

Figure 9

14. CHARLES THOMSON 1729–1824

William Rush 1756-1833

Burnt clay, circa 1795

h. 19¾"

The American Philosophical Society, Philadelphia

Figure 8

15. JACOB DUCHÉ 1738–1798 and his son Thomas Spence Duché

Thomas Spence Duché, Jr. 1763-1790

Oil on canvas, date unknown

d. 18"

The Historical Society of Pennsylvania, Philadelphia

Figure 10

16. JACOB DUCHÉ

The Duty of Standing Fast In Our Spiritual And Temporal Liberties, A Sermon, Preached In Christ-Church, July 7th, 1775. Before the First Battalion of the City and Liberties of Philadelphia. . . .

Philadelphia: James Humphreys, Junior, 1775

The Library Company of Philadelphia

17. JOSEPH WARREN 1741–1775

Attributed to Samuel Okey (active in America 1773-1780) after the circa 1765 oil by John Singleton Copley

Mezzotint, circa 1775

14⅛ x 10⅛

Inscribed: "Major General Joseph Warren/ Who gloriously fell in the defence of American Liberty ye 17th 1775."

Mrs. Henry A. Bosch, Jr.

Figure 11

18. Broadside. "At a Meeting of the Delegates of every Town and District in the County of Suffolk, on Tuesday, the Sixth of September . . . and by adjournment . . . on Friday the Ninth Instant, . . . the following being several times read and put Paragraph by Paragraph, was unanimously voted. . . ." [The Suffolk Resolves.]

Boston: Edes and Gill, 1774

Massachusetts Historical Society, Boston

Figure 12

19. SAMUEL ADAMS 1722–1803

Samuel Okey (active in America 1773-1780) after John Mitchell after the 1770-1772 oil by John Singleton Copley

Mezzotint, 1775

13½ x 9½

Inscribed: "M^r. Samuel Adams J. Mitchell pinx^t. Saml. Okey Fecit./ When haughty NORTH impress'd with proud Disdain,/ Spurn'd at the Virtue which rejects his Chain;/ Hear with a Tyrant Scorn our Rights implor'd,/ And when we su'd for Justice sent the Sword:/ Let ADAMS rest in Warfare nobly try'd,/ His Country's Savior: Father, Shield, & Guide,/ Urg'd by her Wrongs he wag'd ye glorious Strife/ Nor paus'd to waste a Coward Thought on Life./ Printed by and for Chas Reak & Saml Okey— New port Rhode Island. April. 1775."

Massachusetts Historical Society, Boston

Figure 13

20. JOSEPH GALLOWAY 1731–1803
A Candid Examination Of The Mutual Claims Of Great-Britain, And The Colonies: With A Plan Of Accommodation, On Constitutional Principles.
New York: James Rivington, 1775
The Library Company of Philadelphia
Figure 7

21. JAMES DUANE 1733–1797
Robert Edge Pine died 1788
Oil on canvas, 1785
35 x 28½
Mr. and Mrs. James Duane Ireland
Photo: Cleveland Museum of Art
Figure 14

22. EDWARD RUTLEDGE 1749–1800
Attributed to James Earl 1761-1796
Oil on canvas, date unknown
26 x 22
Mr. Edward Rutledge Moore
Photo: Frick Art Reference Library
Figure 15

23. Letter from the Continental Congress to Thomas Gage, October 10, 1774, urging Gage to stop building fortifications in Boston and assuring him that the intentions of the people of Massachusetts were peaceable.
William L. Clements Library, University of Michigan, Ann Arbor

24. EDMUND PENDLETON 1721–1803
William Mercer 1773-1839
Watercolor on ivory, date unknown
1¾ x 1½
Virginia Historical Society, Richmond
Figure 17

25. ROGER SHERMAN 1721–1793
Unidentified artist after the circa 1777 oil by Ralph Earl
Oil on canvas, date unknown
26⅜ x 22³⁄₁₆
National Portrait Gallery, Smithsonian Institution
Figure 18

26. JOHN ADAMS 1735–1825
John Trumbull 1756-1843
Oil on canvas, circa 1793
25½ x 21½
A. Perry Morgan, Jr.
Figure 19

27. JOHN SULLIVAN 1740–1795
Unidentified engraver, probably English
Mezzotint, 1776-1778
14 x 9¾
Inscribed: "peint par Alexander Camphel a Williamsburg en Virginie./ IEAN SULLIVAN/ Major General d'Armee des XIII. Provinces unies/ en Amerique./ Se vend a Londres chez Thom. Hart."
Between 1775 and 1778 a series of mezzotint portraits of American officers were published in London by Thomas Hart, C. Shepherd, and others. Portraits of American heroes were so popular that even these imaginary likenesses by fictitious artists were published in several different states and copies.
Anne S. K. Brown Military Collection, Brown University Library, Providence
Figure 20

28. Declaration of Rights and Grievances passed by the Continental Congress October 14, 1774, in the Rough Journal of the Congress.
From the original in the National Archives

29. *The Association entered into by the American Continental Congress in Behalf of all the Colonies . . . October 20, 1774* [with forty-five signatures of members of the Continental Congress].
Philadelphia: 1774
Rhode Island Historical Society, Providence
Figure 21

30. THOMAS JOHNSON 1732–1819 and his family
Charles Willson Peale 1841-1727
Oil on canvas, 1772
46 x 57½
Private collection
Photo: Frick Art Reference Library
Figure 23

31. Broadside: "Association of the Freemen of Maryland. July 26, 1775. The long premeditated, and now, avowed design of the British Government, to raise a revenue from the property of the colonists without their consent . . ." [with signatures of 112 delegates to the Maryland Convention, signed August 14, 1775].
Annapolis: Frederick Green, 1775
Maryland Hall of Records, Annapolis

32. THOMAS MIFFLIN 1744–1800
Gilbert Stuart 1755-1828
Oil on canvas, circa 1800
29 x 24

Mifflin wears the badge of the Society Of The Cincinnati in the lapel of his uniform.

Private collection

Figure 24

33. Broadside: "Philadelphia, In Congress, Thursday, September 22, 1774. Resolved, That the Congress request the Merchants and Others, in the several Colonies, not to send to Great Britain any Orders for Goods, and to direct the execution of all Orders already sent, to be delayed or suspended, . . . An Extract from the Minutes, Charles Thomson, Sec."

Philadelphia: William and Thomas Bradford, 1774

Library of Congress, Rare Books Division

Figure 22

34. *The Patriotick Barber of New York*

Attributed to Philip Dawe active in London 1750-1785

Mezzotint, 1775

14⅞ x 11

Inscribed: "The Patriotick Barber of New York/ London, Printed for R. Sayer & J. Bennett, Map & Printsellers, N°. 53 Fleet Street, as the Act directs 12 Feby. 1775."

The names of prominent New York Patriots are on the wig boxes in the shop. Hanging on the wall are portraits of William Pitt (Lord Chatham) and Lord Camden, supporters of the colonial cause, and a broadside of the Articles of Association, which discouraged importation of British goods.

The Colonial Williamsburg Foundation

Figure 25

35. *The Alternative of Williams-Burg*

Attributed to Philip Dawe active in London 1750-1785

Mezzotint, 1775

10⅓ x 14¼

Inscribed: "The Alternative of Williams-Burg./ Plate IV./ London, Printed for R. Sayer, & J. Bennett, N° 53 Fleet Street, as the Act directs 16 Feb. 1775"

The "Alternative" facing the Virginia Loyalists was either to sign the Articles of Association or to be tarred and feathered at the hands of the Sons of Liberty.

The Colonial Williamsburg Foundation

36. *A Society of Patriotic Ladies, at Edenton in North Carolina*

Attributed to Philip Dawe active in London 1750-1785

Mezzotint, 1775

18½ x 11½

Inscribed: "A Society of Patriotic Ladies, at Edenton in North Carolina./ Plate V./ London, Printed for R.

Sayer, & J. Bennett, N°. 53 in Fleet Street, as the Act directs 25 March 1775."

The purpose of the ladies' meeting is described on a large document which bears the words: "We the Ladys of Edenton do hereby Solemnly Engage not to Conform to that Pernicious Custom of Drinking Tea, or that we the aforesaid Ladys will not promote yᵉ wear of any Manufacture from England untill such time that all Acts which tend to Enslave this our Native Country shall be Repealed."

The Colonial Williamsburg Foundation

37. Broadside. *An Address to New-England: Written by A Daughter of Liberty*

Boston, 1774

The Historical Society of Pennsylvania, Philadelphia

Figure 16

38. Richard Henry Lee 1732–1794

Charles Willson Peale 1741-1827

Oil on canvas, circa 1795-1805 replica of the 1784 life portrait

30 x 25

National Portrait Gallery, Smithsonian Institution

Figure 26

39. *An Address from the Delegates of the Twelve United Colonies, To The People of England.*

Newport: 1774

Library of Congress, Rare Books Division

40. JOHN JAY 1745–1829

Gilbert Stuart 1755-1828 and John Trumbull 1756-1843

Oil on canvas, probably 1794

50½ x 41½

National Portrait Gallery, Smithsonian Institution

Figure 27

41. *A Letter To The Inhabitants Of The Province Of Quebec from the Minutes of the Congress*

Philadelphia: William and Thomas Bradford, October 1774

Library of Congress, Rare Books Division

Figure 28

42. PATRICK HENRY 1736–1799

Lawrence Sully 1769-1803

Watercolor on ivory, date unknown

2¼ x 1⅞

Museum of Art, Carnegie Institute, Pittsburgh

Figure 29

43. *The Petition of the Grand American Continental Congress, to the King's Most Excellent Majesty*

?, 1774

Library of Congress, Rare Books Division

44. SAMUEL SEABURY 1729–1796

Thomas Spence Duché, Jr. 1763-1790

Oil on canvas, probably painted between 1783 and 1785 when Seabury was in England to be consecrated Episcopal Bishop of Connecticut and Rhode Island

56½ x 47⅛

Trinity College, Hartford

Figure 30

45. SAMUEL SEABURY

The Congress Canvassed: Or, An Examination Into The Conduct of the Delegates, At Their Great Convention, Held in Philadelphia, Sept. 1, 1774. Addressed, To the Merchants of New-York. By A. W. Farmer. Author of Free Thoughts, &c....

New York: James Rivington, 1774

American Antiquarian Society, Worcester, Massachusetts

46. SAMUEL SEABURY

Free Thoughts, on The Proceedings of The Continental Congress, Held at Philadelphia Sept. 5, 1774: Wherein Their Errors are exhibited, Their Reasonings Confuted ... In A Letter To the Farmers, And Other Inhabitants of North America ... By a Farmer....

New York: James Rivington, 1774

American Antiquarian Society, Worcester, Massachusetts

Figure 31

47. SAMUEL SEABURY

A View of The Controversy Between Great-Britain and her Colonies: Including A Mode of Determining their present Disputes, Finally and Effectually; And Of Preventing All Future Contentions. In A Letter To the Author of A Full Vindication Of The Measures of the Congress ... by A. W. Farmer. Author of Free Thoughts, &c ...

New York: James Rivington, 1774

American Antiquarian Society, Worcester, Massachusetts

48. SAMUEL SEABURY

An Alarm to the Legislature Of The Province of New-York, Occasioned By The present Political Disturbances, In North America: Addressed To the Honourable Representatives In General Assembly Convened....

New York: James Rivington, 1775

American Antiquarian Society, Worcester, Massachusetts

49. DANIEL LEONARD 1740–1829

The Origin Of The American Contest with Great-Britain, Or The present political State of the Massachusetts-Bay, in general, and the Town of Boston in particular. Exhibiting the Rise and Progress of the disordered State of that Country, in a series of weekly Essays, published at Boston, under the signature of Massachusettensis....

New York: James Rivington, 1775

The Library Company of Philadelphia

Figure 32

50. MYLES COOPER 1737–1785

John Singleton Copley 1738-1815

Oil on canvas, 1768

29½ x 24½

This was painted when Cooper was president of King's College (now Columbia University).

Columbia University, New York

Photo: John D. Schiff

Figure 33

51. THOMAS BRADBURY CHANDLER 1726–1790

The American Querist: Or, Some Questions Proposed Relative To The Present Disputes Between Great-Britain And Her American Colonies. By a North-American.

New York: James Rivington, 1774

At one time attributed to Myles Cooper

Library of Congress, Rare Books Division

52. THOMAS BRADBURY CHANDLER

A Friendly Address To All Reasonable Americans, On The Subject Of Our Political Confusions: In Which The Necessary Consequences of Violently Opposing the King's Troops, And Of A General Non-Importation Are Fairly Stated....

New York: James Rivington, 1774

At one time attributed to Myles Cooper

Library of Congress, Rare Books Division

53. ALEXANDER HAMILTON 1757–1804

Giuseppe Ceracchi 1751-1801/02

Marble replica of circa 1794 original

h. 22¾

National Portrait Gallery, Smithsonian Institution

Figure 35

54. ALEXANDER HAMILTON

A Full Vindication Of The Measures of the Congress, From The Calumnies of their Enemies; In Answer to A Letter, Under the Signature of A. W. Farmer....

New York: James Rivington, 1774

The Historical Society of Pennsylvania, Philadelphia

55. ALEXANDER HAMILTON

The Farmer Refuted: Or, A more impartial and comprehensive View Of The Dispute between Great-Britain And The Colonies, Intended As A Further Vindication Of The Congress: In Answer To A Letter From A. W. Farmer, Intitled A View of the Controversy

New York: James Rivington, 1775

The Historical Society of Pennsylvania, Philadelpia

56. *Journal of The Proceedings of The Congress, Held at Philadelphia September 5, 1774.*

Philadelphia: William and Thomas Bradford, 1774

The Library Company of Philadelphia

Figure 36

57. THOMAS GAGE 1721–1787

John Singleton Copley 1738–1815

Oil on canvas, 1768/69

50 x 39¾

Mr. and Mrs. Paul Mellon

Figure 37

58. *A Political Lesson.*

John Dixon circa 1730–1803

Mezzotint, 1774

13⅞ x 9¹⁵⁄₁₆

Inscribed: "A Political Lesson./ J. Dixon invenit et fecit/ Published 7 Sepʳ 1774/ Printed for John Bowles, at N⁰ 13 in Cornhill"

This foreboding scene is a direct reference to colonial opposition to the Boston Port Bill. The colonies, symbolized as a rearing horse, cast off British tyranny, personified by General Thomas Gage. The threatening sky reflects the angry mood of the colonists.

Library of Congress, Prints and Photographs

59. Secretary's fair copy of Thomas Gage's memorandum to Lt. Colonel Francis Smith, April 18, 1775, to march "with the utmost expedition and secrecy to Concord, where you will seize and destroy all the artillery and ammunition, Provisions, Tents, & all other military stores you can find...."

Thomas Gage papers, William L. Clements Library, University of Michigan, Ann Arbor

Figure 38

60. Letter from Major John Pitcairn to Lord Sandwich (John Montagu), March 4, 1775, in which he writes "I am satisfied that one active campaign, a smart action, and burning two or three of their towns, will set everything to rights. Nothing now, I am afraid, but this will ever

convince those foolish bad people that England is in earnest."

Victor Montagu

61. Letter from George III to Lord Sandwich, July 1, 1775, agreeing with Pitcairn "that when once those rebels have felt a smart blow, they will submit; and no situation can ever change my fixed resolution, either to bring the colonies to a due obedience to the legislature of the mother country or to cast them off!"

Victor Montagu

62. Handcolored engraving of the uniform of the Royal Welch Fusiliers, one of the British regiments under the command of Lt. Colonel Francis Smith during the expedition to Concord, April 18, 1775, from *Uniforms of the Infantry*, 1768

Prince Consort's Army Library, Aldershot, Hants, England

Figure 44

63. WILLIAM DAWES, JR. 1745–1799

Attributed to John Johnston circa 1753–1818

Oil on canvas, date unknown

35 x 29

Evanston Historical Society, Illinois

Photo: Nickerson

Figure 40

64. JONAS CLARKE 1730–1805

Unidentified artist

Silhouette, date unknown

From Charles Hudson's *History of the Town of Lexington*, 1913, Vol. 1, opposite page 334.

Present whereabouts unknown

Figure 41

65. JONAS CLARKE

The Fate of Blood Thirsty Oppressors, and God's tender Care of his distressed People. A Sermon, Preached At Lexington, April 19, 1776. To commemorate the Murder, Bloodshed and Commencement of Hostilities, between Great-Britain and America ... To Which Is Added, A Brief Narrative of the principal Transactions of that Day....

Boston: Powars and Willis, 1776

Pequot Library, Southport, Connecticut

66. *The Battle of Lexington*

Amos Doolittle 1754–1832

Engraving, 1775

11⅝ x 17¾

Inscribed: "The Battle of Lexington. April 19th 1775. Plate I/ A. Doolittle Sculpᵗ./ 1. Major Pitcairn, at the head of the Regular Granadiers. 2. The Party, who first fired at the Provincials at Lexington. 3. Part of the Provincial Company of Lexington./ 4. Regular Companies on the road to Concord/ 5. The Metinghouse at Lexington/ 6. The Public Inn."

Chicago Historical Society

67. *A View of the Town of Concord*

Amos Doolittle 1754–1832

Engraving, 1775

11⅝ x 17¾

Inscribed: "Plate II. A View of the Town of Concord/ A. Doolittle Sculpᵗ/ 1. Companies of the Regulars marching into Concord./ 2. Companies of Regulars drawn up in order./ 3. A Detachment destroying the Provincials Stores/ 4 & 5. Colonel Smith & Major Pitcairn viewing the Provincials/ who were mustering on East Hill in Concord/ 6. The Townhouse 7. The Meeting House"

In a naive conception of the simultaneity of events, Doolittle included in one scene the arrival of the troops, a close-up of Pitcairn and Smith, and the destruction of military stores. At the left is the Concord Meeting House, which was used by the Massachusetts Provincial Congress.

Chicago Historical Society

68. *The Engagement at the North Bridge*

Amos Doolittle 1754–1832

Engraving, 1775

11⅝ x 17¾

Inscribed: "Plate III. The Engagement at the North Bridge in Concord/ A. Doolittle Scuplᵗ/ 1. The Detachment of the Regulars who fired first/ on the Provincials at the Bridge/ 2. The Provincials headed by Colonel Robinson &/ Major Buttrick./ 3. The Bridge."

Chicago Historical Society

69. *A View of the South Part of Lexington*

Amos Doolittle 1754–1832

Engraving, 1775

11⅝ x 17¾

Inscribed: "Plate IV. A View of the South Part of Lexington/ A. Doolittle Sculpᵗ/ 1. Colonel Smith's Brigade retreating before the Provincials/ 2. Earl Piercy's Brigade meeting them/ 3 & 4. Earl Piercy and Col. Smith. 5. Provincials/ 6 & 7. The Flanck-guards of Piercy's Brigade./ 8. A Field-piece pointed at the Lexington Meeting house./ 9. The Burning of the Houses in Lexington."

Chicago Historical Society

70. HUGH EARL PERCY, SECOND DUKE OF NORTHUMBERLAND 1742–1817

Pompeo Battoni 1708–1787

Oil on canvas, before 1776

28½ x 24

His Grace The Duke of Northumberland, K.G., P.C., T.D., F.R.S.

Photo: R. B. Fleming & Co. Ltd.

Figure 43

71. WILLIAM HEATH 1737–1814

John Rubens Smith 1775–1849 after an unlocated miniature by Henry Williams

Engraving, from *Polyanthus*, Series 2. No. 1, 1813

6 x 4⅛

Library of Congress

Figure 45

72. TIMOTHY PICKERING 1745–1829

Gilbert Stuart 1755–1828

Oil on canvas, September 1808

28 x 22½

Arthur T. Lyman and Essex Institute

Figure 47

73. Alarm letter advising the Colony of Connecticut of the attack on Lexington: "To all the Friends of American Liberty, be it known that this Morning before breake of Day a Brigade consisting of about 1000 or 1200 Men landed at Phip's Farm at Cambridge & marched to Lexington where they found a Company of our Colony Militia in Arms upon Whom they fired without any Provocation and killed 6 Men and Wounded 4 others. . . ." Dated April 19, 1775, this was sent to Christopher Leffingwell of Norwich.

Guthman Collection

Figure 48

74. Alexander McDougall autograph manuscript describing the arrival of the news of the Battle of Lexington and the subsequent action taken in New York, April 23, 1775. Written on the verso of the printed broadside announcing the battle: "New York, Sunday."

From the private library of William H. Scheide, Princeton, New Jersey

75. Broadside. "Baltimore: April 26. We have just received the following important Intelligence viz Watertown, Massachusetts Bay" [Printing of the Lexington Alarm Letter and an ensuing report of the fighting in Concord.]

Baltimore: Mary Katharine Goddard, 1775

Library of Congress, Rare Books Division

Figure 49

76. Broadside. "A Bloody Butchery By The British Troops: Or, The Runaway Fight Of The Regulars."

Salem: E. Russell, 1775

From the private library of William H. Scheide, Princeton, New Jersey

77. Coat of the British 49th Regiment of Foot, circa 1775, possibly worn at the battles of Lexington and Concord.

National Army Museum, London

78. Broadside. "We the Subscribers do hereby solemnly and severally engage and inlist ourselves as Soldiers in the Massachusetts Service . . . " [with forty signatures].

Guthman Collection

Figure 51

79. Broadside. "In Committee of Safety, Cambridge, 1775. To————Sir,————You are hereby empowered . . . to inlist a Company, to consist of 56 able-bodied and effective Men. . . . as Soldiers in the *Massachusetts Service* . . . , for the Preservation of American Liberty. . . . "

Library of Congress, Rare Books Division

80. Broadside. "In Congress, at Watertown, April 30, 1775. Gentlemen, The barbarous Murders on our innocent Brethren on Wednesday the 19th Instant, has made it absolutely necessary that we immediately raise an Army to defend our Wives and our Children . . . signed Joseph Warren."

Massachusetts Historical Society, Boston

Figure 50

81. BENJAMIN CHURCH 1734–1776

A Narrative Of The Excursion and Ravages Of The King's Troops Under the Command of General Gage, On the nineteenth of April, 1775. Together With The Depositions Taken by Order of Congress, To support the Truth of it. . . .

Worcester: Isaiah Thomas, by order of the Provincial Congress, 1775.

American Antiquarian Society, Worcester, Massachusetts

82. An intercepted letter of Dr. Benjamin Church, Loyalist, which begins, "I hope this will reach you. Three attempts have I made without success in effecting. The last man was discovered in attempting his Escape but fortunately my letter was sewed in the Waist Band of his Breeches. . . ." Probably written mid-July 1775.

The Historical Society of Pennsylvania, Dreer Collection, Philadelphia

83. Broadside. *The Address of Liberty, To the Buckskins of Pennsylvania, on hearing of the intended Provincial Congress. . . . From the Temple of Liberty.* January 7th 1775

The Library Company of Philadelphia

Figure 54

84. JOHN HANCOCK 1737/38–1793

John Singleton Copley 1738-1815

Oil on canvas, 1770-1772

29⅞ x 24½

Private collection

Figure 55

85. THOMAS WILLING 1731–1821

Gilbert Stuart 1755-1828

Oil on canvas, circa 1795

29⅜ x 24⅛

Mrs. Arnold B. Chace

Figure 56

86. JAMES WILSON 1742–1798

Jean Pierre Henri Elouis 1755-1840

Watercolor on ivory, circa 1795

2⅝ x 2 1/16

National Collection of Fine Arts, Smithsonian Institution

Figure 58

87. JAMES WILSON

Considerations On The Nature And The Extent Of The Legislative Authority Of The British Parliament.

Philadelphia: William and Thomas Bradford, 1774

Library of Congress, Rare Books Division

Figure 59

88. ROBERT TREAT PAINE 1731–1814

Edward Savage 1761-1817 and John Coles, Jr. 1776/80-1854

Oil on canvas, begun 1802, completed 1822

29¼ x 24¼

Massachusetts Historical Society, Boston

Figure 60

89. *View of the old French Fort, Redoubts and Batteries at Ticonderoga on Lake Champlain and his Majesty's ship Inflexible also the Piers constructed with the Trunks of Large Trees by the American Army for the conveyance of their Troops to Mount Independence taken on the Spot by H. Rudyerd Leut. Corps of Royal Engineers in the year 1777.*

Watercolor, 1777

15½ x 23½

Fort Ticonderoga Museum

Figure 61

90. SILAS DEANE 1737–1789

Charles Willson Peale 1741-1827

Watercolor on ivory, 1776

1 9/16 x 1¼

The Connecticut Historical Society, Hartford

Photo: Frick Art Reference Library

Figure 63

91. BENEDICT ARNOLD 1741–1801

Benoît Louis Prévost 1747-1804 or 1809 after Pierre Eugène Du Simitière

Engraving, 1779

6½ x 4¾

The original Du Simitière portrait of Arnold was done at Philadelphia when Arnold was governor of the city.

The Metropolitan Museum of Art, Bequest of Charles Allen Munn, 1924, New York

Figure 62

92. ETHAN ALLEN 1737/38–1789

A Narrative of Colonel Ethan Allen's captivity, from the time of his being taken by the British, near Montreal, on the 25th day of September, in the year 1775 to the time of his exchange, on the 6th day of May, 1778....

Philadelphia: Robert Bell, 1779

William L. Clements Library, University of Michigan, Ann Arbor

93. Ethan Allen's compass.

2¾ x 1¾ x ½

Fort Ticonderoga Museum

Figure 64

94. Blunderbuss said to have been given by Ethan Allen to Benedict Arnold.

Fort Ticonderoga Museum

Figure 65

95. Powder horn. Inscribed: "Leut. John Brown 1776/ En le petit place dan sub liberate quieten"; with map of Hudson-Champlain route and figure of man holding Magna Carta.

John Brown, a Massachusetts lawyer who served under Ethan Allen, carried the news of the Ticonderoga victory to the Continental Congress.

Fort Ticonderoga Museum

96. GEORGE WASHINGTON 1732–1799

Charles Willson Peale 1741-1827

Oil on canvas, 1782

50 x 40

This portrait is an altered replica of the life portrait of 1779. Commissioned by the Comte de Rochambeau, it commemorates the victory at Yorktown, a view of which can be seen at the left.

Private collection

Figure 66

97. Washington's acceptance of the post of commander in chief, June 16, 1775. In the hand of Edmund Pendleton, except for the phrase "at yᵉ expence of my domesᵗ ease & hap," which was interlined by Washington.

Endorsed: "Gen. Washington's answer/ to the Congress upon his/ accepting the office."

From the original in the National Archives

98. Trunk used by George Washington during the Revolution. Inscribed on brass plate: "Genˡ Washington/ Nᵒ 3"

15 x 33¾ x 19

The Mount Vernon Ladies' Association of the Union

Figure 67

99. Leather pack bag belonging to George Washington; one of a set of three.

13 x 15 x 7½

The Mount Vernon Ladies' Association of the Union

100. George Washington's copy of *The Manual Exercise As Ordered By His Majesty in 1764. Together with Plans and Explanations Of the Method generally practis'd At Reviews and Field-Days.*

Boston: T. and J. Fleet, 1775- (?)

Used to drill the troops in Cambridge.

The Boston Athenaeum

101. HORATIO GATES 1727–1806

Attributed to James Peale 1749-1831

Oil on canvas, date unknown

36⅛ x 27⅛

Maryland Historical Society, Baltimore

Photo: Frick Art Reference Library

Figure 69

102. PHILIP SCHUYLER 1733–1804

Thomas Kelly circa 1795-circa 1841 after the 1792 oil by John Trumbull

Engraving, date unknown

4¾ x 3½

Inscribed: "Painted by J. Trumbull Engraved by T. Kelly./ Major General Philip Schuyler./ Ph: Schuyler"

National Portrait Gallery, Smithsonian Institution

103. JOSEPH REED 1741–1785

Charles Willson Peale 1741-1827

Oil on canvas, 1785 replica after life portrait of 1783

24¾ x 18½

Christopher, Andrew, and Henry Reed

Photo: Frick Art Reference Library

Figure 71

104. Broadside. "By his Excellency The Hon. Thomas Gage ... A Proclamation. Whereas the infatuated Multitudes ... have at length proceeded to avowed Rebellion ... I avail myself of the last Effort within the Bounds of my Duty, to spare the Effusion of Blood; to offer ... his [Majesty's] most gracious Pardon to all Persons who shall forthwith lay down their Arms ... excepting only from the Benefit of such Pardon, *Samuel Adams* and *John Hancock*, ..." June 12, 1775.

Boston: 1775

Massachusetts Historical Society, Boston

Figure 72

105. Broadside. "Boston, May　, 1775 Permit
N Cargarett Iepson [?], together with his Family,
consisting of *Seven* Persons, and *their* Effects, to pass *over
the Line* between Sunrise and Sunset. By Order of his
Excellency the Governor. *To The Field Officer in the Lines.*
No Arms nor Ammunition's allowed to pass. *Nor
Merchandize.*"

Boston: 1775

Massachusetts Historical Society, Boston

Figure 57

106. Manuscript copy of the resolution of the Committee
of Safety and the Committee from Council War "to take
immediate possession of Bunker's Hill and Dorchester
Neck." Headquarters, June 15, 1775

From original at Boston Public Library

Photo: George Cushing

Figure 73

107. Artemas Ward 1727–1800

Raphaelle Peale 1774-1825

Oil on canvas, 1795

General Artemas Ward Museum, Shrewsbury,
Massachusetts, through the courtesy of Harvard
University

Figure 74

108. Artemas Ward's letter to the Continental Congress
accepting his commission as major general, June 30, 1775.

National Archives

Figure 75

109. Sir William Howe 1729–1814

Unidentified engraver, probably English

Engraving, 1777

14⅜ x 10⅜

Inscribed: "The Honble. S^r. W^m. Howe./ Corbutt Delin^t.
et fecit./ Knight of the Bath, & Commander in Chief of his
Majesty's Forces in America./ London: Publish'd as the
Act directs, 10th Novr. 1777, by John Morris, Rathbone
Place."

Anne S. K. Brown Military Collection, Brown University
Library, Providence

See entry for John Sullivan

Figure 78

110. Israel Putnam 1718–1790

John Trumbull 1756-1843

Pencil on paper, 1790

3⅞ x 3½

The Putnam Phalanx, Hartford

Photo: E. Irving Blomstrann

Figure 79

111. Letter from Israel Putnam to John Hancock
requesting money for his troops, April 4, 1776.

National Archives

112. Plan of the fort on Bunker's Hill.

Unidentified engraver

From William Carter's *A Genuine Detail of Several
Engagements*, London, 1784

Massachusetts Historical Society, Boston

Figure 77

113. *The Death of General Warren at the Battle of Bunker's
Hill, 17 June 1775*

John Trumbull 1756-1843

Oil on canvas, 1832-1834 replica after the original
completed in London in 1786

72 x 108

Wadsworth Atheneum, Hartford Museum Purchase

Figure 80

114. Grenadier's hat said to have been worn by a British
soldier killed at the Battle of Bunker's Hill.

Rhode Island Historical Society, Providence

Figure 81

115. British "Brown Bess" musket of the type used by both
British and Patriot soldiers at the Battle of Bunker's Hill.
A standard weapon for over 100 years, its name came from
its brown oxidized barrel.

6½ x 62½ x 4

On lockplate: "GR, Jordan, 1746"; cipher of the British
60th regiment on barrel.

The National Museum of History and Technology,
Division of Military History, William G. Renwick
Collection, Smithsonian Institution

116. *Bunker's Hill or America's Head Dress*

Matthew Darly active 1760-1781

Engraving, March 1776

9½ x 7

A satire on the British uphill struggle as well as the
outsized coiffures of the day.

The Colonial Williamsburg Foundation

Figure 82

117. Revolutionary period drum.

17 x 16½

Guthman Collection

Figure 52

118. Revolutionary period British officer's gorget with royal arms.
Brass and gilt
5½ x 4¾ x 1¼
Guthman Collection

119. Revolutionary period officer's epaulets, probably British.
Guthman Collection

120. Revolutionary period British officer's document box.
Leather-covered wood
5 x 13 x 7¼
Guthman Collection
Figure 129

121. Broadside. "Boston, 26th of June, 1775. This town was alarmed on the 17th instant at break of day, by a firing from the lively ship of war; and a report was immediately spread that the rebels had broke ground and were raising a battery on the heights of the peninsula of Charlestown, against the town of Boston." [British account of the Battle of Bunker's Hill.]
Boston: John Howe, 1775
Library of Congress, Rare Books Division

122. BENJAMIN HARRISON 1726 ?–1791
Unidentified artist
Watercolor on ivory, date unknown
1⁷⁄₁₆ x 1¼
Virginia Historical Society, Richmond
Figure 83

123. WILLIAM FLOYD 1734–1821
Ralph Earl 1751-1801
Oil on canvas, 1793
47 x 35½
From the original in Independence National Historical Park, Philadelphia
Figure 84

124. JOSEPH HEWES 1730–1779
Charles Willson Peale 1741-1827
Watercolor on ivory, 1776
1¾ x 1⅝
Hewes sat for Peale in Philadelphia, March 18-20, 1776.
The reverse of frame is inscribed: "Joseph Hewes S.D.I. To Helen Blair Phila. 1776."
United States Naval Academy Museum, Annapolis
Figure 85

125. PHILIP LIVINGSTON 1716–1778
Thomas McIlworth active 1757-1767

Oil on canvas, 1764 or 1766
29½ x 24½
The Long Island Historical Society
Photo: Frick Art Reference Library
Figure 86

126. CHRISTOPHER GADSDEN 1724–1805
Rembrandt Peale 1778-1860
Oil on canvas, circa 1795-1797
29 x 24
City of Charleston, South Carolina
Figure 87

127. The Mecklenburg Resolutions, adopted by the North Carolina Provincial Congress May 31, 1775, in *The North Carolina Gazette*, New Bern, June 16, 1775.
From the original in the collection of Mrs. John G. Wood, Sr.
Figure 88

128. JOHN DICKINSON 1732–1808
Benoît Louis Prévost 1747-1804 or 1809 after Pierre Eugène Du Simitière
Engraving, 1779
6½ x 4¾
Inscribed: "Drawn from Life by Du Simitiere in Philadelphia/ Engraved by B. L. Prevost at Parice No 11"
The Metropolitan Museum of Art, Bequest of Charles Allen Munn, 1924, New York
Figure 89

129. *A Declaration By The Representatives Of The United Colonies of North-America, Now Met In General Congress At Philadelphia, Seting Forth the Causes and Necessity of their taking up Arms.*
Philadelphia: William and Thomas Bradford, 1775
Massachusetts Historical Society, Boston
Figure 90

130. William Knox's copy of the Olive Branch Petition with his "observations." Knox was British undersecretary of state.
William Knox papers, William L. Clements Library, University of Michigan, Ann Arbor
Figure 91

131. Broadside. "Address to the Soldiers. Gentlemen, You are about to embark for *America*, to compel your Fellow Subjects there to submit to Popery and Slavery. . . ." [An attempt to dissuade the military from taking up arms against the colonists.]
London: 1775
Library of Congress, Rare Books Division

132. GEORGE III 1738–1820
Benjamin West 1738-1820
Oil on canvas, circa 1779
49⅞ x 39¾
The King is portrayed in full armor wearing "The George" of the Order of the Garter and the Star of the Order of the Bath. The Royal Crown appears behind him at left. The ships symbolize his command of Britain's navy as well as her army.
The Cleveland Museum of Art, Gift of Mr. and Mrs. Lawrence S. Robbins
Figure 92

133. Letter from King George III to Lord Sandwich, January 11, 1776, in which he writes, "We must show that the English lion when rouzed has not only his wonted resolution, but has added the swiftness of the racehorse."
Victor Montagu

134. WILLIAM PITT 1708-1778
Richard Brompton 1734-1782
Oil on canvas, 1772
45¾ x 33¾
Trustees of the National Portrait Gallery, London
Figure 95

135. WILLIAM PITT
The Speech of The Right Honourable The Earl of Chatham, In the House of Lords, On Friday the 20th of January 1775. On a motion for an Address to His Majesty, to give immediate order for removing his Troops from Boston....

Philadelphia: John Dunlap, 1775
While reporting of parliamentary debates was often unreliable, and published versions bore little resemblance to what was actually said, this contemporary text "sent over in Manuscript from a Gentleman of Distinction in London" is thought to be an accurate report of Pitt's speech.
The Watkinson Library, Trinity College, Hartford

136. BENJAMIN FRANKLIN 1706-1790
Jean-Baptiste Nini 1717-1786 after a profile sketch by Thomas Walpole, a young English friend of Franklin's
Terra-cotta medallion, 1777
d. 3½
National Portrait Gallery, Smithsonian Institution
Figure 96

137. BENJAMIN FRANKLIN
Hints for Conversation Upon the Subject of Terms That Might Probably Produce a Durable Union Between Great Britain and the Colonies, with Lord Dartmouth's annotations.

The Right Honorable the Earl of Dartmouth and the Trustees of William Salt Library, Stafford, England

138. FREDERICK NORTH, later SECOND EARL OF GUILFORD, known as Lord North 1732-1792
Nathaniel Dance (1735-1811)
Oil on canvas, circa 1767-1770
48 x 36
The Right Honorable the Earl of Guilford
Figure 97

139. EDMUND BURKE 1729-1797
James Barry 1741-1806
Oil on canvas, 1774
49¾ x 38¾
National Gallery of Ireland, Dublin
Figure 98

140. EDMUND BURKE
The Speech of Edmund Burke, Esquire, On Moving His Resolutions For Conciliation With The Colonies, March 22d, 1775.
New York: James Rivington, 1775
American Antiquarian Society, Worcester, Massachusetts

141. Letter from Edmund Burke to the New York (?) Committee of Correspondence, June 7, 1775, telling of Burke's attempt to present a memorial denying Parliament's right to tax the colonies. This letter was intercepted in England.
The Right Honorable the Earl of Dartmouth and the Trustees of William Salt Library, Stafford, England

142. THOMAS HOWARD, THIRD EARL OF EFFINGHAM 1747-1791
Francesco Bartolozzi 1727-1815 after the 1779-1781 original by John Singleton Copley
Pencil on paper, before 1794
5¼ x 4½
This sketch was made for Bartolozzi's line engraving of John Singleton Copley's *The Death of the Earl of Chatham*, published by Copley in 1794. The sketch was formerly attributed to Copley.
The Metropolitan Museum of Art, Morris K. Jesup Fund, 1955
Figure 99

143. SAMUEL JOHNSON 1709-1784
Joseph Nollekens 1737-1823
Plaster cast, 1776
h. 19½"
Herman W. Liebert
Figure 100

144. SAMUEL JOHNSON
Taxation no Tyranny; An Answer To the Resolutions and Address Of The American Congress.
London: T. Cadell, 1775
Library of Congress, Rare Books Divison
Figure 101

145. JOHN WESLEY 1703-1791
William Hamilton 1751-1801
Oil on canvas, 1788
50½ x 40¼
Trustees of the National Portrait Gallery, London
Figure 102

146. JOHN WESLEY
A Calm Address to Our American Colonies.
London: R. Hawes, 1775
Library of Congress, Rare Books Division
Figure 103

147. CATHARINE MACAULAY 1731-1791
Jonathan Spilsbury active 1760-1791 after the undated original by Catharine Read
Engraving, 1764
13⅞ x 9⅛
Inscribed: "Kath. Read Pinxᵗ. J. Spelsbury fecit./ Catharine Macaulay."
Trustees of the National Portrait Gallery, London
Figure 104

148. CATHARINE MACAULAY
Chelsea-Derby, England, circa 1770
Porcelain statuette
h. 13½"
Inscribed on pedestal: "Sydney/ Hampden/ Milton/ Locke/ Harrington/ Ludlow/ Marvel/ Dickenson/ · Burgh/ Wilson." Four volumes of history are labeled: "Macau/ lay's History/ of England/ Vol. 1/ Vol 4/ Vol 6/ Vol 2." In her left hand is a letter "To /Dr. Wilson/ Citizen of London/ & Rector of Walbrook." The base of the pedestal is inscribed "American Congress."
The Metropolitan Museum of Art, The Fletcher Fund, 1944

149. CATHARINE MACAULAY
Chelsea-Derby (?), England, 1768-1770
Porcelain statuette
h. 12¼"
Scroll in left hand is inscribed "Magna Carta/ Bill of Rights."
Dickinson College Library, Carlisle, Pennsylvania

150. CATHARINE MACAULAY
An Address To The People of England, Scotland and Ireland, On The Present Important Crisis of Affairs....
Bath: R. Cruttwell, 1775
Tracy W. McGregor Library, University of Virginia, Charlottesville
Figure 105

151. RICHARD PENN 1735-1811
Joseph Highmore 1692-1780
Oil on canvas, date unknown
48½ x 39½
The Historical Society of Pennsylvania, Philadelphia
Figure 93

152. WILLIAM LEGGE, SECOND EARL OF DARTMOUTH 1731-1801
Nathaniel Hone 1718-1784
Oil on canvas, 1777
30 x 24¾
The Trustees of Dartmouth College, Hanover, New Hampshire
Figure 106

153. Proclamation for suppressing Rebellion and Sedition, issued August 23, 1775, by George III.
Public Record Office, London
Figure 94

154. Broadside. "His Majesty's Most Gracious Speech To Both Houses of Parliament, On Friday, October 27, 1775.... The Authors and promoters of this desperate conspiracy [the Olive-Branch petition] have ... meant only to amuse by vague expressions of attachment to the Present State ... whilst they were preparing for a general revolt."
Philadelphia: Hall and Sellers, 1775
The Library Company of Philadelphia

155. CHARLES WATSON-WENTWORTH, SECOND MARQUESS OF ROCKINGHAM 1730–1782
Studio of Joshua Reynolds 1723–1792
Oil on canvas, date unknown
27¼ x 22
Rockingham is wearing the badge of the Order of the Garter.
Trustees of the National Portrait Gallery, London
Figure 107

156. CHARLES LENNOX, THIRD DUKE OF RICHMOND AND
LENNOX 1735–1806

George Romney 1734–1802

Oil on canvas, circa 1776

32 x 27

Trustees of the National Portrait Gallery, London

Figure 109

157. AUGUSTUS HENRY FITZROY, THIRD DUKE OF GRAFTON
1735–1811 and Prime Minister 1767–1770

Nathaniel Dance 1734–1811

Oil on canvas, date unknown

34 x 28

His Grace The Duke of Grafton

Figure 111

158. CHARLES JAMES FOX 1749–1806

Joshua Reynolds 1723–1792

Oil on canvas, 1784

49 x 40

Lady Teresa Agnew

Figure 112

159. JOHN MONTAGU, FOURTH EARL OF SANDWICH
1718–1792

Joseph Highmore 1692–1780

Oil on canvas, 1740

45 5/8 x 37 3/8

The turban and Turkish costume Montagu is wearing in
this portrait were probably brought back from his tour of
the Mediterranean and visit to Constantinople in 1738 and
1739. The Mosque of Hagia Sophia in Constantinople
appears in the background.

Trustees of the National Portrait Gallery, London

Figure 110

160. GEORGE SACKVILLE GERMAIN, FIRST VISCOUNT
SACKVILLE 1716–1785

George Romney 1734–1802

Oil on canvas, 1778

49 1/2 x 39

L. G. Stopford Sackville

Figure 113

161. Germain's *Memorandum on the Peace Commission of
1776*, which states that "the supreme authority of
Legislature to make laws binding on the Colonies in all
cases whatsoever" cannot be denied.

William L. Clements Library, Knox Papers, University of
Michigan, Ann Arbor

162. WILLIAM WILDMAN BARRINGTON, SECOND VISCOUNT
BARRINGTON 1717–1793

W. A. Grainger, dates unknown, after 1765 original by
Joshua Reynolds

Mezzotint, published in *Engravings from the Works of Sir
Joshua Reynolds*, 2d edition, London, 1865

Lewis Walpole Collection

Figure 114

163. DAVID HARTLEY THE YOUNGER 1732–1813

James Walker 1748–1808 after the 1783 oil by George
Romney

Mezzotint, May 10, 1784

18 x 14

Inscribed on roll on table: "Definitive Treaty with the
United States of America, Sep. 3, 1783." At bottom:
"Engraved by Jas. Walker/ Painted by Geo. Romney/
David Hartley Esq./ Member of Parliament for Kingston
upon Hull./ and His Britannic Majesty's Minister
Plenipotentiary appointed to treat with the Unites States
of America./ Published by S. Watts, No. 50 opposite Old
Round-Court Strand, London"

The British Museum, London

Figure 115

164. ABIGAIL ADAMS 1744–1818

Mather Brown 1761–1831

Oil on canvas, 1785

30 1/4 x 26 1/2

New York State Historical Association, Cooperstown,
courtesy of the White House

Figure 116

165. Flag of the United Train of Artillery, Providence,
Rhode Island, with insignia "Do Not Tread On Me" and
"In God We Hope."

Oil on cotton textile

40 x 50

The Rhode Island Historical Society

Figure 117

166. Broadside. "A Proclamation by his Excellency the
Honorable Wm. Howe . . . Whereas several inhabitants
of this town have lately absconded to join, it is
apprehended, his Majesty's enemies assembled in open
rebellion . . ." [forbidding anyone to leave by land or
water without Howe's permission], October 28, 1775.

Boston: John Howe, 1775

The New York Public Library, Astor, Lenox and Tilden
Foundations, Rare Book Division

167. Broadside. "By His Excellency William Howe . . . As
Linnen and Woolen Goods are Articles much wanted by
the Rebels, and would aid and assist them in their
Rebellion, . . . If after this Notice any Person secretes or
keeps in his Possession such Articles, he will be treated as a
Favourer of Rebels. Boston, March 10, 1776"

Boston: John Howe, 1776
Massachusetts Historical Society, Boston
Figure 121

168. Ballad broadside. *"The Yankey's return from Camp."*
Probably published in Boston, these lyrics, sung to the
tune of "Yankee Doodle," were thought to have been
inspired by a visit to the Patriot camp in Cambridge in
1775.
American Antiquarian Society, Worcester, Massachusetts
Figure 120

169. Henry Knox 1750–1806
Charles Peale Polk 1767–1822 after the 1783 oil by Charles
Willson Peale
Oil on canvas, date unknown
23 x 19
Knox is wearing the badge of the Society Of The
Cincinnati
National Portrait Gallery, Smithsonian Institution
Figure 118

170. John Thomas 1724–1776
Benjamin Blyth circa 1746–1787
Pastel on paper, 1777
24 x 20
Massachusetts Historical Society, Boston
Figure 119

171. *Washington Before Boston* medal.
Pierre Simon DuVivier 1731–1819
Bronze, Paris, 1786
Original striking from the die for a gold medal ordered by
the Continental Congress as a token of thanks for George
Washington's "wise and spirited conduct in the siege and
acquisition of Boston," March 1776.
Obverse: Undraped bust of Washington; inscribed:
"georgio washington svpremo dvci exercitvvm
adsertori libertatis/commitia americana/ DuVivier
Paris"
Reverse: Washington and his staff, mounted, watching
the evacuation of Boston by the British. Inscribed:
"hostibus primo fugatis/bostonium recuperatum
xvii. martii mdcclxxvi"
The American Numismatic Society, New York

172. John Glover 1732–1797
John Trumbull 1756–1843
Pencil on paper, November 13, 1794
4⅞ x 4
From the original in the Park McCullough House
Association, Inc., North Bennington, Vermont

Photo: Frick Art Reference Library
Figure 122

173. Esek Hopkins 1718–1802
Unidentified engraver, probably English
Mezzotint, 1776
12 x 9
Inscribed: "Admiral Hopkins, Commendeur en Chef de
Flotte Americaine des XIII Provinces Unies, peint par
Wilckenson a Boston. Se vend a Londres chez Thom.
Hart." Anne S. K. Brown Military Collection, Brown
University Library, Providence
See entry for John Sullivan
Figure 123

174. Esek Hopkins's silver-mounted sword.
Made by Daniel Henchman 1730–1775
Blade engraved "Esekial Hopkins Scituate."
John K. Latimer, M. D., Sc.D.
Figure 124

175. Two American Revolutionary period cutlasses of the
type used by the navy.
Guthman Collection

176. John Murray, Earl of Dunmore 1732–1809
Joshua Reynolds 1723–1792
Oil on canvas, 1765
96¼ x 56½
Inscription lower left: "John IV Earl of Dunmore/
Captain in Regiment of Foot Guards/ 1755. Governor of
Virginia 1770."
Mrs. Elizabeth Murray
Figure 126

177. Broadside. "By His Excellency the Right Honorable
John Earl of Dunmore, His Majesty's Lieutenant and
Governor General of the Colony and Dominion of
Virginia . . . A Proclamation. [Declaring martial law and
granting freedom to all slaves belonging to rebels who
would join His Majesty's troops.] Given under my Hand
on board the Ship William, off Norfolk the 7th day of
November, in the Sixteenth Year of His Majesty's Reign."
Tracy W. McGregor Library, University of Virginia,
Charlottesville
Figure 127

178. *Map of the Maritime Parts of Virginia*
Robert Aitken 1734–1802
Engraving, printed in *The Pennsylvania Magazine*, 1776
Inscribed: "Map/ of the Maritime Parts of/ Virginia/
Exhibiting the Seat of War and of LD. DUNMORE's
depredations/ in that Colony./ P.E.D. Delint./ R. A.
Sculp./ for the Penns. Mag. p. 184"
The Library Company of Philadelphia

179. Sir Henry Clinton 1738?–1795
Attributed to Andrea Soldi 1703–1771
Oil on canvas, circa 1762
50 x 40
Clinton's uniform is the one he wore when he was aide-de-camp to the hereditary Prince of Brunswick, brother-in-law of George III.
The American Museum in Britain, Bath
Figure 130

180. Sir Peter Parker 1721–1811
Valentine Green 1739–1813 after the oil by Lemuel Francis Abbott
Mezzotint, 1800
24⅝ x 16
Inscribed: "Painted by L. F. Abbott. Engraved by V. Green Mezzotinto Engraver to his Majesty/ Sir Peter Parker Baronet, Admiral and Commander in Chief of his Majesty's Fleet. 1799. Published and Sold by V. Green No. 2, New Road, opposite Fitzroy Square and L. F. Abbot, No. 12 Caroline Street, Bedford Square, London, April 30th, 1800."
The Metropolitan Museum of Art, Bequest of Charles Allen Munn, 1924
Figure 131

181. Charles Lee 1731–1782
Unidentified engraver, probably English
Mezzotint, 1775
14¼ x 9½
Inscribed: "Charles Lee, Esqr./ Major General of the Continental-Army in America./ Published as the Act directs. 31 Octr. 1775. by C. Shepherd. London/ Thomlinson pinx"
National Portrait Gallery, Smithsonian Institution
See entry for John Sullivan
Figure 132

182. William Moultrie 1730–1805
Charles Willson Peale 1741–1827
Oil on canvas, 1782
26½ x 22¼
The seascape in the background represents the attack on Fort Moultrie, South Carolina, by Sir Peter Parker, June 28, 1776.
National Portrait Gallery, Smithsonian Institution
Figure 133

183. Sir Peter Parker's Attack Against Fort Moultrie
James Peale 1749–1831
Oil on canvas, circa 1782
20¼ x 29½

The Colonial Williamsburg Foundation
Figure 134

184. Sir Guy Carleton 1724–1808
Unidentified artist
Oil on canvas, date unknown
30 x 25
The Right Honorable the Earl and Countess of Malmesbury
Figure 135

185. An East View of Montreal, in Canada
Pierre-Charles Canot 1710–1777 after a drawing by Thomas Patten
Engraving, published in London as part of the Scenographica Americana, 1768
20 x 12⅝
Inscribed: "An East View of Montreal in Canada/ Vue Orientale de Montreal, en Canada./ Drawn on the Spot by Thomas Patten/ Engraved by P. Canot./ 1. General Hospital. 2. The Recollects. 3. S. Sulpicius./ London Printed for John Bowles at No. 13 in Cornhill, Robert Sayer at No. 53 in Fleet Street, Thot. Jeffreys the corner of St. Martin's Lane in the Strand, Carington Bowles at No. 69 in St. Pauls Church Yard, and Henry Barker at No. 8 in Cornhill./ 4. The Nunnery. 5. The Jesuits Church. 6. The Fort."
The Public Archives of Canada, Ottawa
Figure 136

186. Benedict Arnold 1741–1801
Unidentified engraver, probably English
Mezzotint, 1776
14 x 9¾
Inscribed: "Colonel Arnold Who Commanded the Provincial Troops sent against Quebec, through the Wilderness of Canada and was Wounded in Storming that City under General Montgomery. Publish'd as the Act directs 26 March 1776 by Thos. Hart London"
Anne S. K. Brown Military Collection, Brown University Library, Providence
Figure 137

187. A Bird's Eye View of the Lower town of Quebec taken from the Bishop's Palace, showing the Citadel & Chateau
Lieutenant James Hunter active 1776–1792
Watercolor, circa 1780
13¾ x 20½
Inscribed on recto in ink: "A Bird's Eye View of the Lower town of Quebec taken from the Bishop's Palace, showing the Citadel & Chateau/ J. Hunter 177[?]"
The Public Archives of Canada, Ottawa
Figure 138

188. Letter from Richard Montgomery to Colonel Bedel concerning the impending attack on Quebec, written at "Camp South Side St. Johns," September 25, 1775.

The Historical Society of Pennsylvania, Dreer Collection. Philadelphia

189. AARON BURR 1756–1836

John Vanderlyn 1775–1852

Oil on canvas, circa 1802–1804

28⁹⁄₁₆ x 22

Yale University Art Gallery, Bequest of Oliver Burr Jennings, B. A. 1917, in memory of Miss Annie Burr Jennings, New Haven

Figure 139

190. Letter from Benedict Arnold to Richard Montgomery introducing Aaron Burr, "a young gentleman of much Life & Activity [who] has acted with great Spirit and resolution On Our fatiguing march . . ." and recommending him for the general's "favor," November 30, 1775.

From original in Maine Historical Society, Portland

Figure 140

191. *The Death of General Montgomery in the Attack on Quebec, 31 December 1775*

John Trumbull 1756–1843

Oil on canvas, 1832–1834 replica of the original completed in London in 1786

72 x 108

Wadsworth Atheneum, Hartford

Figure 141

192. Sword carried by Richard Montgomery when he was killed at Quebec.

Division of Military History, The National Museum of History and Technology, Smithsonian Institution, Julia Barton Hunt Collection

Figure 142

193. Broadside. *Aux Habitants De La Province Du Canada* [telling of the march to Canada and urging the Canadians to form a provincial congress]. "Signe au Nom & par l'Ordre du Congress: John Hancock, President./ A Philadelphie, le 24 Janvier 1776"

Philadelphia: Chez Fleury Mesplet & Charles Berger, 1776

The Library Company of Philadelphia

Figure 143

194. DANIEL MORGAN 1736–1802

Attributed to Charles Willson Peale 1741–1827

Oil on canvas, date unknown

26 x 20

Virginia Historical Society, Richmond

Figure 144

195. DAVID WOOSTER 1711–1777

Johann Martin Will 1727–1806 after unidentified engraver

Mezzotint, 1776–1778

14 x 9⅛

Inscribed: "David Wooster, Esqʳ./ Commander in Chief of the Provincial Army against Quebec./ Ioh Martin Will excud. Aug. Vind."

Anne S. K. Brown Military Collection, Brown University Library, Providence

See entry for John Sullivan

Figure 145

196. THOMAS PAINE 1737–1809

John Wesley Jarvis circa 1780–1840

Oil on canvas, circa 1805

25¾ x 20½

National Gallery of Art, Gift of Marian B. Maurice, 1950, Washington, D. C.

Figure 146

197. THOMAS PAINE 1737–1809

Common Sense; Addressed To The Inhabitants Of America, . . .

Philadelphia: R. Bell, 1776

George Washington's copy.

The Boston Athenaeum

Figure 147

198. Thomas Paine's writing kit.

Huguenot-Thomas Paine Historical Association, of New Rochelle, New York

199. JAMES CHALMERS died 1806

Plain Truth, Addressed To The Inhabitants of America, Containing Remarks On A Late Pamphlet, entitled Common Sense . . . By Candidus. . . .

Philadelphia: R. Bell, 1776

A reply to *Common Sense.*

Library of Congress, Rare Books Division

200. WILLIAM SMITH 1727–1803

Thomas Sully 1783–1872

Oil on canvas, 1855, after the circa 1800 original by Gilbert Stuart

37½ x 51

Robert H. Hicks

Figure 148

201. JOHANN DE KALB 1721–1780

Henry Bryan Hall, Jr. 1808–1884 after the 1781/82 oil by Charles Willson Peale

Engraving, 1872

15 x 12

Inscribed: "Maj-Gen—The Baron De Kalb—/ Etch'ᵈ by H. B. Hall, Morrisania, N. Y. 1872"/ Sign: The Baron de Kalb

Anne S. K. Brown Military Collection, Brown University Library, Providence

202. CHARLES GRAVIER, COMTE DE VERGENNES 1717–1787
Unidentified artist

Oil on canvas, date unknown

31 x 24

Vergennes wears the French order of the Holy Spirit, one of the most coveted orders of knighthood.

Musée National du Château de Versailles

Figure 151

203. LOUIS XVI 1754–1793
Antoine François Callet 1741–1823

Oil on canvas, 1775

111 x 64¾

The King wears state robes and the Order of the Holy Spirit, an order of knighthood founded by Henry III in 1578.

Musée National du Château de Versailles

Figure 150

204. *A View of Savannah*

Pierre Fourdrinier active 1720–1758 after Peter Gordon

Engraving, 1734

16 x 22

Inscribed: "A View of Savannah as it stood the 29th of March 1734./ P. Gordon Inv./ P. Fourdrinier Sculp./ To the Hon.ᵇˡᵉ the Trustees for establishing the Colony of Georgia in America/ This View of the Town of Savannah is humbly dedicated by their Honours/ Obliged and most Obedient Servant/ Peter Gordon/ Vue de Georgia dans la Georgia"

Library of Congress, Prints and Photographs

Figure 153

205. GEORGE WALTON 1741–1804
Charles Willson Peale 1741–1827

Watercolor on ivory, circa 1781

1⅜ x 1⅛

Yale University Art Gallery, The Mabel Brady Garvan Collection, New Haven

Figure 154

206. Broadside. "Resolutions entered into at Savannah in Georgia . . . the 10th day of August, 1774, at a general meeting of the inhabitants. . . ."

Savannah: James Johnston, 1774

Public Record Office, London

207. WILLIAM EDEN, FIRST BARON AUCKLAND 1744–1814
Henry Edridge 1769–1821

Watercolor, 1809

11¼ x 9¼

Trustees of the National Portrait Gallery, London

Figure 159

208. RICHARD EARL HOWE, ADMIRAL OF THE FLEET 1726–1799
Thomas Gainsborough 1727–1788

Oil on canvas, circa 1765

96 x 59

The Right Honorable the sixth Earl Howe, C.B.E., D.L., J.P.

Figure 160

209. RICHARD HENRY LEE 1732–1794

Peter Maverick 1780–1831 and James Barton Longacre 1794–1869 from a drawing by Longacre after an unlocated miniature by an unidentified artist

Engraving, published in John Sanderson, *Biography of the Signers to the Declaration of Independence*, Philadelphia, 1827, Vol. 9

National Portrait Gallery, Smithsonian Institution

Figure 155

210. Resolution of Independence, June 7, 1776, offered by Richard Henry Lee to the Continental Congress on instructions of the Virginia Convention and adopted July 2, 1776.

Half-sheet, verso, endorsed by Charles Thomson

From the original in the National Archives, Washington, D. C.

Figure 156

211. GEORGE MASON 1725–1792

Dominic W. Boudet ?–1845 after the destroyed 1750 original by John Hesselius

Oil on canvas, 1811

30 x 25

S. Cooper Dawson, Jr., great-great-great grandson of George Mason

Figure 157

212. Fairfax Resolves, drafted by George Mason, July 18, 1774.

Virginia State Library, Richmond

213. George Mason's draft of the Virginia Declaration of Rights, circa May 20-26, 1776.

Virginia State Library, Richmond

214. CARTER BRAXTON 1737–1797
Unidentified artist
Watercolor on ivory, date unknown
1 7/8 x 1 3/8
On indefinite loan to the National Portrait Gallery,
Smithsonian Institution, from Donald M. Braxton
Figure 158

215. CARTER BRAXTON
*An Address To The Convention Of The Colony And Ancient
Dominion of Virginia; On The Subject of Government in
general, and recommending a particular Form to
their Consideration....*
Philadelphia: John Dunlap, 1776
The Library Company of Philadelphia

216. THOMAS JEFFERSON 1743–1826
Mather Brown 1761–1831
Oil on canvas, 1786
35 3/4 x 28
When John Adams and Thomas Jefferson were in London
in 1786 on diplomatic missions, each ordered from Mather
Brown, a young American artist working there, a portrait
of the other. There is no earlier known likeness of Jefferson.
Jefferson's portrait of Adams is now in the Boston
Athenaeum.
Charles Francis Adams
Figure 161

217. THOMAS JEFFERSON
A Summary View of the Rights of British America
Williamsburg: 1774
Jefferson drafted this document as suggested instructions
for Virginia's delegates to the First Continental Congress.
Though not officially adopted, it helped establish
Jefferson's national reputation.
The Library Company of Philadelphia

218. *A N.W. View of the State House in Philadelphia taken
1778*
James Trenchard 1747–? after Charles Willson Peale's
drawing of 1778
Engraving, published in *The Columbian Magazine*, I,
July 1787, p. 514
Inscribed: "C. W. Peale delin/ A N.W. View Of The
State House In Philadelphia taken 1778/ J. T. Sculp"
The Watkinson Library, Trinity College, Hartford
Figure 163

219. *Congress Voting Independence*
Edward Savage 1761–1817 after his painting (which may
have been begun by Robert Edge Pine)
Stipple engraving, started after 1796

21 3/4 x 27 5/8
Savage died before completing the plate for this engraving.
His son, Edward Savage, also worked on the plate but
the piece remained unfinished and unpublished. This
impression was pulled (probably from the Goodspeed
printing in 1906) from the copper plate now in the
Massachusetts Historical Society. The setting depicted by
Savage is believed to be the most accurate depiction of
the interior of the State House.
National Portrait Gallery, Smithsonian Institution
Figure 165

220. THE DECLARATION OF INDEPENDENCE
William J. Stone 1798–1865
Engraving, 1823
25 1/2 x 30
Engraved by order of Secretary of State John Quincy
Adams.
All illustrations of the Declaration are from this engraving,
as the original, in the National Archives, has never been
photographed.
University of Indiana Library, Bloomington
Figure 166

221. The Declaration of Independence printed in
Pennsylvanischer Staatsbote, July 9, 1776. This is the first
publication of the Declaration in a language other than
English.
Philadelphia: Henry Miller, 1776
The Library Company of Philadelphia

FURNITURE AND DECORATIVE OBJECTS

222. Rush-bottomed ladderback sidechair and armchair
Maple
44 1/4 x 17; 43 13/16 x 24 1/4
Independence National Historical Park

223. Tin sconce purchased by the Carpenters' Company in
1790.
24 x 11 1/2
The Carpenters' Company of the City and County of
Philadelphia

224. "Bow-back Windsor" armchair, circa 1770
37 x 17 (seat height)
Painted black
The Carpenters' Company of the City and County of
Philadelphia

225. "Comb-back Windsor" armchair used as a Speaker's chair, circa 1770.

53 x 25

The Carpenters' Company of the City and County of Philadelphia

226. Slant-top writing desk, circa 1755–1790

Mahogany and white pine

43 x 42 x 22

Benjamin Frothingham 1734–1809 (paper label)

Frothingham's shop in Charlestown, Massachusetts, was burned in the British attack of June 17, 1775.

Mrs. Frederic A. Milholland

227. Commode, with ormolu mounts and marble top, circa 1780

36 x 56½ x 23

Possibly by Martin Carlin died 1785

Hillwood, Smithsonian Institution

228. Canapé and two sidechairs, gilt wood, circa 1768

Canapé: 36 x 48½ x 25½

Chairs: 35 x 19½

Georges Jacob 1739–1814 (stamped)

Hillwood, Smithsonian Institution

229. Brass snuffer and holder

Herbert Schiffer, Antiques, Exton, Pennsylvania

230. Pennsylvania walnut tavern table

h. 29¼ x w. 26 x l. 40

David Stockwell, Inc., Wilmington, Delaware

231. Two pewter ink standishes

David Stockwell, Inc., Wilmington, Delaware

232. English firescreen, circa 1730, on American mahogany pole, 1755–1780

The Colonial Williamsburg Foundation

233. American bow-back Windsor chair

New England, 1765–1785

The Colonial Williamsburg Foundation

234. Four English Chippendale chairs

The Colonial Williamsburg Foundation

235. Pair of gilded English wall brackets, 1750–1765

The Colonial Williamsburg Foundation

236. Pair of brass English candlesticks, 1740–1770

The Colonial Williamsburg Foundation

237. Pair of silver English candlesticks, 1748–1749, probably by William Gould. Engraved with arms of Lightfoot family of Virginia.

The Colonial Williamsburg Foundation

238. Silver English ink stand, 1753–1754, by Edward Wakelin

The Colonial Williamsburg Foundation

239. Pair of tin candlesticks

Herbert Schiffer Antiques, Exton, Pennsylvania

Index

☆ U.S. GOVERNMENT PRINTING OFFICE : 1976 O—202-319

rmed troops among us : — For protecting them, by a mock Trial, from Punishment for ar

ur Trade with all parts of the world : — For imposing Taxes on us without our Consent :

eas to be tried for pretended offences : — For abolishing the free System of English Laws in

o as to render it at once an example and fit instrument for introducing the same absolute ru

ltering fundamentally the Forms of our Governments : — For suspending our own Legis

He has abdicated Government here, by declaring us out of his Protection and waging War ag

f our People. — He is at this time transporting large Armies of foreign Mercenaries to comp

arcely paralleled in the most barbarous ages, and totally unworthy the Head of a civilized natio

heir Country, to become the executioners of their friends and Brethren, or to fall themselves by their

nhabitants of our frontiers, the merciless Indian Savages, whose known rule of warfare, is an unde

ave Petitioned for Redress in the most humble terms : Our repeated Petitions have been answered

s unfit to be the ruler of a free People. Nor have We been wanting in attentions to our Britti

ble jurisdiction over us. We have reminded them of the circumstances of our emigration and se

y the ties of our common kindred to disavow these usurpations, which, would inevitably in

msanguinity. We must, therefore, acquiesce in the necessity, which denounces our Separat

We, therefore, the Representatives of the united States of America, in

ntions, do, in the Name, and by Authority of the good People of these Colonies, solemnly publis

tates; that they are Absolved from all Allegiance to the British Crown, and that all politica

hat as Free and Independent States, they have full Power to levy War, conclude Peace, co

tates may of right do. — And for the support of this Declaration, with a firm re

nd our sacred Honor.

John

Button Gwinnett

Lyman Hall

Geo Walton.

Wm Hooper

Joseph Hewes,

John Penn

Samuel C

Wm Pac

Thos Sto

Charles Carrol

Edward Rutledge /.

Thos Hayward Junr.

Thomas Lynch Junr

Arthur Middleton

George

Richard

Th Jeff

Benj Ha

Ths Nelson

Francis Ligh

Carter Bra